0750707 7

The Sociology of Mathem

Studies in Mathematics Education Series

Series Editor
Paul Ernest
School of Education
University of Exeter
Exeter

Studies in Mathematics Education Series: 7

The Sociology of Mathematics Education:
Mathematical Myths/ Pedagogic Texts

Paul Dowling

 The Falmer Press

(A member of the Taylor & Francis Group)
London • Washington, D.C.

UK	The Falmer Press, 1 Gunpowder Square, London, EC4A 3DE
USA	The Falmer Press, Taylor & Francis Inc., 1900 Frost Road, Suite 101, Bristol, PA 19007

First published in 1998

A catalogue record for this book is available from the British Library

Library of Congress Cataloging-in-Publication Data are available on request

ISBN 0 7507 0791 7 cased
ISBN 0 7507 0792 5 paper

Jacket design by Caroline Archer

Typeset in 10/12pt Bembo by
Graphicraft Typesetters Ltd., Hong Kong

Printed in Great Britain by Biddles Ltd., Guildford and King's Lynn on paper which has a specified pH value on final paper manufacture of not less than 7.5 and is therefore 'acid free'.

Contents

List of Figures and Tables

List of Figures

List of Tables

Acknowledgments

This book has had a period of gestation of just about a decade. During this time, a very large number of individuals have given me intellectual inspiration, academic and literary advice, and emotional support. Their contributions are woven into the text in ways which are impossible to acknowledge adequately or even to recognize accurately. For the most part, they relate to localized points or periods during the development of the book and, generally, to specialized areas of its content. The presence of three friends and colleagues, however, has spanned the decade and infuses the entire scope of the project. They are Parin Bahl, Basil Bernstein, and Andrew Brown. I have benefitted enormously from the inspirational quality of their own practices and their critical engagement with mine. A mention on this page and, for two of them, anyway, *passim* explicit intertextualities seems parsimonious.

I have been particularly fortunate in having the opportunity to work with a number of colleagues in South Africa during this promising period of that country's history. This work has involved research, teaching and presentations in South Africa over a period of some five years. These activities have proved to be invaluable in the formulation and development of the theoretical dimensions of this book. Paula Ensor, of the University of Cape Town, has been a particularly energetic critic and facilitator, and I must also acknowledge the contributions to my thinking from Jane Coombe, Zain Davies, Jaamiah Galant and Johan Müller, of UCT and Cyril Julie of the University of the Western Cape as well as numerous other staff and students of these and other South African institutions. I am grateful also to the Overseas Development Administration and the British Council for, respectively, funding and managing most of my visits to South Africa to date.

Teaching has had a central place in the development of the ideas in this book. In mediating some of them on doctoral programmes, masters degrees and pre- and in-service teacher education courses it has frequently occurred to me that I, as the teacher, am taking at least as much from the sessions as the most attentive of my students. I am, therefore, grateful to my students on all of these courses at the Institute of Education and at other institutions where I have been given the opportunity to teach. I must also acknowledge the support of colleagues at the Institute in allowing me the space both to develop my teaching and to further my research.

I am grateful to Harvey Goldstein for advice relating to the statistical analysis in Chapter 9; such inadequacies as remain are, of course, my responsibility and not his. I am indebted to Paul Atkinson, Gunther Kress and Valerie Walkerdine for valuable discussion and criticism relating to an earlier version of the core of this work. I am also particularly grateful to Paul Ernest for advice and support during the latter stages of this project and for comments on an earlier draft of the book.

Acknowledgments are owed to Jackie East, for permission to reproduce her illustrations from *Nelson Mathematics*. Also to Cambridge University Press for providing the *SMP 11–16* materials and for permission to reproduce pages from them. I am grateful also to MBTM (Giftware) Ltd, the Metropolitan Police, the School Mathematics Project, and SMILE for permission to reproduce copyrighted items.

Preface by Series Editor

Mathematics education is established world-wide as a major area of study, with numerous dedicated journals and conferences serving ever-growing national and international communities of scholars. As it develops, research in mathematics education is becoming more theoretically orientated. Although originally rooted in mathematics and psychology, vigorous new perspectives are pervading it from disciplines and fields as diverse as philosophy, logic, sociology, anthropology, history, women's studies, cognitive science, semiotics, hermeneutics, post-structuralism and post-modernism. These new research perspectives are providing fresh lenses through which teachers and researchers can view the theory and practice of mathematics teaching and learning.

The series *Studies in Mathematics Education* aims to encourage the development and dissemination of theoretical perspectives in mathematics education as well as their critical scrutiny. It is a series of research contributions to the field based on disciplined perspectives that link theory with practice. The series is founded on the philosophy that theory is the practitioner's most powerful tool in understanding and changing practice. Whether the practice concerns the teaching and learning of mathematics, teacher education, or educational research, the series offers new perspectives to help clarify issues, pose and solve problems and stimulate debate. It aims to have a major impact on the development of mathematics education as a field of study in the 21st century.

With its roots in mathematics, psychology and everyday classroom practice, it might be said that mathematics education is permeated with the ideology of individualism. Perhaps this is an artifact of history. Mathematics education came of age in the era of the Cold War when individualism ruled supreme in the West and communitarianism and social perspectives were backgrounded. In the past decade counterpoising the individualistic voice of developmental psychology a new voice has been heard in mathematics education. This is the voice of sociology and associated social theories. Although a social strand has long been present in mathematics education in such seminal works as Griffiths and Howson (1974), deep applications of sociological theory are as yet rare. Sociology concerns not only individuals and groups and their patterns of inter-relationships. Modern sociology also weaves knowledge and social practice into a complex whole. Until the last decade, studies which recognized this complex character were virtually non-existent in mathematics education. The feminist movement offered a social critique of mathematics, but until works such as Walkerdine (1988), these were under-theorized. Likewise, the multiculturalist and ethnomathematical movements offered valuable social insights for mathematics teaching, and have become widely endorsed vehicles for the reform of mathematics education. But all too often they have been offered uncritically or as under-theorized perspectives. Up to the present day there remains a dearth of fully worked out sociological approaches to mathematics education able to supply the missing theoretical perspectives and critique.

Paul Dowling offers a radical counterbalance to this state of affairs. In this book he provides a defining foray into the sociology of mathematics education. His primary focus is the semiotic analysis of mathematics texts. This is an important innovation which links the sociology of interpersonal and class relations with a central tool in social reproduction through education: the school mathematics text. Identifying the social impact of school texts was presaged by feminist critiques of sexism in mathematics. As in some of those critiques, such as the work of Walkerdine, Dowling's impatience with the construction of various distinct social hierarchies of learners by the institution of school mathematics is apparent. He is also intolerant of easily accepted but thinly theorized views, such as in popular accounts of the applications of mathematics and of multicultural mathematics. In particular, he isolates and identifies a powerful theoretical notion, the colonizing gaze of the mathematician, which appropriates all that it surveys in the name of mathematics. This gaze emanates from an overvaluing of the intellectual, identified by Marx, Sohn-Rethel and other theorists, and looks down upon the manual, practical and other real human practices that it colonizes. It constructs and validates mythical images of the relationship between mathematics and the world in general.

What is really powerful in this work is Dowling's combination of deep underpinning theoretical notions with the very concrete and detailed work in text analysis. Dowling does not desire to be a mere philosopher or theorist, and theory and practice are deeply interwoven in the analysis and interrogation of school mathematics texts. In this emerges another important feature of the work; its methodological innovation. The book develops and exemplifies a systematic approach to the analysis of texts which is extendible to a wide range of empirical settings within mathematics education, to education more generally, and to wider social contexts. It combines quantitative analyses of mathematical texts with penetrating qualitative methods of text analysis based on semiotics. I predict that part of the impact of the work will be due to this powerful methodology, resting on a strong theoretical underpinning.

However the major impact of the book, and I believe that its importance will be widely recognized, must be due to its powerful conceptualization and the resultant social and mathematical critique. In his analysis Dowling draws on a number of leading contemporary social theorists, including Bernstein, Bourdieu, Eco, Foucault, Piaget and Soviet thinkers such as Bakhtin, Luria, Volosinov and Vygotsky. He integrates ideas from these thinkers into a unified theoretical approach which I predict will be influential in a number of ways.

It addresses a central but neglected question concerning mathematics and mathematics education: what is mathematics about? It offers original answers which identify dominant and damaging myths about mathematics. It embodies a critical and iconoclastic approach challenging several received but under-recognized myths associated with mathematics and mathematics education. The text indicates a real political engagement with the consequences of mathematics education in modern society. It distances itself from a range of liberal and progressive perspectives which seek to ameliorate the social status quo without fundamental questioning of the dominant ideologies; thus helping to maintain an unjust system. This critique echoes voices that are emerging in Africa, Australasia and within ex-colonial peoples and minorities the world over. Dowling is very careful to avoid the unconscious eurocentrism that is widespread in mathematics education. Contemporary developments, including the present volume, thus herald not only the theorization of research in mathematics education, but also the globalization of this research. The growing number of researchers world-wide who are sensitive to these issues will welcome their clarification and the associated powerful critique provided by this work.

The book sits squarely within the philosophy of the series *Studies in Mathematics Education*: to further develop the theorization of mathematics education and link it firmly with practice. The book will be very influential, I predict, in both grounding and stimulating further work in this orientation and will be much cited by researchers investigating the sociology of mathematics education and pedagogical texts.

References

GRIFFITHS, H.B. and HOWSON, A.G. (1974) *Mathematics: Society and Curricula*, Cambridge: Cambridge Unviersity Press.

WALKERDINE, V. (1988) *The Mastery of Reason*, London: Routledge.

Chapter 1

Mathematical Myths

This book is, as its title indicates, a sociology. By the use of this term I mean that the theoretical space in which I am interested is concerned with patterns of relationships between individuals and groups and the production and reproduction of these relationships in cultural practices and in action. My principal aim in this book is to introduce a theorizing of this space. This theorizing is a *language of description* which has been designed to enable the analysis of empirical data.[1] I shall refer to my particular language of description as *social activity theory*. I shall present its detailed structure in Chapter 6, following a discussion, in the previous chapter, of work which has been influential in its formulation. Social activity theory has also been designed to be consistent with my general conception of the nature of sociological analysis. I shall refer to this general methodological position as *constructive description*. This position will also be elaborated in Chapter 6.

As well as occupying or establishing a theoretical space, the book is concerned with an empirical space. This space is school mathematics. I shall be making reference to a range of data relating to school mathematics. Principally, however, I shall produce an analysis of the secondary school mathematics scheme, *SMP 11–16*[2]. Arguably, it is through its institutionalized texts that the specificity of any activity is most clearly visible. The social activity analysis of these pedagogic texts will, therefore, enable me to make a number of statements about the nature of the school mathematics activity to which they relate. These statements have to do with the ways in which school mathematics is established as a set of practices and, specifically, the divisions and distributions within mathematics and between mathematics and other practices.

Because the principal data form that I shall be using is textual, this work is also intended to be a contribution to textual analysis. In the main data analysis chapters — Chapters 7–11 — I shall introduce a number of approaches to textual analysis. The emphasis will be on a semiotic approach, but I shall also incorporate quantitative content analysis in Chapters 7 and 9.

So, the book is concerned with particular theoretical and empirical spaces — sociology (social activity theory) and school mathematics, respectively

---

1 This expression was coined by Basil Bernstein and this approach to the relationship between the theoretical and empirical domains has characterized all of his own sociology since the 1960s.
2 Published by Cambridge University Press.

1

— and with general and research methodology — constructive description and textual analysis. I have titled this book: *The Sociology of Mathematics Education*. My contention, however, is that constructive description and social activity theory are of far more general applicability in sociological work. Their generalizability can, I want to claim, extend beyond the empirical space — school mathematics — and beyond the analysis of pedagogic texts. In other words, the book is a localized introduction to a more general language. I hope to be able to demonstrate this as well in the book.

Nevertheless, mathematics in general and school mathematics in particular have been absolutely central in the generation of the more general theory. The choice of school mathematics as the empirical domain is not arbitrary. There are at least three respects in which school mathematics may, on the face of it, at least, be referred to as a critical case. Firstly, it exhibits a highly explicit grammar in respect of what can count as a mathematical utterance and what can count as a true mathematical utterance. This is evidenced by the fact that very few of the answers in the *SMP 11–16* Teacher's Guides or in school mathematics answer books more generally include variations.

Secondly, school mathematics text is at least as distinctive as and arguably more distinctive than that of any other academic school discipline. Halliday (1978) and, following him, Pimm (1987) have made reference to a 'mathematical register' incorporating specialized and reinterpreted terms. The recognizability of elements of this register is substantially a function of the high degree of explicitness of the grammar of mathematics and this has certainly penetrated secondary school mathematics, so that mathematical texts can, generally, instantly be classified as such.

Both the explicitness of its grammar and the consequent recognizability of its texts contribute to the suitability of school mathematics as a critical case for my purposes. This is because an important feature of my analytic work entails distinguishing between mathematical and other practices. The particular forms of realization of the relationship between mathematical and other practices give rise to a *mythology*: mathematics is a mythologizing activity to a degree that is probably unparalleled on the school curriculum. This is the third critical feature of school mathematics.[3]

As a school discipline, mathematics has maintained a prominent place on the curriculum at least since the advent of compulsory schooling in England early on in this century. This prominence is most commonly justified on

3 I should, at this early point, distinguish my use of the expression 'myth' from the prior and highly distinguished work by Roland Barthes (1972). In his analyses in this work, Barthes was concerned to reveal the mechanisms whereby signs participate in ideological or *mythical* reproduction. Barthes' myth could be construed as an operation upon the sign just as I shall constitute *activity* as constituting an operation upon practice, conceived of more generally. However, Barthes provides no motivation for the specificity of the myth. Nor does he need to, because he is interested in the mechanisms of semiosis rather than in sociology. My intention, in this book, is to offer a sociology — a language of description — which is intended to bias, or to motivate, the descriptions which it produces. The mathematical myths introduced in this book constitute an important feature of these descriptions.

utilitarian grounds. That is, mathematics is claimed to be useful, to comprise 'use-values' with respect to diverse economic and domestic practices. This interpretation of mathematics is generally opposed to the elitist view of mathematics as an intellectual endeavour which is substantially isolated from other activities. This position is famously put by G.H. Hardy in his *A Mathematician's Apology*:

> I have never done anything 'useful'. No discovery of mine has made, or is likely to make, directly or indirectly, for good or ill, the least difference to the amenity of the world. [. . .] The case for my life, then, or for that of any one else who has been a mathematician in the same sense in which I have been one, is this: that I have added something to knowledge, and helped others to add more and that these somethings have a value which differs in degree only, and not in kind, from that of the creations of the great mathematicians, or of any of the other artists, great or small, who have left some kind of memorial behind them. (Hardy, quoted by Davis and Hersh, 1981; pp. 85–6)

It is, of course, not universally accepted that society ought to deploy any of its scarce resources towards subsidizing Cambridge dons in order that they might create memorials to themselves. Curriculum developments associated with the modern mathematics movement in the 1950s and 1960s generally located the utility of mathematics within mathematics as an academic discipline: what was wanted was more mathematicians. Such a position differs from Hardy's, but is not necessarily operationally incompatible with it. The current trend, however, is oriented more towards the widespread dissemination of mathematical use-values: not more mathematicians, but a more mathematically competent workforce and citizenry. I want to argue that this latter position, in particular, fails to recognize the social basis of its own epistemology. That is, it generalizes its own practices beyond the context in which they are elaborated, failing to recognize the fundamental implications of moving between contexts.

Alongside the aim of dissemination there has been an increasing amount of writing within the general field of mathematics education that claims mathematics as an essential feature of all human cultures. This view is often explicitly opposed to the elitist view which is often associated with the eurocentric understanding of mathematics as an exclusively European product. Again, I shall claim that this position is no more than a recycling of precisely the same eurocentrism in its failure to acknowledge the social and cultural specificities of the practices that it redescribes in terms of European school mathematics. It might be appropriately referred to as a crude form of mathematical anthropology.

The utilitarian views of mathematics — whether or not mathematics is valued in its own terms — and mathematical anthropology may be associated with a mythology comprising three myths of school mathematics. The myths are, as I hinted at above, concerned with the relationship between mathematics and other cultural practices. I shall introduce these myths in the next three sections of this chapter. In the fourth section, I shall consider a governmental text from a critical political context, the new South Africa. This text represents an attempt to recruit education — clearly including mathematics education — to restructure the socioeconomic sphere via the elimination of its divisions and hierarchies. The text can do this, however, only by establishing its own myth. The question that is raised in the concluding section of the chapter is how can we describe the conditions which make possible the construction of these myths and which constitute them as myths. This is the question that I shall begin to address in Chapter 2 and which is the most central concern of the fundamental sociological thrust of this book.

The Myth of Reference

Mike Cooley (1985) relates the following anecdote:

> At one aircraft company they engaged a team of four mathematicians, all of PhD level, to attempt to define in a programme a method of drawing the afterburner of a large jet engine. This was an extremely complex shape, which they attempted to define by using Coon's Patch Surface Definitions. They spent some two years dealing with this problem and could not find a satisfactory solution. When, however, they went to the experimental workshop of the aircraft factory, they found that a skilled sheet metal worker, together with a draughtsman had actually succeeded in drawing and making one of these. One of the mathematicians observed: 'They may have succeeded in making it but they didn't understand how they did it.' (Cooley, M., 1985; p. 171)

I want to suggest that what is going on here is the propagation of a myth. Cooley is, of course, ironizing the mathematician's utterance in his recruitment of it as reported speech. But the mathematician's voice prior to this refraction is constituting intellectual mathematics as definitive of understanding and so a higher order of activity than the manual tasks of drawing and metalwork. This hierarchy is not to be gainsaid by the contingency of practical success. A division is being established between the intellectual and the manual and the former, represented by mathematics, is constituted as generating commentary upon the latter. Mathematics is mythologized as being, at least potentially, about something other than itself.

But this myth has a basis in social relations. In its way — and from the opposite perspective — the mathematician's pronouncement is as dramatic an illustration of social class hierarchy as is Molière's exclamation by Monsieur Jourdain upon discovering that he had been speaking prose for forty years without suspecting a thing. The successful 'manual' workers' alleged failure to recognize the mathematical nature of their task is constituted as the extent of their lack of understanding. Prose by any other name may perhaps evoke sweet or acrid odours depending upon the relation between utterer and inter-locutor. Here, it is more than a question of style. The moral shock expressed by the mathematician is a response to the possibility of an overturning of the social order, that the hand might succeed very nicely without the head.

Some time ago, I came across another industrial illustration which relates specifically to school mathematics. The Cockcroft Committee of Enquiry into the teaching of mathematics in schools was set up in 1978 as part of James Callaghan's Labour government's response to widespread criticisms of state education, especially from the engineering industry and the writers of the Black Papers (see Kogan, 1978; Lawton, 1980; Salter & Tapper, 1981). The Cockcroft Committee was instructed to pay: '. . . particular regard to the mathematics required in further and higher education, employment and adult life generally . . .' (Cockcroft *et al*, 1982, p. ix).

As part of their response, the Committee set up three research studies. One of these studies was conducted by a team from Bath University. This study focused on the mathematical requirements of the working practices of sixteen-to-nineteen-year-olds. The researchers collected data which they categorized as 'specific tasks incorporating mathematics' (STIM) and 'math-ematics incorporated in specific tasks' (MIST). They found that a great many young employees — a 'vast army of people' — did not appear to require any formal mathematics, not even counting or recording numbers. Neverthe-less, they claimed that 'all these occupations involve actions which could be described in mathematical terms' (Bailey *et al*, 1981; p. 12). The researchers presented a list of these mathematical terms (MIST) as follows:

A set, dis-joint sets.
Mappings, one-to-one, one-to-many, many-to-one correspondences.
Symmetry, bilateral and rotational.
Rotation, reflection, translation and combinations of these[.] Tessellating patterns.
Logical sequences (if . . . . . then . . . . .). (Bailey *et al*, 1981; p. 26)

The terminology used here is very much out of the 'modern mathematics' tradition of the era. The tasks (STIM) to which these MIST items correspond are:

(i)   Articles are sorted into separate collections for packing or on an accept/reject basis.
(ii)   Articles are moved into particular orientations involving moving side-ways, turning over or round.
(iii)   Articles, such as wine glasses[,] are checked for uniformity of shape.
(iv)   Packed articles form regular patterns.
(v)   Assembly tasks can involve matching parts, such as connecting wires to correct terminals.

(vi) Tasks often have to be carried out in particular orders sometimes requiring simple decisions, but which would not often be verbalised. For example, a creeler in a carpet factory: 'Is the spool empty? Yes! Replace with another of the same colour'. Awareness of the consequences of not following the prescribed order may be important. (*ibid*; pp. 25–6)

The researchers are not claiming that creelers need to study formal logic in order to be able to replace a carpet spool when it's empty rather than when it's full. On the contrary, they are clear that such tasks are successfully carried out in the absence of mathematical knowledge. Yet in making this claim, they are, like Cooley's mathematician, establishing a division between the mathematical-intellectual and the manual and constituting the former as generative of commentaries upon the latter. It is as if the mathematician casts a knowing gaze upon the non-mathematical world and describes it in mathematical terms. I want to claim that the myth is that the resulting descriptions and commentaries are about that which they appear to describe, that mathematics can refer to something other than itself. I shall refer to this myth as the *myth of reference*.

This myth is endemic in school mathematics. These mathematical tasks, for example, are taken from the 'Y' series of books in the secondary school mathematics scheme, *SMP 11–16*:

Shopkeeper A sells dates for 85p per kilogram. B sells them at 1.2 kg for £1.
(a) Which shop is cheaper?
(b) What is the difference between the prices charged by the two shop-keepers for 15 kg of dates? (*SMP 11–16 Book Y1*, p. 55)

Britannia best British flour cost £0.71 for 12.5 kg.
Uncle Sam's best American flour cost $1.30 for 3.5 lb.
If 1kg = 2.2 lb and £1 = $1.85, which brand of flour was cheaper, and by how much per kilogram? (*SMP 11–16 Book Y1*, p. 56)

These tasks both recruit a domestic shopping setting. However, it is quite apparent that the tasks are mathematical rather than domestic. This is made clear through a number of devices. The use of the letters A and B to stand, algebra-style, for the shopkeepers, for example, and the reference to an un-likely purchase (15 kg of dates) and an unlikely comparison (cheaper flour hardly justifies a trip across the Atlantic). The stylizing of the names of the brands of flour is also quite obvious. A division between mathematics and domestic activity is maintained so that mathematics is again constituted as generating non-mathematical referents.

The myth of reference, we might say, constructs mathematics as a system of exchange-values, a currency. Mathematical commentaries can be exchanged for the practices which they describe: Coon's Patch Surface Definitions for making an afterburner; formal logic for carpet creeling; ratio and proportion for domestic shopping. The myth encourages us to move between two spheres of activity, one of which is always mathematics. The range of other activities is a measure of the power of mathematics as a currency. School mathematics textbooks often incorporate a considerable diversity of non-mathematical settings, with sequences of tasks moving rapidly from one setting to another. But mathematics is always presented as exchangeable for these settings rather than imbricated by them: you can make an afterburner or you can understand it, but not both.

The Myth of Participation

The myth of reference is not the only myth propagated by school mathematics. Figure 1.1, for example, is also from the *SMP 11–16* series. I want to draw attention to the implausibility of the narratives that are used to constitute the tasks in this section. Firstly, we are asked to believe not only that Jim is stupid enough not to leave any spare tape for fraying and cutting errors, but that he actually manages to buy exactly 90 cm. Presumably, when he goes back to the shop after adding 10 per cent to his original estimate, he asks for 99 cm (although the answer book does give 1 m as an alternative). In task C3, Zola is supposed to calculate the length of baking paper needed to line the tin. In fact, baking paper often comes on a roll of fixed width which would constitute the 'length'; the length to be cut would depend upon the height of the tin and more than one length could be used if the resulting strip was too short; the cake would be unlikely to suffer unduly. Task C6 is on the following page:

> Eve packs rolls of carpet.
> When the carpet is rolled up
> its diameter is about 45 cm.
> Eve puts 3 bands of sticky tape
> round the roll.
> (a)   About how much tape does she need for one band?
> (b)   How much does she need for each roll of carpet?
> (c)   The sticky tape comes in 100 m rolls.
>   Roughly how many carpets can Eve pack with 1 roll of sticky tape?
>   (G7, p. 19; marginal drawing omitted)

Eve apparently packs just one kind of carpet (different pile thicknesses would result in differently sized rolls) and uses just a single turn of tape for each band (the answer in the Teacher's Guide gives 'Accept 145–155 cm' for part (a)) and there is no waste on the roll of tape.

These tasks, it would seem, have been organized according to mathematical priorities and do not follow the contours of the equivalent tasks in the non-mathematical activities. However, the situation is unlike that in the myth of reference. In the cases of Jim and Zola and Eve, the narratives, though short, include more detail than the two shopping cases from the Y

Figure 1.1   SMP 11–16 Book G7 (p. 18)

C   On the safe side

Jim is making a lampshade. Its diameter is 30 cm.	Jim wants to put tape round the top of the shade.	Jim works out he needs roughly 3 × 30 cm, or 90 cm

Jim buys 90 cm of tape.
But 90 cm is not enough.
The tape is a little too short.

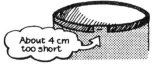

About 4 cm too short

The rule

circumference = 3 × diameter

gives a rough answer for the circumference,
but it is always too short.

To be on the safe side, you can **add 10% to the rough answer.**

C1 Jim works out the circumference as roughly 90 cm.

(a) What is 10% of 90 cm?

(b) How much tape should Jim buy to be on the safe side?

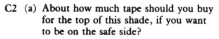

C2 (a) About how much tape should you buy
for the top of this shade, if you want
to be on the safe side?

(b) About how much tape should you
buy for the bottom?

C3 Zola is making a cake.
The recipe says use a 23 cm tin.
That means the diameter
of the tin is 23 cm.
Zola cuts a piece of paper to line the tin.

(a) Roughly what is the circumference of the tin?

(b) What is 10% of your rough answer?

(c) About how long should Zola cut the paper?

18

book. The reader is given names, illustrations are included which, in two
cases, represent the characters of the narrative. These narratives describe a
meaningful practice — making a lampshade, baking a cake, packing carpets —
and incorporate some of the details of these practices — tape, baking paper,
sticky tape. The earlier tasks index shopping practices with far less specificity.
There is, in other words, a substantial residue of the non-mathematical setting

which remains after the mathematical routines have run their course. Further-more, there is, as I shall demonstrate in subsequent chapters of this book, very little in the way of explicit reference to specialized mathematical knowledge anywhere in the G series of books. This is in stark contrast with the Y series. Thus, whilst the Jim/Zola/Eve text recontextualizes the domestic and work settings that it recruits, the recontextualizing activity — mathematics — is, in the G series, substantially invisible other than as a signifier: SMP is an acronym for School *Mathematics* Project.

Mathematics, then, is not so much being constructed as potentially about something other than itself, rather, it is for something else. Mathematics justifies its existence on the school curriculum by virtue of its utility in optim-izing the mundane activities of its students. This is the *myth of participation*. It constructs mathematics, not as a system of exchange-values, but as a reservoir of use-values. A fundamental distinction between exchange-values and use-values is that the former, but not the latter, are constructed in and by a sys-tem. Thus the myth of participation does not need to establish mathematics as systematic knowledge. I will return to this distinction later.

The myth of participation is not an invention of SMP. It is clearly quite fundamental in the motivation which established the Cockcroft Committee. Another of the studies commissioned on behalf of the Committee was carried out by Bridgid Sewell. Again, mathematics is constructed as comprising use-values in respect of non-mathematical activities. Here is an extract from her report:

> Percentages play an ever increasing part in the dissemination of informa-tion, both through the news media and from central government. An under-standing of the national economy assumes a sophisticated comprehension of percentages, as does much of the discussion about pay rises. For the shopper, the ability to estimate 10 per cent can be a valuable 'key' to checking other percentages — even if a precise answer seems too difficult. Since the currency became decimalised, it is a trivial matter to work out 10 per cent of a sum of money, and this can easily be used to estimate other percentages. Those who lack the skill even to calculate 10 per cent are surely handicapped when attempting to understand the affairs of society. (Sewell, 1981; p. 17)

Here, a scenario is presented in which mathematics — in this case percentages — has been incorporated into 'everyday' practices so that the individual who lacks mathematics is effectively 'handicapped' by their own ignorance. The response is to teach mathematics: Sewell, herself, held the post of 'numeracy co-ordinator' for Reading.

Clearly, we can see that 'percentage' is incorporated as a signifier in the practices that Sewell mentions and many other non-mathematical activities. It is likely that some individuals perform calculations within these contexts[4].

---

4   There are also everyday 'uses' of percentages within which calculations would be impossible or meaningless; I'm 99 per cent certain that this is the case.

However, Sewell's assertion that a lack of mathematical skills constitutes a handicap within these contexts is untenable; in fact, mathematical skill is neither necessary nor sufficient for optimum participation within these practices. Firstly, in respect of the necessity of mathematics, there are always alternative resources (price labels, tables showing loan repayments or the effects of tax increases, etc, shop assistants, and so on). Jean Lave (1988; Lave *et al*, 1984), in a rather more sophisticated study, finds that shoppers are highly successful at making best buy decisions and rather less successful at carrying out apparently similar calculations within a mathematical context. Within the supermarket, shoppers resolve problems as and when they arise, making use of elements of the 'arena' of the supermarket itself as well as other resources that constitute their 'activity', itself a dynamic entity. These resources may or may not include mathematics in the school sense.

Secondly, Sewell's assertion that '[a]n understanding of the national economy assumes a sophisticated comprehension of percentages' is a strong statement of utilitarianism only if it implies that this 'sophisticated comprehension' is sufficient to such an understanding. In fact, this is clearly very far from the case. Whilst Jean Lave's study entailed accompanying shoppers to see what they actually did, Sewell's study involved 'presenting [her] interviewees with real life situations' of her own devising (Sewell, 1981; p. 5). Some of these 'real life' situations did appear to be concerned with the 'national economy':

> On the news recently it was said that the annual rate of inflation had fallen from 17.4 per cent to 17.2 per cent. What effect do you think this will have on prices? (If answer 'none') What do you think ought to happen if it had fallen to, say, 12 per cent? (Sewell, 1981; p. 33)

In order to make any sense of this in terms of the effect on an individual's financial situation (ie 'which prices?'), they would have to be in possession of and comprehend details of (amongst other things) the particular type of weighted average upon which the retail prices index is computed. It is also not entirely clear how one might interpret, 'what effect do you think this will have on prices?' Sewell's apparent belief that the rate of inflation has some direct effect on prices (rather than the other way around) seems to suggest that her own understanding of the national economy is somewhat less than sophisticated; this has to do with economics, but not mathematics.

Again, the non-mathematical activity appears to be the focus of a mathematical gaze which organizes its commentary in its own terms. Again, the myth of participation constructs this commentary in utilitarian terms in respect of the recontextualized activity. Jean Lave's description of functionalist psychological theory provides an appropriate metaphor:

> ... mind and its contents have been treated rather like a well-filled toolbox. Knowledge is conceived as a set of tools stored in memory, carried around by individuals who take the tools (eg 'foolproof' arithmetic algorithms) out

and use them, the more often and appropriately the better, after which they are stowed away again without change at any time during the process. The metaphor is especially apt given that tools are designed to resist change or destruction through the conditions of their use. (Lave, 1988; p. 24)

Tools are always for something other than themselves and the notion of a toolbox evokes images of manual work. This metaphor de-intellectualizes the intellectual and appropriately associates the myth of participation with manual labour. This is entirely consistent with the social class principle of the distribution of these two myths which I shall illustrate in my analysis of *SMP 11–16* texts in subsequent chapters.

The prevalence of the myth of participation is not confined to the principal voices of school mathematics represented by school textbooks and numeracy coordinators. Here is an extract from the fieldnotes of Robert Lindsay, who was commissioned to conduct a third study for the Cockcroft Committee[5]:

> . . . every employer he spoke to said the lads don't fill in their time-sheets correctly and therefore find difficulty in seeing how their total money is arrived at. John noted, however, that in the building site dart games these same people can always add and subtract and find out how many more they need to score without any apparent difficulty. They also have a reasonably good idea of how much change they should get, so John infers that the basic ability must be there and it probably hasn't been exercised enough at school. (Shell Centre, nd; p. 585)

The extract reports an interview with a Construction Industries Training Board advisor, John, who pathologizes 'the lads' as lacking in mathematical experience. There are three contexts which are referred to: the completion of time sheets within a working context; the computation of darts scores within a popular leisure context; the practising of arithmetic within a school context. John articulates these contexts via the construction of a set of transferable skills — tools. An alternative analysis might have investigated the different social conditions obtaining within the contexts through which these 'lads' moved, taking note, perhaps, of another study about another group of 'lads' (Willis, 1977). Again, however, the myth of participation is being distributed to manual labour. But class is only one dimension of social structure. There are other myths.

Ethnomathematics and the Myth of Emancipation

The myth of participation 'recognizes' the operation of mathematical tools in diverse practices. It constructs a role for mathematics education in providing

5 Lindsay unfortunately died before he was able to write up these notes as a report. The notes are available from the Shell Centre at Nottingham University.

the toolbox and a pathological lack on the part of the yet-to-be-tutored. In contrast to this pathologizing, a growing body of work seeks to celebrate an alreadiness of mathematical content within the practices of different cultural groups. Within the context of mathematics education, this work has come to be referred to as 'ethnomathematics' — a term originally coined by Ubiritan D'Ambrosio (1985, 1990). I have discussed this work elsewhere (Dowling, 1989, 1995a, 1995b, Brown and Dowling 1989). Here, I shall introduce sufficient of the work to establish my principal argument.

Paulus Gerdes (1985, 1986, 1988a, 1988b), for example, is originally a Dutch educator now working in Mozambique. He has studied non-industrialized production processes in Mozambique — the building of huts, the weaving of fishing baskets and buttons, etc — and traditional sand drawing in Angola. Like the Cockcroft researchers, he has described these practices in terms associated with secondary school mathematics. A pattern in a woven button, for example, signifies Pythagoras' theorem (Gerdes, 1988b). However, unlike the utilitarians, Gerdes does not pathologize the unschooled Mozambicans. On the contrary, he celebrates a mathematical knowledge which is already there, which has been 'frozen' into the button as a kind of 'dead mathematical labour' (to revive Marx's expression). This discovery, Gerdes suggests, might be incorporated into mathematics lessons to stimulate cultural confidence, to emancipate:

> 'Had Pythagoras not . . . *we* would have discovered it'. The debate starts. 'Could our ancestors have discovered the "Theorem of Pythagoras"?' 'Did they?' . . . 'Why don't we know it?' . . . 'Slavery, colonialism . . .'. By 'defrosting frozen mathematical thinking' one stimulates a reflection on the impact of colonialism, on the historical and political dimensions of mathematics (education). (Gerdes, 1988b; p. 152)

Reflection on the impact of colonialism is no bad thing in the Mozambican or, indeed, in any other curriculum. The difficulty is that it appears that a European is needed to reveal to the African students the value inherent in their own culture. When he does so, of course, he does it in European terms, even referring to a European 'mathematician' (Pythagoras)[6]. The African culture, in other words, is not being allowed to speak for itself.

Gerdes' intention is not simply to stimulate cultural confidence, but also to teach mathematics. The mathematics that he wants to teach is very much in the tradition of the contemporary European school. However, he refers to this mathematics as 'world-mathematics' (1988a). He is able to do this via his process of 'defrosting':

> The artisan who imitates a known production technique is — generally — not doing mathematics. But the artisan(s) who discovered the techniques, *did*

---

6 Decontextualizing 'the theorem', it appears to have been known outside of Europe well before the time of Pythagoras (Joseph, 1991), so that the attribution itself is eurocentric.

mathematics, *developed* mathematics, was (were) thinking mathematically. (Gerdes, 1986; p. 12)

Gerdes' 'defrosting' actually denies cultural value (in mathematical terms) to contemporary Mozambicans. At the same time, he is postulating a mathematical originator who created the technology. Gerdes is thus projecting onto African culture not only 'European' mathematics, but also a 'European' capitalist model of 'Fordist' production, in which the worker has no access to the principles of her/his productive processes and is denied creativity (Braverman, 1974; Dowling, 1991a; Hales, 1980; Matthews, 1989), and a 'European', 'great man' model of history which is a distortion even in 'European' terms[7].

Gerdes describes mathematics as 'panhuman' (1988a). Alan Bishop (1988a, 1988b), similarly, describes mathematics as a 'pan-human phenomenon' and marks out six 'fundamental activities' that he describes as 'both universal, in that they appear to be carried out by every cultural group ever studied, and also necessary and sufficient for the development of mathematical knowledge' (1988a, p. 182). These 'fundamental activities' are: counting, locating, measuring, designing, playing, and explaining. I shall refer to just one of these, locating (although a similar argument could be presented in relation to each). Pam Harris has noted that the Aboriginal people with whom she has worked make use of the points of the compass far more frequently than left and right in orienting themselves in space. This preference extends to circumstances in which no European would ever use the points of the compass:

> Even in the most personal and intimate situations related to a person's own body, the Warlpiri still use compass terms and not left and right. Laughren told me of a woman at Yuendumu who, when giving birth to a child in hospital, said that she had a cramp 'warnarri kakarrara'; that is, in the 'east leg'. (Harris, 1991; p. 24)

The Warlpiri knowledge of compass orientations pre-dated the European invasion of Australia. The sensitivity of individuals of this society to their personal orientation with respect to the world is suggestive of quite a fundamental break with the Cartesian epistemology. The latter locates the knowing subject as the frame of reference for the external world; Warlpiri epistemology[8] appears to inscribe the individual within the world. This being the case,

---

7 See, for example, Cockburn (1983, 1985a, 1985b, 1985c) and MacKenzie and Wajcman (1985) for more sociologically aware histories of technology. However, it might be argued that any historiography which constructs events and organizes them as a temporal sequence and/or causal system having a claim on a reality beyond itself is a particularly European mode of self-description.

8 I am, of course, applying the European term 'epistemology' to a non-European culture. However, my intention is to use this European expression to highlight rather than to background differences.

the classification of both European and Aboriginal practices as 'location' is clearly a gross reduction[9].

Ethnomathematics is an area which is now attracting increasing interest on a global scale (see in addition to those mentioned above, for example: Abraham and Bibby, 1992; Fasheh, 1991, 1993; Knijnik, 1993; Maier, 1980). To varying degrees, all of this work succeeds in celebrating non-European cultural practices only by describing them in European mathematical terms, that is, by depriving them of their social and cultural specificity[10]. These authors are able to recognize a practice as mathematical only by virtue of recognition principles which derive from their own enculturation into European mathematics[11].

It would be entirely possible to construct an argument along the following lines. Specific mathematical practices are indicators of psychological states or processes. These states or processes are also indicated by other practices, such as basket weaving, which we would not usually recognize as mathematics. Therefore, the incidence of basket weaving is a valid indicator of the psychological basis of mathematical practices. However, the establishing of such an argument entails a considerable amount of theoretical and empirical work in respect of the elaboration of a psychology and in developing descriptions of both mathematics and basket weaving to the degree that observations can stand as valid and reliable indicators of the theoretical objects. This work has not been attempted. Generally, the work is entirely untheorized. We might speculate that this is a consequence of the pragmatic attitude of a great deal of writing in mathematics education. By this I mean that the work is frequently

9   There exists a body of work on education and Aboriginal cultures which does not reduce Aboriginal cultures to mere exemplars of a global (and essentially European) culture, see, for example: Carroll (1991); Harris, P. (1991); Harris, S. (1988); Ilyatjar (1991); Kearins (1991); McTaggart (1989); Parish (1991); Watson (1988); Wunungmurra (1988). Some, however (for example, Carroll, 1991; Currie *et al*, 1992; Guider, 1991; Kearins, 1991) still seem to prioritise the 'European' school curriculum and focus on difficulties arising out of cultural difference.

10   Mary Harris (1993) argues that my (Dowling, 1989) criticism 'seems harsh' in respect of D'Ambrosio who 'classes western academic mathematics as merely one form of ethnomathematics' (Harris, 1993; no page nos). However, my point is not to accuse D'Ambrosio of an explicit elevation of European mathematics above other practices. Rather, I am maintaining that he implicitly does so by classifying this diversity as mathematics at all. This is because he continues, unreflexively, to use (implicit) recognition principles which derive from his own positioning within European mathematics. Harris's own work (1985a, 1985b, 1987, 1988a, 1988b) is somewhat less susceptible to (but not exempt from) this criticism than most insofar as she foregrounds and celebrates culturally (and industrially) based technologies which are presented as curriculum materials for European students. Most of the other work in the ethnomathematics category is more clearly intended to be *for* non-Europeans.

11   This point is recognized by Bishop in his qualification of his position: 'Perhaps a safer label would in any case be "culturo-centric universals" *i.e.* universals from *our* culturo-centric position, since we are describing the phenomena as "counting", etc this then makes it plain that one can never *establish* the universality of phenomena, one is merely choosing to describe a highly extensive set of similarities in a certain way' (Bishop, 1988b; p. 55). However, this (idealist) admission of cultural relativism is negated by the general line of argument and intentions revealed in his book (Dowling, 1989).

oriented towards practical educational and/or political outcomes rather than towards analysis and theoretically informed description. This, of itself, does not condemn the work. Unless, that is, it parades itself as research. There is a sense in which the whole of this book is concerned with the relationship between context-specific practices. I shall be discussing the particular relationship between educational theory and practice later.

I shall offer a final extract from what was possibly the first piece of work in the 'ethnomathematics' tradition:

> The African adapts his [sic] home admirably to his means of subsistence, to the available materials, and to the requirements of the climate. The circular house in its many versions is found throughout the continent. The circle, of all closed geometric shapes in the plane, encompasses the greatest area within a given perimeter. Confronted by a scarcity of building materials and by the urgency to erect a shelter without professional assistance and in the shortest possible time, the African chooses the circle as the most economical form. He is not unique; round houses are constructed in the Arctic as well as at the Equator. (Zaslavsky, 1973; pp. 155–6)

This extract is from Claudia Zaslavsky's book, *Africa Counts* — a title which is patronizing in both interpretations of the pun. Unlike some of the other writers in this tradition, Zaslavsky is intentionally addressing middle class America. But perhaps this renders the objectification of *the* African even more excruciating. The myth propagated by ethnomathematics entails a celebration of the supposed mathematical practices of non-European societies. Revealing the truly mathematical content of what might otherwise be regarded as primitive practices elevates the practices and, ultimately, emancipates the practitioners. This is the *myth of emancipation*. The construction of the myth is similar to that of the myth of participation. European mathematics constitutes recognition principles which are projected onto the other, so that mathematics can be 'discovered' under its gaze. The myth then announces that the mathematics was there already.

In each case, the recognition of self in the other abstracts descriptions of practices from the constitution of the practices themselves within distinct sets of social relations. A principal difference, however, lies in the nature of the role which the pedagogy constructs for itself. The myth of participation pathologizes the yet-to-be-schooled, but announces the treatment in the provision of use-values. The myth of emancipation denies that there is anything wrong, but implicitly retains the prerogative and principles of diagnosis. When addressing the non-European, the role of school mathematics in the myth of emancipation is that of therapist; a signifier which, in the excision of a space, elides a more appropriate organization of its syllables. Pedagogic action claims to reveal the 'true nature' of the culture of the other: 'what all cultures really, really want, underneath it all, is the Enlightenment phallus of mathematics'. When addressing the European, school mathematics claims to be the champion of the oppressed, but claims also the right to deny the oppressed a voice:

Africans, by the way, can count; Africa counts in the world. Put another way, 'Mathematics Counts'.

I have now introduced three mathematical myths (a fourth will be introduced in Chapter 2 and a fifth and sixth in Chapter 12). The question to be addressed now is, 'precisely what do they mythologize?' As I have argued, the myth of reference constructs mathematics as a system of exchange-values which can be exchanged for practices relating to non-mathematical activities. The principle of exchange, however, entails a differentiation. That mathematics can be exchanged for shopping is contingent upon mathematics incorporating recognition and realization principles that facilitate the exchange: this mathematical string for that retail transaction, and so forth. This is what I mean by the 'gaze'. However, we know that the principles which regulate mathematics and those which regulate shopping constitute distinct systems. One may recruit elements of the other: a shopper may use a memory of a multiplication table; a mathematics textbook may incorporate a domestic setting. But precisely what is recruited is regulated by the recruiting rather than the recruited practice. Mathematics is not about shopping because the shopping settings which appear in mathematical texts are not motivated by shopping practices. Mathematics is no more about shopping than Picasso's *Les Demoiselles d'Avignon* is about prostitution. In its pure, ideal-typical form, the myth of reference consumes the non-mathematical setting within a mathematical play leaving only a trace to remind us that there is something outside of mathematics[12]. This is why the settings in the extracts from *SMP 11–16 Book Y1* are so pruned of non-mathematical specificity. The merest residue is sufficient to the purpose of the myth which is to claim an external motivation for mathematics. Behind the myth lies mathematics as a self-referential system. Its utterances are not references, but simulacra (see Baudrillard, 1993, 1994).

The myth of participation is realized through far more extensive non-mathematical residues. Settings must exhibit a strong non-mathematical modality, that is, they must make a strong claim to a non-mathematical reality which they faithfully represent[13]. Failure in this regard would negate the claim to non-mathematical utility. It will be noticed, for example, that the modality of the Jim/Zola/Eve extracts is high in comparison with that of the two brief shopping extracts from *SMP 11–16 Book Y1*. Unlike exchange, the principle of use-value is not differentiation but unification: tools must fit their purpose. Any claim that the tools are generalizable is simply an extension of the unified domain: it is not merely mathematics and shopping which are unified, but mathematics and any sphere of activity in which it might be of use. This is precisely the nature of the myth: the claim to a unity of culture which is, thereby, incomplete without mathematics. This is why mathematics is necessary for the optimizing of non-mathematical practices. Behind this myth again lies mathematics as a self-referential system, now more effectively concealed.

---

12   The motivation for this expression is in Saussure's poetics interpreted by Baudrillard (1993).
13   See Hodge and Kress (1988) for a discussion of modality.

The myth of emancipation must generate dual settings. Firstly, it must claim to represent a non-mathematical setting. Secondly, it must redescribe it in mathematical terms and assert that the two describe the same object, which is an essential mathematical competence. Mathematics, then, appears as the universal law. Again, the myth is one of unification. But what makes its utterances possible is precisely the same gaze that constitutes the two other myths. The principles of realization of this gaze are mathematical.

Of the three myths, only the first, the myth of reference, represents the cultural domain as divided. Since the myth speaks the 'voice of mathematics', it of necessity constitutes a hierarchy, prioritizing mathematics over other activities. Furthermore, since mathematics is an intellectual activity, it of necessity reproduces the intellectual/manual hierarchy whenever its object is other than intellectual (which is very often the case). By contrast, the myth of participation and the myth of emancipation represent the cultural domain as unitary and so deny the divisions and hierarchies constructed by the myth of reference. But the denial is itself mythical, because the myths are concealing the self-referential origin of the gaze which constructs their texts.

Myths and Utopias: A Political Text

Of the three myths, only one — the myth of reference — maintains a visible distinction between the mathematical and the non-mathematical. The myth is consistent with the form of utilitarianism that I have associated with the modern maths movement, because both entail a celebration of mathematics as systematic knowledge of and for itself, but potentially about something else. The myth is also operationally compatible with Hardy's elitism for much the same reason: it does not, ultimately, challenge the integrity of mathematical knowledge. Insofar as it sustains the principle of disciplined academic knowledge, the myth calls for an extended apprenticeship. The university — itself associated with an elite organized on the basis of social class — is an entirely appropriate centre for such an apprenticeship. Utility, such as it is, is inevitably deferred and uncertain: a half-hearted promise.

I want to look, now, at a text which presents a challenge to this myth on both utilitarian and unificatory grounds. The text in question is an extract from the first *White Paper on Education and Training* from the South African government which was elected in 1994. I have chosen a South African text because the defeat of the apartheid State has resulted in the democratic election of an ANC-dominated government with a massive popular mandate for revolutionary change in the social sphere and with a perceived need for urgent and extensive economic regeneration. The ANC itself is, of course, no stranger to revolutionary political action. These are good grounds for treating South Africa as a critical case with respect to political action. We might reasonably expect that its challenges to the old colonial order and its associated mythology will be most vigorous and most explicit. The text comprises paragraphs 4, 5 and 6 in Chapter 2 of the White Paper, 'Why Education and Training?'

4 An integrated approach implies a view of learning which rejects a rigid division between 'academic' and 'applied', 'theory' and 'practice', 'knowledge' and 'skills', 'head' and 'hand'. Such divisions have characterised the organisation of curricula and the distribution of educational opportunity in many countries of the world, including South Africa. They have grown out of, and helped to reproduce, very old occupational and social class distinctions. In South Africa such distinctions in curriculum and career choice have also been closely associated in the past with the ethnic structure of economic opportunity and power.

5 Successful modern economies and societies require the elimination of artificial hierarchies, in social organisation, in the organisation and management of work, and in the way in which learning is organised and certified. They require citizens with a strong foundation in general education, the desire and ability to continue to learn, to adapt to and develop new knowledge, skills and technologies, to move flexibly between occupations, to take responsibility for personal performance, and to set and achieve high standards and to work co-operatively.

6 In response to such structural changes in social and economic organisation and technological development, integrated approaches toward education and training are now a major international trend in curriculum development and the reform of qualification structure. An integrated approach to education and training will not in itself create a successful economy and society in South Africa. However, the Ministry of Education is convinced that this approach is a prerequisite for successful human resource development, and it is thus capable of making a significant contribution to the reconstruction and development of our society and economy. (Department of Education, 1995; p. 15)

The first sentence of paragraph 4 sets up a number of oppositions: academic/applied; theory/practice; knowledge/skills; head/hand. These are being established as equivalents and clearly resonate with the intellectual/ manual opposition which I have associated with the myth of reference and with academic elitism. In the second sentence of the extract, these equivalents are being located in the past ('such divisions *have* characterised . . .') and generalized ('. . . in many countries of the world . . .'). The third sentence associates both the origins and effectivity of these oppositions with social class divisions, which are, again, *passé* (they are 'very old'). The final sentence of the paragraph specializes the South African context, again, looking back; the introduction of the term 'power' indicates, if it were not already apparent, that we are not talking about mere divisions, but about hierarchies. This paragraph, then, associates the theory/practice or intellectual/manual division with South Africa's apartheid past.

So, the text has constituted a nexus of equivalent practices: theory/practice; class structure; apartheid. These are located in the past. Paragraph 5 shifts the temporal frame. The subject of the first sentence is notionally in the present: 'successful modern economies and societies'. However, these economies and societies are not indexed. Indeed, nor can they be; their localizing would invoke their specificities which may challenge the nexus of equivalents established in the previous paragraph. Japan, for example, might be interpreted as a successful modern economy and society, however, its educational practices might be described as exhibiting precisely the divisions that are being located in the past. In other words, a virtual subject is being established, a subject which can be attributed with all of those qualities which are to be advocated in the text, a utopia. Utopias are always located outside of the present temporal frame. The past having been established as a dystopia, the utopia lies in the future.

This utopia has requirements, specifically the elimination of 'artificial hierarchies'. The hierarchical divisions of the past nexus are, then, artificial. Just as apartheid itself constitutes an artificial racial hierarchy, just as capitalism (a word which must remain unspoken) constitutes an artificial class hierarchy, so theory/practice constitutes an artificial hierarchy of knowledge. If it is artificial, then it can be removed and, indeed, its removal is required by the utopia. The utopia also has requirements of its citizens who must have certain attributes and dispositions. Most crucial of these, perhaps, is the need 'to take responsibility for personal performance'. The utopia has requirements in terms of both the organization of the social, the workplace, and the school, and in terms of the attributes and dispositions of its citizens who must be responsible for their own performances within the organization. What is missing is the explicit recognition of the subject of organization and management, that is, the bureaucratizing state, the principal voice of the text. The position for this voice is nevertheless established through the need associated with the requirements of the utopia.

Paragraph 6 explicitly attaches the principal voice to the achievement of the utopian requirements, that is, to the elimination of the nexus of the past dystopia. This is more difficult, because it is no longer simply a matter of critical association and the construction of utopias and dystopias. The text must claim authority for a practical governmental strategy — all political texts must assert their authority with respect to the reader. To claim authority for a practical strategy would seem to demand empirical evidence. This can be achieved connotatively, thus, the first sentence of paragraph 6 describes 'integrated approaches to education and training' as 'a major international trend'. However, to assert, directly, that such approaches developed in advance of economic and structural developments within the international field would beggar belief. Rather, the major international trend towards an integrated approach is constituted as a 'response' to such economic and structural developments. But the second sentence in this paragraph initiates a rotation of this line of cause and effect: 'an integrated approach . . . will not in itself create a successful economy and society . . .' This should be obvious, if the latter causes the former, but doubt is being introduced. The final sentence completes the turn: 'However, the Ministry of Education is convinced that this approach is a prerequisite for successful human resource development and it is thus capable of making a significant contribution to the reconstruction and development of our economy and society'. Causality has been reversed, so that the authority of the principal voice of the text is established in relation to a specific governmental strategy.

My reading of these three paragraphs illustrates two principal categories that I shall develop in Chapter 6. Essentially, my approach derives from a theoretical position which guides my interpretation. In simple terms, I shall propose that the social comprises relations and practices which are organized as empirically definable 'activities'. School mathematics is describable as an example of such an activity. An activity is a structure of relations and practices which, essentially, regulates who can say/do what. It constitutes positions which are always hierarchical (although not necessarily simply hierarchical). The practices of the activity are distributed within this hierarchy. Activities are produced by and reproduced in human subjects — who move, routinely, between activities — and by texts. I shall try to signify the dialectical nature of production/reproduction through the use of the expression, (re)production. If texts are to (re)produce activities, then they must establish textual positions (voices) with respect to each other and distribute textual practices (messages) in relation to the structure of positions. Texts must constitute positioning and distributing strategies.

The above text positions its own voice through the invoking of utopia. It also positions the voice of the good citizen, which affiliates to the utopia, and the bad citizen, which affiliates to the past. The voice of the bad citizen has yet to be made explicit, but the message that is distributed to it constitutes the past nexus, including the theory/practice hierarchy. The message of the principal voice of the text is the requirement of the utopia which is the governmental strategy to be implemented: the integrated approach. The message of the good citizen is responsibility and compliance.

The voice of the bad citizen is made explicit in a subsequent part of the text, here are paragraphs 12 and 13:

12 The Working Group includes representatives of the Departments of Education and Manpower, the National Training board, organised business and organised labour. The Working Group recognises that the prospect of an integrated approach to education and training has alarmed some professionals in both the formal education and the skills training camps. Some training practitioners are concerned that the specific requirements of occupational skills training will be swamped by unreasonable demands for the inclusion of general or academic courses. Some educators are concerned that the intrinsic values of general or academic education will be over-ridden by a narrow vocationalism or a merely economic approach to learning.

13 To some extent, such concerns probably reflect past divisions between the education and training sectors, and may not be fully informed by the most advanced international practice in the design and assessment

of learning programmes, either in industry or in educational institutions. Nevertheless, they are not unreasonable and they need to be addressed seriously. Enabling the National Qualification Framework to be developed in an evolutionary, participatory, and consensual way, within clear policy guidelines, will be the best way of implementing the new strategy. The organised teaching profession, and the representative bodies of the university, technikon and college sectors, as major stakcholders, will be invited to become fully involved in this process. (Department of Education, 1995; p. 16)

The 'Working Group' has been introduced as an agency of the dominant voice, nominally the Ministry. In these two paragraphs the bad citizen is nominated as 'some training practitioners' and 'some educators'. The use of these terms associates the voices with precisely the past practices (that is, distributes these practices to them) that are rejected by the dominant voice. They are concerned about being 'swamped' or 'over-ridden'. These are negative terms which might be associated with a dictatorial, antidemocratic mode of government, another unspoken voice.

Paragraph 13 opens with a distributing strategy which associates the bad citizen with the past nexus and a positioning strategy which establishes them as ignorant in respect of the utopian practices which have already been introduced. Ignorance, however, is not necessarily culpable and can be overcome. The paragraph names the bad citizens more explicitly: 'the organised teaching profession, and the representatives of the university, technikon and college sectors'. It also distributes their responsibilities. Development which is 'evolutionary, participatory' and is 'consensual' — provided that it is 'within clear policy guidelines' — optimizes implementation. The 'new strategy' itself is non-negotiable, but (reformed) bad citizens may assist in applying it.

The subject of political action is represented by the dominant voice of the text. It claims authority in the name of a post-Fordist utopia within which social divisions and hierarchies have been eradicated and economic productivity has been assured. The utopia naively ignores the fact that economic production is predicated upon the negative entropy of the unequal distribution of scarce resources; this is why it is a utopia and not a programme. The myth, however, resides not in the inevitable unachievability of utopia. Rather, the myth is the construction of the managerial practices of the State in respect of education and training as use-values with respect to the engineering of social relations. This is an inversion of a crude Marxism which constitutes a cultural superstructure as a mere reflection of the relations of production which comprise the base. Here, the State claims to be able to manipulate culture and effect changes in social structure. The State has to make such claims, of course, in order to conceal its self-referential impotence. But, in this text, the self-consciousness of a young and residually honest government shows through in the visibility of its somersault in paragraph 6 of the first section of the extract.

The crunch comes with the realization that what is to be achieved by the text is no more than the replacement of one myth by another. A substitution which leaves untroubled the comfortable hierarchy of intellectual and manual labour. Out is to go the elitism of the academic disciplines with their myths of reference which have failed to deliver on their half-hearted promises. In come the practices of management in education and training. These practices, equally intellectual, are now to be operated by corporatist elites: '[t]he organised teaching profession, and the representative bodies of the university, technikon and college sectors, as major stakeholders, will be invited to become fully involved in this process'. The State can dissolve academic educational content, but only by replacing it with educational management which will not, of course, be transmitted in the schools alongside the new vocational curriculum. In this most critical of contexts, the existing social order, described in terms of the intellectual/manual hierarchy, remains, perhaps, remarkably unscathed. I shall return to reconsider this in the final chapter of this book.

Towards a Demystification of Myths

The myths that I have described are all concerned with the relationship between what I want to maintain are different activities. The myth of reference constructs mathematics (for example) as a distinctive practice, but one which can be systematically exchanged for other practices. Mathematics is able to constitute principles of recognition and realization which enable it to project a gaze onto non-mathematical practices and redescribe them in its own terms. Because the gaze is systematic as is mathematical knowledge itself, the latter is (mythically) understood to comprise exchange-values in respect of (potentially all) other activities.

The myth of participation elides the distinctive nature of mathematics. The latter is constructed as tools — as use-values — with multiple purposes. The effect is to unify the domain of cultural practices. The myth of emancipation achieves the same unification, but is a somewhat different way. The myth of participation pathologizes culture as incomplete without an explicit mathematical education. The myth of emancipation claims that such an education must always have been a component of all cultures, because they all entail mathematics. Both of these myths commonly cast their gaze upon manual activities. Both of them effectively conceal the intellectual activity which constitutes their principles of recognition and realization. Unlike the myth of reference, they effectively ideologize the intellectual/manual hierarchy.

The South African government, more so than most, needs to present itself as engineering socioeconomic transformation. In the extract from its White Paper, it effectively and correctly identifies the intellectual/manual hierarchy as fundamental to the class structure of the society. It sets out to dissolve this hierarchy, but is unable to do so. It simply replaces one realization of it by another. Its own myth proclaims the effectivity of its managerial practices in social transformation. That this claim is mythical of necessity entails that the transformation is utopian. The White Paper makes just another claim for the power of mind over matter: mathematics over shopping; managerial practices over apartheid. This is the myth that is at the core of all of the myths that I have identified in this chapter. Ideologically, the myth serves to conceal the self-referential nature of intellectual activity. Hardy wanted an intellectual memorial. Mythically, his memorial is a monolith, a phallus with the power to create and transform. How is such a myth possible, what are the conditions of its existence? This is the question that I shall begin to address in Chapter 2.

Juggling Pots and Texts

In Chapter 1 I introduced three myths which are constructed in and by mathematics education. The myths are concerned with the relationship between mathematics and non-mathematical activities. I also considered an extract from a South African White Paper on education and training. The extract represented an attempt to challenge social and cultural divisions through the imposition of what are effectively managerial practices. I argued that the result constituted a mythologizing of these practices as effective in respect of social engineering. This is no more than the replacement of mythologized academic knowledge by mythologized managerial practices. The social structure indexed by the intellectual/manual hierarchy remains unchallenged by this move. My intention in the first chapter was to call into question the assumption that the sociocultural terrain can in any meaningful sense be regarded as a unity. I wanted to challenge the core myth that practices which are organized and developed within one activity can be effective, even transformative, within another.

The general position that I intend to argue in this book is that insofar as an activity can be empirically described as exhibiting a particular structure of social relations, then this structure will tend to subordinate to its own principles any practice that is recruited from another activity. I want to refer to this position as the *principle of recontextualization*. As a simple illustration, school mathematics may incorporate domestic settings in its textbooks, but the structure of the resulting tasks will prioritize mathematical rather than domestic principles. Alternatively, domestic practices may recruit mathematical resources, but the mathematical structure will be to a greater or lesser extent subordinated to the principles of the domestic activity. Illustrations of this recontextualization were introduced in Chapter 1, more will be given later in the book.

In this chapter I want to begin to develop a description of the ways in which contexts may differ in respect of their structure. This will enable me to introduce a key term in my language of description, *discursive saturation*. I also want to draw out some of the implications for mathematics education and, in particular, to introduce another myth: the *myth of construction*. I shall begin with an illustration from a non-mathematical text intended for self-instruction. I shall then describe two ideal types of pedagogic relations. I shall move from this typology to a brief analysis of some primary school mathematics materials and the introduction of the myth of construction. This will enable me to construct a third ideal type of pedagogic relation. Again, the theoretical framework which informs the work of this chapter will be developed more fully in Chapters 5 and 6.

Juggling

In an attempt to annoy some of my friends, I bought them each a set of juggling balls, together with instructions, for Christmas[1]. The initial result was a resounding success: 'You bastard!', was the response of one, 'now I'll have to learn how to do it'. Unfortunately, I had been unable to resist buying an additional set for myself. I found myself hoist by my own petard, caught by the balls.

The instructions are organized along the classic lines of what B.F. Skinner referred to as 'shaping'. First you learn how to throw and catch one ball, then two, then two whilst holding a third, then you throw the third — anywhere — then you try to catch the third ball. Finally, you just keep going. The task is simplified and instruction moves progressively towards the final form. Apart from its behaviourist pedagogy, what is interesting about the instructions is the diagrams, one of which is shown as *Figure 2.1*. You will notice that the trajectory of the balls defies gravity. Those of us who have studied kinematics know that the trajectory of a projectile in a parallel field is a parabola, which is a symmetrical curve. The trajectories in the diagram look rather more like skewed frequency distributions. Of course, if the diagram showed the balls following parabolic trajectories, they would appear on the same curve and so would collide (*see Figure 2.2*). The text overcomes this by pretending that the balls can boomerang back on themselves. This trajectory also has the advantage of providing two target points in the corners of the box which is shown in the diagram. So, what happens when you actually throw the balls? Do they collide? Obviously not, as we know from the fact that experienced jugglers contrive to extend their performances beyond the collision of the first two balls that they throw in the air. Furthermore, I can provide empirical evidence of the success of this text as a self-instruction manual: I and the friends to whom I gave juggling balls and instructions are now proficient at juggling with three balls.

I would not wish to claim that all juggling manuals misrepresent the physical world in this way. But I have another which includes even more extreme distortions of the parabolic trajectories[2]. My question is, 'how is it possible to learn the practice from a self-instruction manual which misrepresents it?'

---

1 The juggling balls and instructions are produced by More Balls Than Most Ltd, London. The instruction booklet is titled *A Short Course in Life Enhancement Volume 2*, and is dated 1994.
2 Dingman, R. (1994) *The Little Book of Juggling*, Philadelphia: Running Press.

Figure 2.1   A Short Course in Life Enhancement Volume 2 (Source: London: More Balls
Than Most, 1994, Figure 2)

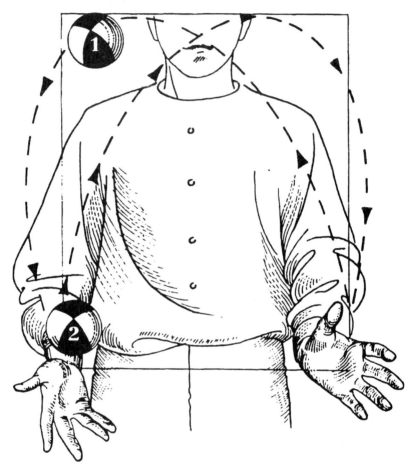

In fact, success is achieved because we can assume a certain minimal
degree of hand-eye co-ordination on the part of the learner. If you aim at the
corner of the box (*Figure 2.1*), then the ball will return to its initial level
beyond the position of the catching hand as it is shown in the diagram. The
juggler must move the hand outwards in order to catch the ball. There is then
a 'natural' tendency to move the hand back towards the body so that the
throw is made from the original position. The juggler's hands thus move in
circles. This is apparently contradicted by the text which advises: 'keep your
hands low at the bottom corners letting the balls fall into them'[3]. The text,

---

3   In another diagram, the hands are shown to move inwards, although it is not clear whether
    this is simply indicating a throwing action. Nowhere does the text explicitly mention the
    circular movement of the hands.

Figure 2.2 Alternative juggling diagram

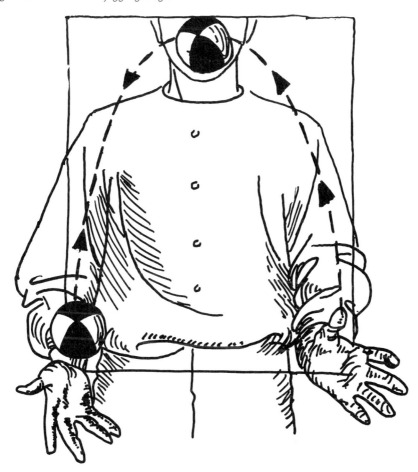

then, has misrepresented not only the physics of the situation, but also the action of the skill itself. Plausibly, this has been done in order to simplify the instructions. The fact that one can still learn to juggle using a text which describes an imaginary skill in an imaginary universe is attributable to the physical nature of the situation together with the assumed generic physical skills of the learner. Since a novice can't juggle whilst looking in a mirror, you will not be in a position to notice that you are not doing it as it shows it in the diagrams until you are already proficient.

Although there is a pedagogic text, here, this is about self-instruction to the extent that the learner is free to recruit and interpret the text according to criteria over which they have control. There is, in other words, no pedagogic relationship involved. Included among the learner's criteria will be those relating to the adequacy of performance. These criteria will have been constituted by a gaze cast by the learner on the performances of others, that is, on the performances of jugglers, as well as by reading the instructions. Further development will include practice, but it will also include the development of these criteria. Devices for achieving this might include the use of additional instruction books, the opinions of critical others, or apprenticing oneself to a juggler. A pedagogic relationship is inaugurated upon the advent of an other. I want now to move to a consideration of modes of pedagogic relationship.

Modes of Pedagogic Relationship: First Steps Towards an Ideal-typical Schema

My intention is to generate ideal types of pedagogic relationship. The method of ideal types was introduced by Max Weber who used it to generate categories of, for example, social action (instrumental- and value-oriented) and authority (traditional, charismatic, bureaucratic) (see Weber, 1964). Ideal types are categories which originate from observation, but which have been made conceptually coherent. In referring back to the empirical, it is important to remember that concrete instances are likely to combine elements of more than one ideal type, so that the latter are unlikely to be found in their pure form. It is also important to stress that the construction of ideal types is a theoretical exercise, albeit with some grounding in observation; as Blau and Meyer (1971) point out, the method of ideal types is intended to be a guide to empirical research, not a substitute for it[4]. Crucially, the generation of ideal types may be considered as a step in the dialogue between a developing theory and empirical observation and this is the sense in which it is being used here. Both the theoretical and empirical domains will be developed further in subsequent chapters.

The discussion on juggling, above, was concerned with self-instruction. Self-instruction denotes a relationship between an individual — the learner — and a practice which they wish to acquire, but which is interpreted from their perspective. There is no interaction. Pedagogic action, by contrast, involves the relationship between two subjective positions. Conventionally, it is assumed that one of these positions is adept in respect of the to-be-acquired practice, and the other is a novice. As I shall argue, this situation does not always obtain. Where it does, I shall refer to the form of pedagogic relationship as one of *apprenticeship*.

In an apprenticeship relation, the adept may be described as the *subject* of the practice which the novice is to acquire. Here, I am using 'subject' in a sense similar to its meaning in 'the subject of a sentence'. Figuratively, the adept 'speaks the voice' of the practice. This, of course, does not make the adept a free agent. On the contrary, to be the subject of the practice means to

---

4   The danger of a descent into theoreticism which is immanent in the ignoring of these methodological issues is illustrated by Hunter (1994) who reifies Weber's 'bureaucratic authority' in his positivist critique of liberal and radical accounts of schooling (see Dowling, 1994/5).

be subjected by its regulative principles, in the same way as to be a speaker of English entails a certain subjugation to its grammar and lexicon. The novice is to become subjected to the discipline of the practice in order also to become its subject. The novice is, furthermore, the object of pedagogic action. This entails, crucially, that the evaluative criteria are controlled by the adept and not by the novice. The self-learner must satisfy their own criteria for success: the apprentice must satisfy someone else's.

As I have indicated, the self-instructor's criteria are at least partially derived through a recontextualizing of performances which are generated within the site of production relating to the practice to be acquired. I recognize adequacy in my juggling because I have seen the performances of acclaimed jugglers. But the site of evaluation of my performances is different. There is, in other words, a displacement between the site of pedagogic action (myself, my juggling balls, and my instruction book) and the site of production of performances (the juggler that I watch and applaud with the crowd in a market in Durban). This is not the case with respect to apprenticeship as this mode is to be understood here. The criteria that are to be applied to the performances of the novice are, at least ultimately, the same as those which are applied to the performances of the adept. These performances enter into the same field of relations. In the case of commodity production, that field is an economic field. Acquisition is to occur within the context of the elaboration of that which is to be acquired: there is a coincidence of pedagogic action and pedagogic content; the adept is teaching the practices in which they are adept.

Traditional apprenticeship occurs in Japanese *mingei* folk pottery. Apprenticeship in this site is described by John Singleton (1989). The early stages of this form of apprenticeship often involve working around the edges of the practice and observing, what Lave and Wenger (1991) refer to as 'legitimate peripheral participation'. This form of involvement may last for a very long time, even years, especially where the adept is being paid a regular fee for what amounts to allowing the novice to act as unskilled (but unpaid) labour. Eventually, the would-be potter is allowed to try their hand on the wheel. One of the first tasks that they have to perform is to produce ten thousand *sake* cups to the model produced by the adept. Initially, most if not all of the apprentice's output will be returned to the clay pit to be recycled.

> An apprentice may spend six months or more making the first simple shape at the wheel, after his other chores have been attended to, not actually counting to see if the goal of ten thousand has been reached. When the potter begins to select some of the cups for firing, to be finished and sold as unsigned products of the shop, the apprentice has moved from practice to production. It is an important change of status, though there are still other forms to practice and master. (Singleton, 1989; p. 20)

Throughout this process there is very little explicit instruction; learning is achieved by observation. The practice is regulated by and within the concrete situation. Under these circumstances, we might expect that actions, including linguistic utterances, will be highly localized, highly context-dependent.

The apprenticeship of these craft potters takes place within the context of the production of pots as commodities. Performances — including the early successes of the *mingei* apprentice — enter into economic relations with other performances. The form of their evaluation is, like the instruction, tacit. The whole practice is regulated tacitly. I refer to such practices as exhibiting low *discursive saturation*, because there is a low degree of saturation of the non-discursive by the discursive. I will discuss this concept more fully in Chapter 5. Here, it is sufficient to indicate that, essentially, I am referring to 'the discursive' as the domain of the linguistic. Because neither the instruction nor the performances are strongly regulated within this domain, the specialization of language cannot be expected to be high, limited, perhaps, to argots. We might suppose that juggling would also be an example of a practice of this kind. This might explain the difficulties apparently experienced by the authors of the instruction booklet in transcribing a substantially non-discursive practice into discursive form. A transcription which is not ultimately achievable.

To summarize, the mode of pedagogic relation that I have described is characterized as apprenticeship. This involves a relationship between an adept as a subject of the to-be-acquired practice and a novice as the object of pedagogic action. The intention of pedagogic action is the establishing of a new adept, the establishing of subjectivity. The mode of pedagogic action is compatible with the mode or relationships into which performances enter, that is, substantially non-discursive. The practice is therefore described as exhibiting low discursive saturation; this will be denoted by DS$^-$.

The term 'apprenticeship' is generally associated with manual occupations. However, I have defined this mode simply in terms of an adept/novice relationship and a coincidence of the site of pedagogic action and the site of the production of performances relating to the pedagogic content (the apprentice potter is apprenticed by the potter in the pottery). This does not specialize the mode to manual or intellectual occupations. My extension of the term will therefore allow me to include the supervision of PhD theses as an example of apprenticeship.

There are a number of similarities between doctoral supervision and traditional craft apprenticeships. Acquisition is concerned with the practice in which the teacher is an adept. The student may not be required to produce ten thousand papers, but the evaluation of their early output will be undertaken in private discussion between student and supervisor. Later, the student will often be encouraged to present papers to their peers. Ultimately — often shortly before submitting their thesis for examination — the student will be invited to deliver a paper at a conference or open seminar. Indeed, this may happen on numerous occasions if the production of the thesis is prolonged. Furthermore, there are aspects of the transmission of research skills which resemble craft apprenticeship in the comparatively tacit nature of their acquisition. This is most obviously the case in the area of research methodology.

One acquires skills in interviewing and in the practical analysis of qualitative data, for example, through observation and practice. One might imagine that there are corresponding areas within the natural sciences and even mathematics. Explicit instruction may provide pointers, but is ultimately insufficient. Books on research methods are notoriously vague when it comes to the nitty gritty of what you actually do. A good piece of analysis often leaves one with a sense of its inevitability, even simplicity, which nevertheless mystifies its actual production.

However, there is a fundamental difference between the craft site and the research site. Specifically, performances in the former are commodified; they enter into economic relations with each other. They are, in this sense, evaluated according to a system of exchange-values that cannot be sensitive to the discursive form. Only in very special cases — such as meta-analysis — are the performances of academic research treated as directly comparable and even here there is no commodification. In general, the performances of this site enter not into economic relations but into discursive relations with each other. The intertextuality of research papers is always at least partially explicit in the bibliography. Research always incorporates and bears upon and interrogates previous research explicitly, which is to say, within language.

It is true that there are features of the evaluation of research production which constitute an economy of performances. The evaluation of academic performance in terms of a quantitative measure of publications output, for example. Nevertheless, the nature of research production itself is centrally discursive and, indeed, the discursive evaluation of research output precedes such economic evaluation in the selection — including refereeing — of papers submitted to journals and conferences. It is also true that academic research, in common with all other cultural practices, takes place within the context of the prevailing conditions of the economic configuration. However, unless we are to revert to a rigid scientific Marxist analysis, we must understand these conditions as setting limits to the nature of culture, but not as ultimately determining its content.

The performances of the doctoral student are always evaluated discursively. As the student's research proceeds, the context of this evaluation approaches the context within which the performances of the supervisor, *qua* researcher, are evaluated. There is thus a coming together of the supervisor *qua* supervisor and the supervisor *qua* researcher; a suturing of pedagogic action and pedagogic content. The performances of the student and, in particular, the thesis itself, must conform to the principles which are established by and within the discipline. In contrast with the situation in craft pottery, these principles are available within discourse. They are realized in the explicit interrogation of research texts by research texts. The form that this interrogation takes will be more or less specific to the disciplinary area of the thesis, but will be relatively independent of the specific problem addressed or methodology employed by the thesis. This is why the supervisor is able to supervise a range of theses (although some degree of specialization is clearly necessary). Thus research apprenticeship constitutes an initiation into a mode of discursive interrogation, the principles of which are relatively independent of the specificities of the particular piece of research[5]. Performances within such a practice must be relatively independent of their immediate context of production; they must be generalizable. I refer to such practices as exhibiting high discursive saturation, denoted by DS^+, because there is a relatively high level of saturation of the non-discursive by the discursive. They are capable of generating generalizable theoretical structures which can be applied across a range of settings. They are, in other words, substantially self-referential.

This facility is clearly a feature of mathematics and of sociology and of academic practices in general. It derives from the public and discursive nature of the relations between performances. For example, my own work originated in the analysis of secondary school mathematics texts. However, it has been and is being extended to the analysis of primary mathematics texts; classrooms; teacher education; home-school communication in the primary phase; texts in the further education sector; texts in the field of academic development; and the relationship between pedagogic practices and community structure. Similarly, mathematics can describe almost anything. This is evidenced in the diverse non-mathematical settings incorporated by school textbooks, in textbooks and courses in mathematical modelling, in writing in the area of 'ethnomathematics', and in research investigating the uses of mathematics.

There is, however, a price to be paid for this panoptic potential. Essentially, generalizable descriptions lose the specificity of that which they describe. They constitute not so much representations as myths. This was the argument that I presented in the first chapter. Mathematics and, indeed, sociology mythologize the world, creating public domains of their own expression. This is precisely because and to the extent that mathematical and sociological performances are evaluated discursively and within the context of the production of mathematical and sociological knowledge. There is, of necessity, a dislocation between these academic contexts and the contexts of evaluation of the practices which are mythologized. There may, indeed, be a discontinuity in mode of evaluation: domestic practices, for example, are frequently mathematized, but are evaluated within a field which exhibits low discursive saturation. Thus, DS^+ activities are able to cast a wide gaze, but the recontextualizing that such a gaze achieves effectively isolates the gazing from the gazed contexts. I will develop a theorizing of the nature of this isolation in Chapters 5 and 6.

In fact both DS^+ and DS^- activities isolate themselves with respect to other activities. In the case of DS^- activities, such as craft pottery, this is achieved via the context-dependency of the practices. These activities are specialized in terms of the physical organization (and often the physical location) of the space in which they are elaborated. Because they do not impose a high degree

---

5 See Dowling (1996a) for some thoughts on the form that such a mode of interrogation might take within educational research. See also Brown and Dowling (1998).

of system upon language, utterances are also likely to be highly context-dependent, that is, they are likely to suffer severe semantic depletion outside of their context of immediate production. Very substantially, then, DS⁻ activities constitute a division of labour which is predicated upon physical site. They are characteristic of what is commonly referred to as manual labour.

DS⁺ activities are isolated via a mechanism which operates in the opposite direction. That is, they generate texts which exhibit a high degree of context independence. This entails, however, that the texts only weakly articulate with contexts. Mathematized shopping is very different from domestic shopping; mathematized engineering cannot, it would seem, make an afterburner. These texts are the product of, in these cases, a mathematical gaze. The tendency to construct such texts as context-dependent rather than as context-independent mythologizes mathematics as being about or for or implicated within other activities. These are the myths of reference, participation, and emancipation. Such texts recontextualize the activity upon which the gaze has been cast — the objectified activity. To the extent, however, that they are represented as if they were texts of the objectified activity, they mythologize the latter. In particular, the myth of participation frequently mythologizes domestic practices; the myth of emancipation mythologizes diverse non-industrial cultures.

As I indicated at the start of this section, apprenticeship is not the only mode of pedagogic relation. In order to establish an alternative form, I shall give some further consideration to school mathematics texts.

School Texts and the Mythologizing of the Student

In the first chapter, I contrasted the myth of reference with the myth of participation. The former might be described as a colonizing of non-mathematical activities as a source of illustrations of the (mythical) referential nature of mathematics. The myth of participation, on the other hand, presents mathematics as a necessary condition for the optimizing of participation in apparently non-mathematical practices. Yet both myths entail the recontextualizing of non-mathematical practices. In the SMP text involving Jim and Zola (*Figure 1.1*), the mundane practices of DIY and cooking are arranged, not as people actually act in concrete, everyday settings, but according to mathematical principles. It is as if mathematics were casting a gaze on people's lives, reorganizing them according to its own structures and then handing them back: you see how much better life would be if we were all mathematicians. But it wouldn't be better, because mathematized solutions always fail to grasp the immediacies of the concrete settings within which, as Jean Lave (1988) points out, problems and solutions develop dialectically. The mathematical gaze generates a virtual reality, a mythical domesticity within which all is rational and all is calculable.

This is more insidious than the colonizing of the myth of reference. It is a moralizing of domestic space and of the mundane generally. This is a common message in school mathematics for the 'lower ability' students and also in the area of adult basic numeracy. It is apparent, for example, in Bridgid Sewell's, work which was cited in Chapter 1:

> Those who lack the skill even to calculate 10 per cent are surely handicapped when attempting to understand the affairs of society. (Sewell, 1981; p. 17)

But, school mathematics as represented by the myth of participation is clearly not transmitting skills that will be of assistance in understanding the affairs of society, or even in baking a cake. The text is mythologizing these activities.

All texts can be described in terms of their construction of their readership. Textbooks are directed at students. The SMP text in *Figure 1.1* is taken from a textbook which is intended for use with 'lower ability' students. This text, therefore, constructs its reader as 'low ability'. The textbook also constructs a teacher who is to recruit it for use in their classroom. The teacher must, therefore, constitute the text as appropriate for use with their students and so must have made an assessment of them as of 'lower ability'. As I shall illustrate in my more detailed analysis of the SMP materials, this evaluation constitutes a number of attributions, including short attention span, inability to cope with complex situations and difficulty in following instructions. Facility with assessment practices is constructed as an aspect of the skill of the teacher *qua* teacher.

The Teacher's Guides to the 'low ability' books make a great deal of the need for relevance. It is suggested that the teacher might make the work more directly relevant to the actual lives of the students:

> We hope that much in the G materials will act as a 'model' for work of your own devising. Work on timetables, map-reading, shopping and so on is far more motivating for pupils if it is seen to be 'real'. Blagdon[6] can never substitute for your own town! So in a sense, we hope that some chapters in the books never get used by pupils. They are written to be replaced by work which is firmly based on the pupils' own environment. Of course, replacement may not always be possible, but work based on the pupils' own school, town or surroundings may be added to a particular chapter. (G1TG, p. 8; my footnote)

As I have illustrated, the 'model' that the books provide mythologizes pupils' own environment by subordinating it to mathematical rationality. The teacher, then, is enjoined to direct the mathematical gaze onto the students' lives in much the same way.

Thus, the student as both an intellectual and a social being is objectified by the text which also recruits the teacher as an agent of objectification. A principal role of the teacher is to cast a pedagogic and mathematical gaze onto

6 The name of an apparently fictional town referred to frequently in the SMP texts. There is no obvious reference to Blagdon in Avon or Blagdon in Devon.

the student, to measure them, as it were, in terms of the curriculum. This objectification marks a fundamental distinction between this mode of teaching, on the one hand, and apprenticeship, on the other. As I have suggested, apprenticeship entails the creation of subjects via an initiation of the novice into the area of expertise of the adept. Teaching, as it is constructed in these texts, entails the objectification of the student in terms of the curriculum by the teacher. Apprenticeship reproduces subjects: teaching constitutes objects.

In my definition of apprenticeship, I indicated that in this mode there is a coincidence of pedagogic action and pedagogic content: the adept is teaching that at which they are an adept. The situation in teaching as described above, however, is rather different. In fact, the objectification of the student in and by teaching is rendered possible precisely by a displacement between pedagogic action and pedagogic content. The teacher's expertise lies within teaching, their skill incorporating, for example, diagnostic assessment. However, the teacher is not teaching the student to be a teacher. Rather, the teacher is, in principle, teaching the student to perform in mathematics. In contrast with the situation in apprenticeship, the student's performances do not enter into either economic or discursive relations with other performances. Rather, they enable the teacher to define the student, both intellectually and in terms of their adequacy in domestic and other mundane practices.

The SMP text in *Figure 1.1* is, as I have noted, intended for 'lower ability' students. I also pointed out, in Chapter 1, that the mathematical principles that structure the tasks in this text are substantially invisible. A similar invisibility is a feature of some primary mathematics texts adopting the principle of pedagogic constructivism. This principle entails, in general terms, the assumption that the student learns by individual cognitive action upon appropriate experiences. The resonance in form, if not in principle, between texts intended for 'lower ability' students and texts for younger students is a feature that occurs within the SMP scheme, as I shall demonstrate later. Here, however, I want to give a little closer attention to a primary mathematics text in order to clarify the third ideal type of pedagogic relation, that of teaching. The main text that I shall focus on is amongst the most popular in the UK, *Nelson Mathematics*. I shall use examples from the 'Teacher's Resource File', *Towards Level 2*, which is intended for use with students in the lower primary school[7].

There was a time when a great deal of primary mathematics teaching was concerned with the rote learning of facts, such as multiplication tables, and the drilling of algorithms, mostly in arithmetic. The 'modern mathematics' movement of the 1960s was an attempt to organize the school curriculum on the more principled basis of the Bourbakiists. Thus set theory provided the entry into primary mathematics and the language of sets and Venn diagrams pervaded the curriculum (see Moon, 1986). A more recent trend has tended to reject this knowledge-centred approach. This trend grounds pedagogic practice upon a 'constructivist' understanding of the learner.

---

7   The scheme is published by Thomas Nelson and Sons, Walton on Thames and is dated 1992.

The Nelson scheme reflects this approach in the explicit assumptions it makes about the teaching of mathematics:

- children need concrete experiences if they are to acquire sound mathematical concepts;

- like adults, children learn best when they investigate and make discoveries for themselves;

- children refine their understanding and develop conceptual structures by talking about their own thinking and what they have done; (page 5)

The expressions 'experiences' and 'conceptual structures' are examples of what Jay Lemke (1995) refers to as 'condensation'. This, Lemke argues, is a common feature of 'technical' and 'technocratic' texts. The category 'technical texts' includes scientific writing such as that of Jean Piaget and his colleagues which was the original inspiration of constructivism[8]. In Piaget's work, 'experience' and 'conceptual structures' have specific and technical meanings which are bound up with other technical concepts such as autoregulation, equilibration, structuralism, and genetic epistemology. Condensation in technical texts gives access to those readers who are familiar with these intertextual resources, but tends to deny it to those who are not.

The introduction in the Nelson teacher's file is closer to a technocratic text. Here, condensation effects the unexamined recruitment of these technical terms. It also conceals a shift in the meaning of the terms as they move from Piagetian psychology (which Piaget certainly describes as 'constructivist') to what I have referred to as 'pedagogic constructivism'. Specifically, there has been a shift from 'mathematico-logical experience' and 'schemata', in Piaget, to concrete, which is to say practical experiences and understanding. This is partially achieved by the association of 'experience' with 'concrete', in the above extract. The latter term is another reinterpreted term, the meaning of which has shifted from a position within the developmental sequence concrete operations/formal operations to having a meaning associated with practical or physical.

The reinterpretation of 'conceptual structures' is achieved in the third assumption in the above extract: 'children refine their understanding and develop conceptual structures'. Refining/development are achieved 'by talking about their own thinking and what they have done', so that there is an equivalence established between understanding and the development of conceptual structures. In one of Piaget's (1953) famous 'experiments', he asks a young child to say whether they have the same amount to drink after orangeade has been poured from a tall narrow glass into a short wide one. He argues that the

---

8 See, for example, Piaget (1953, 1971, 1972a, 1980a, 1995); see Walkerdine (1984) for a discussion of the recontextualizing of Piaget within primary educational practice.

nature of the responses depends upon the level of cognitive development that the child has achieved. At one level, the child may answer that there is now less to drink, focusing only on the single perception of the height of liquid in the glass. At an intermediate stage, the child may answer that there is the same amount. When asked to explain, they may, for example, coordinate the two perceptions, height and width. They will not, however, make reference to the necessary identity of quantities which results from the fact that nothing has been added or taken away from the original amount. Responses employing this form of reasoning indicate the next stage in cognitive development. At this stage, children are said to be able to *conserve* quantities[9]. In Piaget's discourse, we could not assert that non-conserving subjects did not understand what was happening when the orangeade was poured from one glass to another, even if their answer was, in conventional terms, incorrect. We would say merely that their understanding was not predicated upon conservation.

Thus psychological discourse is replaced by the discourse of primary mathematics, which is concerned with practical activities, discovery and talk. A space is created for the teacher as the provider of experiences, that 'children need concrete experiences . . .' suggests that they won't get them unless the teacher — guided by the Nelson scheme — provides them. Indeed, it seems to deny that children have already had concrete experiences. This constitutes a moralizing, a mythologizing of the student which corresponds to the moralizing/mythologizing in the secondary mathematics curriculum which was described earlier. Secondary mathematics for the 'less able' pathologizes domestic practice as inadequate without mathematics. Primary mathematics, as represented by this text, pathologizes domestic practice as inadequate in terms of the provision of concrete experiences for children. In this case, the teacher/text takes over from the home. A different strategy is employed by another widely adopted scheme, IMPACT. Here, the domestic space and parents are recruited in the provision of 'appropriate' experiences, but in a way which excludes parents from access to the principles which structure the experiences (see Brown and Dowling, 1993; Brown, 1993, 1994).

The next two assumptions listed in the Nelson introduction refer to differences in students:

- individual children develop at different rates, some finding certain elements of mathematics difficult, whilst others understand them quickly;

- children learn in different ways; mathematics teaching should provide a rich and wide variety of experiences; (page 5)

---

9   The form of reasoning is far more important than the immediate response relating to whether or not there is the same amount to drink. This is why Piaget employed the clinical interview in his empirical work, in order to encourage the subject to elaborate their reasoning. The importance of reasoning and of the clinical interview is underplayed in much subsequent work claiming to show that children develop at a faster rate than is apparent from Piaget's research (see, for example, Donaldson, 1978; Hughes, 1986; see also Light, 1986).

It is the responsibility of the teacher to measure these differences in terms of the curriculum:

> A significant part of a primary teacher's day is spent on the informal evaluation of a child's or group's learning and in deciding what the next learning experiences should be. (page 17)

The introduction points to the value in children's recording of the work:

> Children's recordings are also useful to the teacher for assessing children's progress. But to be really useful they must indicate the thought processes that the child went through to solve a problem.
>
> Encouraging children to do all the working out for an algorithm 'in rough' and to present only the 'finished product' is to miss valuable assessment and teaching opportunities.
>
> A teacher interested only in answers might have seen this, from seven-year old Mary, and just marked it right:
>
> $25 - 18 = 7$
>
> Fortunately, Mary's teacher was interested in processes, encouraging the children to write everything down. This is what she actually got from Mary.
>
> $25 - 18$ is 5 take away 8 is 5 steps forward and 8 steps back, that's -3. 20 take away 10 is 10. 10 and -3 is 7. 7 is the answer.
>
> From this she learnt that Mary had a good 'feel' for numbers and an understanding of place value and negative numbers (although we would not necessarily expect the latter at this level, nor does the National Curriculum require it). (page 18)

This extract presents an opposition of bad and good practice. Bad practice allows children to record only the final answers. Good practice recognizes that this results in missed opportunities. Instead, it encourages students to record their thought processes. This is an enjoinment to confess. The example illustrates the objectification of Mary's mind by the teacher/priest; '"feel"' and 'understanding' are not elaborated, but they are clearly positive values in respect of the curricular elements: numbers; place value; and negative numbers.

As I have suggested, this objectification is made possible by the displacement of pedagogic action with respect to pedagogic content. The former objectifies the student with respect to the latter. This objectification is iconized in the teacher's resource file for this level of the Nelson scheme. The file includes seventy-five photographs of active children; only four of these photographs include the teacher. It is worth noting that none of these photographs illustrates or represents any need for control intervention on the part of the teacher. These are idealized — mythologized — classrooms in which the teacher's responsibility is to facilitate experiences and activities and then to observe the students.

The term 'algorithm', used in the last extract, is clearly not limited to standard methods and embraces the idiosyncratic strategy used by Mary. The inclusion of the term is another example of condensation. It invokes the tension between the constructivist pedagogy, in which students are encouraged to develop their own methods, and the pedagogic practice, which constructivism seeks to oppose, in which students are drilled in standard methods. This is a second opposition of good and bad practice. It is again made explicit in the assumptions:

- children will become more mathematically able if allowed to develop reliable personal methods of working; the formal recording used by mathematicians is very difficult for most children to understand;

- the conventions of mathematics should be taught only when children are confident in their own knowledge, concepts and skills; (page 5)

The text incorporates the assumption that the formal recording and conventions of mathematicians do not change the essential nature of mathematical activity, so that the latter can be developed independently of them. The premature transmission of these conventions is pathologized by the constructivist text. This, of course, constitutes a curricular hierarchy between what we might refer to as informal and formal mathematics. We might project this hierarchizing across to the ethnomathematical claim that the same mathematical principles underlie European academic mathematics and the apparently non-mathematical practices of non-industrialized societies. This projection generates an enhanced racism in which the 'to-be-emancipated', non-industrial societies are effectively infantilized: their 'mathematics' is necessarily prior to the European form.

In contrast with the work ethic of the knowledge-centred pedagogy, pedagogic constructivism as represented by the Nelson text places great importance on children's play. Play has particular importance in the history of primary education. Ian Hunter (1994) describes the emphasis placed upon the school playground by the nineteenth century British educationalists David Stow and Samuel Wilderspin, Stow states it thus:

A playground is in fact the principal scene of the real life of children . . . the arena on which their true character and dispositions are exhibited; and where, free and unconstrained, they can hop and jump about, swing, or play at tig, ball, or marbles . . .
With such a machinery in operation, and surrounded for several hours a day by such a world of pupils, it is the province of the shrewd, intelligent, and pious superintendent, to watch and direct all their movements; and whilst

he daily participates in their juvenile sports, he in consequence *gradually* gains a thorough knowledge of their *true* dispositions, which, at the proper time and season, he applauds or condemns . . . (David Stow quoted by Hunter, 1994; p. 81)

This explicit moralizing of the students by the teacher as observer has some resonance with the latter day teacher's objectifying practices as indexed above. Hunter describes the role of the nineteenth century teacher as being as unobtrusive as possible and letting 'the environment do the teaching' (Hunter, 1994; p. 72). The Nelson teacher's file describes an arrangement for a modern playground:

> Playgrounds can be marked with paint or chalk to show different shapes such as pentagons and hexagons, for children to walk or skip around. A hopscotch grid can have numerals chalked in, which are part of a number pattern, such as even and odd numbers of a pattern of fives. A maze or pathway, with right-angled turns can be used by the children to give each other instructions for moving along it. (page 14)

One of the activities in the Nelson materials suggests using a photograph of children playing in a geometrically marked playground (provided) to 'pose problems' such as:

> If the children who are sitting talking join the skippers, how many children would be skipping altogether? (page 56)

Samuel Wilderspin had his playgrounds planted with fruit trees 'which in offering a continuous temptation to misconduct, formed part of a constant incentive to self-reflection and self-regulation' (Hunter, 1994; p. 72), Wilderspin outlined the principle in his evidence to the parliamentary Select Committee on the Education of the Poorer Classes:

> . . . that is the way in which we endeavour to appeal to the child's judgement; he moves in a society of trained beings, and the next time he stops and looks at a fine cherry he looks about to see whether there is anybody within view. Doubtless he is restrained from taking the cherry by fear, but in process of time, by moving among restrained playfellows, he has that command over himself which enables him to resist temptation. (Samuel Wilderspin quoted by Hunter, 1994; pp. 72–3)

The modern learning environment may be deforested, but is structured, nevertheless, for improvement and, always, assessment; the Nelson materials suggest that:

> Play offers opportunities for teachers to observe and assess children's knowledge and understanding. A set of coloured rods placed in a haphazard pile, could be used to assess the children's developing understanding of pattern by observing how they sort, order and use them. (page 14)

Trees laden with fruit have become piles of coloured rods. Ian Hunter's 'genealogy' of education describes the recruitment of the technologies of Christian pastoralism by the bureaucratic apparatuses of the State. Wilderspin's playground facilitates the imposition of a morality-power. Whether or not students acquiesce to the code forbidding cherry-picking, they are open to its evaluation. The modern playground and classroom represented by the Nelson text transform the code, but not the principle. The students are continually open to the gaze of the teacher whose responsibility is to classify their activities according to the curricular code.

A good deal of the 'play' has rather more explicit structure than leaving coloured rods lying around the place; this is the procedure for 'Numeral Lotto':

> This activity is for two children. They set out the numeral cards for 1 to 9 in a row. One child says, 'One (or two or three) more', rolls the dice, counts on one (or two or three), and points to the correct numeral in the row. The children alternate turns. Encourage them to say a full addition sentence at the end of each go, for instance, 'one more than five is six'. (page 37)

The activity has the name and superficial form of a game: a dice is used; children take turns. But the Nelson scheme recruits the play setting as a mathematical 'experience'. This is not really a game at all. There is no competition, no strategy. But the instructions are presented as an algorithm. Indeed, ironically, what has derived from a constructivist pedagogy nevertheless begins to look rather like drill.

Sometimes, the relationship between the mathematical structure and the 'play' element can be almost entirely arbitrary as in the example in the use of the copymaster 'number and pattern woodlouse'. A large line drawing of the animal comprises mainly spaces which can be used for sequences of number operations and so on. The image invokes a (masculine) childish predilection for creepy-crawlies — there is another activity called 'Mathsy Centipede'. The mathematical task merely occupies the spaces on the drawing[10].

Under observation and structuring by the teacher, play becomes recontextualized play, subordinated to mathematical structure in much the same way as domestic practices are by the SMP text discussed earlier. A mathematical gaze is cast onto children's activities. However, the mathematical principles of the gaze rest with the teacher. To the extent that they are not made explicit, a doubt must be raised about the plausibility of transmission. As an illustration, compare the three images in *Figures 2.3*, *2.4* and *2.5*. The lolly sticks in *Figure 2.3* have dots on them. The sticks represent sets, the elements of which are to be combined in addition. The spike abacuses in *Figure 2.4* are introducing place value, so beads on the left-hand stick have a value which is different from those on the right-hand stick. The two columns on the worksheet in

---

10 Of course, this strategy also has an economic rationality: you have to buy the woodlouse copymaster.

Figure 2.3   Nelson Mathematics: Towards Level 2, Teacher's Resource File
(Source: Walton on Thames: Nelson, 1992, from p. 36)

Figure 2.5 represent occurrences of different outcomes of an action (tossing a coin). Each is constituted by the scheme as an embodiment of a different mathematical content. However, the embodiments look very much the same. What are the mechanisms by which the student comes to know what the embodiments are embodiments of?

To answer this question, we might recall that the constructivist pedagogy is, at root, a recontextualizing of the psychology of Jean Piaget. However, it is a recontextualizing which transforms the basically Kantian epistemology of Piaget into something more closely resembling the empiricist epistemology of John Stuart Mill. Mill argued that we acquire mathematics through our physical interactions with the world[11]. We acquire number concepts, for example, by activities such as juggling with pebbles. A naive interpretation of Mill's epistemology, however, attributes mathematical properties to physical objects or actions as essential qualities. This attribution is clearly inappropriate as soon as we realize that any number of mathematical categories — numbers, geometrical shapes, etc — can be assigned to any given physical object. A button, for example, might be assigned the number one, or the number corresponding to the number of its holes, or two (two sides), or any number at all corresponding to its circumference in absolutely any units. Two buttons may be assigned the number one — one category, buttons. To the extent that mathematics and its categories and gaze is, as I have argued, regulated discursively, they must be acquired within language.

It is interesting to note that the cover illustration of the Nelson teacher's resource file shows a passive and an active snowperson, the latter juggling with its buttons. This image of juggling is as inaccurate as the one in the juggling manual. The four buttons are arranged in an arch over the snowperson's head between its upstretched arms. To juggle with four balls you either juggle with two balls in each hand, or you pass two balls between the

11   See Bloor (1976) for a brief critical account of Mill's epistemology; there is also a brief discussion in Ernest (1991).

Figure 2.4   Nelson Mathematics: Towards Level 2, Teacher's Resource File
(Source: Walton on Thames: Nelson, 1992, from p. 63)

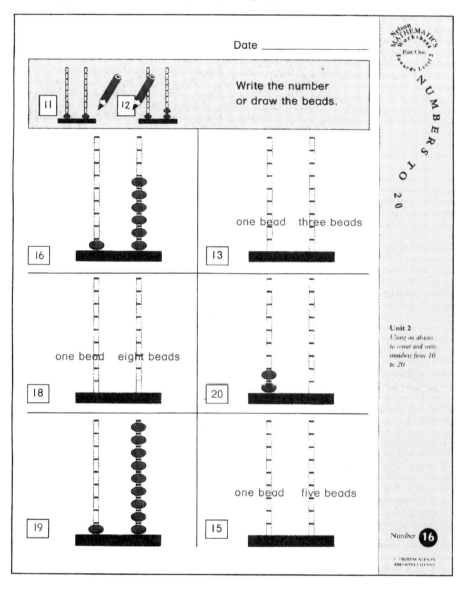

hands at the same time, one passing above the other. The misrepresentation of juggling here, however, is far less appropriate. The juggling manual can misrepresent juggling and get away with it because juggling is dependent upon the physical nature of the act; it is a practice which exhibits low discursive saturation. The discursive commentary on juggling — the instruction book — gets you into the activity and then the physicality of the action takes over.

Figure 2.5 Nelson Mathematics: Towards Level 2, Teacher's Resource File
(Source: Walton on Thames: Nelson, 1992, from p. 118)

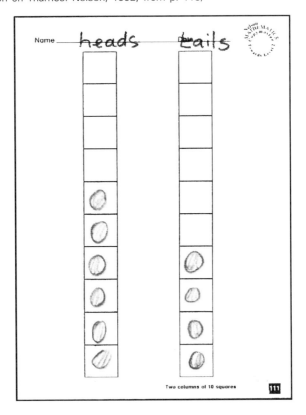

Pedagogic constructivism, then, is revealed as a myth. This strategy that presumes that mathematical knowledge is to be acquired predominantly through physical experiences is an inversion of the juggling situation. Mathematics is, as I have argued, a DS^+ activity. That which regulates mathematical knowledge is fundamentally discursive and not physical. Whilst the physical world may provide starting points, the mathematical interpretation of these starting points must be made explicit by the only person in the classroom who is able to make them explicit: the teacher. Mathematics comprises principled knowledge. Whether or not we accept that there is a fundamental structure to the ways in which we develop cognitively, the detail of mathematical knowledge is essentially a sociocultural arbitrary. Sooner or later, if someone is going to learn mathematics, someone else is going to have to tell them about it.

It may be possible to reconcile a form of constructivism with the essentially linguistic understanding of mathematical knowledge that I am adopting here. I shall indicate this briefly since it is not within the principal compass of this study. The approach involves adopting a broadly Vygotskian interpretation of cognitive development rather than one which is tied to Piaget's non-linguistic categories. As I shall discuss more fully in Chapter 5, Vygotsky (1978, 1986) adopts a linguistic model of cognitive development wherein speech provides the structure for thought. Development occurs as thought grasps new linguistic tools and operates with them in its own restructuring. This occurs within a 'zone of proximal development', which might be understood as that region within which linguistic tools are available that have yet to be consolidated. It is a zone of uncertainty which provides a disequilibrating tension, urging the learner forward, as it were.

My use of the expression 'disequilibrating' is deliberately intended to recall Piaget's equilibration (see, for example, Piaget, 1980b). Piaget's concept also suggests an eternally unstable subject whose cognitive attempts to establish equilibrium are perpetually thwarted. The difference between the two, however, is that Vygotsky's construction, but not Piaget's, refers to linguistic instability and thus allows for the development of an epistemology which constitutes rationality as socially constructed. There are difficulties with Vygotsky's evolutionary model, as I shall argue in Chapter 5. Nevertheless, it does suggest a route for a productive articulation of theories of cognitive development and the kind of sociological model that I am developing in this study. As far as pedagogic action is concerned, the Vygotskian approach demands that instruction be explicit; this is entirely consistent with my criticism of pedagogic constructivism.

I have described constructivism as a myth. The myths that I introduced in Chapter 1 each mythologized mathematics. The myths of reference, participation, and emancipation mythologized mathematics as being, respectively, about, or for, or implicated in non-mathematical activities. The myth of construction also mythologizes mathematics. In this case, mathematics is mythologized as a codification of human cognitive structure. This is the case whether cognitive structure is held to be invariant, as is the case with Piaget's constructivism, or whether it is constructed as specific to the individual, as is the case in respect of radical constructivism (see, for example, Glasersfeld, 1987). In all four cases, what is concealed is the possibility of mathematics as primarily self-referential.

Modes of Pedagogic Relationship: Extending the Ideal-typical Schema

In addition to revealing a fourth mathematical myth, my discussion of these mathematical texts has enabled me to extend the schema that I began in the section above on *Modes of pedagogic relationship: First steps towards an ideal-typical schema*. In the earlier section, I restricted my discussion to apprenticeship. This is defined as a relation between an adept and a novice within which there is a coincidence of pedagogic content and pedagogic action: the adept is transmitting that in which they are an adept. The situation with respect to the teaching of 'lower ability' or very young students, as it is represented in these texts, is somewhat different. Here, the teacher is constructed, not as an expert in mathematics, but as an expert in teaching, most particularly in respect of the practice of assessment. The teacher's expertise resides, in this respect, in classifying students' actions in terms of a mathematical code and in prescribing the appropriate tasks for the students.

The displacement between pedagogic content and pedagogic action is made possible by the particular form that the institutionalizing of schooling has taken. That is, curriculum content is officially regulated to a considerable extent. This was the case in England and Wales in advance of the advent of the National Curriculum through, for example, the standardizing of textbooks and public examination syllabuses. This regulation of the curriculum also constitutes a regulation upon the teacher so that the teacher functions as a relay. In the textual illustrations that I have given thus far, the mathematics curriculum seems to have developed evaluative principles which objectify the student and/or their lives, but which are not explicitly transmitted to the student. Thus, the SMP student is provided with recontextualizings of their domestic practice. The form of presentation of these recontextualizings elides, as I have indicated, the mathematical principles of their construction. The Nelson student is provided with tasks and experiential opportunities. The student's performance on these tasks and opportunities is then available to be measured in terms of mathematical knowledge which is again not made visible to them. In neither case is the student initiated into the mathematical principles. The teacher is not apprenticing the student into mathematical practices so much as measuring the student in terms of these practices. This is a relaying pedagogic action as distinct to an apprenticing pedagogic action.

The invisibility of the mathematical principles from the perspective of the student is not necessarily a general feature of school mathematics. As I shall demonstrate, the principles are more likely to be made explicit in respect of older and 'higher ability' students. Thus, apprenticing pedagogic action is increasingly present where students are increasingly intellectually mature. The mode of pedagogic action is thus distributed on the basis of some function of age and the attribution of ability. In Chapter 3 I shall give some attention to the nature of 'ability' from a sociological perspective. To conclude this chapter, I want to extend the discussion of school teaching as an activity in respect of its location in the ideal-typical schema that I have introduced.

The schema differentiates modes of apprenticeship according to whether they exhibit high or low discursive saturation. Firstly, I have indicated that school teaching is not, in the sense that I have defined it, an apprenticeship mode of pedagogic relation. But is it best characterized as DS^+ or as DS^-? In my discussion of apprenticeship, the distinction turned on the mode of relationships entered into by performances. In terms of their official relationships with each other, the performances of school students are economized via schemes of assessment. Their work is graded in such a way that it can be directly compared with the work of other students. This is most obviously the case with respect to national assessments and public examinations. However, this also applies, to a greater or lesser extent, to the marking of students' work more regularly and informally. Initiatives such as the Graded Assessments in Mathematics (GAIM, 1987) and the development of standard reporting forms for parents' use in the IMPACT project (see Brown, 1994) are illustrations of the more formal end of the economy of students' work. There are even examples of the formalizing of assessment for pre-school use as in the *All About Me* materials (Wolfendale, 1990).

In contrast with the performances of apprentices, those of school students are generally valued as indicators of something other than themselves, that is, of some attribute of the student. A clear illustration of this is given by the fundamental differences between the PhD examination and school examinations. In the former case, the thesis is judged on the basis of its merits as a performance in the field. In UK universities, no grade is awarded. The examiners hold a *viva voce* examination during which the thesis is defended by the candidate and after which the examiners produce a written report which is generally made available to the candidate. If the thesis is inadequate, then there can be no allowance for compensating circumstances, such as the ill health of the candidate or poor quality guidance by the supervisor; there are no aegrotat awards at doctoral level. The successful thesis will be placed in the university library and will be recorded in the index of theses, the latter constituting an important source in the production of literature reviews for academic work.

The school student's examination script, on the other hand, is submitted to the examination process and retained for a short period of time after which it is disposed of. Examination performances are generally not returned to the candidates. They are ultimately reduced to a grade which constitutes a measurement of the candidate. The candidate will, of course, be made aware of this grade, but the examiners will not, generally, enter into any discussion with the candidate regarding their reasons for assigning this grade. If, however, the candidate has a doctor's letter certifying that they were seriously incapacitated as a result of illness during the examination, or if a part of the candidate's script is lost, then the examiners are able to adjust the grade on the basis of an assessment of what might have been achieved under more favourable circumstances. It is, after all, the candidate and not the script that is being assessed.

None of this discussion stands in the place of the systematic empirical study of the teaching process which would be necessary in order to establish the level of discursive saturation of school teaching. Nevertheless, it does suggest the possibility that it may be appropriate to regard school students' performances as entering into economic relations with each other on the basis of systems of exchange-values established by schemes of assessment, reporting and examination. To this extent, at least, school teaching comes to resemble the craft activity more than it resembles the academic. In school teaching, however, the student is objectified as a product. In craft and academic activities, the student aspires to the subjectivity which will effect their alienation from their material and symbolic products.

That component of pedagogic action which comprises assessment practices may thus be described as constituting economies of students by establishing means of translating general attributes and actions into categories within what are, of necessity, comparatively simple structures. Such structures are, by virtue of their simplicity, unlikely to be able to sustain the degree of discursive complexity of DS^+ practices, they are more properly referred to as DS^-. It is likely that this also refers to the practical issues of classroom control and management strategies which are also components of pedagogic action (see, for example, Dowling and Brown, 1996; Ensor, 1994; Johnston, 1993). Within the context of mathematics schooling, that which is to be relayed — the pedagogic content — is mathematics which, as a practice, exhibits DS^+. We therefore have a situation in which DS^+ practices are to be relayed, at least in part, through DS^- practices. We might expect that the latter will act as a filter. Mathematics, under such circumstances can be relayed only as DS^-. It will be argued that this is indeed the case with respect to the mathematical content which is distributed to 'lower ability' students. It is to the nature of 'ability' that I shall turn in Chapter 3.

Chapter 3

Sociology, Education and the Production of 'Ability'

In Chapter 2 I mentioned 'ability' as a variable in the distributive principles of the mathematics curriculum. The *SMP 11–16* materials, in particular, are explicitly differentiated in respect of categories of 'ability'. The curriculum in the UK has always been explicitly differentiated, in one way or another, within any given age cohort[1]. The currently fashionable expression 'differentiation' gives official sanction to this process and is incorporated in the current national criteria for initial teacher education as a competence to be acquired. The rationale behind 'differentiation' entails the assumptions that, firstly, students differ from each other and, secondly, pedagogic action and, generally, pedagogic content must be correspondingly differentiated in order to maximize actual performances. The first of these assumptions is not being challenged here; it would clearly be absurd to claim that all students are identical in every respect. The second assumption demands a measurement of these differences in terms of the curriculum, suggesting that the curriculum comprises legitimate exchange-values for student differences. The form of these exchange-values and of their relationship to the student varies. The Norwood Report[2] of 1943, for example, perceived students falling into three categories for which there should properly correspond three qualitatively different curricula:

> In a wise economy of secondary education pupils of a particular type of mind would receive the training best suited for them and that training would lead them to an occupation where their capacities would be suitably used; that a future occupation is already present in their minds while they are still at school has been suggested, though admittedly the degree to which it is present varies. Thus, to the three main types sketched above there would correspond three main types of curriculum. (Norwood Report, quoted by Gordon and Lawton, 1978; p. 30)

The three types of curriculum denoted by the Report are commonly referred to as academic, technical and practical and correspond to the tripartite

---

1 This is not universally the case. In Greece, for example, differentiation within a cohort is illegal.
2 The Norwood Report was the Report of the Secondary Schools Examinations Council of the Board of Education, published in 1943. See Gordon and Lawton (1978).

system of schools — grammar, technical and modern — proposed by the earlier Spens Report[3] and established after 1944. The types of curriculum were explicitly related to expected occupational destination and so directly related to social class. The rhetoric, however, differentiated students in terms of their 'particular type of mind'. More recently, the official position has moved away from the qualitative differentiation of curricula to a quantitative differentiation, that is, a differentiation in terms of pacing. This should be varied, now, according to students' individual 'abilities'. The Cockcroft Report (1982), for example, proposed building the mathematics curriculum from the 'bottom up', starting with a 'foundation list' which should comprise the basic curriculum for all students and the curriculum *in toto* for the 'least able'. This quantitative differentiation of the curriculum has informed and structured the National Curriculum. Thus, the Secretary of State wrote, in his letter to the National Curriculum Mathematics Working Party:

> I am looking to you to recommend attainment targets which set out the knowledge, skills and understanding which pupils of different abilities should be able to achieve by the end of the school year in which they reach one of the key stages. They should allow scope for the very able, those of average ability, and the less able to show what they can do. So far as possible I want to avoid having different attainment targets for children of different levels of ability. (DES, 1988a; p. 94)

The quantitative differentiation retains a direct link with occupation insofar as the periods of compulsory and subsequent free schooling are fixed in terms of students' age and insofar as occupational choices are linked to level of certification. Students moving through the curriculum at a slower pace will achieve lower terminal levels of certification and so have restricted occupational options. In the practice of mathematics teaching, curricular differentiation remains qualitative, as will be clear in my analysis of the *SMP 11–16* materials. Thus, the economy of students constituted by the curriculum remains rather more complex than a simple hierarchy of pacing.

Whatever the form of its differentiation, the assumption that the curriculum can and should express real differences between students, that students are properly economized by the curriculum, is, in the UK, long-standing and frequently goes unchallenged. Indeed, one might imagine that a typical response to my comments on curricular differentiation in Chapters 1 and 2 might be along the following lines: 'well, of course the teacher must shape the curriculum to the individual needs of the students, just as a medical practitioner matches the treatment to the condition of the patient'. The sociology that I am developing in this book, however, questions this position. I shall want to argue

3 The Spens Report was the Report of the Consultative Committee of the Board of Education with Special Reference to Grammar Schools and Technical High Schools, published in 1938. See Gordon and Lawton (1978).

that although students differ one from another in objective terms, the curriculum does work in order to recontextualize these essentially non-educational differences as differences in educational attributes and performances.

A key term, in this respect, is 'ability'. Essentially, schooling recontextualizes social differences as differences in 'ability', thereby producing its own hierarchy of educational outputs. In this chapter I want to provide some orientation to this kind of argument through a discussion of some selected work in the sociology of education. The sociology of education has rarely directed its attention at mathematics education. Indeed, this is the principal reason for including the material in this chapter which is intended to serve as an introduction to sociology. If I am to refer to substantive research, however, this entails that few of the examples that I shall use will focus specifically on mathematics. First, however, I want to consider some of the ways in which curricular differentiation has been described and realized in respect of major dimensions of social inequality.

Curriculum Differentiation: Some Images

In 1867 Robert Lowe (a one-time Vice President of the Committee of Council on Education and subsequent Chancellor of the Exchequer and Home Secretary) announced:

> The lower classes ought to be educated to discharge the duties cast upon them. They should also be educated that they appreciate and defer to a higher cultivation when they meet it: and the higher classes ought to be educated in a very different manner, in order that they may exhibit to the lower classes that higher education to which, if it were shown to them, [they] would bow and defer. (quoted by Gordon, 1978; p. 121)

'Class', here, is clearly a position into which one is born and for which there corresponds a particular form of curriculum. The nineteenth century concern with the engineering of populations saw a combination of the eugenicist programme of race improvement and the developing science of statistics. Francis Galton — the founder of the eugenics movement and influential statistician — constituted the population as normally distributed in terms of 'civic worth'. His drawing of a typical bell-shaped curve, reproduced by Mackenzie (1981) is labelled showing those having increasing amounts of 'civic worth'. The lowest in this quality are 'criminals, paupers, etc', next are the 'poor and low-paid', then the ' "respectable" working class', then 'skilled workers, foremen, clerks, small tradesmen, etc', and with the most 'civic worth', 'independent professionals, large employers, etc'. We are familiar with this distribution as reflecting the current evaluation of 'civic worth' in terms of remuneration (although we might feel that 'criminals' are more widely distributed in this respect). But the same distribution is also found in respect

Figure 3.1   Copy of ' "Ability" Distribution' observed on a deputy headteacher's noticeboard circa 1980

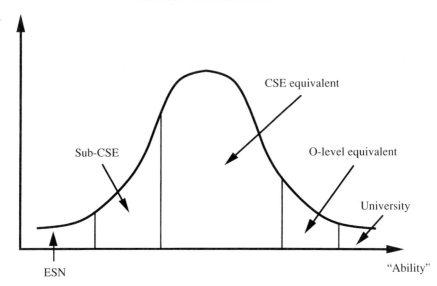

"ABILITY" DISTRIBUTION

of educational 'ability'. *Figure 3.1* is a copy (from a drawing that I made at the time) of a chart that I found on a secondary school deputy headteacher's wall in the early 1980s. This chart remains a distribution of social class insofar as the manual and intellectual occupations are associated with lower and higher levels of educational certification, respectively.

As I have noted, the National Curriculum constitutes a quantitative differentiation of the curriculum, mapping pacing onto 'ability'. In an earlier study (Dowling, 1990), I made a calculation on the basis of readings which I took from a graph published in the report of the Task Group on Assessment and Testing (DES, 1988b). The graph shows the relationship between levels of achievement, age and ability. The last category is included through the use of dotted lines showing the range of achievement between the 10th and 90th percentiles in the 'ability' range. My calculation, which was intended to highlight and challenge the assumptions implicated in the graph, resulted in the following formula giving the relationship between a student's age in years (A) and their 'ability' in terms of percentile (a) upon attaining the expected terminal achievement level[4].

$$A = \frac{2213}{a} - 89$$

4   That is, level 6/7: the expected terminal achievement at the end of compulsory schooling for the student of average 'ability'.

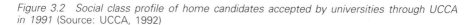

Figure 3.2   *Social class profile of home candidates accepted by universities through UCCA in 1991* (Source: UCCA, 1992)

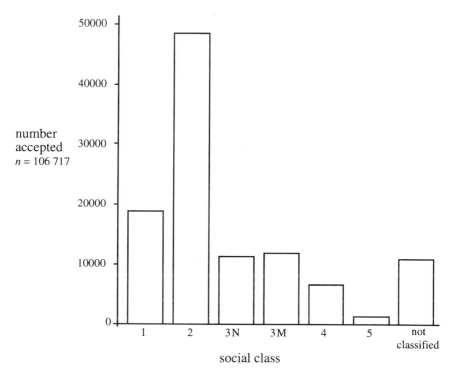

From the formula, whilst the average student achieves this terminal level at about age 16 — the end of compulsory schooling — a student at the 90th percentile will have achieved it at age 12.4 years and a student at the 10th percentile would need to remain at school until the age of 22.3 years. The practice, of course, is the reverse of this. Those students designated as more 'able' actually tend to remain in full-time education for longer than those who are said to have lower 'ability'. That these results at least correlate with social class is strongly suggested by the figures represented in *Figure 3.2*. This graph shows the social class profile of home (*i.e.* UK) candidates accepted to universities through the Universities Central Council on Admissions (UCCA) in 1991. I have converted these figures to give an estimate of the proportional representation of each social class of the candidates accepted, yielding the results shown in *Figure 3.3*.[5] Clearly, then, although 'class' has substantially

5   In *Figures 3.2* and *3.3*, the category 'social class' is scaled as follows: 1 — professional; 2 — intermediate; 3N — skilled non-manual; 3M — skilled manual; 4 — partly skilled; 5 — unskilled. *Figure 3.3* was constructed as follows. The number of admissions (in hundreds) for each definable social class shown in *Figure 3.2* was divided by an estimate of the proportion (as a percentage) of the population in each of the respective social classes. The figures for the social class composition of the population relate to people in employment in 1994 (CSO, 1995). There are some potential incompatibilities between these data and those represented in

Figure 3.3 *Relative representation of each social class in home applicants accepted by universities through UCCA in 1991* (Sources: CSO, 1995 & UCCA, 1992)

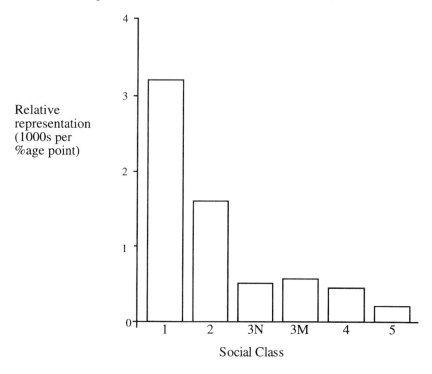

disappeared from the official rhetoric of educational policy, there remains a sense in which one of the effects of schooling is to recontextualize social class differences into differences of educational achievement mediated, it would seem, by the construct 'ability'.

Curricular differentiation according to gender is also long standing as is its criticism. George Eliot, in her novel published in 1860, constructs a scene

Figure 3.2 other than those relating to the time difference (the latter being a result of a decision taken on the basis of the data which was reasonably readily available on the grounds that the social class composition of the population does not change radically over a span of four or five years). Specifically, it is likely (but not certain) that the attributions of social class made by UCCA will tend to have been most commonly made on the basis of the father's rather than the mother's occupation. The principal differences between the social class composition of the male and female populations are in respect of the categories IIIN (skilled non-manual) and IIIM (skilled manual). 11.8% of men and 36.8% of women are recorded in IIIN, whilst 31.3% of men and 8.1% of women are recorded in IIIM. However, using the figures for men, rather than for men and women, does not significantly alter the general shape of the graph in *Figure 3.3*. It should also be noted that the social class composition refers only to people in employment. Clearly, this includes some people who will certainly not be the parents of university applicants (16–35-year-olds, for example) and excludes others who may be (retired and unemployed people, for example). However, the purpose to which these data are being put in this chapter are purely illustrative and are in no sense being presented as definitive.

in which Maggie is visiting her brother, Tom, who is having some difficulty with his lessons:

> Nevertheless it was a very happy fortnight for Maggie, this visit to Tom. She was allowed to be in the study whilst he had his lessons [. . .]
> Mr Stelling liked her prattle immensely, and they were on the best terms. She told Tom she should like to go to school to Mr Stelling, as he did, and learn just the same things. She knew she could do Euclid, for she had looked into it again, and she saw what A B C meant: they were the names of the lines.
> 'I'm sure you couldn't do it, now,' said Tom; 'and I'll just ask Mr Stelling if you could.'
> 'I don't mind,' said the little conceited minx. 'I'll ask him myself.'
> 'Mr Stelling,' she said, that same evening when they were in the drawing-room, 'couldn't I do Euclid, and all Tom's lessons, if you were to teach me instead of him?'
> 'No; you couldn't,' said Tom, indignantly. 'Girls can't do Euclid: can they, sir?'
> 'They can pick up a little of everything, I daresay,' said Mr Stelling. 'They've a great deal of superficial cleverness; but they couldn't go far into anything. They're quick and shallow.'
> Tom, delighted with this verdict, telegraphed his triumph by wagging his head at Maggie behind Mr Stelling's chair. As for Maggie, she had hardly ever been so mortified. She had been so proud to be called 'quick' all her little life, and now it appeared that this quickness was the brand of inferiority. It would have been better to be slow, like Tom. (George Eliot, 1981, *The Mill on the Floss*, Oxford: Oxford University Press; p. 150)

Maggie's dismay would have been even greater had she been aware of the 'scientific evidence' which supported the denial of education to females:

> One book published in America in 1873 by an 'expert', Dr Edward H. Clarke, went rapidly through seventeen editions and set forth the argument that education directly caused the uterus to atrophy. (Dr Clarke was also concerned about the ill-health of factory women, but he thought factory work less damaging to women than education because in the factory it was the body that was occupied and not the brain.) In support of his contention that educated women were damned, Dr Clarke produced cases from his own practice. One young woman, a student at Vassar, had fainting spells during her menses, which were painful and scanty. When she graduated, it was as an invalid with constant headaches; her reproductive system had its development arrested because of her concentration on education. (She was also flat-chested.) (Oakley, 1981; p. 121)

Given the interest in eugenics at the time and the rapid expansion of industrialization it is, perhaps, unsurprising that it was the reproductive apparatus

Table 3.1: Gender distribution of students and staff at universities in Great Britain

	Biological, Mathematical & Physical Sciences		Language, Literature & Area Studies*		Education		All Subjects	
	females (%)	males (%)	females (%)	males (%)	females (%)	males (%)	females (%)	males (%)
Full-time Undergraduates	45	55	70	30	77	23	50	50
Full-time Postgraduates	34	66	52	48	54	46	43	57
Lecturers	19	81	39	61	44	56	27	73
Readers & Senior Lecturers	5	95	19	81	21	79	12	88
Professors	2	98	12	88	16	84	5	95

* The data for students refers to Languages only
Source: The data for students is for 1994–5 (compiled from Higher Education Statistics Agency, 1996). The data for staff is for 1993–4 (compiled from University Statistical Record, 1994).

of middle class women rather than the well-being of women manual workers that was of primary concern. Social restructuring on the basis of education took a somewhat different approach in the post war period of the twentieth century. Girls should now be educated, but schooling should be mindful of their position within society:

> ... the prospect of courtship and marriage should rightly influence the education of the adolescent girl ... her direct interest in dress, personal experience and in problems of human relations should be given a central place in her education. (Crowther Report, 1959, quoted by Wolpe, 1981; p. 151)

> The main groups of occupations most widely taken up by girls — jobs in offices, in ships, in catering, work in the clothing industry and other manufacturing trades — can all provide material for courses at more than one level of ability. (Newsam Report, 1963, quoted by Wolpe, 1981; p. 152)

The differential performances of boys and girls in school mathematics have been well documented elsewhere (see, for example, Burton, 1986; Walkerdine *et al*, 1989). The general pattern seems to be that girls generally outperform boys in primary mathematics and that this situation is reversed at 16+ examination level, so that boys are slightly ahead of girls in terms of GCSE performances in mathematics. This male advantage expands, thereafter, so that the ratio of male to female undergraduates in mathematical sciences is about 1.7:1. In most other subjects, girls consistently outperform boys throughout the primary and secondary phases of schooling. For example, the ratio of female to male undergraduates in languages is approximately 2.4:1. After the point of university entrance, however, females are consistently 'frozen out' in terms of their representation in the academic hierarchy. *Table 3.1* shows the gender distribution of students and staff at Universities in Great Britain. The interpretation of *Table 3.1* is hampered by its collapsing (even inversion) of the career timescale in terms of the periods to which the data relate. Nevertheless, the steady and very substantial decrease and increase in the percentage figures as one moves down the female and male columns, respectively, is certainly illustrative of this 'freezing out' process.

Patterns of educational inequality are also to be found with respect to race and ethnicity. In some respects, this inequality is particularly pronounced in mathematics. For example, in one metropolitan authority, the percentages of white and black Caribbean pupils gaining A–C grades in mathematics were 35.2 per cent and 7 per cent, respectively (Gillborn and Gipps, 1996). More generally, these patterns are complex and reflect the interaction of variables including social class and gender with ethnicity. Furthermore, available data is often less than adequate as a result of crude and incompatible definitions applied to ethnicity and the dispersion of some ethnic groups which produces very small numbers in any given area. Partly because of this, the strength of

Table 3.2: Average examination scores by social class, ethnic origin and gender (1985)

Ethnic and social class group		Average exam score		Number of Cases
		Male	Female	
African Caribbean	Professional	27.1	24.9	12
	Intermediate	21.1	18.1	68
	Manual	14.3	15.6	115
Asian	Professional	30.7	27.8	17
	Intermediate	27.2	25.9	95
	Manual	23.3	22.5	189
White	Professional	30.4	32.3	2,118
	Intermediate	23.7	25.6	3,903
	Manual	17.6	20.6	5,218

Source: Gillborn and Gipps, 1996, Table 2.1

the association between social class and educational performance, in particular, can often simulate or conceal ethnic differences. As Gillborn and Gipps point out:

> Social class is strongly associated with achievement regardless of gender and ethnic background: *whatever the pupils' gender or ethnic origin*, those from the higher social class backgrounds do better on average. (Gillborn and Gipps, 1996; p. 17)

Gillborn and Gipps reproduce a table summarizing the results of a Youth Cohort Study. The table, reproduced here as *Table 3.2*, illustrates some of the complexity of the situation as well as providing clear evidence of inequality of performance in ethnic terms.

Of course, the broad classifications that are necessary in the production of quantitative data themselves perpetuate symbolic violence on the delicate and interactive textures of class and gender and ethnicity. It seems likely, however, that the current official rhetoric, is one of denial:

> We are concerned that undue emphasis on multi-cultural mathematics [. . .] could confuse young children. Whilst it is right to make clear to children that mathematics is the product of a diversity of cultures, priority must be given to ensuring that they have the knowledge, understanding and skills which they will need for **adult life in employment in Britain in the twenty-first century**. We believe that most ethnic minority parents would share this view. We have not therefore included any 'multi-cultural' aspects in any of our attainment targets. (DES, 1988a; p. 87)

The totalizing of what is more appropriately interpreted as a socio-culturally relative position is precisely what I have been referring to in

Chapters 1 and 2 as mythologizing. A shift to a slightly less familiar position may make the effect more visible. The French government recently gave official support to schools which had banned the wearing of headscarves by Moslem girls. The grounds for this act were that the Napoleonic Code insists upon a rigid division between educational and religious activities; the latter are illegal in schools. To allow Moslems to adopt practices in schools which were in contradiction to the requirements placed upon school students in general would constitute an overriding of a secular code by a religious one within an institution in which only the former is allowed to have a standing. The imposition of the Napoleonic Code, however, constitutes a totalizing of a division which is wholly unacceptable within the Islamic faith. Islam maintains that religion is and must be the foundation of every aspect of one's life. The expression 'Islamic State' is an oxymoron in France and pleonastic within such a State. The French Moslems are in an impossible position[6].

The French regulation and the English and Welsh National Curriculum are differentiated in respect of ethnicity by their denial of the voice of the other. This is the same kind of differentiation that constructs disability as a dimension of social and cultural inequality. That is, assumptions about, for example, physical capabilities are built into the architecture and the pedagogic practices of schools, thereby totalizing, or mythologizing the 'normal' human being. This, of course, progressively excludes individuals who deviate further from this constructed norm. But the voice of 'disability' is excluded yet more subtly. *Figure 3.4* shows the front cover of a SMILE card[7]. On the next page, the text reads: 'Work through this card to find out how much space the average person needs and then study the problems of the disabled.' There are illustrations which show a masculine figure in a leotard stretching his arms upwards and outwards. The student is required to find the dimensions of the box that these actions generate when they perform them themselves. Then they are to repeat the process from a sitting position — the leotarded figure is now shown sitting on a standard school chair: 'If you were confined to a wheelchair what do you think you might be able to reach?'

The point is that 'disability' is recognized, but is given no voice. Instead, the text defines its voice for it. 'the problems of the disabled' are concerned with reach and space, that is, they are to do with the 'mathematical' acts

6 As are another group of Moslems. As I write this, on Bastille Day, President Chirac is calling on the United Nations to aid the Bosnian Moslems against Bosnian Serbian aggression. We should be careful not to accuse the French State of being anti-Islam. Bosnia is, of course, a long way from Paris.

7 The SMILE scheme (Secondary Mathematics Individualised Learning Experience) has been in operation in a significant number of secondary schools, mainly in and around the former Inner London Education Authority (ILEA) area. It comprises around eighteen hundred cards plus other materials. The cards are graded by topic and level. Students work through the cards on an individual basis arranged as sequences of 'matrices' of about ten cards at a time set by the teacher. This card was discussed in Brown and Dowling (1989).

Figure 3.4   SMILE, card 1328 (front cover)

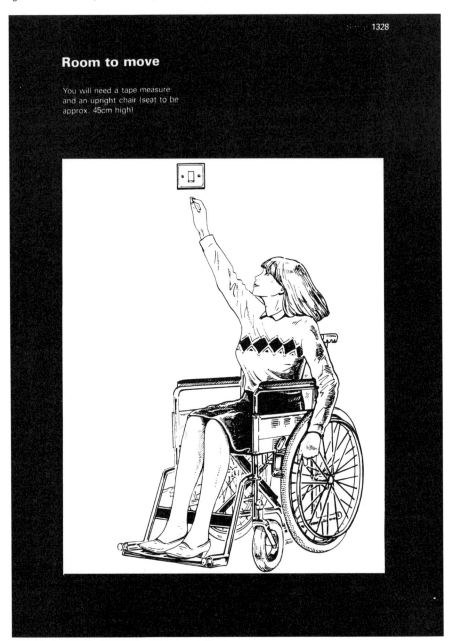

of measurement. It is measurement, of course, which is the real object of interest: the disabled individual is being measured. In fact, even this is an overstatement. It is not the disabled individual, but the student who is being measured. The student is necessarily not confined to a wheelchair as they have to be able to stand up and then sit in a chair which is certain to be of very different dimensions from those of a wheelchair. The student is further alienated from the wheelchair by the text — '*If* you were confined to a wheelchair . . .' — and by the connotations of fitness and health associated with the leotard.

If the card or the student were really interested in 'the problems of the disabled', they might feel inclined to speak to some people who were attributed to this category (which, of course, extends beyond and also excludes some users of wheelchairs). Unfortunately, this might lead to the act of measurement being somewhat backgrounded if, as I would predict, very few such individuals claimed that their major problem was that they generated a box of such and such dimensions when they waived their arms about.

It gets worse. Returning to the image on the front of the card (*Figure 3.4*), we note that the girl in the wheelchair (whose visible and well-defined gastrocnemius muscles suggest that she hasn't been sitting in it for very long) is currently experiencing a problem reaching for a light switch. I am only an inch or two above average height for an adult male in the UK. Nevertheless, I can reach a light switch placed at the usual height whilst sitting on the floor. The authors of the card have not, it would appear, even bothered to look at someone sitting in a wheelchair! 'The disabled' are as objectified as my use of quotation marks suggests. only 'normal' people have a voice, here.

In this section I have been referring to the differentiation of the curriculum in relation to major dimensions of social inequality, that is, social class, gender, ethnicity and ablebodiedness. The differentiation takes different forms across time and with respect to the different dimensions. Nevertheless, there is considerable continuity in the construction of the dominant category in education, and generally, as middle class, male, pale and hale! This has been well known for some time. I do not propose to give a summary of the diverse approaches adopted by sociologists to the issue of the production and reproduction of social inequality in and by education. This has been done often enough[8]. In the rest of this chapter, I want to provide an orientation to the kind of argument that informs my own position which I will then develop more fully in subsequent chapters. The selection of research for discussion here has not been made on the basis of that which has been most influential on my own (although the final piece of work discussed certainly has been influential). I shall discuss my own theoretical antecedents in Chapter 5. Rather, the work introduced here has been chosen because it seems to me to be well suited to the purpose of orientation.

8 See, for example, discussions in Whitty (1985).

The Production and Reproduction of Educational Inequality: Some Examples from the Sociology of Education

My contention, then, is that an important aspect of the work of schooling is the recontextualizing of objective, but essentially non-educational differences between students as differences in educational attributes and performances. Ray Rist describes the situation as follows:

> There occurs within the classroom a social process whereby out of a large group of children and an adult unknown to one another prior to the beginning of the school year, there emerge patterns of behaviour, expectations of performance, and a mutually accepted stratification system delineating those doing well from those doing poorly. (Rist, 1970; pp. 412–3)

Rist conducted a longitudinal study, following a group of black children through their first two-and-a-half years of schooling in an urban ghetto school in the US in the late 1960s. The kindergarten teacher had access to various sources of information about the children prior to their entry into her class. However, as Rist points out:

> It should be noted that [none] of these [. . .] sources of information to the teacher was related directly to the academic potential of the incoming kindergarten child. Rather, they concerned various types of social information revealing such facts as the financial status of certain families, medical care of the child, presence or absence of a telephone in the home, as well as the structure of the family in which the child lived, *i.e.*, number of siblings, whether the child lived with both, one, or neither of his [sic] natural parents. (*ibid*; p. 418)

During the first few days at school, the teacher was also able to observe the children's mannerisms, physical appearance, and performance on early tasks. Within 'a few days', one group of children were marked out by being called upon, exclusively, to perform high status tasks, such as leading the class, taking messages, and so forth. This group were placed closest to the teacher, at 'Table 1'. A hierarchy of three tables was established by the eighth day:

> As one progressed from Table 1 to Table 2 and Table 3, there was an increasing dissimilarity between each group of children at the different tables on at least four major criteria. The first criterion appeared to be the physical appearance of the child. While the children at Table 1 were all dressed in clean clothes that were relatively new and pressed, most of the children at Table 2, and with only one exception at Table 3, were all quite poorly dressed. The clothes were old and often quite dirty. (*ibid*; p. 419)

The other criteria mentioned by Rist are, firstly, interactional behaviour: those children who were beginning to develop as leaders were placed at Table 1. Secondly, the children at Table 1 spoke to the teacher more often than the others and displayed a greater use of Standard American English in contrast to the other children who spoke less frequently to the teacher and commonly in black dialect. Finally, the children differed in terms of a range of 'social factors' which were known to the teacher in advance of her construction of the seating arrangements. These factors included family size and income and parents' education. The children from the smaller families with higher incomes and more extensive educational background tended to be on Table 1, those in the larger, poorer families with less formal education on Table 2 and, especially, Table 3.

Essentially, this hierarchical arrangement remained substantially undisturbed throughout the period of the research during which the children moved into the first and second grades. In particular, in relation to their second grade reading groups:

> Initial expectations of the kindergarten teacher two years earlier as to the ability of the child resulted in placement in a reading group, whether high or low, from which their appeared to be no escape. The child's journey through the early grades of school at one reading level and in one social grouping appeared to be pre-ordained from the eighth day of kindergarten. (*ibid*; p. 435)

Rist argues that the kindergarten teacher's assessment of the children was principally based on a:

> . . . roughly constructed 'ideal type' as to what characteristics were necessary for any given student to achieve 'success' both in the public school and in the larger society. These characteristics appeared to be, in significant part, related to social class criteria. (*ibid*; p. 414)

The kindergarten teacher's initial translation of the children's personal and social characteristics into an academic hierarchy effectively became the basis for future evaluations and curriculum differentiation: a self-fulfilling prophecy.

More recently, Keith Sharpe (1992) followed up on the findings of a series of comparative studies in the 1980s which found that there was far greater homogeneity of practice amongst primary school teachers in French schools than amongst their British counterparts. Specifically, the practices in British schools displayed a far greater tendency to depend upon the socioeconomic backgrounds of the students. Sharpe conducted an 'ethnographic' study within two schools in an industrial town in northern France, one in an affluent area and the other in an educational priority zone, situated on a 'run-down municipal housing estate'. Sharpe found that there did indeed appear to be considerable homogeneity in practice between the two schools. In his analysis he associated this with a national context which incorporates a fundamental commitment to equality of treatment in ideological, policy and institutional terms. This is in marked contrast to the diversity which is actually encouraged by the same Education Reform Act that installed a National Curriculum in England and Wales. The homogeneity in French pedagogic practices is also clearly in contrast with the differentiation found by Rist. However, there is a paradox, as Sharpe points out:

> . . . on the one hand it is arguable that the established French approach based on homogenous provision in practice discriminates against children from family backgrounds which do not prepare them to benefit from schooling and that to treat everyone 'the same' when they are, in fact, very different is effectively to deny them equality of opportunity. On the other hand, there is evidence that where teachers are free to decide what should be offered to which children they may, albeit unwittingly and with the best of professional intentions, predetermine the success of some and the failure of others. (Sharpe, 1992; p. 346)

The latter eventuality is evidenced by Rist's study and others which are indexed by Sharpe. With respect to the former, Sharpe describes the system of appointments which effectively distributes the most experienced and successful teachers to the affluent areas, leaving the younger and older less successful teachers in precisely those areas in which children might be expected to be most in need of good teaching.

Rachel Sharp and Tony Green's *Education and Social Control* reported on another study focusing on the production of academic differentiation within the primary school classroom, this time, in England. Their book was published in 1975 during a period of increasing interest in Marxist perspectives within the sociology of education. They were concerned to demonstrate that social structures, specifically social class relations, were reproduced within the classroom behind the teacher's back, as it were. Thus the rhetoric of the progressive pedagogy in the infant school expressed concern for the needs of every individual. However, a stratification of opportunities arose out of patterns of sponsorship of certain pupils but not others. Essentially, such sponsorship was distributed on the basis of social class as a result of a concordance between the middle class child and the middle class teacher expectations. The outcome, then, was much in line with that found by Rist. A principal difference lay in Sharp and Green's focus on the contradiction between the rhetoric and practices of progressive education.

The year following that of the publication of Sharp and Green's book saw the appearance of *Schooling in Capitalist America* by Samuel Bowles and Herbert Gintis (1976). The political nature of the argument in both books is quite apparent in their respective titles. Bowles and Gintis adopted a more scientific Marxist perspective whereby the nature of cultural practices, specifically schooling, are of necessity in more or less direct correspondence with the structure of economic relations. Through this structural correspondence, schooling helps to integrate young people into the economic system.

Thus blacks and other minorities are concentrated in schools whose repressive, arbitrary, generally chaotic internal order, coercive authority structures, and minimal possibilities for advancement mirror the characteristics of inferior job situations. Similarly, predominantly working-class schools tend to emphasize behavioural control and rule-following, while schools in well-to-do suburbs employ relatively open systems that favour greater student participation, less direct supervision, more student electives, and, in general, a value system stressing internalized standards of control. (Bowles and Gintis, 1976; p. 132)

In a study which is, perhaps, influenced more by a Gramscian interpretation of Marx (see Gramsci, 1971), Jean Anyon analysed the treatment of economic and labour union developments during the period from the Civil War to World War I by history textbooks used in American secondary schools. She found that the books presented the capitalist mode of production as natural, eliminating virtually all traces of oppositional discourse. Anyon concludes that:

The school curriculum has contributed to the formation of attitudes that make it easier for powerful groups, those whose knowledge is legitimized by school studies, to manage and control society. Textbooks not only express the dominant groups' ideologies, but also help to form attitudes in support of their social position. (Anyon, 1981a; pp. 32–3)

Anyon appears to be making the assumption that dominated groups more or less readily succumb to the hegemony of the dominant groups. Working from an explicitly Gramscian perspective, Bob Connell and his co-authors argue that the ideology of possessive individualism of the school comes into conflict with working class culture which, they claim, tends to emphasize co-operative rather than individual action. The result is alienation:

. . . the attempt to get most kids to swallow academic knowledge produces insurmountable problems of motivation and control. Not only because of the abstractness of the content, but also as a consequence of the formal authority relations of its teaching. (Connell *et al*, 1982; p. 199)

The response to this has been an attempt to make school knowledge more 'relevant and meaningful'. However, this has generally been motivated by the need to overcome control problems and has resulted in restricted and restricting curricula. The authors signal the emergence of a third approach which, they claim, offers potential in what radical educators in nineteenth century England referred to as 'really useful knowledge' (see Johnson, 1981):

The approach neither accepts the existing organization of academic knowledge nor simply inverts it. It draws on existing school knowledge and on what working-class people already know, and organizes this selection of

information around problems such as economic and collective action, hand-
ling the disruption of households by unemployment, responding to the
impact of new technology, managing problems of personal identity and
association, understanding how schools work, and why. (Connell *et al*, 1982;
pp. 199–200)

This oppositional curriculum is contingent upon the development of
teachers who are 'organic' to the working class, that is, teachers who are
socio-culturally located within the working class. There remain tensions in
this programme, however, Connell (1985) describes one teacher's work:

[Jack Ryan's] work is mainly with stroppy boys, who are the more conspicu-
ous problem in his school. It probably does not work as well with stroppy
girls. Jack's own brand of masculinity easily gets him on a wavelength with
teenage boys, with interests like billiards, camping and cars; but could equally
be an obstacle to relations with teenage girls. He is familiar with the rough,
male-dominated sexuality of the neighbourhood kids — the drunken weekend gang-bangs, the unpredicted but unpreventable pregnancies (he reports
that the girls won't take the pill because it makes them fat) — and is pretty
uneasy with it. His practice does not give much grip on these issues. (Connell,
1985; p. 65)

The struggle for a working class counter hegemony via practices which
sustain patriarchal relations might, indeed, be interpreted as inevitably counterproductive. In Heidi Hartmann's Marxist-feminist analysis, patriarchy legit-
imates class hierarchies amongst men 'by allowing men of all groups to control
at least some women' (Hartmann, 1981; p. 206).
     In all of the work that I have described so far, in this section, the emphasis
is placed, in one way or another, on something that is done to the student
by the curriculum. Differential treatment of different social groups by Rist's
kindergarten teacher; apparently similar treatment of what might be presumed
to be differentially prepared students in the French educational system which,
paradoxically, distributes the 'better' teachers to those students whom might
be expected to be best prepared; the distribution of sponsorship on the basis
of social class in Sharp and Green's study; the imposition of regulation or the
fostering of responsibility on a class basis in Bowles and Gintis; the transmission of a class-specific ideology by the textbooks studied by Jean Anyon; and
Connell's alienated working class for whom an alternative treatment might
(or might not) prove counter hegemonic.
     We might say that the studies all make important empirical claims.
However, they all construct a dualism between the social practices which
constitute the curriculum, on the one hand, and the student as the object upon
which the curriculum operates. This dualism is theoretically inadequate. In
order to theorize the impact of social practices upon human subjects, the
subject must be conceptualized in terms of those social practices, thus dissolv-
ing the dualism. To take an analogy from school level physics, to claim that

a body will continue in its state of rest or uniform motion unless acted upon by a force — Newton's first law — is to imbricate the constructs 'body' and 'force' within each other: a body is that which is susceptible to a force in this way; a force is that which has this effect upon a body. The second law further elaborates the relationship in its assertion that the extent of the effect of a force upon the motion of the body is proportional to the magnitude of the force and inversely proportional to the magnitude (the mass) of the body. Sociologists rarely claim that the effect of the curriculum upon the student is mechanically deterministic. The result is an indeterminate residue of subjectivity, that is, an untheorized subject.

The understanding of subjectivity that I shall adopt in this book will be developed in Chapters 5 and 6. Here, I shall begin the introduction of my position via a brief description of some work which is theoretically closer to my own and which also picks up on the theme of gender inequality which was raised in the discussion of Bob Connell's research.

Valerie Walkerdine has produced a considerable body of empirical work relating to gender as a dimension of social inequality. This work includes a number of studies carried out by the Girls and Mathematics Unit at the Institute of Education, University of London into the area of girls' attainment in mathematics. This work, focusing on girls at pre-school, primary and secondary school ages, is reported in Walkerdine *et al*, 1989 (see also Walden and Walkerdine, 1982, 1985; Walkerdine, 1984). For my present purposes, that which is of greatest interest in this work is its rejection of socialization theories. These presume, to a greater or lesser extent, the effectiveness of the action of primary socialization in the home or secondary socialization in the school. This socialization is assumed to produce in girls peculiarly feminine cognitive and/or affective properties which distinguish them from boys and result in differential performances in school mathematics.

Drawing on the work of Michel Foucault (which will enter into the discussion in Chapter 5), Walkerdine argues that the mistake is to look to girls themselves for explanations of their own lack of success in school mathematics. Indeed, the school studies fail to find evidence of boys outperforming girls, often, the opposite is the case, up until the sixteen-plus public examination. Walkerdine argues that it is not girls' performances as such that are the problem. Rather, it is the interpretation of their success as the result of hard work that denies them the attribute of real ability, or flair in mathematics. On the other hand, boys' poorer performances can be attributed to a lack of care which might actually be taken to be an indicator of real ability. In the primary school, the rhetoric of progressivism and its implication of a version of Piagetian psychology can be interpreted as supporting this construction of the higher educational value of play (boys) with respect to work (girls) (see Walkerdine, 1984).

Thus, school practices and knowledges construct gendered positions which can be occupied by children: successful girls are constructed as lacking that which even relatively unsuccessful boys can possess, that is, rationality — in this case, mathematical ability. The apparatuses of the modern order construct the rational man as the normal state and counterpoise this with irrational woman:

> We claim that knowledges and apparatuses define femininity as a perpetual exclusion from the qualities necessary to produce a rational subject, the rational man, and that beneath this lies a terror. That these strategies are founded not upon a certainty but on a necessity to produce order against a constant threat of rebellion. There is a long history of the oppression of those knowledges in which women had powerful positions, and of the poor, the exploited and the oppressed attempting to rise up against an order which proclaimed a freedom for which they were the price. (Walkerdine *et al*, 1989; p. 205)

It can be claimed that Walkerdine's images of femininity are heavily dominated by expectations relating specifically to the white middle classes and that taking account of the dimension of ethnicity produces a more complex analysis (Ensor, 1991, 1993, 1994; see also Mac an Ghaill, 1988). Nevertheless, this work clearly represents an advance in terms of theoretical development in relation to much of the other work described here.

Differentiation: A Calculus of Social Inequality

In this chapter I have attempted to provide an orientation to the kind of analysis of schooling which I am developing in this book. I have introduced some of the ways in which curriculum differentiation has been described in respect of major dimensions of social inequality. I then considered some attempts to describe this articulation within the sociology of education. I want now to summarize, in general terms, my understanding of the action of schooling in relation to the social construction of ability.

In Chapter 1 I described sociology as being concerned with patterns of relationships between individuals and groups — the social — and the production and reproduction of these relationships in practices and in action — the cultural. Schooling comprises cultural institutions, practices and beliefs which are constituted by and are constitutive of the relations which characterize the social. Specifically, schooling in general, and school mathematics in particular, is organized on the basis of the distribution of pedagogic content and action in terms of student attributes. In the early stages of the development of mass schooling the principles of this distribution were commonly explicitly stated in terms of social class and gender. More recently, the rhetoric has tended to background these social considerations in favour of categories such as ability, achievement and needs. Nevertheless, it seems that the differentiation of the curriculum remains more or less closely associated with the social stratification of the student population.

In stark terms, my position is that there is no such thing as 'ability' or 'achievement' or 'needs' insofar as these are interpreted as substantive predicates of individual students. Rather, these are variables which are constituted in and by the practices of schooling. They are not to be interpreted as referring to or as measuring students in terms of their qualities as students. On the contrary, they are constituted within a substantially self-referential system which also relates them to images of social relations in terms of social class, gender, ethnicity, ablebodiedness and so on. Students must connote these images in their appearances, officially constructed life histories, and behaviours. It is this that enables them to be classified within the system of schooling and, indeed, to recognize themselves within the context of schooling. This is not to claim that 'failing' students must recognize themselves as inadequate in the manner of Bernard Coard's (1971) West Indian children who were *made* 'educationally subnormal' in the British school system. On the other hand, it may, finally, imply that the assertion of self-esteem entails the rejection of schooling.

Chapter 4

The Analysis of School Texts: Some Empirical Antecedents

Most of the research that I introduced in the previous chapter focused on the classroom as their empirical site. The main focus of my study is school mathematics textbooks. In this chapter I shall give some consideration to antecedent research which has focused on school texts.

A search of the English language literature reveals very little interest in the sociological analysis of school textbooks. The analysis of textbooks more generally is, however, a very large area. Within this capacious category would fall readability and evaluation studies, for example. Almost none of this work is of direct relevance here. I will, therefore, consider, firstly, work which focuses on the analyses of specifically mathematics textbooks and, secondly, I shall consider 'sociologically-orientated' analyses of textbooks in other curriculum areas. This second category includes, for example, analyses in terms of gender, ethnicity and class and ideological analyses of textbooks. The work in these two categories bears, at most, an indirect relevance to my project. Finally, I shall discuss, in rather more detail, two studies of science textbooks which seem, in different ways, to come closest to my own work.

Mathematics Textbooks

A search of the research literature reveals very little interest in this area. Analysis of specifically mathematics textbooks is almost non-existent and none of the work that has been produced enters the particular sociological field of interest of this study. An earlier search (Garcia *et al*, 1990) looking for work investigating the portrayal of 'females and minorities' in mathematics texts notes that:

> What was surprising in conducting this search was the absence of major studies examining the portrayal of females and minorities in elementary and secondary mathematics books. (Garcia *et al*, 1990; p. 3)

In fact, Garcia *et al* found only one study (Nibbelink *et al*, 1986 — see below) in respect of the representation of females and none relating to the portrayal of ethnic minorities. Their own study looked at illustrations and 'story problems' in elementary mathematics texts. They concluded that there had been a reduction, over a period of a decade, in the degree to which texts could be described as 'sexist' and that the textbooks that they analysed were appropriately described as 'multicultural'. Their main criticism of the texts concerned a common lack in the featuring of careers in mathematics.

My own search has revealed a small number of other studies focusing on the gendering of mathematics texts. Jean Northam (1982), for example, analysed textbooks published between 1970 and 1978. She concluded that '[t]here is a clear tendency in the books studied to define mathematics as the province of males, and especially adult males' (p. 14). Northam points to stereotypical images of males and females, the virtual absence of adult women from the texts and a steady decline in the representation of girls as the target age range moved from 3 to 13 years. Another study of sex-role stereotyping in mathematics textbooks was produced by the New Zealand Department of Education (1980). This study looked at six primary school textbooks and twenty-five secondary school textbooks and, again, concluded that there was strong evidence of bias in favour of males. Maggie McBride (1989) includes a brief discussion of stereotyping in mathematics textbooks in her 'Foucauldian analysis of mathematical discourse', although without presenting any systematic analysis.

In a paper which incorporated a response to McBride, I illustrated three 'textual strategies' in the gendering of mathematics texts (Dowling, 1991b). The first strategy is illustrated in the original series of the secondary school mathematics scheme produced by the School Mathematics Project (SMP). *SMP Book 1* makes use of the following metaphors to introduce the mathematical topic 'rotation':

> When your mother does the weekly wash, she probably uses a wringer or spin dryer to remove most of the water from the clothes, and your father probably uses a screw driver, a spanner and a drill to help do odd jobs about the home. (SMP, 1965, *SMP Book 1*, London: CUP; p. 54)

This extract invokes a cultural database of connotations which we might refer to as a 'domestic code'. The code might be illustrated in a Venn diagram as in *Figure 4.1*.

The elements in bold can be read more or less directly from the text, 'responsibility for the home' arising as a consequence of the father 'helping': whom is he helping; the mother is not helping[1]. The other elements are intertextual connotations of the extract. 'Father' and 'mother' clearly connote 'male' and 'female', respectively and 'boy' and 'girl' (schoolboy and schoolgirl)

---

1 It is important to note that, in this form of analysis, I am not claiming to produce the definitive reading of the text, but simply to demonstrate the workings of the text internally and intertextually. It is clearly possible to interpret 'helping' as signifying a subordinate role, that is as tending to invert the patriarchal hierarchy between women and men: faith in such an interpretation may, however, require somewhat Olympian feats of the imagination.

Figure 4.1   The gendering of 'rotation' (Source: Dowling, 1991b)

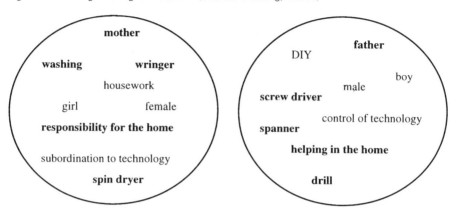

in terms of their origins. 'Washing' and the sequence 'a screw driver, a spanner and a drill' connote 'housework' and 'DIY' (do-it-yourself) respectively[2]. The connotations 'subordinate to technology' and 'control of technology' obtain because of the relative task dedication of wringers and spin dryers compared with screw drivers, spanners and drills. 'Subordination' is particularly associated with the spin dryer (and to an even greater extent with the modern equivalent) in that the housewife must wait for it to finish its cycle[3]. The reading of the piece of text thus partitions not just mothers and fathers, but (school)girls and (school)boys who are respectively associated — through the text and its intertextual connotations — with domesticity and subordination to technology, on the one hand, and activity outside the domestic sphere (the father is only 'helping' in the house) and technological control, on the other. The further connotation of technology with the more erudite aspects of mathematics facilitates the definition of female and male students as, respectively, alienated from and associated with erudite mathematics.

Two important points must be made. Firstly, the emphasis here is on the construction of female and male students within school mathematics rather than on whether or not the text provides 'appropriate role models' for girls (and boys). The text contributes, through its internal structure and external relations, to what it means to be female/male. Secondly, the SMP text is not to be held entirely responsible for this meaning: the gender codes always

2   It is interesting that 'housework' does *not* connote DIY, despite the fact that there would appear to be a logical correspondence between, for example, the opposition of 'DIY' to 'paying a plumber to repair the central heating', on the one hand, and that of 'housework' and 'employing a cleaner', on the other. Each opposes doing-it-yourself to getting-someone-else-to-do-it. Of course, plumbers and cleaners are also gendered: a firm distinction must be made between 'logical' and cultural principles of classification; the former constituting a sub-category of the latter.

3   Subordination/control is not an essential feature of the technology but must generally be understood contextually: my relationship to my wordprocessor is not the same as that between an office clerk and hers [sic] (see Dowling, 1991a).

already pre-date the text and enable its reading[4]. The function of the text is to reproduce patriarchal relations in the context and through the elements of school mathematics so that the gender structuring of society is dyed-in-the-wool of mathematics education.

Because of the dialectical nature of the masculine-feminine relationship, that is, 'masculine' is defined, principally anyway, in opposition to 'feminine', a text need not draw explicit contrasts between the genders. *The Mathematical Experience* by Davis and Hersh (1981) includes sixty-six pictures of mathematicians (including one of each of the authors, on the dust jacket) precisely none of which are images of women. Furthermore, as far as I can see, there is no reference to a female anywhere in the book and the expected gender of a mathematician (and that of a mathematician's student) is quite apparent in the authors' choice of pronoun:

> . . . the mathematician regards *his* work as part of the very structure of the world, containing truths which are valid forever, from the beginning of time, even in the most remote corner of the universe.

> *He* rests *his* faith on rigorous proof; *he* believes that the difference between a correct proof and an incorrect one is an unmistakable and decisive difference. *He* can think of no condemnation more damning than to say of a student, '*He* doesn't even know what a proof is'. Yet *he* is able to give no coherent explanation of what is meant by rigour, or what is required to make a proof rigorous. In *his* own work, the line between complete and incomplete proof is always somewhat fuzzy, and often controversial. (Davis and Hersh, 1981; p. 34; my emphasis)

and so it carries on[5]. Every instance of a masculine image or name or pronoun invokes its absent other which is feminine; the opposition is always already present within the intertextual connotations of 'masculine'. But the book is about erudite mathematics where, clearly, the feminine has no place. This alienation from mathematics is part of the meaning of femininity and, through connotation within the school, constructive of the female student.

The most recent edition of the SMP materials, *SMP 11–16*[6], illustrates a third possibility by placing masculine and feminine images, names or pronouns in contexts which appear to defy the patriarchal connotations described above, the following examples are taken from *Book B2*:

> Thomas did some shopping in a supermarket. The bill came to £14.47. When he got home he found he had been charged £5.39 for a joint which should have cost £3.59. What should his total bill have come to?

4   Roland Barthes purports to escape from this apparent determinism through the notion of 're-reading' which '. . . alone saves the text from repetition (those who fail to re-read are obliged to read the same story everywhere)' (Barthes, 1974; p. 16): in this sense, this book is a re-reading of school texts.
5   Despite the status of mathematics as the *queen* of sciences!
6   I will introduce a systematic analysis of books from this scheme in subsequent chapters.

> An architect is designing a house . . . *she* wants the three spaces marked S to be of equal width . . .

> A van driver leaves a shop. *She* has to deliver packages to four houses and return afterwards to the shop . . .

> A police*woman* is keeping a lookout on an empty house. She sees a man enter the house at 8:50 am . . . (SMP, *SMP Book B2, passim*, my emphasis)

Shopping connotes domesticity and therefore femininity[7]; architect and van driver connote masculinity and the default connotation for police *constable* is masculine, this being underlined by the use of the initials PC (police constable) and WPC (*woman* police constable), the 'W' being, otherwise, a clear pleonasm. As is commonly the case in English, the feminine term is 'marked'; other examples are: *woman* athlete; *woman* doctor; and *lady* golfer; and feminizations such as actress and authoress. In general, the marked term indexes the subaltern[8]. The SMP text, then, sets up a dissonance between its own juxtapositions, on the one hand, and intertextual connotations, on the other: a potential site for the worthwhile disruption of patriarchy. However, this dissonance is occasional and never explored. The text is structured as a relentless sequencing of tasks. Activity on these tasks is clearly to be maintained if the primary goal — the acquisition of mathematical knowledge and skill — is to be approached. The connotative dissonances are suppressed. The *goal* concerns the elaboration of mathematical techniques; the *means* involves tasks, some of which happen to serve the ancillary function of providing an alibi for sexism[9].

The suppression of connotative dissonances allows the latter — at most — to emerge, briefly, as jokes which are, of course, counterproductive in terms of antisexism: the following sequence, from the same book, seems ideally suited as an illustration:

> A Viking chief and his three sons raided a castle and made of with 2714 gold pieces. The chief took 893 himself and shared the rest equally between his sons. How many did each son get?

> Another chief and his four sons stole some gold pieces. The chief took 267 himself and each son got an equal share of the rest. If each son got 176 pieces, how many pieces were stolen?

7 And as is so common when token males are placed in feminine positions Thomas gets it wrong: he can't even count his change before he leaves the shop.
8 Which is equally the case with *male* nurse. The masculine is here being marked as the deviant form in the context of a feminized occupation.
9 I am making reference, here, to Leont'ev's hierarchy of activity wherein 'actions', which are related to 'goals', are more fundamental than 'operations' which concern 'means', the latter being characterized by a degree of arbitrariness. In the development of my language of description in Chapters 5 and 6 I shall introduce an alternative hierarchy which is more appropriate in the context of sociological textual analysis.

Yet another chief and his *daughters* stole 6941 gold pieces. The chief took 2417 and his daughters shared the rest equally. If each daughter got 348 pieces, how many daughters were there? (SMP, *SMP BOOK B2*; my emphasis)

An unusual way, perhaps, to count your daughters.

It may be that the suppression of context is so effective as to elide even comedy. On visiting a second-year secondary class working on an *SMP 11–16* booklet, I spoke to a girl who was working, on her own, through the activity in *Figure 4.2*.

The student was working diligently, answering the questions correctly and without any apparent difficulty. I pointed to the statue of George Eliot[10].

PD:	Who's this?
Student:	It says it's George Eliot.
PD:	Do you know who George Eliot is?
Student:	Is he a scientist?
PD:	So who's that on top of the pedestal?
Student:	Florence Nightingale?
PD:	She's moved over to George's pedestal, has she?
Student:	Yes.

The hiatus had only opened up at all because I had intervened, disrupting the flow of activity. Furthermore, it was easily sutured by the student who readily substituted a dissonance of syntax (the name on the pedestal not being the name of the individual represented) for a dissonance of connotation (a masculine name cannot signify a female[11]). A picture of George Eliot might connote a society in which a woman cannot become publicly successful unless she is believed to be a man: a picture of a *statue* of George Eliot seems to reflect a cosy image of a contemporary culture which is quite prepared to celebrate the lives and products of the good and the great, their femininity notwithstanding. In any event, such intertextual connotations must precede the reading; this clearly did not obtain in the case of the student in question. Deliberate pedagogic action is demanded, but this, of course, would detract from the goal which is mathematics.

Three textual strategies with respect to gender have been considered in this discussion. The first celebrates the social construction of the feminine/masculine opposition and reasserts its correspondence with 'user of technology'/'controller of technology' and, therefore, the affinity of the masculine with erudite mathematics in contrast with the alienation of the feminine; the subject is constituted through the reinforcing of the gender code. The second strategy excludes as a positive presence the feminine from mathematics, confirming it in its alienation as a negative trace of otherness. The third strategy makes a ritual genuflexion to the discourse of equal opportunities and so

---

10 The dialogue which follows was recorded in field notes.
11 On another occasion, another student resolved the dissonance by suggesting that George Eliot might have been a priest, presumably wearing clerical robes.

Figure 4.2   SMP 11–16, Turning (p. 8)

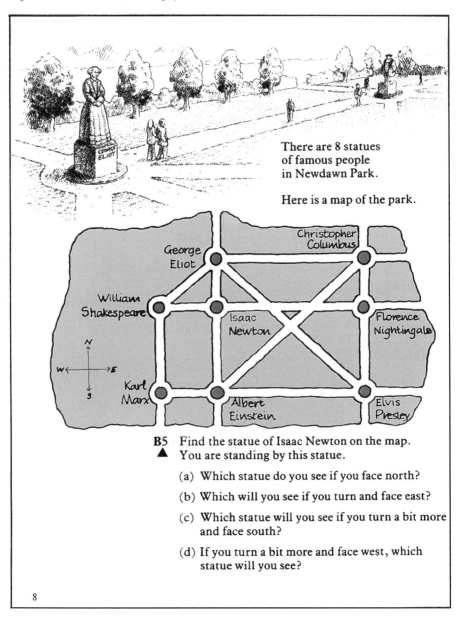

There are 8 statues
of famous people
in Newdawn Park.

Here is a map of the park.

B5 Find the statue of Isaac Newton on the map.
▲ You are standing by this statue.

(a) Which statue do you see if you face north?

(b) Which will you see if you turn and face east?

(c) Which statue will you see if you turn a bit more
and face south?

(d) If you turn a bit more and face west, which
statue will you see?

8

defuses antisexist petards. The possibility of actual critique within the text,
however, is suppressed through the rigid structuring of what the text is really
about and through the failure to confront gender as a social structure. Any
residual connotative dissonance emerges as a joke or is easily repaired within
available discursive resources.

The social is already structured by gender codes. But by leaving the hierarchical organization within this code untouched or by actively reinforcing it, these three strategies within school mathematics texts facilitate the articulation of a gender hierarchy to a curricular one. They define the masculine as mathematical and the feminine as anti-mathematical. These constitutions of subjectivity are not contingent upon the respective natures of females and males as is supposed by McBride (1989). This author's 'Foucauldian analysis' actually misrepresents Foucault's 'subject positions' as 'roles' and essentializes the feminine through the attribution of gendered cognitive styles. The constructions of subjectivity in and by these textbooks are part of what it means to be male or female. School mathematics texts do not cause girls to fail. Rather, they reproduce and augment what it means to be a girl. Whatever their actions, girls must either be confirmed in their femininity and therefore as lacking anything more than moderate 'ability' in mathematics, or they must be labelled as gender-freaks. Girls and, by the same token, boys are thus doubly bound into a social structure which delimits possibilities.

This argument regarding the construction of gender in the context of school mathematics clearly resonates with the position adopted by Walkerdine which was outlined in the previous chapter. In the second part of the paper in which it was originally presented, I included a discussion of the construction of ability in school mathematics texts in terms of social class (see, also, Dowling, 1990a, 1991c, 1993, 1994a, 1995a, 1996b). I shall not further elaborate this here as the position which I introduced in these earlier publications has been considerably developed and will form a significant component of the textual analysis which I shall present later in this book. Rather, I shall complete my survey of research on school mathematics texts.

I have already mentioned the work of Jean Northam (1982). The analysis reported in this paper was undertaken as part of a mathematics diploma course for primary teachers. Work looking at representations of gender in mathematics textbooks is commonly directed at practitioners rather than at researchers. The discussion in Burton *et al* (1986) of gender stereotyping in mathematics textbooks, for example, appears in a pack for teachers produced collaboratively by the Open University and the Inner London Education Authority (ILEA). The ILEA's Centre for Learning Resources (1985) produced its own publication looking for bias in primary mathematics materials. Morehead's (1984) consideration of the illustrations in three textbook series appears in the UK professional journal, *Mathematics in School*, and Nibbelink's (1986) analysis of problems in elementary school mathematics textbooks appears in the US professional journal *The Arithmetic Teacher*.

The ILEA publication (1985) also addresses the issue of the representation of ethnic minority groups in mathematics texts. In this area: Hudson (1985) looks at 'militarist', sexist and ethnocentrist bias in mathematics textbooks and computer software; Rivers (1990) considers the portrayal of females and ethnic minorities in first year algebra textbooks; the Garcia paper (*op. cit.*) has already been mentioned.

Other studies of mathematics textbooks have focused on issues of mathematical subject content or problem-solving. Remillard (1991a, 1991b), for example, evaluates the conceptions of problem-solving in elementary mathematics texts and Donald Freeman and others (Freeman *et al*, 1983a, 1983b, 1983c; Freeman and Porter, 1989) have analysed elementary mathematics textbooks in terms of mathematical content and pedagogic intention; these analyses were compared with analyses of lessons and of standardized tests. Cairns (1984) has produced a content analysis of *SMP 7–13* in comparison with two other schemes in terms of subject content and sequencing. Kim (1993) has compared, briefly, the measurement and geometry content in American and Republic of Korean textbooks, seeking some explanation for outperforming of American students by Korean students in the Second International Mathematics Study.

In his PhD thesis, Wing (1989) draws on theoretical resources from the fields of semiotics (Eco and de Saussure) and philosophy (Heidegger) and on his own experience in using school mathematical texts as well as interview data with primary school children. Wing argues that, in their use, these texts necessarily become authoritarian in character, so as to preserve, impart or emphasize a 'textual' mathematics. Although this work draws on some of the semiotic resources that inform the language of description used in my own work, it cannot be described as a sociological study.

Finally, in relation to mathematics textbooks, the studies of Barry Cooper (1983, 1985) and Bob Moon (1986) should be mentioned. Cooper's work is concerned with the development of 'modern mathematics' and specifically with the success of the School Mathematics Project in the secondary school curriculum. This work clearly relates to textbooks, but does not, itself, constitute an analysis of textbooks. Similarly, Moon's study is concerned with the 'new maths curriculum controversy' in elementary education. This work is directly relevant to the development of mathematics textbooks in the UK, specifically, the Nuffield Project texts. However, as is the case with Cooper's work, there is no analysis of the texts themselves.

Other Curriculum Areas — 'Sociological' Analyses

Moving beyond mathematics as a curriculum area, textbooks have attracted some attention in the area that might be broadly described as 'sociologically-orientated' studies. Notably, Michael Apple (1986, 1989) considers the conditions of the production of textbooks at a higher level of analysis even than obtains in the studies by Cooper and Moon. Apple's answer to the question 'how is "legitimate" knowledge made available in schools?' is:

> By and large it is made available through something to which we have paid too little attention — the textbook. Whether we like it or not, the curriculum in most American schools is not defined by courses of study or suggested programs, but by one particular artefact, the standardized, grade-level-specific

text in mathematics, reading, social studies, science (when it is even taught), and so on. The impact of this on the social relations of the classroom is immense. It is estimated, for example, that 75 per cent of the time elementary and secondary students are in classrooms and 90 per cent of their time on homework is spent with text materials [. . .]. Yet even given the ubiquitous character of textbooks, they are one of the things we know least about. (Apple, 1986; p. 85)

However, Apple concentrates on the 'ideological, political and economic sources of the production, distribution and reception' (*ibid*; p. 86) of school textbooks and does not analyse any empirical texts. Lorimer and Keeney (1989) are also interested in the macroeconomic context of textbook production. They draw on analyses of the thematic and ideological content of elementary language art readers and of science textbooks in their description of the role of multinational publishing companies in 'defining' the Canadian school curriculum.

I have mentioned the work of Jean Anyon (1979, 1981a, 1981b, 1983) in Chapter 3. In her ideological analysis, she claims to have determined that the history texts that she analysed were biased in favour of the priorities of dominant groups. However, she fails to present the principles of her description of these texts or of the social which, in terms of 'interests', is being represented by them. In this sense, she is not detecting bias so much as introducing it through her treatment of the texts as transparent with respect to her own interpretations.

Joel Taxel (1981, 1983) analysed the content and narrative structure of thirty-two children's novels about the American Revolution, published in four periods between 1899 and 1976. He concluded that a 'simplistic, selective, and conservative conception of the Revolution' (1983, p. 74) was also reinforced by the narrative structure of the novels, for example, in the coding of the characters along the good/bad opposition. Taxel also compares his own analysis with Wright's analysis of Western films and finds 'remarkable similarities' in the results. Taxel argues that the novels and films serve to legitimate the structure of socioeconomic relationships. He rejects a determinist model in favour of a 'sensitivity to the historic specificity of culture and classroom life' (*ibid*; p. 85). However, although he genuflects to theorists such as Bernstein, Bourdieu and Willis, Taxel fails to provide any structuring to his 'sensitivity', while Anyon needs her analysis of textbooks to provide her with an image of the social:

An examination of school knowledge as a social product suggests a great deal about the society that produces and uses it. It reveals which groups have power, and demonstrates that the views of these groups are expressed and legitimized in the school curriculum. It can also identify social groups that are not empowered by the economic and social patterns in the society: they do not have their views, activities, and priorities represented in the school curriculum. The present analysis suggests that the United States working

class is one such group, [. . .] the poor may be another. Omissions, stereotypes, and distortions that remain in 'up-dated' social studies textbook accounts
of Native Americans, blacks, and women reflect the relative powerlessness of
these groups. (Anyon, 1983; p. 49)

I am adopting the position that, at least in its final form, a sociological
analysis of texts should present a coherent theoretical account of those aspects
of the social that are to be described and should generate a language which
enables the movement between social structure and textual reading. The
approach, here, should also be distanced from the apparent ontological com-
mitments of ideological analysts, such as Anyon and Taxel; as Rob Gilbert
describes 'structuralism':

. . . structuralism as a method does not require a transcendental generating
force beyond the structure itself. No necessary ontology need be implied in
the construction of a structuralist reading of text. To construct a model of
the rhetorical elements and relations of a text need not be to reify that structure, or to deny that the model itself could be subjected to a similar analysis.
The exercise can just as easily be seen as a translation of one discourse into
another, the notion of structure being a means of representation rather than
a reality beyond discourse. (Gilbert, 1989; p. 67)

Gilbert refers to his own position as 'in some respect post-structuralist'
(*ibid*; p. 71). I shall refer to my analysis as '(post)structuralist' to indicate that
it is not non-structuralist or anti-structuralist, but that it has learned from the
criticisms of much structuralist work as essentialist (see, for example, Laclau
and Mouffe, 1985). Thus, in contrast to ideological textual analysis, I am not
seeking to uncover bias, but to translate pedagogic texts into a sociological
language. The bases and elements of this language are presented in Chapters
5 and 6.
A number of other 'ideological' analyses of textbooks were discovered in
the literature. Also found were a number of items focusing on the detection
of bias in textbook representation of gender and/or ethnicity. These may be
of interest and are referenced in an earlier publication (Dowling, 1995a); they
are also included in the bibliography of this book. However, the approach
being adopted here is very different, being concerned with the development
of a systematic language for the sociological description of pedagogic texts in
terms of their regulation of 'who' can say or do 'what'. There is a very small
amount of literature which, on the face of it, is related to this project. I shall
end this chapter with a discussion of two such pieces in greater detail.

Two Studies

In surveying the literature I paid some attention to textbooks in the field of
'English for Specific Purposes' (ESP). A review of the articles published in

the journal of that name reveals that most are concerned with the difficulties of students having a language other than English as their first language in working with textbooks in the medium of English (Chimombo, 1989; Love, 1991; Marshall and Gilmour, 1993). These articles are clearly directed towards the amelioration of these difficulties. In this respect, they are adopting an 'engineering' approach to textual production. In a slightly different vein, Kuo (1993) considers possible principles for the selection and development of materials in English for Science and Technology for use at university level in Taiwan. Tadros (1989) presents a model of discourse analysis which is used to analyse the instance of predictive categories in university law textbooks. Myers (1992), however, offers an analysis of university science textbooks which explicitly invokes sociology; he asserts that:

> To understand what makes textbooks different from other academic texts, and perhaps what makes them problematic for our students, we need to see what they do in the social structure of academic disciplines, how writing and reading them reproduces knowledge and reproduces academics. We need to ask some sociological questions. (Myers, 1992; p. 3)

Myers first considers the role of textbooks in the life histories of scientists. He rejects a position (which he attributes to Thomas Kuhn) in which 'early training in textbooks makes alternative views of phenomena unthinkable, so that there can be no rational comparison of competing paradigms' (*ibid*; p. 5). This view, he argues, ignores the importance of craft knowledge in the work of a scientist and also the critical relationship to textbooks which is adopted by some scientists (exemplified by James Watson, one of the discoverers of the structure of DNA)[12].

Myers then considers a 'more useful' line of thinking in which textbooks are seen 'as the end of the development of a fact, not as the beginning of the development of a scientist' (*ibid*; p. 6). Here, Myers contrasts the textbook with the research journal article. Journals constitute an arena for conflicting views and claims. The textbooks, however, establishes a selection of these claims as 'facts' which are incorporated into a particular kind of order. Myers produces an analysis of two short sections of text which are related in terms of content, one from a university textbook on genetics and the other from a journal article on RNA processing. The texts are compared in terms of their respective uses of personal and impersonal subjects, verbal tense, modality[13], cohesion, references to other texts, and illustrations. The following is an extract from the comparison of modality:

12 Kuhn's (1970) argument also ignores any empirical reference to the readers of textbooks or to teachers.
13 'Modality' is a term that has been introduced in Chapter 1. It refers to the strength of the claim on the reality of a situation which is represented in a text. Modality may be weakened by the use of 'hedging', thus: 'the rain in Spain falls mainly on the plain' becomes 'the rain in Spain *perhaps* falls mainly on the plain'; the latter exhibiting a reduced modality via the inclusion of the hedging term, 'perhaps'.

Nonscientists may be surprised to find just how often the statements in the scientific article are modified.

> Analogous intervening sequences *appear* to interrupt . . . (2)
> The possibility that this precursor represents a transcript of the beta-globin gene including intervening sequences is *attractive* because . . . (6)

I have argued [. . .] that almost all new claims are hedged. In contrast, the textbook represents these claims as accredited facts that need no hedging:

> The coding region of most eukaryotic structural genes is interrupted by non-coding sectors . . . (1)

The textbook uses some hedges too (although fewer), but it usually reserves them for matters of representation about which there is not yet a clear consensus:

> *perhaps* most appropriately called precursor mRNA . . . (8)

Other hedges indicate remaining uncertainty:

> they *appear* never to leave the nucleus . . . (11)

A student who knows only the way textbooks use hedges for uncertainty is unprepared for the ways articles use them in polite statements of claims. (*ibid*; p. 11)

These differences are constitutive of distinct genres which are motivated by their respective roles in what Myers refers to as the 'social structure of academic disciplines' (*ibid*; p. 3). Thus:

> Authors of textbooks try to arrange currently accepted knowledge into a coherent whole, whereas authors of journal articles try to make the strongest possible claim for which they think they can get agreement. (*ibid*; p. 9)

It is arguably possible to reconcile Myers' view of the textbook[14] as in some sense, 'the end of the development of a fact' with Bernstein's (1990) concept of recontextualization[15]. Bernstein has contrasted the 'primary context' of the production of scientific knowledge with the 'secondary context' of its reproduction[16]. The relationship between 'discourse' within the primary context of production and discourse within the secondary context of reproduction is described by Bernstein as 'a complex transformation from an original [*i.e.* unmediated] to a virtual/imaginary discourse' (p. 185). This involves the delocation and relocation of scientific knowledge via the process of 'recontextualization'. Essentially, the recontextualizing of primary discourse is achieved by 'pedagogic discourse'. Pedagogic discourse is constituted by the recontextualizing principles of the 'pedagogic device', which constitutes and sustains the relations of power and principles of control within a pedagogic relationship, effecting differential transmission and acquisition.

14 More correctly, the incorporation of the textbook into empirical classroom practices.
15 Bernstein's concept and my own use of the term are further discussed in Chapters 5 and 6.
16 Although Bernstein is referring, primarily, to the school as the site of reproduction.

It would be appropriate to describe the texts that Myers analyses as differentially implicating certain resources in certain strategies which are constitutive of reader-author relationships which are appropriate to their respective contexts. The strong modality of the textbook sustains its authority within the secondary context of reproduction. It stands as a surrogate for the teacher/student relationship. The weakening of modality within the journal article is no mere politeness. On the contrary, within the primary context of the production of knowledge, the validity of all claims is to be judged by the academic community which constitutes the 'peer' group refereeing and readership of research articles. The modality of the text is weakened because the authority of the author is weakened in favour of that of the reader. The vector of evaluation is reversed.

Myers' interest, however, is in the application of linguistic tools in cataloguing the characteristics of respective genres. Within the field of applied linguistics, these tools are certainly constituted as well-developed and coherent languages. Myers' recruitment of the sociology of scientific knowledge enables him to provide a plausible explanation for the generic differences which he identifies. However, the principles of the sociological apparatus are far less explicit and coherent than the linguistic language. They are also substantially dislocated from that language, meeting only in terms of their mutual reference to an epistemology (albeit sociologically defined). My project is the development of a more fully explicit and coherent sociological framework which will enable the operational analysis of texts in terms of their (re)production of the structure of the context within which they are deployed. In respect of the textbook, I am identifying that context as pedagogic rather than epistemological or linguistic.

Lynn Mulkey (1987) describes her work as 'sociological'. She has produced a content analysis of 187 science textbooks used in middle and working class districts of New York at different age-grade levels. The analysis assesses the 'functional/dysfunctional role [of textbooks] in socialization for scientific careers' (p. 511). The general hypothesis to be tested was that:

> ... textbook content for middle-class districts and higher grades would be organized so that knowledge was more facilitative of the acquisition of the intellectual and emotional characteristics of scientists than for working-class districts and lower grades. The consequences are that if children in working-class districts are being socialized into nonparticipant roles they are less likely to contribute to scientific advancement than those children in middle-class districts who are being socialized into participant roles. (Mulkey, 1987; pp. 512–3)

The first point to be made is that Mulkey is clearly making precisely the kind of assumptions about the effectiveness of socialization that were challenged by Walkerdine in the work described in Chapter 3. However, I want to focus on a different aspect of the work, here. The concept 'textbook content' consisted of six dependent variables which Mulkey describes as follows:

... (1) orientation to cognitive flexibility (knowledge supportive of the ability to make connections between ideas in novel ways (2) orientation to abstract thinking (knowledge supportive of the ability to apply rational ideas to empirical ends to produce generalized and systematic schemes (3) orientation to communicative fluency (knowledge supportive of the ability to acquire the social and cognitive conventions of science) (4) orientation to autonomy (knowledge facilitative of self-direction in new situations (5) orientation to goal achieving (knowledge supportive of the ability for personal mastery of an event), and (6) orientation to positive imagery (knowledge which influences the perceptions of students about scientists so that entry into the scientific professions results). The degree of 'participant organization' (grouping of content conducive to the acquisition and development of the cognitive and personality precursors of scientific roles) versus 'non-participant organization' (grouping of content that is not conducive to the acquisition and development of the cognitive and personality precursors of scientific roles) was measured on a variable nine-point scale. (*ibid*; pp. 513–4; brackets as in original)

The results of the analysis did not produce statistically significant differences, in general, between textbooks used in middle class districts in comparison with those used in working class districts, although differences were found between the grade levels (higher grade textbooks provided higher degrees of participant organization). The results also offered 'minimal support' for the hypothesis that the greatest degree of participant organization would be provided by upper grade middle class textbooks[17].

Mulkey compared her findings to those of another study (by Harrington) which found differences between middle class and working class political science texts, but found less pervasive differences between grade levels. Mulkey postulates that the differences between the studies are produced by the differences between the disciplines with which they are concerned. Scientific ideas, she contends, 'retain a universality uncommon in other areas of human enterprise and are unprecedented except by mathematical ideas' (*ibid*; p. 519). Thus, science textbook writers might be expected to have a consistency of approach which is relatively impervious to the effects of social class. On the other hand, 'the complex cognitive skills and accompanying motivational factors that are required in order to do science' (*ibid*) would necessitate the grade-development in all aspects of orientation to participation in science books; presumably, these skills and factors are not understood, by Mulkey, to conceptualize political science. It is also worth noting that Mulkey's finding that the science textbooks were effectively class-blind and her explanation in terms of the nature of science and mathematics is directly challenged by the findings of my analysis of UK mathematics textbooks.

Mulkey's explanation for her finding that the highest degree of orientation to participation is provided by upper grade middle class textbooks is

---

17 Although the differences were statistically significant only in respect of 'orientation to cognitive flexibility'.

predicated upon the assumption of a model of cultural deprivation on the part of textbook writers and selectors. It is suggested that these agents presume a greater degree of preparedness for orientation to cognitive flexibility on the part of older middle class students than would be the case for working class students of the same age.

In terms of specific research methodology, Mulkey's analysis gives a very high-level description. The unit of analysis is the individual textbook which is assigned a single value on each of the dependent variable indicator scales described above. Each textbook was also assigned a value on the two independent variable scales, that is, middle class/working class[18] and grade level. In the light of her use of such a coarse instrument of analysis, her failure to find very much may not be surprising, despite the fact that there is a sense in which she knew what she was looking for.

My interest is in the production of a much closer form of textual reading and, to this extent, my project is closer to that of Myers. Myers, however, ultimately deserts sociology in favour of linguistics. My intention has been to generate a purpose-built language of description out of an engagement between a general sociological orientation — to be described in Chapters 5 and 6 — and an empirical text. Unfortunately, the dynamics of this production are, of necessity, elided, to a certain extent, in the presentation of the language and the analysis as artifacts.

The intention of Mulkey's analysis is to provide an instrument of evaluation to assist with the production and selection of 'functional' as opposed to 'dysfunctional' textbooks. This general methodological perspective of Mulkey's work is inconsistent with that to be adopted here. A distancing is to be announced in relation to both the 'engineering' intention of Mulkey's analysis and its explicit and naive functionalism. The position that I am adopting in my approach to textual analysis is that the textbook participates, tacitly, in the (re)production of social structure. The analysis of the textbook entails the description of the nature of this participation. That is, my analysis addresses the question: 'how does the textbook select and distribute the modes of relay of mathematical knowledge'?

Mulkey seems to treat that which ought to be transmitted by the textbook as basically unproblematic. Her ideal textbook seems to have something of the quality of a superconductor. As a teacher of ESP, Myers project is, ultimately, pedagogic. That is, he wants to be able to identify and transmit genre-specific textual characteristics thus:

> If we, as teachers, keep several genres in mind, instead of focusing on textbooks as the genre that students first encounter, we may be able to help

---

18 The exclusivity of the class value of the textbooks seems odd: 'Of the total 187 books reported used extensively and occasionally by middle- and working-class districts, the three middle-class districts accounted for 64 per cent ($n = 119$) and the working-class districts only 36 per cent ($n = 68$).' (Mulkey, 1987; p. 515).

students respond more easily, and more critically, to the texts they encounter later in their careers. (Myers, 1992; p. 9)

Like Mulkey, then, he also has in mind an ideal text, although in his case, his ideal (ESP) text is a product rather than an assumption of his analysis. In both cases, the production of appropriate materials is interpreted as essentially a technical problem and their application is intended to engineer a pedagogy which is more efficacious in terms of intentions which can be made explicit. This interpretation, however, denies the contingent specificity of the social which inscribes educational researchers and sociologists as fully as it does textbook writers and teachers (including teachers of ESP). I want to assert that the pedagogic text (any pedagogic text) constructs both its message and its readers in a form which is consistent with the social conditions within which it participates. As I will demonstrate — and authors' expressed intentions notwithstanding — this must entail alienation as well as apprenticing.

In this chapter, I have summarized some of the approaches that have taken a broadly sociological interest in the analysis of school textbooks. In general, it can be said that these studies have tended to restrict themselves to the issue of the representation of different social groups, either by exclusion/inclusion, or by the use of stereotypes, or, as is the case in the more sophisticated work of Anyon and Taxel, in terms of the representation of the interests of dominant groups in ideological terms. The 'sociological' studies by Myers and by Mulkey are both, ultimately, motivated by an 'engineering' imperative which actually leads to their ignoring of the constitutive impact of social structure. None of these studies derive a systematic and detailed analysis from a coherent and explicit theory of the social. In representing some of my own earlier work, here, I have intended to suggest the general direction of the (post)structuralist methodology that I shall be elaborating in the next two chapters.

Chapter 5

Towards a Language of Description: Some Theoretical Antecedents

This chapter and the one that follows will derive and lay out the language of description: which is the central achievement of this study. In subsequent chapters, this language will be used to present an analysis of the *SMP 11–16* texts. The language of description has been generated, firstly, via a consideration of theoretical issues and, secondly, through an extensive and intensive engagement with the empirical texts. Thus, both deductive and inductive processes have been involved. In this exposition, however, the language will be presented in deductive form. The work of this chapter, therefore, is to generate the theoretical propositions from which the language of description will be derived in Chapter 6.

These propositions will be generated out of a discussion of work which has been central in providing inspiration for the work as a whole. Clearly, there are problems associated with the presentation of such a discussion, both in terms of selection and ordering. The necessary limitation on space has a bearing on each of these problem areas. The selection of work has been made on the basis of my perception of its importance in the development of the language of description. The general theoretical position outlined at the end of this chapter does not follow the same order as the chapter as a whole. Clearly, it would have been possible to arrange the main discussion in the chapter so that it coincided with the structure of the summary. However, this would have resulted in a very much longer exposition and a certain measure of redundancy (or an unmanageable amount of cross-referencing). I have, therefore, decided to organize the discussion around three interrelated themes. The discussion within each theme will begin with a consideration of antecedent work and will develop some of the ideas that have been introduced in earlier chapters.

The first theme concerns the distinction between the abstract and the concrete. This is an opposition which has received a great deal of attention across a range of disciplines in the social sciences during the twentieth century and it corresponds to a distinction which is crucial in this work. The elaboration of this theme will open with a brief consideration of the discursive/ non-discursive distinction indexed by Michel Foucault. I will then move to a discussion of some of the ways in which the modality of the discursive has been treated in the literature. Out of this discussion, I will establish the scaling of practices in terms of *discursive saturation*. This concept was introduced in the generation of an ideal typography of pedagogic modes in Chapter 2. It constitutes a fundamental dimension in my language of description.

The second theme concerns the production of subjectivity. Here, my approach was adumbrated in the discussion of the social construction of ability in Chapter 3. In this discussion I shall make use of the term 'ideology', which is a familiar expression. In the construction of my language of description, I shall be defining an analytic space which will enable me to describe the empirical as constituted by the division of labour in general. Within the empirical domain, this space is always 'ideologized'. That is, it is always inscribed within a particular division of labour. In referring to my analytic space, therefore, I shall use the alternative term — 'activity' — which I have already defined loosely in Chapter 1. The term will be more fully elaborated in Chapter 6 and will be used in the formulation of the theoretical statements in the summary of the present chapter.

The third and final theme to be discussed in this chapter is concerned with the contextualizing and recontextualizing of practices. This theme was introduced in the discussion of mathematical myths in Chapter 1. Out of this discussion, I will establish a second fundamental dimension of the language of description. The chapter will close with a summary statement from which the language of description will be derived in Chapter 6.

Abstract and Concrete Practice

The Discursive and the Non-discursive

Michel Foucault is rather ambivalent about the distinction that I want to make, here, that is between the discursive and the non-discursive. In his later work, for example, he introduced the term 'apparatus' (*dispositif*) which he described in an interview in the following terms:

> What I am trying to pick out with this term is, firstly, a thoroughly heterogeneous ensemble consisting of discourses, institutions, architectural forms, regulatory decisions, laws, administrative measures, scientific statements, philosophical, moral and philanthropic propositions — in short, the said as much as the unsaid. The apparatus itself is the system of relations that can be established between these elements. (Foucault, 1980; p. 194)

Foucault's interviewers subsequently press him on the issue of the non-discursive:

> *J.-A. MILLER:* With the introduction of 'apparatuses' you want to get beyond discourse. But these new ensembles which articulate together so many different elements remain nonetheless *signifying* ensembles. I can't quite see how you could be getting at a 'non-discursive' domain.

FOUCAULT: In trying to identify an apparatus, I look for the elements which participate in a rationality, a given form of co-ordination, except that . . .

J.-A. MILLER: One shouldn't say rationality, or we would be back with the *episteme* again.

[. . .]

FOUCAULT: The term 'institution' is generally applied to every kind of more-or-less constrained, learned behaviour. Everything which functions in a society as a system of constraint and which isn't an utterance, in short, all the field of the non-discursive social, is an institution.

J.-A. MILLER: But clearly the institution is itself discursive.

FOUCAULT: Yes, if you like, but it doesn't much matter for my notion of the apparatus to be able to say that this is discursive and that isn't. If you take Gabriel's architectural plan for the Military School together with the actual construction of the School, how is one to say what is discursive and what institutional? That would only interest me if the building didn't conform with the plan. But I don't think it's very important to be able to make that distinction, given that my problem isn't a linguistic one. (*ibid*; pp. 197–8)

Such nonchalance is, perhaps, to be expected in one who rarely makes explicit the principles of his descriptions. Descriptions which would thereby lay claim to a certain transparency of data, were it not for their stunning originality. Foucault clearly needs to index a discursive/non-discursive differentiation, because therein lies the inevitability of the 'failure' of 'programmes' which are realized in purely discursive terms. These programmes are associated with 'technologies' which extend beyond the discursive and, therefore, beyond its control. The result is the subjectless 'strategies' discussed by Foucault in the interview cited above[1]. Foucault's originality lies precisely in his use of such terms. The breadth of these concepts, however, of necessity allows a great deal of scope for idiosyncratic interpretation. Again, Foucault's originality resides in his organizing strategies rather than in the precision of his histories. His ultimate refusal to establish a clear distinction between the discursive and the non-discursive is, possibly, a consequence of his recognition of a paradox: were he to provide such a distinction, then he would either have defined the limits of the discursive within discourse itself[2], or he would have rendered the non-discursive discursive.

In recognition of this paradox, the discursive/non-discursive distinction can only be a heuristic distinction and it is in this sense that it will be made here. Thus, we can assert that there always exists an excess of human practices over the strictly linguistic; an excess which corresponds to Heidegger's 'background'. This excess can never be fully realized in language, although its extent will vary between different aspects and instances of practice. The importance of this heuristic proposition is that it enables me to differentiate

1   See Gordon's discussion in the afterword to the same volume (Gordon, 1980).
2   An impossibility also recognized by Wittgenstein (1961).

between different modes of practice within the discursive in terms of the extensiveness of the non-discursive excess. Thus, practices which minimize the non-discursive excess are, by definition, those which are most fully realizable within language. Such practices must tend to make explicit the principles of their regulation in order to minimize reliance upon the unsayable. On the other hand, practices which exhibit a comparatively high degree of non-discursive excess are less capable of making explicit their regulating principles; they are, substantially, non-discursively regulated. As I announced in Chapter 2, these modes of practice will be described as exhibiting high and low *discursive saturation* (DS⁺ and DS⁻) respectively. In order to give more substance to this distinction and to acknowledge its intellectual pedigree, I shall now consider some other work which has made a corresponding differentiation of practice within the discursive level.

The Modality of the Discursive

There is, throughout the social sciences, a persistent dichotomizing of modes of practice or of cognition which can be formulated at the level of discourse. An early example is to be found in the work of Lucien Lévy-Bruhl who 'was the first to point out the qualitative features of primitive [sic] thought and the first to treat logical processes as products of historical development' (Luria, 1976). Lévy-Bruhl was thereby making a distinction between the modes of practice in societies at different stages of development, 'primitive' and modern. Yu. M. Lotman distinguishes between 'grammar-oriented' and 'text-oriented' societies which are described by Umberto Eco as follows:

> There are cultures governed by a *system* of rules and there are cultures governed by a *repertoire* of texts imposing models of behaviour. In the former category texts are generated by combinations of discrete units and are judged correct or incorrect according to their conformity to the combinatorial rules; in the latter category society directly generates texts, these constituting macrounits from which rules could eventually be inferred, but that first and foremost propose models to be followed and imitated. (Eco, 1976; pp. 137–8)

There is also a developmental relationship between these two forms, Eco continues:

> Lotman suggests that text-oriented societies are at the same time expression-oriented ones, while grammar-oriented societies are content-oriented. The reason for such a definition becomes clear when one considers the fact that a culture which has evolved a highly differentiated content system has also provided expression-units corresponding to the content-units, and may therefore establish a so-called 'grammatical' system — this simply being a highly articulated code. On the contrary a culture which has not yet differentiated its content-units expresses (through macroscopic expressive groupings: the texts) a sort of *content-nebula*. (*ibid*, 1976; p. 138)

This distinction between rule-governed practices and practices which draw upon a repertoire of exemplary texts, or perhaps a repertoire of techniques, resonates with my distinction between high and low discursive saturation. My differentiation, however, is intended to distinguish modes of practice within a society rather than to classify societies in total. Furthermore, there are questions to be addressed relating to both the acquisition and the application of either rules or exemplars, that is, to the issues of pedagogy and context. These issues are discussed in other sections of this chapter.

Alfred Sohn-Rethel (1973, 1975, 1978) introduces a differentiation which is intra-societal. He focuses his attention on the familiar distinction between intellectual and manual labour as a fundamental division in class societies:

> Clearly the division between the labour of head and hand stretches in one form or another throughout the whole history of class society and economic exploitation. It is one of the phenomena of alienation on which exploitation feeds. (Sohn-Rethel, 1978; p. 4)

For Sohn-Rethel, intellectual labour is necessarily social insofar as it is predicated upon 'necessary abstractions' from the form of social relationships. For example, the introduction of coinage inaugurates an abstraction whereby the object of the coin must stand for something other than itself. Sohn-Rethel's project is to demonstrate that 'a true identity exists between the formal elements of [this] social synthesis and the formal constituents of cognition' (*ibid*; p. 7). Sohn-Rethel argues that his materialist theory of cognition 'accounts for the historical emergence of the clear-cut division of intellectual and manual labour associated with commodity production' (*ibid*). His study of the genesis of this division is intended to reveal the preconditions for its disappearance in the advent of a socialist mode:

> When we distinguished 'societies of production' and 'societies of appropriation' we made the point that on the basis of primitive communal modes of production, as they preceded commodity production, the social practice was rational but the theory was irrational (mythological and anthropomorphic), while on the basis of commodity production the relation was reversed; namely, the social practice has turned irrational (out of man's control) but his mode of thinking has assumed rational forms. What Marx has in his mind's eye [. . .] is man's historical potentiality of achieving a rational practice and a rational theory combined, which is simply another way of speaking of communism. (*ibid*; pp. 133–4)

In this extract, however, we can see evidence of another distinction which resonates with that of Lévy-Bruhl, that is, between irrational, mythological and anthropomorphic 'theory' and rational 'theory', elsewhere referred to as 'science' (the 'logic' of which is 'mathematics'). The cognition of 'primitive' people is irrational as are the practices of manual labourers[3]. Viewed from the perspective of Sohn-Rethel's particular version of Marxism, this may be the case. 'Rationality', however, has meaning only within discourse. 'Rational' intellectual labour and 'irrational' manual labour thus have some correspondence with high and low discursive saturation. But this correspondence is not an identity: the whole of social practice must, for Sohn-Rethel, finally become realizable in discourse in the ultimate rationality of communism. In this sense, Sohn-Rethel certainly denies the ontology of the non-discursive[4] and apparently prioritizes the intellectual over the manual. This priority is, however, undermined by his historicizing of rationality and by his apparent rejection of the rational in the last sentence of his book:

> Above all it must be seen that it is not the recourse to the acclaimed neutrality of intellect and intellectual judgement but, on the contrary, the revolutionary commitment of our exposition that yields the truth. (*ibid*; p. 204)

A third position is to be adopted here, one which neither lays claim to detached neutrality nor predicates its validity on faith. Rather, the intention is to elaborate an empirical description alongside the principles that make the description possible. Sohn-Rethel's developmental model is securely grounded in very high level theory. His engagement with the empirical, however, has a pre-digested quality which obscures its own genesis. Nevertheless, the association of the modality of practice with the division of labour is an important advance on the non-sociological classification of Lévy-Bruhl and is reflected in the model being developed here.

Lev Vygotsky (1978, 1986) and his colleagues, Alexander Luria (1976) and Aleksei Leont'ev (1978, 1979) also adopted a Marxist methodology in their studies of cognition. For Vygotsky, ontogenesis is achieved as thought appropriates speech and progressively structures itself. However, speech is a social phenomenon the level of development of which is contingent on the level of development of society. The social thus facilitates and delimits cognitive development. A major distinction is made by Vygotsky between thinking in 'complexes' and thinking in 'concepts'[5]. Vygotsky argues that the former has been found to characterize the thinking of 'primitive' people (by Lévy-Bruhl), of 'the insane' (by Storch) and of children (by Piaget). Each of these groups displays the trait of 'participation', whereby objects are classified

---

3 The attribution of rationality (at least, in a global sense) to the social practice of 'primitive' people also comes into conflict with Bourdieu's description of such practice as 'polythetic' (see the discussion below).

4 Ontology is clearly important if one is attempting to change the world in a prescribed way.

5 Another distinction made by Vygotsky is that between 'spontaneous' and 'non-spontaneous' (or 'scientific') concepts. Insofar as the former are acquired in use and the latter in formal instruction — *i.e.* via definitions — this distinction resonates with that made by Bourdieu between practical and formal logic (see below). In Vygotsky, however, the relationship between the two is dialogic and developmental, whereas, for Bourdieu, the objectivism of formal logic is inconsistent with practical logic.

together on the basis of 'bonds unacceptable to adult logic' (Vygotsky, 1986; p. 129). Thus, Vygotsky argues:

> . . . the child, primitive man, and the insane, much as their thought processes may differ in other important respects, all manifest participation — a symptom of primitive complex thinking and of the function of words as family names. (*ibid*; pp. 129–30)

Whereas Vygotsky's own empirical work focused on the cognitive development of the 'normal', modern individual, Luria (*op. cit.*) carried out some work in peasant (*i.e.* comparatively 'primitive') societies. Most of Luria's subjects were unschooled and illiterate. Luria drew on the work of Vygotsky, Goldstein and others to distinguish between different kinds of cognitive action. Thus:

> In abstract or categorial classification, the normal subject forms a distinct category by selecting objects corresponding to an abstract concept. This kind of classification yields instances of abstract categories such as *vessels*, *tools*, *animals*, or *plants* in an appropriate group, no matter whether the particular objects are ever encountered together. (Luria, 1976; p. 48)

Such classification, Luria argues, exploits the higher capacities of language associated with literacy. By contrast:

> Subjects who gravitate towards [concrete or situational thinking] do not sort objects into logical categories but incorporate them into graphic-functional situations drawn from life and reproduced from memory. These subjects group together objects such as a table, a tablecloth, a plate, a knife, a fork, bread, meat, and an apple, thereby reconstructing a 'meal' situation in which these objects have some use. (*ibid*; p. 49)

In his empirical work, Luria found that the illiterate subjects did indeed tend to employ situational thinking in classification activities, whereas those who had received even a small amount of elementary schooling tended to classify objects taxonomically. Responses to questions involving syllogisms also separated his subjects. Thus the literate individuals generally recognized the logical connection between the major and minor premises of a syllogism and drew the correct conclusion independently of any reference to their own practical knowledge. Luria's illiterate subjects most frequently referred back to their own experience or lack of it. For example, Luria presented a thirty-seven-year-old illiterate peasant with the following problem: 'Cotton can grow only where it is hot and dry. In England it is cold and damp. Can cotton grow there?' (*ibid*; p. 108). The subject first said that he didn't know, that he had never travelled outside of his region. When pressed, he drew on his practical knowledge of growing crops:

> If the land is good, cotton will grow there, but if it is damp and poor, it won't grow. If it's like the Kashgar country, it will grow there too. If the soil is loose, it can grow there too, of course. (*ibid*)

When asked, finally, 'what do my words suggest?', the peasant replied:

> Well, we Moslems, we Kashgars, we're ignorant people; we've never been anywhere, so we don't know if it's hot or cold there. (*ibid*)

Luria concludes that the subject is unable to make use of the higher facilities of language which enable a distancing from immediate experience through the constitution of what is effectively a self-referential system. For Luria, syllogistic reasoning and categorial thinking are facilities which are natural in the sense that they are a function of the most highly advanced form of social structure. This is a materialist epistemology as is that of Sohn-Rethel. It is apparent, however, that both the Vygotsky/Luria schema and that of Sohn-Rethel have limited affinities with Marx. Neither seeks to specify a form of consciousness which is unique to the capitalist mode of production. Sohn-Rethel refers his necessary abstraction to the commodity form and to coinage. Luria's empirical differentiation is predominantly made on the basis of elementary schooling. Luria's work does, however, touch more closely upon the current project in that it moves to a focus on language and, therefore, towards the possibility of empirical description.

The distinction between the context-dependency of concrete thinking (in terms of 'graphic-functional situations') and the comparative context-independence of abstract thinking (things can be classified together even if they are never encountered together) is also crucial in the development of the expression, discursive saturation. Practices which exhibit low discursive saturation are, of necessity, context-dependent, since they do not incorporate explicit regulatory principles. On the other hand, the availability of such principles in practices which exhibit high discursive saturation, renders them comparatively independent of any immediate context[6].

The work of Valerie Walkerdine has been highly influential, both in this project and in the wider field of mathematics education, to which this project relates. I shall discuss, at some length, an early paper (1982) in which she adopts a distinction between 'formal' and 'practical' reasoning which is similar to Luria's differentiation[7]. In this paper, Walkerdine turns her attention to a

---

6 My use of 'context', here, refers to the unrepeatable event or its sedimentation as a 'graphic-functional situation'.

7 In *The Mastery of Reason*, Walkerdine distinguishes between 'instrumental discourse' and 'pedagogic discourse' in analysing 'mother-initiated exchanges' between mothers and young children: 'Instrumental referred to tasks in which the main focus and goal of the task was a practical accomplishment and in which numbers were an incidental feature of the task, for example in cake-making, in which the number *two* might feature in relation to the number of eggs needed and so on. In the pedagogic tasks numbers featured in quite a different way: that is, numbers were the explicit focus of the task' (Walkerdine, 1988; p. 81). This distinction

critique of developmental psychology as represented by Margaret Donaldson (1978)[8]. Walkerdine argues that it is inappropriate for Donaldson to draw conclusions about children's abilities to operate with logical relations on the basis of tasks which 'call up' familiar practices involving games with teddy bears etc. She argues that:

> In practical reasoning we determine the truth or validity of a statement in terms of its correspondence to the rules of a practice, whereas in formal reasoning truth is determined in terms of the internal relations of the statement itself. (Walkerdine, 1982; p. 138)

Formal reasoning, is to be understood as 'an act performed upon language; it is a peculiar one which is not in any sense of the term "natural", and we do not have to seek explanations in terms of the structures of the child's mind' (*ibid*; p. 140). From Walkerdine's theoretical perspective the challenge on Donaldson is valid. However, a similar criticism could not be made of Luria and Vygotsky. This is because, for them, cognitive development is essentially tied up with language development which constitutes rather than expresses it. Luria's illiterate subjects are cognitively limited because they have had no access to the higher capacities of language. For Vygotsky, the development associated with such access is necessarily spread out in time, so that a developmental sequence is inevitable.

Furthermore, it is clear that Piaget, himself regarded rational thought as 'natural' in the sense that it constitutes the telos, albeit never achieved, of unconstrained equilibration. This process is, for Piaget, characteristic of all living beings by virtue of their essential property of autoregulation (Piaget, 1980a). Like Vygotsky and Luria, Piaget (1995) was also influenced by Marx. Piaget seems to make a liberal interpretation of Marx which locates subjectivity within social relations, but which pretends that such establishment of relational subjectivities can, ultimately, be achieved without the operation of power. Piaget opposes relations of constraint to relations of co-operation. The former may characterize 'primitive', gerontocratic societies as well as families or classrooms in which knowledge and/or morality is invested with the authority of the parent or teacher. Here, thought is sociocentric, a distorted mode which reinforces the early egocentrism of the child, inhibiting the development of rational thought. The replacement of constraint by co-operation or reciprocity enables and is enabled by the uninhibited play of equilibration via the reconciliation of points of view. In the individual, this facilitates the

---

is clearly related to the formal/practical opposition. It also has some resonance with Leont'ev's hierarchy, in activity theory, between goal-directed 'actions' and means-oriented 'operations' (1978, 1979; see also Zinchenko, 1979). There is also a resonance with Heath's (1986) study of school and home language. In relation to the mode of participation of numbers in the discourses and tasks described by Walkerdine and by Zinchenko, this work also relates to the strategy/resource hierarchy that I shall introduce in the next chapter.

8   Paul Light (1986) offers a critique of Donaldson and of some of his own earlier work which clearly draws on this paper by Walkerdine.

development of operational thought; in society, it gives rise to science. The development of social thought moves from technique (practical, non-reflective action on the world) through sociocentric thought (myths, religions, ideology) to science as constraint is progressively overcome. Individuals within liberal, co-operative societies, develop from the sensori-motor stage, through egocentrism to reflective thought; ontogenesis thus corresponding to sociogenesis. Clearly, then, there is a sense in which science and rational thought can be interpreted as 'natural' within Piaget's scheme as it can within the Vygotskian tradition. Ultimately, Walkerdine's claim that formal reasoning is 'not *in any sense of the term* "natural"' betrays the culturalist reductionism of her position in this early paper.

Walkerdine also proposes a theory of instruction in her paper. This theory proposes that instruction involves the disembedding of mathematical tasks which are originally embedded within other more familiar 'discourses' via a stripping away of the 'metaphoric' associations of the non-mathematical context and a maintenance of the 'metonymic' structure of the mathematical statements. This is a useful image in relation to pedagogy and informs my own conception of this process. However, I should also note, now, that I intend to move from a conception of metaphor and metonym in Jakobson's sense as constituting orthogonal axes to a simplification of Eco's (1976, 1979) construction in which metaphors are facilitated by subjacent chains of metonyms. I shall describe an action of pedagogy as the construction of metonymic chains between the non-mathematical and the mathematical, between the student and the teacher. Equally, metonymic chains may be constructed within mathematics. Metaphors are to be understood as 'shortcircuiting' metonymic chains.

Walkerdine uses the term 'discourse' in a way which is different from that of her source for the term, Michel Foucault (1972, 1977a)[9]. Walkerdine distinguishes between the discursive and the material, the former constituting a form of realization of the latter; 'discourse' can also refer to everyday speech, thus:

> Children do not have raw experiences of concrete objects: meaning is created at the intersection of the material and the discursive, the fusing of the signified and signifier to produce a sign. These meanings are located in, and understood in terms of, actual social practices, represented in speech as discourse. It is by analysing the form and content of discourse, the processes of selection and combination, of metaphor and metonymy, that we can account for the origins and processes of reasoning. Young children are able to shift in and out of discourses from an extremely young age and I have examined some of the ways in which they adopt different discursive positions. (Walkerdine, 1982; p. 153)

Foucault is not concerned with everyday utterances which, in any event, would generally be unavailable in the context of historical studies. Rather, he is concerned with the conditions of existence of what Dreyfus and Rabinow

---

9 Which is not to say that Foucault is entirely consistent in his use of the term and of associated terms.

(1982) have translated as 'serious speech acts' (archaeology) and in the dia-chronic tracing through of the play of power (genealogy). Foucault's objects of study are always very large scale affairs: 'a history of insanity in the age of reason' (1965); the human sciences (1970); clinical practices (1973); 'the birth of the prison' (1977a); sexuality (1978, 1984, 1986). These all seem a long way from playing with teddy bears (which might constitute a 'discourse' in Walkerdine's study).

The distinction is important because the small scale 'discourses' that Walkerdine is interested in are not regulated or regulating in the same way as are the discursive formations and apparatuses which are of concern to Foucault[10]. This is precisely because Walkerdine's discourses are never archived other, that is, than in recontextualized forms in research such as her own. Rather, these local practices are negotiated within the context of their immediate elaboration. This is not to say, of course, that such practices are anarchic. Practices such as shopping, for example, are always elaborated within the context of a physical and linguistic matrix. This is also the case in respect of children playing at shopping. However, discourse associated with shopping is unlikely to be appropriately described as regulated to the same extent as, for example, discourse associated with school mathematics[11], the latter being institutionalized in a way that the former is not[12]. It is precisely this sort of distinction that I want to make.

Thus, 'formal reasoning' corresponds to high discursive saturation and 'practical reasoning' to low discursive saturation. The distinction rests on the extensiveness of the excess of the non-discursive over the discursive, that is, on the extent to which the regulation of the practice lies within or outside the linguistic. In my terms, playing with teddy bears is not a discourse to the extent that its principles are always context-dependent and so non-explicit. School mathematics, on the other hand, is more discursive, because its principles are comparatively explicit and context independent. However, this does not render the former 'natural' and the latter 'unnatural'.

Walkerdine, in this paper, also differs from Foucault in her conception of the non-discursive. As I noted above, Walkerdine is conceptualizing discourse as a form of realization of material actions. However, she appears to refer to the words that are uttered (or diagrams that are drawn) as 'signifiers' for physical actions which are the corresponding 'signifieds'. She also refers to this relationship as metaphorical. Thus in an interaction between a teacher and a young child, the teacher:

> ... puts the blocks in two piles on the table, and as she says 'put them all together' she moves them together with her hands. This [is] her first relation

10 Although the distinction is, perhaps, less striking in respect of Foucault's work on sexuality.
11 See Lave (1988; Lave *et al*, 1984) and Fiske (1989) which very differently describe negotiation in shopping practices.
12 Elsewhere, Walkerdine herself describes some of the regularities of school mathematics, in relation to developmental psychology (1984; Corran and Walkerdine, 1981) and in relation to gender (1989; Walden and Walkerdine, 1982, 1985).

of signified (moving the blocks) and signifier (saying the words). The task is practised a second time and then the teacher makes an interesting move in discourse:

T: Good boy, let's count them altogether. One-two-three-four-five-six-seven. So Nicola had four, Debbie had three, so three and four make . . . (*she puts the blocks together*)
Ch: Seven.

She repeats the same exercise of putting the blocks together, but this time the phrase that she uses refers to the blocks *implicitly* but makes no reference in language to them, so that she introduces the children to the 'disembedded' form of the statement: 'three and four make . . .' (Walkerdine, 1982; p. 146)

Thus 'discourse' appears, here, to be being represented as comprising only signifiers and physical actions are signifieds[13]. Clearly, there is a need of some modification of Saussure (1983)[14] since Walkerdine is focusing her attention upon speech (*parole*) rather than on language (*langue*), which was Saussure's object of study. Nevertheless, such a sundering of the sign seems too radical. Volosinov, for example, who also prioritizes *parole* over *langue*, argues that the notion that 'the expressible is something that can somehow take shape and exist apart from expression; that it exists first in one form and then switches to another form' (Volosinov, 1973; p. 84) is untenable, that the dualism is invalid, 'after all, there is no such thing as experience outside of embodiment in signs' (*ibid*; p. 85)[15].

Walkerdine needs to distinguish between the discursive and the non-discursive because she wants to make use of more delicate linguistic tools in her analysis (metaphor, metonymy, signifier, signified) and to locate formal reasoning as 'an act performed upon language'. However, this has still not resulted in the production of a language of description which is adequate to the task to be undertaken in the present study. One move might be to refer all utterances (spoken and written) to interpretants[16], so that all texts are to be interpreted in relation to interpretive bases which themselves are to be described. This move indexes the discussion of context in the section on *Context and Recontextualization* later in the present chapter.

13 Walkerdine is not entirely consistent in this. Elsewhere in the article, she states that 'formal reasoning draws its validity from, and depends entirely upon, reflection on the metonymic axis — on the relations between signs and not on their metaphoric content' (p. 141). Nevertheless, there remains a suggestion that the discursive is exclusively governed by syntagmatic principles and that the semantic is alienated. The signified is thus present, but in an impoverished form.
14 Walkerdine cites the 1974 edition.
15 This last statement would be true if we were to assume that the sign was stable. My heuristic distinction between the discursive and the non-discursive, however, asserts an inevitable degree of context-dependency which denies the final closure of any signifying system: there is always an excess of material contingency.
16 In Peirce's sense (1931–8). See, also, Eco (1973, 1976, 1984, 1990).

Despite her separation of the material from the discursive, Walkerdine nevertheless describes practical reasoning as rule-governed as is illustrated by the first extract from her paper cited above. This raises the question of whether the rules are in the minds of the participants or whether they are *post hoc* constructions (or potential constructions) in Walkerdine's own (potential) analysis. This question is addressed in Pierre Bourdieu's critique of the object-ivism of structuralism (one of several recurring themes in his work):

> The generative formula which enables one to reproduce the essential features of the practices treated as an *opus operatum* is not the generative principle of the practices, the *modus operandi*. If the opposite were the case, and if practices had as their principle the generative principle which has to be constructed in order to account for them, that is, a set of independent and coherent axioms, then the practices produced everything according to perfectly conscious gen-erative rules would be stripped of everything that defines them distinctively as practices, that is, the uncertainty and 'fuzziness' resulting from the fact that they have as their principle not a set of conscious, constant rules, but practical schemes, opaque to their possessors, varying according to the logic of the situation, the almost invariably partial viewpoint which it imposes etc. Thus, the producers of practical logic are rarely entirely coherent and rarely entirely incoherent. (Bourdieu, 1990; p. 12)

More simply (and less precisely) put:

> The science of myth is entitled to describe the syntax of myth, but only so long as it is not forgotten that, when it ceases to be seen as a convenient translation, this language destroys the truth that it makes accessible. One can say that gymnastics is geometry so long as this is not taken to mean that the gymnast is a geometer. (*ibid*; p. 93)

For Bourdieu (1977)[17], structuralist accounts of, for example, gift ex-change remove the necessary temporal dimension within which such practices are embedded. Pure reciprocity can only ever be available if the exchange is instantaneous. That this is never the case introduces a degree of uncertainty regarding the circumstances under which reciprocal action will take place, or even if it will take place at all. Indeed, the interval itself becomes an arena in which and on which the strategies of the actors can play. Practices of this kind are more properly understood as following a 'practical logic'. This has the quality of being 'polythetic', that is, it cannot be reduced to a consistent structure because it relates to involvement in practices which are fundament-ally corporal and oral and local and thereby incommensurable: they are context-dependent. The individual's apprenticeship into such polythetic practices, the

---

17   See also Robbins (1991).

habitus[18], constitutes the embodying of the structures of the world, 'that is, the appropriating by the world of a body thus enabled to appropriate the world' (Bourdieu, 1977; p. 89).

The regulation of 'polythetic practices' is more non-discursive than discursive and, in that sense, it is appropriate to refer to them as exhibiting low discursive saturation. The acquisition of such practices is, according to Bourdieu, mimetic:[19]

> So long as the work of education is not clearly institutionalized as a specific autonomous practice, and it is a whole group and a whole symbolically struc-tured environment, without specialized agents or specific moments, which exerts an anonymous, pervasive pedagogic action, then the essential part of the *modus operandi* which defines practical mastery is transmitted in practice, in its practical state, without attaining the level of discourse. The child imitates not 'models' but [sic] other people's actions. (Bourdieu, 1977; p. 87)

Opposed to practical logic, however, is not one, but three 'modes of theoret-ical knowledge' (*ibid*; p. 3) which 'may be described in a dialectical advance towards adequate knowledge' (*ibid*). He describes the first two of these modes in the following terms:

> The knowledge we shall call *phenomenological* [. . .] sets out to make explicit the truth of primary experience of the social world, *i.e.* all that is inscribed in the

18 *Habitus* serves a similar purpose for Bourdieu as does the concept of 'structuration' for Giddens (1984; Cohen, 1987), by allowing for both dispositions and creativity. There are also clear resonances between this term and Wittgenstein's (1958) notion of a 'language game', Gadamer's (1976) structure of 'prejudices' and Dasein in Heidegger (1962). It is curious that Bourdieu nowhere in this publication (although he does in a later work) appears to cite the previous use of this unusual term by Marcel Mauss, whose paper was first published in the *Journal de Psychologie Normale et Pathologique* 35e année, 1935, pp. 271–93. Bourdieu does refer to a publication in which the paper is included, but in fact acknowledges Mauss in a very restricted way and nowhere in relation to *habitus*. Mauss states: '. . . I have had this notion of the social nature of the '*habitus*' for many years. Please note that I use the Latin word — it should be understood in France — *habitus*. The word translates infinitely better than '*habitude*' (habit or custom), the '*exis*', the 'acquired ability' and 'faculty' of Aristotle (who was a psychologist). It does not designate those metaphysical *habitudes*, that mysterious 'memory', the subjects of volumes or short and famous theses. These 'habits' do not vary just with individuals and their imitations; they vary especially between societies, educations, proprieties and fashions, prestiges. In them we should see the techniques and work of col-lective and individual practical reason rather than, in the ordinary way, merely the soul and its repetitive faculties' (Mauss, 1979; p. 101). This extract is from a section of Mauss's book entitled 'Body Techniques'. *Habitus* is here very much associated with physical dispositions — gait, posture, etc. It thus suggests a differentiation between discursive and non-discursive regulation of dispositions. This is a distinction which is, perhaps, lost in Bourdieu's later use of Mauss's expression which becomes less of a concept and more of an arena for Bourdieu's perpetual reinterpretations.

19 Although the notion of 'imitation' seems, perversely, to exclude the social and to exclude creative potential. A similar point was made, in Chapter 1, regarding Gerdes' (1986) descrip-tion of non-industrialized production processes.

relationship of *familiarity* with the familiar environment, the unquestioning apprehension of the social world which, by definition, does not reflect on itself and excludes the question of the conditions of its own possibility. The knowledge we shall term *objectivist* [. . .] constructs the objective relations (*e.g.*, economic or linguistic) which structure practice and representations of practice, *i.e.*, in particular, primary knowledge, practical and tacit, of the familiar world. This construction presupposes a break with primary knowledge, whose tacitly assumed presuppositions give the social world its self-evident, natural character [. . .]. It is only on condition that it poses the question which the *doxic* experience of the social world excludes by definition — the question of the (particular) conditions making that experience possible — that objectivist knowledge can establish both the structures of the social world and the objective truth of primary experience as experience denied *explicit* knowledge of those structures. (Bourdieu, 1977; p. 3)

'Phenomenological' knowledge excludes reflection on the conditions of the possibility of primary experience. 'Objectivism' does reflect on these conditions in setting out 'to establish objective regularities [. . .] independent of individual consciousnesses and wills [and so] introducing a radical discontinuity between theoretical and practical knowledge' (1990; p. 26). The distinction between polythetic, practical logic, on the one hand, and objectivist thinking, on the other, is made in terms of the modality of the action of power. Polythetic practices are constituted within the context of individualized and localized power operating through the play of personal strategies exercised in primary contact. Objectivist thinking, on the other hand, is predicated upon the establishment of institutions which minimize personal power in favour of a more generalized power action. However, objectivism cannot interrogate these conditions of its own possibility. Bourdieu, therefore, proposes 'a second break, which is needed in order to grasp the limits of objectivist knowledge' (*ibid*) to constitute an 'adequate science of practices' (*ibid*):

Just as objectivist knowledge poses the question of the conditions of the possibility of primary experience, thereby revealing that this experience (or the phenomenological analysis of it) is fundamentally defined as *not* posing this question, so the theory of practice puts objectivist knowledge back on its feet by posing the question of the (theoretical and also social) conditions which make such knowledge possible. Because it produces its science of the social world against the implicit presuppositions of practical knowledge of the social world, objectivist knowledge is diverted from construction of the theory of practical knowledge of the social world, of which it at least produces the lack. (Bourdieu, 1977; p. 4)

We might conclude that Bourdieu is hovering dangerously between the abyss of the infinite regress and the annihilatory self-deconstruction of the postmodern. Derek Robbins describes Bourdieu's position in rather more concrete terms:

> Bourdieu's main problem during the 1980s has been to sustain his symbolic power whilst simultaneously undermining the scientificity on which it was originally founded. Some would say that he has tied the noose around his own neck and kicked away the stool from beneath his feet. (Robbins, 1991; p. 150)

However, this ignores the plausibility of a division of labour within sociology between the construction and deconstruction of ('objectivist') interpretive frameworks. Such a division clearly penetrates most concrete sociologists dialogically and might be described as the partial trammelling of what Feyerabend (1975) has referred to as 'epistemological anarchy'. Bourdieu's work, perhaps better than most, exemplifies the productivity of such dialogue. However, his insistent critique of 'objectivism' denies him the possibility of constructing a language of sufficient precision and stability for the purposes of textual analysis. Basil Bernstein (1971a, 1977, 1990, 1996; see also Atkinson, 1985) gets much closer to what is required here in his work on speech codes:

> The simpler the social division of labour, and the more specific and local the relation between an agent and its material base, the more direct the relation between meanings and a specific material base, and the greater the probability of a restricted coding orientation. The more complex the social division of labour, and the less specific and local the relation between an agent and its material base, the more indirect the relation between meanings and a specific material base, and the greater the probability of an elaborated coding orientation. (Bernstein, 1990; p. 20)

The distinction draws on Durkheim's (1984) distinction between mechanical and organic solidarity which exhibit relatively simple and relatively complex division of labour respectively. The empirical realization of coding orientations often bears a strong resemblance to the responses of Luria's subjects. Thus, when asked to classify different types of food, lower working class children had a tendency to reconstruct meals, whilst middle class children favoured taxonomic classification. Bernstein achieves the provision of a material base for the different modes of response in terms of the Durkheimian model. Unlike Durkheim, however, Bernstein does not attempt to characterize society as a whole as exhibiting mechanical or organic solidarity. Rather, he uses these concepts to describe different forms of the division of labour which coexist within societies. Individuals within such a hybrid configuration are likely to be located predominantly within one form of the division of labour, but may be expected to move routinely between locations. The relationship between the individual and speech codes, therefore, is one of orientation and not confinement. Thus the fundamental distinction between restricted and elaborated code is not so much developmental (as is Durkheim's own work and the 'Marxist' account of Luria) as locational; orientation is, essentially, distributed by social class.

An orientation towards restricted code means an orientation towards context-dependent meanings[20]. That is, the meaning of an utterance is given only in the enactment of the practice within which it occurs. The meaning would be radically altered (and almost certainly ambiguous) if, for example, the utterance were to be recorded and played-back under different material circumstances. Restricted codes are highly context-dependent, highly localized. Elaborated codes, by contrast, generate utterances which are more explicit at the level of language, so that they are less context-dependent and more generalized.

Because of their relationship to different forms of the division of labour, Bernstein's speech codes are of considerable heuristic value in the present sociological account. However, as I shall discuss in the next section, my emphasis is on the analysis of (pedagogic) texts and upon subjectivity as (re)produced by texts. It would, therefore, be inappropriate to graft these concepts onto my own model (which would inevitably transform them). My own conceptual framework will be specified in the following chapter.

A series of oppositions has been discussed in this section. Each opposition marks out, in a particular way, a distinction between the concrete and the abstract within the level of the discursive. The specificity of 'primitive' thought as distinct from that of 'modern' individuals, described by Lévy-Bruhl. Lotman distinguishes text- from grammar-oriented societies. Sohn-Rethel marks out manual from intellectual labour. Vygotsky and Luria distinguish between thinking in complexes and thinking in concepts via the notion of participation. Walkerdine describes practical and formal reasoning. In Piaget, technique/sensori-motor would be opposed to both sociocentric/egocentric and science/reflective thought within social/individual knowledge. Bourdieu differentiates practical logic from three modes of theoretical knowledge. Bernstein constructs restricted and elaborated codes. Corresponding oppositions are also made, for example, by Lévi-Strauss (1972), in the distinction between bricolage and science and by Freud (1973a, 1973b) in that between the id and the ego. Each of these oppositions clearly displays a uniqueness which derives from the theoretical framework within which it is embedded. Each construction is also more or less adequately fitted to its empirical or (in the case of Sohn-Rethel) political purpose. Nevertheless, each opposition resonates with the modality of the discursive which is being defined here for its own specific purposes. Each of these oppositions, in other words, can be mapped onto the scaling of discursive saturation as low or high (this mapping is summarized in *Table 5.1*). Practices exhibiting high discursive saturation are associated with a degree of context-independence or generalization; practices exhibiting low discursive saturation are associated with comparative context-dependency or localization.

Mathematics is clearly a case of high discursive saturation, a practice which is highly organized at the level of discourse and so produces generalized

---

20 In relation to contexts, which are defined in terms of 'classification' and 'framing'; see pages 116–19.

Table 5.1:   *The dual modality of practice*

Author	Abstract *Context-independent* *Generalization* *DS⁺*	Concrete *Context-dependent* *Localization* *DS⁻*
Bernstein	elaborated code	restricted code
Bourdieu	formal/theoretical logic	practical logic
Foucault	programmes	technologies
Freud	ego	id
Lévi-Strauss	science	bricolage
Lévy-Bruhl	modern thinking	primitive thinking
Lotman	rule-governed practice	repertoire of exemplary texts
Luria	abstract thinking	situational thinking
Piaget	sociocentrism/egocentrism science/reflective thought	technique/sensori-motor
Sohn-Rethel	intellectual	manual
Vygotsky	conceptual thinking	complex thinking
Walkerdine	formal reasoning	practical reasoning

utterances. The development of such practices is, as Bernstein suggests, indicative of a complex division of labour. Domestic and manual practices are examples of low discursive saturation, because they are not generally highly organized at the level of discourse and so they produce localized utterances[21]. These practices exhibit a simple division of labour. Of necessity, no practice can be fully realized within discourse. If there really were nothing but discourse, it would not be possible for the pre-linguistic child ever to enter the domain of the linguistic. Even higher mathematics is dependent upon what I might (temporarily) refer to as a mathematical component of *habitus*, as Livingston (1986) has illustrated. This *habitus* consists of the 'yet-to-be-discursive'. However, Livingston's discursive indexing of the tacit assumptions in Gödel's inconsistency theorem[22] still cannot exhaust the practice; there is always an excess of the material over the discursive. The distinction is one of relative saturation of a material practice by discourse.

The Production of Subjectivity

In the previous section, my discussion focused attention on the modality of practices rather than on the subjects of those practices[23]. I now need to consider

21 Other examples of comparatively low saturation in a discursive practice are to be found in spectator sports. In cricket, for example, even apparently technical terms such as 'wicket' and even 'bat' and 'ball' have no unambiguous meaning.

22 In his introduction, Livingston indexes tacit assumptions in the more widely familiar proof concerning the relationship between the angles subtended at the centre and at the circumference of a circle. See, also, Knee (1983) who points to similar tacit assumptions in Euclid's *Elements*.

23 Although subjectivity is clearly not ignored by the authors whose work was discussed.

the nature of subjectivity and its production via pedagogic action. I want to adopt a concept of subjectivity in which the subject is inscribed within, or constructed by, social practices and relations. This is broadly consistent with the notion of the subject in the work of Foucault, (see, also, Henriques *et al*, 1984; Laclau, 1984; Laclau and Mouffe, 1985). As I announced at the beginning of this chapter, I shall, for the time being, make use of the term 'ideology' to identify that which is constitutive of subjectivity. In developing the concept of ideology and the production of subjectivity via pedagogic action, I shall have need of heuristic models which I shall draw from Althusser and Eco in the first three Sub-sections of this section. In the fourth Sub-section, I shall introduce the concept of the textual subject which is necessary for the form of textual analysis to be adopted.

Althusser and Ideology in General

Ideology, for Althusser, is material: '. . . an ideology always exists in an apparatus and its practice, or practices. This existence is material' (Althusser, 1971; p. 156)

The material is ultimately rooted in physical matter, in human terms, the body and its physical environment. This does not entail a prioritizing of the physical over the intellectual, rather, an insistence that ideology, cast in these terms, exceeds the discursive. This is clearly consistent with the position adopted above. For Althusser, ideology constitutes individuals as subjects via the 'process' of interpellation. Althusser introduces a metaphorical scenario in which 'interpellation' is described as a hailing in the street; this metaphor is worthy of some consideration:

> Assuming that the theoretical scene I have imagined [the interpellation of concrete individuals by ideology] takes place in the street, the hailed individual will then turn round. By this mere one-hundred-and-eighty-degree physical conversion, he [sic] becomes a *subject*. Why? Because he has recognised that the hail was 'really' addressed to him, and that 'it was *really him* who was hailed' (and not someone else). (*ibid*; p. 163)

This interpellation of the individual as subject entails their subjection to the Subject, the metaphor for which is God, the transcendental signified. Becoming a subject of necessity entails subjection, as Foucault puts it:

> There are two meanings of the word *subject*: subject to someone else by control and dependence, and tied to his [sic] own identity by a conscience or self-knowledge. Both meanings suggest a form of power which subjugates and makes subject to. (Foucault, 1982; p. 212)

For Althusser, who is describing ideology *in general* and not specific ideologies, '*individuals are always-already subjects*' (*op. cit*; p. 164). Thus, the metaphor, 'interpellation', entails a heuristic introduction of an imaginary temporal dimension. Subjects in general, however, are not always-already subjects in particular. Specifically, an apprenticing relationship must (at least as an ideal type) comprise different subjects/subjectivities. Initial recognition of the adept subjectivity by the apprenticed subjectivity must be of otherness: they confront one another. At the completion of the apprenticeship, they must stand together. There is still a 180 degree turn by the apprentice. However, this is now of necessity extended in real time and, furthermore, Althusser's directions are reversed: the subject becomes rather than worships her/his God.

The 'interpellation' of ideology in general, then, is to be replaced by (apprenticing) 'pedagogic action' which effects a 'symbolic violence' in the imposition of a cultural arbitrary (Bourdieu and Passeron, 1977) which might be thought of as a specific ideology. This is not the original establishing of the subject, but the apprenticing of an always-already subject into a new subjectivity. It is through this process that, for example, a university student becomes a mathematician. The question now to be addressed is, what is the nature of this subjectivity, this specific ideology?

Ideology-in-Particular

In his *Sociological Studies* Piaget's (1995) liberal gaze has produced a pedagogic theory which opposes direct instruction as in, for example, the didactic exposition of mathematical knowledge. This mode is characterized by constraint and so is likely to reinforce egocentric thought and thereby inhibit the development of rational thinking. However, if power is reinstated as necessarily characteristic of the social, then the generation of any particular knowledge structure as a 'point of view', a specialism within the division of labour, is, both socially and individually, a political act. It is, furthermore, one which is of necessity extended in time. If reciprocity entails dialogue, then dialogue entails a plurality of positions each of which must be achieved within the context of a structure of power and which thereby serves to reproduce that structure. Piaget fails to see this because he reduces discourses to single points in space and their propositions to mathematical symbols. Struggle can succeed, at best, only in the reconfiguration of power, not its annihilation. Piaget's liberal optimism, which fails to recognize the ubiquitousness of power, leads him to acquiesce in the reproduction of traditional social hierarchies: primitive/advanced societies; rural/urban communities; manual/intellectual labour; and, elsewhere (Piaget, 1932), female/male sexes. Indeed, these hierarchies are legitimated by the evolutionary relation between ideology and science. For Piaget, ideology is constrained knowledge and is always, ideology-in-particular. Rational knowledge can exhibit no enduring discursive structure, because this would signify constraint and the inhibition of equilibration. This position is clearly being rejected in the sociological theory being developed here.

For purely heuristic purposes, I want to postulate (drawing inspiration from Eco, 1976, 1979) the notion of a *Global Semantic Universe* (GSU). The universe should be thought of as comprising all possible cultural units as proto-signs. Conceived of in this way, the universe is the imaginary space in which semiosis proceeds. The GSU, itself, is devoid of semantic expression or content, which are only to be understood in relational terms, that is, within the context of semiotic action. Within this space, an 's-code' (Eco, 1976) is (always-already) established as the articulation of units as a relational totality. Where the units are signifiers (Saussure, 1983[24]) the s-code constitutes a plane of expression; where they are signifieds, it defines a plane of content. A code is a specific correlation of an expression plane with a content plane, that is, a correlation of two s-codes (Eco, 1976)[25]. It is this 'code' which, in my interpretation, corresponds to ideology-in-particular. Eco describes *langue* as follows:

> A code as '*langue*' must therefore be understood as a sum of notions (some concerning the combinatorial rules of the expression items, or syntactic markers; some concerning the combinational rules of the content items, or semantic markers) which can be viewed as the *competence* of the speaker. However, in reality this competence is the sum of the individual competences that constitute the code as a collective convention. What was called 'the code' is thus better viewed as a *complex network of subcodes* which goes far beyond such categories as 'grammar', however comprehensive they may be. One might therefore call it a *hypercode* [. . .] which gathers together various sub-codes, some of which are strong and stable, while others are weak and transient, such as a lot of peripheral connotative couplings. In the same way the codes themselves gather together various systems, some strong and stable (like the phonological one, which lasts unchanged for centuries), others weak and transient (such as a lot of semantic fields and axes). (Eco, 1976; pp. 125–6)

Eco's lack of sensitivity to sociological structuring is apparent in his use of the term 'sum' to conceptualize langue as the aggregate of individual competences and in his description of the 'hypercode' as that which 'gathers together' various subcodes. The potential for describing relationships between individuals and groups would seem to be very limited within this schema. This does not pose a problem for Eco, whose principal interest lies in the exploration of the workings of what are essentially discursive systems. Thus:

> . . . it is not up to semiotics to establish whether [factual judgements] are true or false, but it is up to semiotics to establish whether or not they are socially acceptable. Many factual judgements seem unacceptable, not because they are false, but rather because to accept them would mean to impose a restructuration of the Global Semantic System or large parts of it. This explains

---

24 This translation of Saussure inexplicably replaces the conventional terms 'signifier' and 'signified' with 'signal' and 'signification', respectively. I intend to retain the more familiar terms.

25 I am not making an ontological distinction between expression and content planes, although expression and content can always be distinguished in context.

why, under particular historical conditions, physical proof of the truth of certain judgements could not stand up before the social necessity of rejecting these same judgements. Galileo was condemned not for logical reasons (in terms of True or False) but for semiotic reasons — inasmuch as the falsity of his factual judgements is proved by recourse to contrary semiotic judgements of the type 'this does not correspond to what is said in the Bible' (Eco, 1979; pp. 84–5)

Eco has no language adequate to the description of the social in sociological terms. Nevertheless, via a reinterpretation of *langue* as an ideology-in-particular, a workable structure begins to emerge. That is, an ideology (in particular) is to be understood as a specific articulation of cultural elements. Cultural elements are here understood to extend beyond the discursive to include what has been referred to as *habitus*. The ideology is also understood to comprise subordinate structures at a level corresponding to that of Eco's 'subcodes', but not necessarily described in the same way. Ideology as '*langue*' must constitute 'speaking' subjects and their 'utterances'. Conceived of in this way, an ideology is instantiated as individual subjectivities and as texts[26]. To concretize: school mathematics (say) as an ideology consists of the totality of its texts and the subjectivities of school mathematics teachers and students *qua* school mathematics teachers and students.

The questions now to be addressed concern the production of text and subjectivity by or in ideology. Before I can proceed to an answer, however, I must take a brief diversion, in order to consider the forms of articulation of the elements which comprise ideology. I shall describe these articulations in terms of the tropes 'metaphor' and 'metonymy'.

Metaphor and Metonymy

I noted in the section above on *Abstract and Concrete Practice* that Walkerdine[27] was using the relations 'metaphor' and 'metonym' in the sense given by Jakobson, thus:

> The development of a discourse may take place along two different semantic lines: one topic may lead to another either through their similarity or through their contiguity. The metaphoric way would be the most appropriate term for the first case and the metonymic way for the second, since they find their most condensed expression in metaphor and metonymy respectively. (Jakobson, 1956; p. 76)

26 Because an ideology is to be defined (in the next section) in sociological terms, the postulation of a collective subjectivity as the totality of its individual subjectivities and texts does not pose the difficulties for sociological description that obtain in the case of Eco's 'hypercode'.

27 See also the discussions in Henriques *et al* (1984) on this interpretation of these tropes. See also Atkinson (1990) on the use of metaphor and metonymy in ethnographic writing.

Jakobson associates metonymy with Freud's mechanisms of defence, including 'displacement' and 'condensation'[28], and metaphor with the Freudian processes, 'identification' and 'symbolism'. With reference to literature, Jakobson describes 'romanticism' as being closely linked with metaphor and 'realism' with metonymy. Metaphor and metonymy are also seen as the lines of 'least resistance' for poetry and prose, respectively. This orthogonal organizing of the two tropes also recalls Saussure's 'syntagmatic' and 'associative' relations, otherwise, the syntagmatic and paradigmatic axes of language. Useful as this interpretation has undoubtedly been, it has a tendency to prioritize the grammatical, that is, the linearity of written or spoken language, in its description of metonymy as being concerned with relations of contiguity.

This interpretation also has a superficial appeal with reference to school mathematics (which was also the context of Walkerdine's discussion[29]). Insofar as mathematical 'utterances' are regarded as strings of mathematical symbols, ideally exemplified in a mathematical equation or proof, mathematics would seem to be characterized as 'metonymic'. On the other hand, school mathematics often involves reference to non-mathematical objects and relations. These seem to stand in 'metaphorical' relationship to mathematical objects and relations. However, such a construction is problematic in two respects. Firstly, it seems to demand that there are practices which 'legitimately' occur in school mathematics but which are, in fact, not mathematics (this indexes the discussion in the next section of this chapter). Secondly, it ignores mathematics as a relational totality, capable of producing strings as utterances, but not confined to such instances. Ideology is not, ultimately, reducible to the syntagmatic.

Alternatively, we might consider what constitutes the condition for a metaphorical relationship. To take a specific instance that I have used elsewhere (Dowling, 1993): how can I interpret the statement, 'her face was an aspirin'? This is undoubtedly a metaphor. However, it can only work as a metaphor because 'her face' and 'aspirin' have shared associations: whiteness or pallor; roundness; sickliness; hardness, perhaps. These associations stand in metonymic relationship with 'her face' and with 'aspirin'. The metaphor achieves a selection of possible qualities or associations of the two terms, that is, it is conditional upon metonymy. It seems inappropriate to describe dependent tropes in a perpendicular relationship, the latter being a geometric condition for independence. Eco describes an alternative arrangement:

> A metaphor can be invented because language, in its process of unlimited semiosis, constitutes a multidimensional network of metonymies, each of which is explained by a cultural convention rather than by an original resemblance. The imagination would be incapable of inventing (or recognizing) a

---

28 The latter being described as synecdoche, interpretable as a species of metonymy.

29 See, also, Corran and Walkerdine (1981). 'Metaphor' has been widely discussed with reference to mathematics education; see, for example: Brown (1981); Janvier (1987); Liebeck (1986); Otte (1983, 1986); Pimm (1986, 1987, 1990, 1995); Rotman (1985); Tahta (1985).

metaphor if culture, under the form of a possible structure of the Global Semantic System, did not provide it with the subjacent network of arbitrarily stipulated contiguities. The imagination is nothing other than a ratiocination that traverses the paths of the semantic labyrinth in a hurry and, in its haste, loses the sense of their rigid structure. The 'creative' imagination can perform such dangerous exercises only because there exist 'Swedish stall-bars' which support it and which suggest movements to it, thanks to their grill of parallel and perpendicular bars. The Swedish stall-bars are Language {*langue*}. On them plays Speech {*parole*}, performing the competence. (Eco, 1979; p. 78)

Eco also describes metonymy as a relationship of contiguity. However, this is not limited to syntagmatic contiguity, but can include semantic or even phonetic proximity. The relationship between metaphor and metonymy in this conception is one in which the former constitutes a 'short-circuiting' of the latter: metaphors are always 'provable' by metonymic substitution. As Eco notes, relations of metonymy are cultural conventions. In the schema which is being developed in this book, these relations are regulated, which is to say 'rarefied' (see Foucault, 1972) within particular ideologies. In this sense, then, ideology is the condition of possibility of metaphor.

The articulation of the signifying elements which comprise an ideology can thus be described as metonymic or as metaphorical. I want to move on, now, to consider the production of ideological realizations in texts and subjectivities.

Text, the Reader and Pedagogy

Hodge and Kress describe the relation between text and system as 'dialectical':

Terms in a system have value by virtue of their place in that system. At the same time, a system is constantly being reproduced and reconstituted in texts. Otherwise it would cease to exist. So texts are both the material realization of systems of signs, and also the site where change continually takes place. (Hodge and Kress, 1988; p. 6)

Ideology is realized in texts which are themselves the sites of both the reproduction and the transformation of ideology: texts produce and reproduce ideology. In order to sustain the dynamic intention of this definition, I am, as I announced in Chapter 1, adopting the expression '(re)production' in refer-ring to this relationship. I should make two observations before proceeding. Firstly, I must re-emphasize that ideology and therefore text is understood to exceed the discursive. Texts, therefore, are not to be understood purely in lin-guistic terms. Secondly, in order to foreground the transformative potential of the text, I could have chosen to focus my attention upon empirically con-tested readings. Hodge and Kress (1988), for example, provide a description of a cigarette advertisement which has been paid some attention by an oppositional campaign. The wording of the advertisement, for example, has been transformed by politically intentioned graffitists from 'New. Mild. And Marlboro.' to 'New. Vile. And a bore.' Within the context of school mathematics texts, I could clearly have looked at readings produced by different groups of students, teachers, etc. I have chosen not to do this, but to produce an analysis of a text from a single perspective. This is because the principal task that I have set myself is the production of a language for the sociological description of pedagogic texts which are, in this case, mathematical. As the principles of the description are sociological, the reading of the text is made from a position which is outside of the context of the production of the text as a work (see Barthes, 1981a). Thus, the language, in constructing its description, constitutes the text as a site of contestation: the analysis is of necessity critical. I shall develop this argument in the next chapter.

Texts in general and pedagogic texts in particular must, of necessity, presuppose a readership, in Eco's terms:

> To organize a text, its author has to rely upon a series of codes that assign given contents to the expressions he [sic] uses. To make his text communicative, the author has to assume that the ensemble of codes he relies upon is the same as that shared by his possible reader. The author has thus to foresee a model of the possible reader (hereafter Model Reader) supposedly able to deal interpretatively with the expressions in the same way as the author deals generatively with them. (Eco, 1979; p. 7)

The analysis of pedagogic texts will thus entail the inference of the model reader. The language of description which is to be developed must provide the terms in which categories of model reader are to be described. Again, this is not to say that the model reader resides within the work, but within the critical reading of the work. Similarly, the text (or, rather, its reading) constructs its author:

> In a communicative process there are a sender, a message, and an addressee. Frequently, both sender and addressee are grammatically manifested by the message: 'I tell you that . . .'
>
> Dealing with messages with a specific indexical purpose, the addressee is supposed to use the grammatical clues as referential indices (/I/ must designate the empirical subject of that precise instance of utterance, and so on). The same can happen even with very long texts, such as a letter or a private diary, read to get information about the writer.
>
> But as far as a text is focused *qua* text, and especially in cases of texts conceived for a general audience (such as novels, political speeches, scientific instructions, and so on), the sender and the addressee are present in the text, not as mentioned poles of the utterance, but as 'actantial roles' of the sentence (not as *sujet de l'énonciation*, but as *sujet de l'énoncé*) . . . (*ibid*; p. 10)

Eco describes both 'author' and 'model reader' as 'textual strategies'. It is in this sense that I will interpret the categories, author and reader; they are, in other words, the products of the principled analysis of the text. They are thus to be distinguished from the empirical author and reader which are not to be the focus of attention (in line with the decision outlined above). However, it should be noted that, even if interviews with authors and classroom observations etc were to be carried out, the 'empirical' author and reader emerging from the subsequent analysis would be no less fictive in their dependence upon the principles through which they were to be described. Furthermore, every analysis must bound its text. For the principal object of analysis in this study I have chosen to bound my empirical terrain so as to constitute a monologic text[30]. That is, a text which constructs a unitary authorial position; in this case, a school mathematics scheme of textbooks. An alternative might have been, for example, to analyse the textbooks in use in a classroom situation. However, under these circumstances, it is almost certainly the case that the text would better be described as dialogic. For example it might be expected that student utterances would be more or less difficult to reconcile with those of the model reader constructed by the analysis of the textbook alone. It may also be expected that the teacher would impose selection and recontextualizing principles upon the textbook which, again, might be more or less difficult to reconcile with the model author. It is unlikely that the resulting complex might be appropriately constituted within a unitary ideology-in-particular so that that which would be being described would already be a contested text.

In (re)producing ideology, a text thus constructs textual subjects which are associated with that ideology. It is these textual subjects which are my concern and which are to be produced within the textual analysis which is the main empirical work of this volume. A consideration of the relationship between textual subjects and empirical subjects (actual human beings) involves two issues, one theoretical and one methodological. The theoretical issue concerns the introduction of an interactional dimension. This dimension is suppressed within the model and analysis as presented in this and the next section of the book, because the focus is on monologic texts. However, an indication of where this dimension may be introduced is given in the final section of Chapter 6. The methodological issue relates to questions of validity and reliability of the analysis, which turn on the status of the text in relation to the particular ideology under consideration. This issue will also be addressed in Chapter 6. The nature of the association between the textual subjects and the ideology is contingent upon the nature of the texts which, in this study, are pedagogic.

From my perspective, a pedagogic text is an utterance within the context of a pedagogic relationship which implicates a pedagogic subject and one or more pedagogic objects. Both or all of these are textual subjects, or *voices*, in the terminology being adopted here and are, respectively, the subject and

---

30 The distinction between monologic and dialogic texts is inspired by, but differs somewhat from, Bakhtin (1981).

object or objects of pedagogic action. Pedagogic subject and object(s) are thus to be interpreted as, respectively, authorial and reader voices of the pedagogic text. In the terms used in this chapter, apprenticing pedagogic action[31] entails (ideally) the apprenticing of the pedagogic object into an ideology. The author/ pedagogic subject is the agent of the ideology which is (re)produced by the text[32]. As I have indicated, the authorial position is unitary within a monologic text. The reader/pedagogic object of necessity connotes an otherness with respect to this ideology, yet is the addressee of pedagogic action. Author and reader as subjectivities thus stand in metaphoric relationship to one-another. Apprenticing pedagogic action can therefore be described as the provision of metonymic links between these subjectivities. The reader is a potential author. It is this potentiality that must be realized in and through the apprenticeship. It is not supposed that ideology can be acquired all in one go. Apprenticeship therefore entails the provision, extended in time, of metonymic links between pedagogic subject and pedagogic object. The adept has completed the 180 degree turn through which the apprentice is transcribed from the floor of the classroom to the teacher's desk.

Context and Recontextualization

What remains to be done is to discuss the multiplicity or the contextualizing of ideology. In the preceding discussion I have referred to ideology in the particular rather than in the general sense. In the general sense, the subject is always-already a subject of ideology. This applies to the apprentice as much as to the adept. The apprentice must, therefore, already be a subject of a particular ideology which is other than that of the adept. The implication is clear, that is, that there exist multiple ideologies. Ideologies are, as discussed above, (re)produced by subjectivities which must, in empirical terms, be instantiated in human individuals. Since human individuals must, of necessity, traverse the ideological space, such individuals must be constituted as multiple subjectivities (see Henriques *et al*, 1984; Laclau, 1984; Laclau and Mouffe, 1985). This is a necessary feature of my general methodology and is clearly germane to the understanding of pedagogic action and apprenticeship as outlined above. However, since I am concerned with textual subjects, I shall not, at this stage, develop my theory of empirical individuals beyond this basic assertion of multiplicity. I shall, however, return to this issue in the next chapter.

The notion of the multiplicity of ideologies resonates with Walkerdine's use of 'discourse'. Bakhtin (1981) describes language as 'heteroglossic'. This stands in critical relationship to Saussure's notion of the object of linguistic

---

31   As opposed to relaying pedagogic action; see Chapter 2.
32   This is not to deny contradiction within ideology.

analysis which Volosinov[33] describes as 'an objective system of incontestable, normatively identical forms' (Volosinov, 1973; p. 67). For Bakhtin/Volosinov the utterance is the proper object of study. However, unlike Saussure's *parole*, the utterance is not an act of individualized will, but reflects the material conditions of its production:

> All the diverse areas of human activity involve the use of language. Quite understandably, the nature and forms of this use are just as diverse as the areas of human activity. This, of course, in no way disaffirms the national unity of language [. . .] Language is realised in the form of individual concrete utterances (oral and written) by participants in the various areas of human activity. These utterances reflect the specific conditions and goals of each such area not only through their content (thematic) and linguistic style, that is, the selection of the lexical, phraseological, and grammatical resources of the language, but above all through their compositional structure. All three of these aspects — thematic content, style, and compositional structure — are inseparably linked to the *whole* of the utterance and are equally determined by the specific nature of the particular sphere of communication. Each separate utterance is individual, of course, but each sphere in which language is used develops its own *relatively stable types* of these utterances. These we may call *speech genres*. (Bakhtin, 1986; p. 60)

Corresponding to Eco's 'model reader', 'speech genre' exhibits a model addressee:

> Thus, addressivity, the quality of turning to someone, is a constitutive feature of the utterance; without it the utterance does not and cannot exist. The various typical forms this addressivity assumes and the various concepts of the addressee are constitutive, definitive features of various speech genres. (*ibid*; p. 99)

The materialist critique of Saussure is regarded here as entirely appropriate and the importance of the addressee/reader has already been acknowledged. However, Bakhtin's overriding emphasis on the utterance is as limiting for a sociological study as is Saussure's exclusion of *parole*. For Saussure there is no specificity to the empirical text. For Bakhtin, there is no possibility describing regularity, that is, of specifying context.

Foucault (1981) speaks of a contextualized domain of discourse. This domain is regulated by three main kinds of procedures. Firstly, 'procedures of exclusion' include: the prohibition of certain kinds of speech; the opposition between reason and madness; and the opposition between truth and falsehood. Secondly, internal procedures of 'rarefaction' include principles such as: the commentary; authorship; and the discipline. Finally:

33 'Volosinov' may or may not have been a 'flag of convenience' for Bakhtin (see the discussion in Hirschkop, 1989). For my purposes, however, the works cited constitute a plausibly unitary position.

There is, I believe, a third group of procedures which permit the control of discourses. This time it is not a matter of mastering their powers or averting the unpredictability of their appearance, but of determining the condition of their application, of imposing a certain number of rules on the individuals who hold them, and thus of not permitting everyone to have access to them. There is a rarefaction, this time, of the speaking subjects; none shall enter the order of discourse if he [sic] does not satisfy certain requirements or if he is not, from the outset, qualified to do so. To be more precise: not all the regions of discourse are equally open and penetrable; some of them are largely forbidden (they are differentiated and differentiating), while others seem to be almost open to the winds and put at the disposal of every speaking subject, without prior restrictions. (Foucault, 1981; pp. 61–2)

Foucault's gaze is, as usual, cast very broadly. His organizing principles are clearly of great value in speaking of the discursive field in general and enable him to mark out specific 'positivities' (1972). It is not at all clear, however, how he might make sense of a single text. Nor is it always clear how he selects the texts upon which he bases his 'histories' (although he claims exhaustive coverage of extant contemporary texts relating to sexuality in ancient Greece (1984)). Nevertheless, his work begins to suggest a way forward for the current project.

Foucault's procedures for the control of discourse clearly operate, firstly, on what can be said and secondly upon who can say it. They also distinguish between relatively public and relatively private regions of discourse. Furthermore, the relatively private discourses are never entirely closed-off: 'they are differentiated and differentiating'. One of the principal mechanisms of this differentiation is formal education:

Although education may well be, by right, the instrument thanks to which any individual in a society like ours can have access to any kind of discourse whatever, this does not prevent it from following, as is well known, in its distribution, in what it allows and what it prevents, the lines marked out by social distances, oppositions and struggles. Any system of education is a political way of maintaining or modifying the appropriation of discourses, along with the knowledges and powers which they carry. (Foucault, 1981; p. 64)

My project is more modest than the analysis of an education system, far less the field of discourse in general. However, Foucault's broad brush strokes at this high level of analysis sketch the outline of two heuristic questions. Firstly, how do we distinguish between public and private ideologies? Secondly, how can a pedagogic text be described as distributing the content of a specific ideology so as to constitute included and excluded subjectivities? The following extract from Bourdieu, addresses the first of these questions and also introduces a third:

> Knowledge does not only depend, as an elementary relativism suggests, on the particular viewpoint that a 'situated and dated' observer takes up *vis-à-vis* the object. A much more fundamental alteration — and a much more pernicious one, because, being constitutive of the operation of knowing, it inevitably remains unnoticed — is performed on practice by the sheer fact of taking up a 'viewpoint' on it and so constituting it as an object (of observation and analysis). And it goes without saying that this sovereign viewpoint is most easily adopted in elevated positions in the social space, where the social world presents itself as a spectacle seen from afar and from above, as a representation. (Bourdieu, 1990; p. 27)

The additional question concerns the relationship between ideologies: how does one 'view' another? The 'elevated positions' to which Bourdieu refers clearly include those that are elevated by the educational system. Those positions that are characterized, in our society, by formal, objectivist thinking, rather than the polythetic thinking of practical logic. In addressing these questions, I want to refer, again, to Bernstein's work, principally to his concept of 'classification'. The first question, introduced above, refers to the specializing of discourse, Bernstein argues that:

> If categories of either agents or discourse are specialized, then each category necessarily has its own specific identity and its own specific boundaries. The speciality of each boundary is created, maintained and reproduced only if the relations between the categories of which a given category is a member are preserved. What is to be preserved? The *insulation between the categories*. It is the strength of the insulation that creates a space in which a category can become specific. (Bernstein, 1990; p. 23)

The strength of the insulation is referred to as 'classification'.[34] Different strengths of classification relate to different principles of the social division of labour because insulation 'presupposes *relations of power* for its creation, reproduction, and legitimation' (*ibid*; p. 24). As is made clear in the above extract, classification can be used to measure the degree of specialization of any social category[35]. My interest here concerns education:

> We can regard the social division of labour of a school to be composed of categories (transmitters and acquirers) and categories of discourse ('voices'). If the coding principle is one of strong classification, then there is strong

34 See also Bernstein 1971a, 1971b, 1977.
35 In an earlier, unpublished paper I made use of this notion to examine transformation in Cuban society since the Revolution in respect of educational categories and of the categories of gender and race. I concluded that: '. . . with the possible (and uncertain) exception of race, many of the principles of classification that obtained prior to 1959 remain intact in Revolutionary Cuba, the basis of this conclusion is the maintenance of many pre-Revolutionary boundaries between social categories. This is not to deny the enormous improvements that have been made in the lives of the majority of the population [for example, the abolition of] the conditions that give rise to a culture of poverty' (Dowling, 1985; pp. 9–10).

insulation between educational discourse ('voice') and non-educational discourse ('voices'). Discourses are strongly insulated from one another, each with its own specialized 'voice' so that transmitters and acquirers become specialized categories with specialized 'voices'. Within the category of transmitter there are various 'sub-voices', and within the category of acquirer there are various 'sub-voices': age, gender, 'ability', ethnicity. In the process of acquiring the demarcation markers of categories (agents/discourse) the acquirer is constituted as a specialized category with variable sub-sets of voices depending upon age, gender, 'ability', ethnicity. (Bernstein, 1990; p. 26)

I have three qualifications to make to Bernstein's conception in moving towards establishing my own use of it. The first is a product of my working within a general framework which is heavily influenced by structural linguistics and it is this: Bernstein refers to classification as a measure of the strength of boundaries or insulation between categories (of agents/discourse). If we refer to school subjects — mathematics, English, history, physics, etc — as the relevant categories, then it is clear that the term 'boundary' has some significance. For example, different subjects are often taught in different physical spaces which are insulated from each other. It is also the case that we can, metaphorically, consider mathematics, for example, as historically having established a space for itself which is distinct from, say, physics. However, this 'space' is here being conceptualized as a particular articulation of a notional Global Semantic Universe. This being the case, the metaphors 'boundary' and 'insulation' are not appropriate (although, of course, physical boundaries may be incorporated, semiotically, into the establishing of the space). The difference between the two positions may be indexed by the question, where is the boundary between the north and south poles of a bar magnet?

I have described the articulations between signifying elements within an ideology as metonymical and metaphorical. It is possible to describe articulations between ideologies in the same way. That is, an element in one system can be considered to be metonymically, or connotatively, linked with elements in other systems. Where the availability of such connotative links between the elements of two ideologies is high, we can describe the strength of classification between them as low. Where the availability of connotative links is low, or, alternatively, where such connotations are predominantly ones of 'otherness', the strength of classification is high. Concretely, the following mathematical expression minimizes non-mathematical connotations:

$$2(P) \equiv (\exists x)(\exists y)[P(x).P(y).x \neq y.(z)(P(z) \supset. z = x \lor z = y)]$$

Clearly, some of the symbols connote signifiers in standard English. However, even these connotations are minimized by the immediate context. This 'text', then, indicates strong classification of mathematics with respect to other ideologies.

The above example leads to the second qualification that I need to make regarding my use of Bernstein's concept of classification. Thus, whilst it is the case that the above mathematical expression minimally connotes the non-mathematical, it is possible to present it in an alternative form which weakens the classification, thus:

> . . . there are two Ps if and only if there are x, y such that x is P and y is P and x is not the same thing as y and for all z, if z is P then z is the same thing as x or z is the same thing as y . . .

The denotative content has remained unchanged[36]. Now, however, the mode of expression is less specialized, so that there is a slight increase in the availability of non-mathematical connotations: 'thing', for example, is not specific to mathematics. The classification has been weakened. Furthermore, if I note that both expressions constitute a definition of the number 2, classification is weakened still further.

In other words, the strength of classification of mathematics is not a fixed quality of mathematics, but varies, depending upon the particular mathematical content under consideration, or upon the manner in which it might be expressed. Ideologies, generally, are thus presumed to be regionalized in terms of their strength of classification with respect to each other.

The third qualification relates to Bernstein's use of 'sub-voices' which, in the case of the 'acquirer', are exemplified as: age, gender, 'ability', ethnicity. My point here is that these categories are not sociologically equivalent (and Bernstein clearly recognizes this in his use of quotation marks around 'ability'). I want to maintain (and shall produce evidence to this effect) that, in the context of school mathematics, age and ability are explicit variables relating to competence and performance. Gender and ethnicity and, indeed, social class, are not. For example, school mathematics generally produces different curricula for students of different ages and abilities; it generally does not (at least, not in the UK at the present time) produce curricula which explicitly index students of different genders and different ethnic groups. Indeed, contemporary texts may go to great lengths (not always successfully) to be 'politically correct' in their treatment of categories which differ in these respects. I have illustrated this, in Chapter 4, in relation to tokenist strategies employed in the *SMP 11–16* texts. The structuring of curricula in gender and ethnic terms is commonly implicit rather than explicit. I shall also argue that social class is an implicit variable.

Gender, ethnicity and social class are, in other words, certainly interpreted by the ideology under examination. Arguably, these fundamental categories are interpreted by all ideologies. In this respect, however, they should be understood as constituting resources in the elaboration of the ideology and not as generative principles. This is a consequence of my construction of an analytic space. There is no doubt that the division of labour is 'ideologized' along class, gender and ethnic dimensions. These are not, however, being construed

36   The 'translation' is provided by Benacerraf and Putnam (1983, p.15).

as the 'motors' of the social, but as describing its contingent, material state. This being the case, they are certain to be implicated within all 'ideologies-in-particular'. The subjectivities constructed by ideologies are, therefore, implicitly rather than explicitly defined in terms of these major dimensions of social structure. This will be the case other than in very particular cases (for example, gender is likely to be an explicit principle in domestic ideologies).

Classification refers to relations between categories. Bernstein introduces the concept 'framing' to refer to the form taken by control within categories. Bernstein defines framing as follows:

> Framing refers to the principle regulating the communicative practices of the social relations within the reproduction of discursive resources, that is, between transmitters and acquirers. Where framing is strong, the transmitter explicitly regulates the distinguishing features of the interactional and locational principles, which constitute the communicative context. Where framing is weak, the acquirer has a greater degree of regulation over the distinguishing features of the interactional and locational principles that constitute the communicative context. This may be more apparent than real. (Bernstein, 1990; p. 36)

I shall not make use of the category 'framing'. In the present study, the 'transmitter' and 'acquirer' are both textual categories. It is certainly germane to discuss the nature of the relationship between these categories as constructed by the text. However, the acquirer as acquirer must always be objectified by the pedagogic text and thereby denied control in terms of pedagogic action. Consider, for example, a text which instructs the student to 'discuss' a mathematical pattern with a colleague. There is an apparent handing over of control to the student insofar as there is no direction over the nature or content of the ensuing discussion. Clearly, an empirical student might choose to discuss last night's football match or might discuss the aesthetic rather than the mathematical qualities of the pattern. The textual student, however, cannot make such choices. 'Discussion' must be included as a task by virtue of some presumed pedagogic (even therapeutic) value. The student is objectified as the site of this activity. The location of control with the textual acquirer is always 'more apparent than real'. Framing, therefore, might be appropriately interpreted as a measure of the extent of the coincidence of the textual students and the empirical student. I will comment on this relationship in the next chapter, but its elaboration is beyond the empirical scope of this book.

I have introduced concepts relating to the first of the three questions raised earlier. The private and the public in ideology can be distinguished in terms of the theoretical/practical logic described by Bourdieu. This distinction essentially differentiates between ideal types of ideologies. That is, between those exhibiting high and low discursive saturation respectively. This distinction is also relevant in differentiating within ideologies, as I shall argue in the next chapter. The private and the public can also be distinguished in terms of the strength of classification of forms of expression and content. Again, this measure is capable of differentiating within and between ideologies. Its principal use here, however, will be in describing structure within ideology.

The second question concerns the distribution of ideology in the construction of included and excluded categories of subject. I have argued that the production of subjectivity is the achievement of pedagogic action. We can define the transmitter in the pedagogic relationship as already subjectified by the relevant ideology, that is, as being in possession of its principles (both in formal and practical terms). I have also referred to apprenticeship as the provision of metonymic links which enable the apprentice to 'rotate' between positions of subjectivity, or to participate within a proto-subjectivity. Metonymic chains may, for example, provide links between the everyday and the mathematical, or they may be confined within regions of mathematics which are either strongly or weakly classified with respect to the non-mathematical. Alternatively, links may be made metaphorically rather than metonymically. These different modes of link will facilitate or deny access to the regulating principles of the ideology, which access is the condition for subjectivity. In either case, the pedagogic action will be subject to the regulating principles of the ideology. The latter will either be 'visible' or 'invisible'.

Bernstein (1977, 1990) has introduced the term 'visible pedagogy' to refer to a form of pedagogic action which emphasizes the evaluation of performance in terms of explicit principles. 'Invisible pedagogy' refers to pedagogic action which focuses on the elaboration and development of competence under circumstances in which the principles are implicit. Thus, from my perspective, we can define *visible pedagogic action* as generating metonymic chains which enable access to the principles of the ideology. *Invisible pedagogic action* can then be defined as metaphoric and so not generating such chains.

Finally, in addressing the third question (how does one ideology view another) I want to draw again on the work of Bernstein (1990). The 'recontextualizing rules' of Bernstein's 'pedagogic device' constitute 'pedagogic discourse' which is:

> ... a principle which removes (delocates) a discourse from its substantive practice and context, and relocates that discourse according to its own principle of selective reordering and focusing. In this process of the delocation and the relocation of the original discourse the social basis of its practice, including its power relations, is removed. In the process of the de- and relocation the original discourse is subject to a transformation which transforms it from an actual practice to a virtual or imaginary practice. Pedagogic discourse creates imaginary subjects. (Bernstein, 1990; p. 184)

Bernstein's construct is incorporated into a tightly defined theoretical framework. Thus, as was the case in respect of his work on speech codes, it is not possible to implant his concept into my theory. However, Bernstein's description of the action of pedagogic discourse has informed my own conception of the way in which one ideology 'views' another. Retaining the visual metaphor, I shall use the term *gaze* to refer to a mechanism which delocates and relocates, that is, which *recontextualizes* ideological expression and content. The result of such recontextualizing is to subordinate the recontextualized ideology to the regulating principles of the recontextualizing ideology. In other words, the recontextualized ideology is constituted as a virtual ideology and its subjects as virtual subjects, which is to say, as objects. This gaze is the device which produces the myths which I introduced in the first two chapters of this book.

I have described a specific ideology as a particular articulation of a notional Global Semantic Universe. With respect to any given ideology, there will be regions for which the forms of expression and/or content must be comparatively weakly classified with respect to other ideologies; this was discussed above. Nevertheless, the realization of these forms of expression and contents in texts must, to a greater or lesser extent, conform to the general principles of the ideology. To concretize: there are, as I illustrated in Chapter 1, regions of school mathematics which involve forms of expression and content (signifiers and signifieds) relating to domestic ideology such as shopping. We can say that the *gaze* of school mathematics *recontextualizes* shopping practices. In doing so, 'shopping' is constituted as a set of virtual practices, it is mythologized. The principles governing texts which incorporate recontextualizations will first and foremost be those relating to school mathematics. The domestic principles regulating shopping practices must be subordinated, to a greater or lesser extent, to those of school mathematics. This generalization describes the production of the myths of reference, participation and emancipation which were introduced in Chapter 1. However, it has now been derived from the theoretical description of the social which has been presented in this chapter.

This now concludes my discussion of the theoretical work which has been most influential in generating the theoretical propositions upon which my language of description is based. In the final section of this chapter, I shall present the propositions.

Summary: Theoretical Propositions

I shall now summarize the key points in the preceding discussion in order to present a concise image of my conception of the sociocultural as it has been developed in this chapter. The summary will constitute the theoretical propositions that form the basis for the development of my language of description in Chapter 6. I have used the term 'ideology' throughout this chapter, because of its familiarity. As I signalled at the start of this chapter as well as in Chapter 1, however, I intend to use the alternative term, *activity*, in my own language of description. This is because my language of description establishes an analytic space and not an empirical one. I shall reintroduce the alternative term at this point; its formal definition and categories will be discussed in Chapter 6.

Activity (-in-general) is to be understood as that which is produced by and that which produces the division of labour so that it constitutes the contextualizing basis of all social and cultural practices. Activity (-in-particular) may be conceived as that which regulates who can say or do what, which is to say, it comprises *positions* and associated *practices*. The term 'regulation' is being used in a descriptive, which is to say symmetrical sense. Alternatively, then, human subjects' practices constitute regularities which are recognized as activities. It is this dialectical relationship between activities and action which I am attempting to capture through the use of the expression (re)production. Because human subjects routinely participate in multiple activities and because these activities constitute and are constituted by ((re)produce) human subjectivity, the latter is of necessity constituted as multiple. This is not to say, however, that human subjectivity is radically schizoid; I will return to this point in the next chapter.

Any given bounded empirical terrain is being referred to as a text which may be actional and/or discursive. All texts constitute, in their reading, *voices* and, in particular, authorial and readerly voices. A pedagogic text is an utterance within the context of a pedagogic relationship. A pedagogic text thus constructs one or more textual pedagogic subjects or transmitters and one or more textual pedagogic objects or acquirers. Texts may be monologic or they may be dialogic; monologic texts constitute single authorial voices, whereas dialogic texts constitute multiple authorial voices. A single authorial voice can clearly be contained within a single activity. For this reason, a monologic text has been chosen for the analysis in the next part of this book in which the language of description is to be employed. In the next chapter I shall also give some indication as to how dialogic or interactional texts might be addressed.

A given activity may be conceived of as a particular articulation of a notional Global Semantic Universe, the latter comprising discursive and extra-discursive forms of expression and contents as relational totalities. Activities vary internally and one-from-another according to the extent of the saturation of material practice by discourse, that is, their *discursive saturation* may be high (DS$^+$) or low (DS$^-$). Discourse can never exhaustively saturate practice. In discursive terms: activities exhibiting DS$^+$ can give rise to relatively generalizable utterances; DS$^-$ activities can generate only localized utterances.

I should emphasize at this point that the level of discursive saturation is not being conceived as an essential property of the practices of any activity. Rather, it constitutes a major dimension in terms of which positions (and so activities) mark out their affiliations to what might be broadly polarized as the intellectual or the manual via, respectively, the weakening or strengthening of context-dependency. That is, practices are always strategic[37]. By way of an

---

37 Or, in some instances, tactical. See de Certeau (1988) for an interesting distinction between strategic and tactical action.

illustration we (in the South Eastern region of the UK, anyway) may have encountered a derisive 'middle class' rationalizing of a supposed 'working class' tendency to punctuate conversation with the expression 'know what I mean?' as indicative of a lack of apprenticeship into grammatically correct English. Such a middle class imagining of language as conforming to rules which are independent of the context of its use contrasts with an actual usage which is always understandable by empirical interlocutors. An example of an effective riposte might be, 'Well, you can ponce up your language as much as you like, but then you drive a secondhand Escort and I've got a P-reg B-Mer'. The particular selection within this kind of response, however, must be context-dependent.

Activities also vary internally (and one-from-another) with respect to the strength of classification of their forms of expression and content. A weakening of classification within a zone of activity implies that forms of expression and/or content have been *recontextualized* from another activity via the *gaze* of the recontextualizing activity. The principles of the recontextualizing activity always effect a transformation upon the forms of expression and contents which are recontextualized.

Articulations between signifying elements of an activity may be metonymic or metaphoric. The distinction concerns the visibility or explicitness of the denotations and connotations which establish the articulation. Metonymic chains render visible, or explicit, metaphorical relations. Subjectivity in relation to specific activities are achieved by pedagogic action, which establishes metonymic links between the adept and the apprentice. Pedagogic action may be visible or invisible depending upon the accessibility to the apprentice of the regulating principles of the activity. Visible pedagogic action renders the principles available via metonymic rather than (or at least as well as) metaphoric links. This may be achieved ostensively or verbally, depending upon the level of discursive saturation. Successful apprenticeship to an activity is achieved (metaphorically) upon the completion of a one-hundred-and-eighty-degree rotation of the apprentice who thereby 'moves' from 'outside' to 'inside' the activity and becomes its Subject.

In the next chapter, I shall introduce the main terms and structure of my language of description. The language will be further elaborated and illustrated in the subsequent chapters in the next part of the book, which contain the analysis of the selected monologic empirical texts.

Chapter 6

Constructive Description and Social Activity Theory

In this chapter I shall move to the presentation of the central features of my language of description, which I shall refer to as *Social Activity Theory*. The language of description is derived from the theoretical propositions that were summarized at the end of the last chapter. First, however, I shall discuss the general methodological position with reference to which the language of description and its analyses are generated and are to be interpreted.

Constructive Description

The idea of a language of description is explicitly proposed by Bernstein in *Pedagogy, Symbolic Control and Identity* (1996). However, the notion is implicit (at least) in all of his work and much of that with which he has been directly associated since the 1960s. Bernstein introduces the concept as follows:

> Briefly, a language of description is a translation device whereby one language is transformed into another. We can distinguish between internal and external languages of description. The internal language of description refers to the syntax whereby a conceptual language is created. The external language of description refers to the syntax whereby the internal language can describe something other than itself. (Bernstein, 1996; pp. 135–6)

The nature of and relationship between internal and external languages of description provides the basis for the interrogation of research. This is far more sophisticated than a simple consideration of concepts and indicators. Bernstein clearly places the emphasis on relational structures at both levels. The internal language produces theoretical descriptions. The external language is derived from the internal language in such a way that the former can facilitate the production of a description of an empirical setting. This is not to say, however, that Bernstein is advocating theoreticism. The internal language must also develop and this will come about via the dialogic relationship between the external and internal descriptions and via the constitution of the external description as:

. . . an interpretative surface, or the means of dialogue between the agency
of enactments and the generating of the internal language of the model.
(*ibid*; p. 138)

Here, Bernstein is concerned to give space for the voice of the researched
to announce the specificity of its text, enabling the internal language to
develop empirically. Clearly, the internal language can also be developed
in terms of its own internal consistency and in dialogue with other languages
of description.

The language that I am introducing in this book is clearly indebted to
Bernstein's work. Nevertheless, there are significant divergences between his
position and mine. Some of these have been described in the previous chapter,
others will emerge in the present one. Many of these differences are at the
level of general methodology, which is to say, they relate to the theoretical
propositions derived in the previous chapter and, indeed, to epistemological
assumptions that frame these propositions. I shall have a little more to say
about epistemology later. Here I wish to refer to a pragmatic distinction, *viz*
the specific form of the development of my language has not incorporated a
clear distinction between its internal and its external systems. In part, this is
because much of this development took place before the chapter of Bernstein's
book from which the above extracts are taken was written[1].

This is not to say that Bernstein's analysis cannot be applied to my
language in order to resolve it into external and internal components. This
certainly could be achieved and such an achievement could constitute a reading of my language into Bernstein's metalanguage, that is, an evaluation of
my language according to the principles of another. Since my current project
is to assert the positivity of my own language, such an evaluation is not my
immediate concern. On the other hand, it is appropriate to recontextualize
Bernstein's conception with respect to the current development of my general
methodological framework. I shall attempt this by addressing a general question concerning the relationship between the theoretical structures that I have
developed and the empirical claims that are being or which might be made.

Thus, a number of theoretical propositions have been introduced in the
previous chapter and these will be developed and augmented, to a certain
extent, in the present one; to what extent is the textual analysis which is to
follow a test of these propositions? I can address this question, initially, by
referring again to the process by which the language of description was generated. Essentially, this involved, on the one hand, an engagement with literature relating to social theory and to textual analysis. This literature constitutes
the theoretical antecedents which are represented by the work discussed in the
previous chapter. On the other hand, there was an engagement with an

---

1   It is probably accurate to say that the level of development of Bernstein's conception of a
    language of description (or, at least, my interpretation of it) that obtained at the point of the
    first significant theoretical developments of my own work is that given in Chapter 5 of Bernstein
    (1996).

Figure 6.1   Schema for the language of description and its analysis

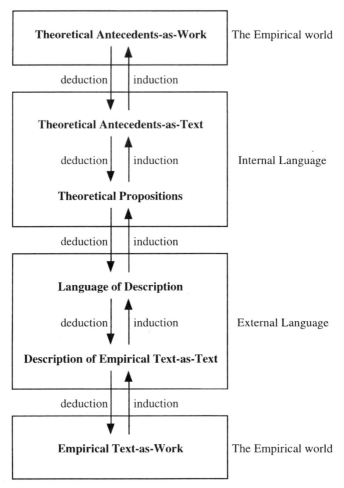

empirical text. The language of description emerged in a complex synthesis of deductive theoretical construction and inductive empirical reading. The theory and the description which it produces are therefore produced together, so that their separation is itself an analytic exercise. At this stage, it is possible, as I have suggested above, to forge a distinction between the propositions and the specific details of the language of description as, respectively, internal and external languages. The former would be more closely, but not exclusively, associated with the theoretical antecedents, the latter would be more closely associated with the empirical text. This would produce the schema illustrated in *Figure 6.1*.

It will be apparent that 'the empirical world' is introduced at both the uppermost and lowermost points of the schema and that each level is articulated to subjacent and superjacent levels by downward deduction and upward induction. It will also be noticed that a distinction is being made between 'theoretical antecedents' and 'empirical text' each as 'work' or as 'text'. This latter distinction corresponds to the distinction made by Barthes (1981a) whereby the text is to be understood as that which is produced by the reading. The work is taken up and produced as a text in its reading. To this extent, reading is always writing. The present work must establish its position within a field of academic production. This field is constituted by this positioning as more general than the work itself, so that my particular product is to be derived from that field. However, the field itself is also to be inaugurated by the work. In other words, I must act selectively upon a notional set of available discursive resources, just as the reader must impose selection principles of some kind in taking up a book. There is, therefore, an inductive relationship between my emerging text and the field which I am constituting and which is constituting my text. Thus, in producing my theoretical antecedents as text, I am also constituting an exteriority, a work of which my product is a reading.

The lowest articulation of the schema illustrated in *Figure 6.1* constitutes an equivalent dialectic. The language of description must be capable of describing more than a single text, so that it is at a higher level of generality. In the inauguration of my description of the empirical text I must impose more or less rudimentary selection principles of recognition of what is to count as an object and of realization of how that object is to be realized as data. There is, in other words, a deductive relationship between the description of the empirical text-as-text and the empirical text-as-work. However, to constitute this relationship as purely deductive would be to construct the present work as pure theory which would dissolve into solipsistic musings if, in addition, the deductive link with theoretical antecedents as work were to be denied.

The specificity of the empirical text and, indeed, of the academic field, as work must be constituted by the approach being developed here. However, this is not to succumb to naive realism. To the extent that an epistemological positioning may be instructive, it is more appropriate to recontextualize the neo-Kantian philosophy of Jean Piaget. This will entail some restating of points made in Chapter 5. In his chapter, 'Egocentric thought and sociocentric thought', Piaget (1995) constitutes the development of rationality as the interaction between three systems: the sensori-motor; the operational; and the symbolic. None of these systems is reducible or can be represented by any of the others, although the sensori-motor and the symbolic systems are necessary interfaces, so to speak, whereby the ratiocinating subject can interact with the world. Piaget relates these three systems to three different socialization processes. Firstly, there is the development of technical skill through physical imitation. Secondly, the exchange of ideas within the context of non-authoritative relations of mutual respect, which gives rise to rational or scientific thought. Thirdly, the incorporation of the ideas of others as one's own within the context of constraint or unilateral respect, which gives rise to egocentric thought.

These processes of socialization are related to the three forms of collective thought which were referred to in Chapter 5, respectively, technique, science and ideology. Then, just as science is concerned with the liberation of thought from ideological distortion, rational or operational thought is concerned with the liberation of thought from egocentric distortion. This relationship between science and ideology is a clear reference to Marx, whom Piaget cites explicitly. Unlike Marx, Durkheim is, according to Piaget, unable to distinguish between sociocentric and scientific forms of thought. This is, essentially, because Durkheim fails to recognize struggle and conflict[2]. Wallon, on the other hand, claims to recognize the distinction to be made, but attempts to develop rationality out of egocentric verbal thinking, thus again collapsing what Piaget regards as two essentially distinct modes.

Individual cognitive development occurs in a process of equilibration which is the essential quality of the human subject (indeed, potentially any form of life) as an autoregulative being (Piaget, 1980a). Disequilibrium occurs constantly via conflict arising between cognitive structures, out of interpersonal experience and out of new internalized actions. Equilibration, then, is the process whereby cognitive structures develop hierarchically in the resolution of such conflict. Piaget (1980a) describes three levels of equilibration: the dialectically related processes of assimilation and accommodation with respect to specific cognitive structures; the specialization of cognitive structures; and the formation of new global structures at a higher level of abstraction.

There are two principal obstacles to the assimilation of Piaget's position (as I have interpreted it) to my own or to my accommodation to his. Firstly, as I suggested in the previous chapter, Piaget's appropriation of Marx is a liberal recontextualization, which fails to recognize Marx's insistence on the constitutive and so timeless nature of power. A line from the *Grundrisse* is helpful:

> The human being is in the most literal sense a ζῷον πολιτιχόν[3], not merely a gregarious animal, but an animal which can individuate itself only in the midst of society. (Marx, 1973; p. 84)

The contextual 'individuation' of human subjects is precisely what constitutes and is constituted by relations of power: no power, no society, so no human subjects. This is essentially the same argument as might be used to criticize a naive optimism in economics which fails to understand economic activity as precisely the constitution of scarcity and not the production of plenty.

Equilibration of necessity presupposes a state of equilibrium which is therefore predicated of the equilibrating subject. Figuratively, the inauguration of

---

2 It is not clear that this criticism of Durkheim is entirely justified, although it is widely made. In *The Division of Labour in Society*, for example, (which Piaget does not cite) Durkheim (1984) explicitly points to social antagonism which distinguishes society from the organism. A distinction which, itself, may be less than secure, given current biological understanding of the self-destructive potential of auto-immune systems.

3 Political animal.

the human individual within the disequilibrating state of life must be consti-tuted, by Piaget, as an expulsion from Paradise. The psychoanalyst Ignacio Matte-Blanco (1988; see, also, Rayner, 1995) constitutes precisely such an edenic state as 'being' which characterizes the deepest level of the unconscious. The human individual's earliest experiences of life, for example, in Kleinian terms (1975), the good breast and the bad breast, disturb this contented slumber in the generation of asymmetry. Subsequent asymmetric differentiation constitutes the higher levels of the unconscious and, ultimately the state of 'thinking' which characterizes the consciousness of the now social subject. The agonistic nature of the social world (and, in Matte-Blanco's argument, the three-dimensional nature of the physical world) cannot contain the symmetrical logic (and infinite dimensionality) which characterizes the unconscious which is precisely the reason for the conscious/unconscious division and what Matte-Blanco describes as the 'fundamental antinomy between human beings and the world'.

Matte-Blanco's formulation appears to have more potential in terms of the reinstatement of power as constitutive of (conscious) subjectivity. Else-where (Dowling, 1996b) I have initiated a recontextualizing of Matte-Blanco's work in an attempt to introduce a notion of a social unconscious[4]. I shall return to some consideration of the potential of this idea in the concluding chapter to this book.

The second obstacle is Piaget's employment of what is arguably an under-developed understanding of language as naively representational, in other words, it is less of a system than a lexical collection. I want to recognize language as comprising multiple, non-closed systems, which we might refer to as discourses. This is to say that any notional or empirical domain that we might want to constitute as language as a whole or as a specific discourse is both self-referential and also refers outside of itself. This exteriority obtains precisely because of the limit to the saturability of the non-discursive by the discursive and because of the contextual nature of discourse both of which I discussed in the previous chapter. Since language and discourse is thus open to the contingent and the non-discursive, it is necessarily being conceived of as dynamic and partial. Indeed, Piaget's systems cannot be constituted as entirely closed with respect to each other. Were they to be so conceived, it is inconceivable that they could interact. It seems plausible, then, to envisage the development of rationality as arising out of the interaction or 'dialogue' between discursive and non-discursive systems between and within human subjects. Further, dialogical interaction between these systems entails their prior formation or internalizing within the dialogic or, shall we say, equilib-rating subject. Under these circumstances, what Piaget refers to as sociocentric thought, acquired under at least some degree of constraint or unilateral respect, is a necessary condition for dialogue and so for development; the specificity of the discourse must be permitted to speak.

---

4 This is to be distinguished from and is not in any clear sense dependent upon Carl Jung's (1959) conception of the 'collective unconscious'.

This discussion of my interpretation of Piaget's work is intended to motivate rather than to ground the general methodological perspective which should be taken to contextualize the theoretical and empirical constructions presented in this book. Firstly, then, and to backtrack just a little, the language of description is a discursive structure which has been forged out of a constructive dialogue with antecedent theory and with an empirical text. By the end of this book, the language of description will have been presented at its current state of development. In this temporary state of completeness, the language of description is construed as a technology, the purpose of which is the analysis of texts as expressions of social relations and the cultural practices which (re)produce them. This is achieved in the construction of empirical texts-as-texts from empirical texts-as-works. Collaterally, the language of description also constructs the academic field-as-texts from the academic field-as-works.

Secondly, whilst the language of description as technology constitutes the central subjectivity for the descriptions (texts-as-texts) that it constructs, it of necessity confronts each new text-as-work with a degree of surprise. This is to say, the focus of attention on the new text-as-work inaugurates a disequilibrating conflict. The text-as-work, then is being conceived as another discourse. There is, then, equilibrating work to be done. This work takes the form of a dialogue between the developing language of description and the textualizing text-as-work. Thirdly, however, as the language is repeatedly applied to more new texts-as-work, we must expect its descriptive power to increase precisely because it is modified in order to facilitate the description of an increasing diversity of texts-as-work. We must expect, therefore, that developments will increasingly occur at the level of detail rather than fundamental structure[5].

Thus, the theoretical discourse in relation to its empirical and theoretical terrain is being construed as an equilibrating system for the production of textual description. It is appropriate to refer to this conception of general methodology as *constructive description*. The products of constructive description are not facts, nor are they representations of the world. Rather, constructive description produces systematic order. The extent to which a particular scheme of constructive description — a given language of description — is useful is a function of the extent to which and the consistency with which it is used. There is, then, a sense in which this book is more appropriately conceived as a marketing strategy than as a representation of the way things are. This being the case, it will be apparent why some of the language that is employed may tend to encourage precisely the opposite interpretation.

Social Activity Theory

As I have already announced, I intend to avoid using the term 'ideology', because of its own ideological baggage. Instead, I am using the term *activity*.

5   This is, essentially, the assumption of the procedure of analytic induction (which is, of course, a methodology rather than an epistemology). However, analytic induction is empiricist in its intention, whereas my position allows for more genuinely theoretical development.

It is important to specify that activity constitutes an analytic space. Activity is always ideologized in the empirical. That is, activities are, themselves, constituted by (and (re)productive of) the division of labour in society. Since the language of description is to be derived from the theoretical propositions summarized at the end of the previous chapter, there is a need for a certain amount of repetition in the presentation which follows.

Activity is to be understood as the contextualizing basis of social practice. Thus, firstly, any particular activity must specialize *practices*. This is achieved as a particular articulation of a notional Global Semantic Universe. An activity thus regulates what can be said or done or meant. Secondly, an activity establishes one or more positions which can be occupied by human individuals; these are specialized *positions*. These are not construed as 'roles' in G.H. Mead's sense (Turner, 1987) or as either 'roles' or 'social positions' in Giddens' use of these terms (Cohen, 1987). Positions are understood, here, to be constitutive of human subjectivity rather than syndromes of expected behaviours, whether or not associated with a determinate physical locale. Concrete human *subjectivities* are to be interpreted as articulations of multiple positions. The relationship between the practices and positions associated with a particular activity is as follows: practices are distributed within the array (potentially hierarchical) of positions. That is, an activity regulates who can say or do or mean what. For example, school mathematics constructs a hierarchy of positions, such as teacher and students of different ages and abilities. This is achieved via the distribution of school mathematics practices (mathematical and pedagogic knowledge) within the hierarchy.

The practices and positions of an activity are also realized in *texts*. A text is an utterance (linguistic and/or non-linguistic) or set or sequence of utterances made within the context of one or more activities. The empirical object of analysis of the present work is a school mathematics scheme. This scheme consists of a set of utterances of the activity school mathematics. The chapters that follow are concerned with the analysis of these utterances and not with the interactions between them and what may occur in a classroom within which they are used nor, indeed, with what happens when an empirical reader takes up the texts. Thus, the empirical text is being constituted as monologic. All texts construct authors and readers; a monologic text constructs a single author and so can be read in relation to a single activity. All texts (re)produce, in part, the practices of the activity (or activities) of which they are utterances. *Pedagogic texts*, which are my immediate concern, construct authors as transmitters and readers as acquirers. The transmitter is in possession of the regulative principles of the practices of the activity which the acquirer is to acquire. Transmitter and acquirer are textual constructions which are textual realizations of positions. The practices and positions of an activity are thus instantiated in pedagogic texts. The instantiation of *practices* will be referred to as *message*; the instantiation of *positions* will be referred to as *voices*.

I have now introduced two levels. At one level, activity constructs positions via the distribution of practices to a range of positions. At this level, activity is (re)produced by human subjectivities which articulate multiple positions. Individual human subjectivity is not my primary concern in this study. However, I shall return to a brief consideration of it in the final section of this chapter. At the second level, activity is (re)produced by texts and, in particular, by pedagogic texts. Pedagogic texts distribute message over a range of voices and so (re)produce the practices and positions of activity. Activity and human subjectivity comprise the structural level; text constitutes the level of event. The relationship between these two levels is not one of simple reproduction or correspondence. Rather, the relationship between the structural and evental levels corresponds to that between *langue* and *parole*, where this relationship is conceived of as dialectical (see the discussion in Hassan, 1992a; see also Derrida's discussion of the *a* motif in his term *différance*[6]). I have tried to establish this through the use of my term *(re)production*: texts (re)produce activities and human subjectivities.

As is the case with linguistics, the structural level (activity and human subjectivity or *langue*) is accessible only via the level of events (text or *parole*). I will refer to the level of events as the textual level of the language of description. Text as a material instance of activity is the empirical object of the study. Both activity and text are theoretical objects of the study, as has been discussed above.

My programme for the remainder of this chapter is as follows. Firstly, I will discuss the composition of the structural level of the language: activity; its practices and their characterizing; and positions. Secondly, I will introduce the language at the level of the text: the (re)production of practices and subjectivity via the construction of message and voice by textual strategies. This section will be followed by the introduction of a third level of the model, that of resources. In these sections I shall be referring, in the main, to DS^+ activities, principally, school mathematics. In the final section of the chapter I shall give some attention to DS^- activities and to the programmatic issues of dialogic texts, human subjectivity and institutional level.

The Structural Level: Activity

Practices: Domain and Gaze

The GSU comprises forms of expression and contents relating, respectively, to signifiers and signifieds. These are articulated as relational totalities which

6 'The activity or productivity connoted by the *a* of *différance* refers to the generative movement in the play of differences. The latter are neither fallen from the sky nor inscribed once and for all in a closed system, a static structure that a synchronic and taxonomic operation could exhaust. Differences are the effects of transformations, and from this vantage the theme of *différance* is incompatible with the static, taxonomic, ahistoric motifs in the concept of *structure*. But it goes without saying that this motif is not the only one that defines structure, and that the production of differences, *différance*, is not astructural: it produces systematic and regulated transformations which are able, at a certain point, to leave room for a structural science. The concept of *différance* even develops the most legitimate principled exigencies of "structuralism"' (Derrida, 1981; pp. 27–8). See also the discussions in Sturrock (1979, 1986) and Bannet (1989).

constitute activities, that is, their practices and positions. I am asserting that school mathematics specializes its practices and subjectivities sufficiently to be referred to as an activity. However, it is of the nature of a relational totality that it resists all attempts at *a priori* definition. The positivity of school mathematics as an activity must emerge within the context of its description as an activity. In advance of this, however, it is also to be used as the principal reservoir of exemplary illustrations. Consider the following four extracts, which are all taken from the *SMP 11–16* scheme[7].

EXTRACT A

Solve   (a) $18x + 92 = 137$ (b) $0.7x + 3.2 = 4.88$
          (c) $2.9x - 3.5 = 19.7$ (d) $0.4x - 4.6 = -2.0$

(*SMP 11–16 Book Y1*, p. 66)

EXTRACT B

A4 What is the bill for each of these shopping lists?
     Work out each bill in your head.
(a) 1 kg potatoes   (b) 2 oranges   (c) 2kg spuds   (d) 1kg bananas
     1 grapefruit   1 cauli   100g mushrooms
                                                               1kg bananas
(e) 1 grapefruit
     1 orange

(*SMP 11–16 Book G1*, p. 14; original shopping lists drawn as fragments of paper)

7   I have noted that the structural level of the model is empirically 'accessible' only via the level of events, that is, that activity is describable only in terms of its instances. There is a common tendency to disregard this on the part of grand theorists of social structure. Where social structure is described other than formally, theorists often make use of 'imaginary' texts, or 'texts' which have already undergone an implicit analysis. For example, Bowles and Gintis (1986; 1988) sketch out the structure of the social universe in terms of 'sites' of social practice. These sites are differentiated on the basis of their principal axes of power distribution. Bowles and Gintis offer 'government closes tax loopholes' as an illustration of a 'distributive' practice within the site of the 'liberal democratic state'. Just what makes such an action 'distributive' rather than 'political' or 'cultural' or 'appropriative' is not elaborated. Nor is the action described at the level of concrete practice, but at a sort of metatextual level. The actual texts (*i.e.* as work) which are associated with government actions are not introduced. Nor is it at all clear how Bowles and Gintis would be able to deal with them, given the highly general nature of their language: they have no language of description. A similar criticism can be made of Marx's analysis in *Capital* (1976). Bowles and Gintis' earlier work, *Schooling in Capitalist America* (1976) does not exhibit precisely the same problem, because empirical data is given. Again, however, there is no language of description. Their thesis is advanced on the basis of a 'correspondence principle' bolstered by a residual argument. (See also Bowles and Gintis, 1988). The limiting of exposition on structure to imaginary or pre-digested texts seems, to me, to be an error. It demands a suspension of disbelief concerning both the genesis and application of the model. I shall, therefore, make use of empirical texts in the introduction of the structural level of my model, even though I have not yet described the tools which will enable their analysis.

EXTRACT C

A café orders p white loaves and q brown loaves every day
for r days.
What does each of these expressions tell you?
(a) $p + q$ (b) pr (c) qr (d) $(p + q)r$
                                                      (*SMP 11–16 Book Y1*, p. 32)

EXTRACT D

Here is a machine chain.

You find the output
from the first machine ...

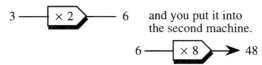

and you put it into
the second machine.

                              (*SMP 11–16 Book G1*, p. 41; indexical borders and shading
omitted, font standardised)

Extract *A* is relatively unambiguously a (school) mathematics text in terms of both its form of expression and its content. There are equations involving arithmetical symbols, positive and negative numbers, and unknowns (signified by 'x'); 'solve' is clearly to be interpreted as a mathematical process and not, for example, in the sense of solving a crime ('discover who was responsible for the following inscriptions'!). This kind of text exhibits comparatively strong classification or specialization of mathematical knowledge. Extract *B*, by contrast, clearly has some of the characteristics of a school mathematics text, but appears to index something else. The other that is indexed by this extract is the domestic practice of shopping. There is an absence of specialization of either forms of expression or content. This extract signals weak classification of mathematical knowledge. Extract *C* is a hybrid. The content of the task is non-mathematical. That is, the context is an economic practice (running a café). However, the task incorporates specialized mathematical algebraic expressions. The content of these expressions — their principal denotations — are non-mathematical: $p + q$, for example, signifies the total quantity of loaves ordered each day. The content thereby signals weakly classified mathematical knowledge. The form of expression of the algebra, on the other hand, refers to strongly classified mathematical knowledge. Finally, extract *D* is the other way around. Here, the context is comparatively unambiguously mathematical: all of the signifiers in the text principally denote mathematical objects. However, one of the signifiers, 'machine' is a non-mathematical expression; it introduces a metaphor, machine for arithmetic

Figure 6.2   Domains of practice

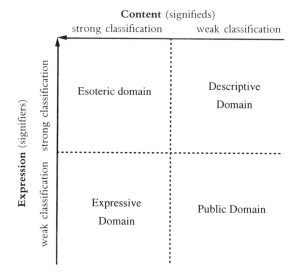

operation. In this case, a non-mathematical form of expression has been embedded within a mathematical context: the content represents strong classification, the expression (which has been foregrounded) represents weak classification.

These four examples illustrate the characteristics of each of four *domains* of school mathematics practice. The four domains can, in fact, be derived directly from the theoretical propositions at the end of Chapter 5 in respect of any activity. Since the form of expression and content can be measured separately in terms of strength of classification, strong or weak, the product of these two scales generates the space illustrated in *Figure 6.2*.

The *esoteric domain* of practice refers to the region of an activity which is most strongly classified with respect to other activities. Both forms of expression and content are specialized. The esoteric domain may itself comprise subregions corresponding to Eco's 'sub-codes' (1976), these will be referred to as *topics*. School mathematics, for example, consists of topics such as algebra, statistics and probability, arithmetic, Euclidean geometry, transformation geometry, and so on. Topics exhibit a certain degree of positivity, but are multiply interconnected (otherwise the activity itself could not exhibit positivity). Because ambiguity is minimized in the esoteric domain, specialized denotations and connotations are always prioritized. It is, therefore, only within this domain that the principles which regulate the practices of the activity can attain their full expression. The esoteric domain may be regarded as the regulating domain of an activity in relation to its practices.

However, all activities must look beyond themselves for pedagogic if for no other reasons. Bernstein has made this point with great clarity, albeit in a different methodological framework:

> If the culture of the teacher is to become part of the consciousness of the child, then the culture of the child must first be in the consciousness of the teacher. (Bernstein, 1971a; p. 65)

If an activity were to make no references outside of itself, then it would be unable to create apprentices. The esoteric domain of an activity is therefore conceived as casting a *gaze* beyond itself. The gaze lights upon external practices which are *recontextualized* by it. Recontextualizing entails the subordination or partial subordination of the forms of expression and/or contents of practices of one activity to the regulatory principles of another. Extract *B*, above, provides a textual illustration of the effects of such a recontextualization. Whilst the forms of expression and content derive from domestic activity, they have been referred, by the mathematical gaze, to mathematical interpretants, in this case, arithmetical interpretants.

The general effect of the recontextualizing gaze is the production of a domain of practices which exhibits comparatively weak classification in terms of forms of expression and content. This is to be referred to as the *public domain*. The public domain has the appearance of non-specialized practice as is illustrated by extract *B*. However, it remains, to a greater or lesser extent, subject to the regulative principles of the esoteric domain. These principles, however, cannot be adequately expressed within this domain, because there can be no certainty of the prioritizing of specialized denotations and connotations. Nevertheless, this domain is a crucial component of the practices of an activity, because, as I have suggested above, it is the domain through which apprentices must enter the activity.

I should emphasize, at this point, that the public domain is not external to the practice; it comprises practices which have been or are being recontextualized from other activities. The relationship between these recontextualized practices and their pre-recontextualized correlates corresponds to the relationship between text-as-text and text-as-work under the operation of a language of description.

An alternative mode of recontextualization occurs where the gaze combines non-specialized forms of expression with specialized content. In order to recognize, textually, the product of this mode of recontextualization it is necessary to analyse a sufficiency of text. In extract *D*, for example, there is a sufficiency of context to enable its recognition as mathematical in terms of content, so that 'machine' appears as a non-mathematical element at the level of expression. Thus, the non-mathematical element is being recontextualized within mathematical practice in order to give expression to a mathematical content. This domain of practice is, therefore, referred to as the *expressive domain*. Again, the regulative principles of the esoteric domain cannot be fully expressed within this domain.

Finally, the gaze may recontextualize a non-specialized setting the contents of which are described in terms of mathematical forms of expression. Thus, extract *C* describes quantities of bread, which constitute the content in terms of algebraic symbols as the form of expression. This domain or practice is referred to as the *descriptive domain*. Here, the specialized expression is being imposed upon the non-specialized content from the position of the esoteric domain. Nevertheless, the esoteric domain must signify differently because of the recruitment of a non-mathematical setting, so that, once again, the principles of the esoteric domain cannot be made fully explicit within this domain.

I shall next consider the implications of the distinction that I have made in terms of discursive saturation.

Practices: Discursive Saturation

In the previous chapter, I spent some time in a discussion of various conceptions of the modality of practice which led to the notion of *discursive saturation*. I argued that, whilst all practices are material, some practices minimize their dependency upon the material via the production of highly developed and articulated — that is, highly systematized — discursive structures. Part of the value of taking mathematics as a case study is that it is often construed as exhibiting the highest form of systematicity. Foucault describes mathematics as:

> . . . the only discursive practice to have crossed at one and the same time the thresholds of positivity, epistemologization, scientificity, and formalization. The very possibility of its existence implied that [that] which, in all other sciences, remains dispersed throughout history, should be given at the outset: its original positivity was to constitute an already formalized discursive practice (even if other formalizations were to be used later). Hence the fact that their establishment is both so enigmatic (so little accessible to analysis, so confined within the form of the absolute beginning) and so valid (since it is valid both as an origin and as a foundation); hence the fact that in the first gesture of the first mathematician one saw the constitution of an ideality that has been deployed throughout history, and has been questioned only to be repeated and purified; hence the fact that the beginning of mathematics is questioned not so much as a historical event as for its validity as a principle of history: and hence the fact that, for all the other sciences the description of its historical genesis, its gropings and failures, its late emergence is related to the meta-historical model of a geometry emerging suddenly, once and for all, from the trivial practices of land-measuring. (Foucault, 1972; pp. 188–9)

This is, perhaps, an undue mythologizing of mathematics. It certainly dismisses the non-discursive in mathematics. Nevertheless, Foucault is probably correct in his assertion that '[m]athematics has certainly served as a model for most scientific discourses in their efforts to attain formal rigour and demonstrativity' (*ibid*)[8]. It may be, then, that it is easier to demonstrate the

8   The text immediately following this extract reads: 'but for the historian who questions the actual development of the sciences, [mathematics] is a bad example, an example at least from which one cannot generalize' (*ibid*). My interest, of course, is not in the development of the sciences, so I shall take it that Foucault's caveat is not directed at me.

high level of discursive saturation of mathematics[9] than of other school disciplines or of other activities in general. However, the discussion in Chapter 5 was intended to justify the assertion that discursive saturation is a quality which is generalizable beyond mathematics. Therefore, although school mathematics continues to be used as the principal exemplar, the contention is made that this aspect of the language of description as well as the others are of value more generally.

The crucial distinction between practices exhibiting high and low discursive saturation is the extent to which their regulating principles are realizable within discourse. This entails that practices exhibiting high discursive saturation (DS⁺) are, at the level of discourse, highly complex and exhibit comparatively complete articulation. They are, furthermore, highly organized; discursive objects (signs) are always defined more or less formally and within discourse[10]. That is, any sign may be objectified within discourse, so that it is always possible to produce abstractions. It has already been established that regulating principles are only fully realizable within the esoteric domain of an activity. Therefore, the esoteric domain of a DS⁺ activity is characterized by a degree of discursive closure[11].

The high degree of discursive organization of the esoteric domain of a DS⁺ activity facilitates the generation, by such an activity, of languages of description having highly explicit realization principles. This concerns the application of the gaze. The descriptive power of the esoteric domain preconceptualizes practices which are recontextualized, so that these are easily subordinated to the grammar of the recontextualizing esoteric domain. Indeed, such subordination is to a large extent necessary, because of the relative inflexibility of the grammar of the recontextualizing esoteric domain. Such activities are, therefore, capable of producing highly abstracted descriptions both within and outside of the esoteric domain. School mathematics provides an obvious example of such an activity as the discussion on mathematical myths, in Chapter 1, illustrates.

The gaze itself must incorporate recognition principles. However, there is no logical necessity that these be discursively explicit to the extent that the gaze is, first and foremost, concerned with pedagogy, that is, with the creation of subjectivity. It is probably more appropriate to understand the recognition principles of the gaze as deposited in the extension of a set of exemplars (cf Kuhn, 1970) rather than as being prefigured by intensional precepts. Apprenticeship into the principles of the gaze, however, must entail that the abstractive features of the exemplars are made visible through

---

9 There is an assumption, here, of at least a degree of continuity between school and academic mathematics.

10 In Vygotsky's (1986) terms, signs (more correctly, perhaps, signifieds) are generally constituted within such practices as 'scientific concepts'.

11 Although there is always a necessary openness at both the discursive and non-discursive levels since connotations can never be excluded. I am not, therefore, proposing 'closure' in the Piagetian/mathematical sense (Piaget, 1971).

metonymic reduction. In the case of school mathematics, it is not at all clear that there are any limits on recognition. The arithmetic of the natural numbers, for example, seems to be universally applicable (although not, of course, universally useful). The prevalence of the view that 'mathematics is everywhere' again attests to this:

> Maths is everywhere, isn't it? Maths — number concepts and such — is in everything the children do, right from the beginning. Don't you agree? (Primary school headteacher quoted by Corran and Walkerdine, 1981; p. 35)

Activities whose practices exhibit low discursive saturation (DS⁻) are characterized by implicit regulating principles. That is, specialization is at the level of the non-discursive, but not, to any great extent, at the level of the discursive. These activities may be described as being characterized by what Bourdieu terms 'polythetic' thinking. Thus utterances within these activities are, of necessity, highly particularized or context-dependent (Bernstein, 1990). This latter term requires a little elaboration. All utterances are context-specific, in the sense that they must be interpreted within the context of a particular activity. However, an utterance within a DS⁻ activity is also context-*dependent*, to the extent that it cannot be unambiguously interpreted outside of the context of its immediate production. Activities that are characterized by DS⁻ include those that are commonly (although not necessarily) referred to as 'manual' activities.

It is also the case that comparatively low levels of DS are represented by texts in more conventionally 'intellectual' activities. For example, insofar as it is concerned with student control, school mathematics can apparently lack discursive organization. The following two extracts are taken from the transcript of an interview with a mathematics teacher[12]:

> After having Jason who was on his own, working with Elaine, they seemed to get on OK, so I tried them together again and that seems to be working reasonably. Jason is quite capable but wanders all the time. Elaine struggles a bit and Robyn and Ann are quite strong so I put them altogether because they also seem quite considerate of the others' needs.
> [. . .]
> Over here I felt that Cyril he's reminded me of a lot of kids I see, particularly black boys, they come in and they are very capable but within a few months they start drifting off for some reason. There is something wrong there, so I've put him in with two very strong boys.

It would appear that the teacher, who was aware of the interviewer's expertise in education, has no recourse to a specialist language in describing his classroom organization strategies. Such a language is clearly lacking in the

---

12   The interviews were conducted by Jayne Johnston as part of the empirical programme of her doctoral research at the Institute of Education, University of London. Students' names have been altered.

first extract: 'they seemed to get on OK, so I tried them together again . . .'. The second extract bespeaks a more or less explicit racism, but even this is not consistent as other black boys were described by the same teacher as exhibiting notable stability. The teacher is bricolaging his responses, which is to say, making use of resources that are at hand in formulat   his discourse (cf Lévi-Strauss, 1972). It may be that the researcher will   loy a well-developed language of description to organize the teacher's p   discursively. However, the teacher does not appear to be likely to achieve this himself. This is 'because the expertise of the secondary mathematics teacher resides in [school] mathematical discourse and not in didactics' (Dowling, 1993).

I have now introduced the terms which enable me to talk about practices. These are to be described in terms of *domain* and *discursive saturation*. As I noted earlier, activities also construct *positions*. I shall now turn to this element in the final part of this section.

Positions

Pedagogic activities, such as school mathematics, must logically construct a hierarchy of positions. That is, they must construct transmitting and acquiring positions. Since pedagogic action is extended in time, such activities must also construct a hierarchy within the category 'acquiring position', minimally in terms of the degree of advancement, or career. Additionally, however, not all acquirers become even potential transmitters. Pedagogic activities, therefore, construct hierarchies within the category 'acquiring position' which are not entirely defined by career. Such activities are, in other words, selective. Pedagogic activities may also construct hierarchies within the category 'transmitting position'. There are, thus relatively dominant and relatively subaltern positions. The most dominant position, we might say, exhausts the practices of the activity and is its *subject*. The more subaltern positions are aptly described as being, to a greater or lesser extent, objectified by the activity. The teacher in the interview transcripts quoted above is clearly objectifying the students, even if not in any consistent way.

Thus dominant and subaltern positions are constructed via the distribution of practices. The activity, in effect, regulates 'who' can say or do or mean 'what'. Clearly, the activity must provide for the generation of new subjects. As I have argued in Chapters 2 and 5, the process of subject generation is appropriately referred to as 'apprenticeship'. Certain of the positions constructed by the activity can be described, therefore, as 'apprenticed positions'. These positions are partially objectified by the activity, but they must be attributed a residual subjectivity in terms of their potential as future subjects and in terms of the actions that they must engage in in order to achieve this future position. The most sensitive region of practice must be the esoteric domain and its gaze. In the case of a DS$^+$ activity, such as school mathematics, the apprenticed position must be recruited into the regulative principles of the esoteric domain and the realization principles of the gaze at the level of discourse.

The residual subjectivity of other, more subordinated positions, by contrast, is more marginalized. This may be because they are not constructed as potential subjects or, in terms of career, because they are at a greater distance from such subjectivity, the ultimate achievement of which is, therefore, less certain. Acquiring positions must clearly be attributed some degree of subjectivity. However, insofar as the more subordinated positions are not attributed potential subjectivity of the activity itself — that is, they are not apprenticed — their residual subjectivity remains dependent upon the subjectivity of the activity. These may be referred to as 'dependent positions'.

It is thus possible to describe pedagogic action in relation to apprenticed positions following on from the discussion in the previous chapter. The initial 'hailing', or 'interpellation' must take place within the public domain. Pedagogic action then proceeds via the construction of metonymic chains which must enter the esoteric domain. In order to establish the semiotic complexity of the DS^+ esoteric domain, pedagogic action must render accessible, again metonymically, the regulative principles and organizational structure of this domain, which must entail establishing explicit links within and between topics. In thus establishing the apprenticed position as a limited subjectivity with respect to any region of the esoteric domain, the apprenticed position will have undergone what can, metaphorically, be described as a 180-degree rotation from the public to the esoteric domain. The operation of the gaze may then be made accessible in the production of exemplars. The essential ingredient of apprenticeship is a visible pedagogic action.

The dependent position must, correspondingly be denied access to, at least, the regulative principles of the esoteric domain. This may entail restriction to the public domain. Where esoteric domain practices are introduced, the dependent position must be denied access to its systematic complexity. The distribution of practices to the dependent position, therefore, is likely to be characterized by an interrupted esoteric domain. In this way, the lack of access to the regulative principles of the activity achieve perpetual dependence upon the subject.

I have already announced that the activity must constitute a public domain. This region is comprised of practices which are recontextualized from other activities. Thus, extract *B*, above, illustrates the recontextualizing of domestic practices by school mathematics. The activity must also construct positions which relate to such recontextualized practices. In the case illustrated, for example, the activity must construct a position of 'shopper'. Such positions are neither apprenticed nor dependent. They are, in other words, attributed no subjectivity. Rather, they are fully objectified by the activity. These public domain positions are identified as *objectified* positions.

This completes the discussion of the structural level of the language of description which is summarized in *Figure 6.3*. I shall now introduce the textual level. Rather than give extensive illustrations from the textual analysis here, I shall limit myself to a few orienting examples. The details of the textual level will become clarified in the following chapters.

Figure 6.3 Social activity theory: The structural level

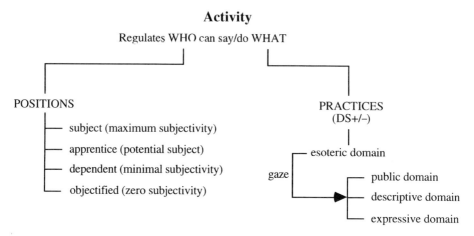

The Textual Level

Corresponding to practices and positions, at the structural level of activity, are *message* and *voices*, at the textual level. The use of different terms for the two levels emphasizes the difference in theoretical status. Message and voice are the direct products of the analysis of a particular text, which is to say, the production text-as-text from text-as-work. Whilst the text-as-work is bounded, and although the language of description is, in my formulation of its presentation, constituted as prior to its reading of the text-as-work[13], there is, nevertheless, an inevitable uncertainty in the relation between text-as-work and text-as-text. That is, it cannot be asserted that the particular reading that is presented is the only reading that could have been generated by the language of description. The degree of stability of the reading which is presented corresponds to the more conventional measures, validity and reliability. The validity of the analysis is a function of the degree of explicitness of the presentation of the language of description. The reliability of the analysis is a function of the sampling procedures which have been applied to the text. The mode of analysis being applied here is predominantly qualitative. Validity and reliability are, therefore, not to be understood as quantitative measures. Rather, they are arenas within which claims are to be supported and contested.

Practices and positions, which are features of the structural level are to be inferred from the analysis. The question, here, concerns generalizability and is a function of the standing of the analysed text within the archive of all extant texts. The practices and positions of an activity are structuring

---

13 This is the case even though the language of description was generated in the dialogical manner which I have described above. This is because of the particular formulation of this presentation of the language of description and the analysis that it produces. This is intended to foreground its potential in subsequent readings rather than simply catalogue the results of the particular analysis that participated in its generation.

resources in the production of texts which, themselves, are produced as well as reproduced by texts; the relationship is dialectical. Activities are thus (re)produced by texts and, in particular, by pedagogic texts. Pedagogic texts must, therefore, (re)produce the various features of activity described in the previous section. I shall denote the various mechanisms by which they achieve this as *textual strategies*. Barthes (1974) describes a text as a 'weaving of voices' (his 'voices', not mine). In my language of description, a pedagogic text is a weaving of textual strategies which position voices and distribute message. It is these strategies and the patterns of voices and message that must be identified in and by the analysis. The principal categories of textual strategy are introduced below.

Voices and Positioning Strategies

Any given monologic text will constitute a range of voices corresponding to a subset of the range of positions constructed by the activity. Typically, we might expect the *authorial voice* of the text to correspond to the subject position of the activity. However, as I shall illustrate in the textual analysis in subsequent chapters, the text may also constitute a spurious or *displaced authorial voice* which acts as a mask with respect to the authorial voice. The text must also constitute one or more reader voices to which a greater or lesser degree of potential authorship is attributed. Authorial voices are dominant and reader voices are subaltern voices. The latter may be organized hierarchically. Thus, pedagogic texts may construct both *apprenticed* and *dependent* voices, each with the possibility of being further hierarchized according to career. Insofar as it incorporates public domain message, the text must also construct *objectified* voices. The analysis of the text must produce a description of its voice topography in these and related terms.

It will be recalled that the activity regulates who, in terms of positions, can say or do what, in terms of practices, the latter being differentiated with respect to domain and level of discursive saturation. Correspondingly, the voices of a monologic text are differentiated in terms of message. The text must, therefore, incorporate *distributing strategies* which effect the distribution of message across the voice topography. *Positioning strategies*, on the other hand, operate by establishing relationships between voices more directly. This may be achieved in various ways. For example, an authorial voice may directly address another voice. For example, the teacher in a classroom may claim (or attempt to claim) authorship of the lesson by walking to the front of the room, standing behind the teacher's desk and announcing in a loud and clear voice, 'Good morning, class'. This initiating action at once *authorizes* the teacher — the authorial voice — and interpellates the students as subaltern voices. The positioning strategy operates via the recruitment of the social organization of the classroom. In particular, the teacher faces the class all of whom are seated so as to face the teacher; the teacher is exclusively authorized to address the class collectively.

Alternatively, the teacher may recruit other features of the social organization of the classroom in constituting her or his utterance as, for example, a question, an instruction, an evaluation or an admonition and so forth. Some of these resources are available for recruitment in similar ways by a written text — such as a textbook. Thus, the text may incorporate greetings, ask questions, impose tasks. Other resources must be recruited differently by a written text. Thus, a textbook may incorporate an evaluation only insofar as it precodes responses to its tasks. The physical arrangement of the classroom is available, but again, not interactively; it must be represented iconically or in verbal text. A textbook may, for example, incorporate a picture of a classroom in which students are working from copies of the textbook itself.

The positioning strategies that I have been referring to thus far all interpellate the subaltern voice as subject to the authority of the authorial voice. This authority entails the direction of transmission and evaluation. I shall refer to this mode as *interpellation*. Alternatively, positioning strategies may establish identification between voices. For example, in constituting a public domain setting, a text may construct a character with whom the reader is identified either in terms of a projected career or within a contemporary relational nexus. An example of the former might be the introduction of a junior in a company as an occupational voice that the reader might possibly occupy after leaving school. Alternatively, the text might construct a domestic narrative which includes characters who might stand as textual surrogates for the reader's family.

Positioning strategies which operate on the reader voice in this way are referred to as *identifications*. The construction of objectified voices, such as characters in public domain settings, is referred to as *objectification*. The identification of the reader voice with an objectified voice is, of course, also an objectification of the reader voice.

Identifications need not be confined to the public domain. The text may, for example, construct a career identification between the reader voice and the authorial voice. This would clearly be an apprenticing strategy. Public domain identifications are more likely to be associated with dependency or objectification strategies, although this is contingent upon how the text incorporates distributing strategies to move between domains. As I shall illustrate in the analysis of the *SMP 11–16* texts, differentiation in public domain identification also enables the 'recognition' of apprenticed and dependent voices in terms of social class.

The authorial voice may, itself, constitute an identification with another voice. For example, the text may claim an association with professional mathematicians. I will refer to an authorial identification of this sort as an *affiliation*. On the other hand, the authorial voice may identify itself with the reader so as to constitute a displaced author; this is a *displacement*. The text might achieve this by claiming empathy with the reader's difficulties. This is to be distinguished from an identification of the reader voice with the authorial voice. In a displacement, the authorial voice moves, figuratively, towards the reader voice; in being identified with the author, the reader voice moves.

Commonly, positioning strategies do not operate in isolation from the message. This is clearly the case in, for example, public domain identification. Identification would obviously be impossible without the production of public domain message. More concretely, as I have often pointed out to student teachers, getting the class's attention is of little value unless you have something to say to them. I shall now move on to consider the categories of distributing strategies and how these may combine with positioning strategies to constitute authorizing, apprenticing, dependency and objectification.

Message and Distributing Strategies

I have described the practices of the activity in terms of domain and in terms of discursive saturation. In its production, a text may vary in terms of the extent to which it claims authority over or gives access to the domains of practice and, in DS$^+$ activities, the principles of its discourse. Firstly, then, distributing strategies may expand or limit the *range* of the message. *Expanding* strategies broaden the message being distributed to a given voice in terms of the range (intensive and extensive) of esoteric domain topics and recontextualized (public domain) settings. *Limiting* strategies effect the narrowing of the message in terms of topics and settings.

Limiting may be effected via the *exclusion* of message relating to the esoteric domain. As I will illustrate in Chapter 7, this strategy is employed very substantially by the series of *SMP 11–16* textbooks which are targeted at 'lower ability' students. These books very rarely enter the esoteric domain and, when they do, they implicate a very limited range of topics. This strategy is clearly associated with a more subordinate, dependent voice. However, exclusion is also employed in certain areas of the textbooks which are targeted at the highest 'ability' level. This occurs, for example, in the treatment of the topic probability by the *SMP 11–16* textbooks. These texts rarely enter the esoteric domain in relation to this topic, so that probability is presented as an almost exclusively public domain message. This is shown by the results of the content analysis in Chapter 7 (see also Dowling, 1995a). It may be speculated that this topic is being constituted as too difficult for students in this age range. In this sense, the apprenticeship is being paced in terms of career by the exclusion strategy.

Exclusion from the public domain is also an important strategy. As I have indicated above, the public domain constitutes the portal through which apprentices enter the practices of an activity, with the descriptive and expressive domains constituting links between the esoteric and the public domains. Thus the use of highly technical (esoteric domain) language to a lay audience is clearly an excluding strategy. In this case, it is appropriate to refer to the voice that is constructed by such a strategy as *alienated*. Two points should be made in relation to the alienated voice. Firstly, I have described it as an achievement of a distributing strategy. A corresponding positioning strategy would constitute the denial of a voice as a reader voice. This is either an objectifying strategy, or simply a failure to interpellate. There is, in other words, no separate category of 'alienation' as a positioning strategy. Secondly, since the alienated voice is attributed zero subjectivity by the text, it corresponds to the object position at the structural level. There is, then, no separate category of 'alienated' position.

Other than in isolated topics, such as probability, it might appear that expanding strategies should generally be associated with authorizing and apprenticing, whilst limiting strategies would seem to be more appropriate for dependency strategies. However, the association between these distributing strategies and the voice structure of a text is contingent upon their combination with other distributing strategies which are concerned with the *discourse* of the activity. In this regard, I want to distinguish between *principling* and *proceduralizing* strategies. It will be useful to give an illustration. According to David Pimm:

> Too much algebra teaching is solely syntactic, in that much mathematical practice is coded into precepts which operate entirely on the symbols, rather than being combined with a meaning (and hence a purposeful goal), an interpretation in which the requisite transformations make some sense. (Pimm, 1987; p. 174)

Pimm's language is inconsistent with that being used here; the notion of a meaningless symbol clearly does not fit in with the semantic structuring of school mathematics that I am employing. Nevertheless, the notion of the 'coding' of mathematical practice into a precept or procedure is instructive. Take, for example, the procedure which is commonly employed in the division of fractions: turn upside-down and multiply. The effect of such 'coding' of mathematical discourse as an algorithm is to particularize mathematical knowledge, to reduce its level of abstraction. The general quality which distinguishes principled from procedural discourse is that the former exhibits connective complexity, whereas the latter tends to impoverish this complexity, minimizing rather than maximizing connections and exchanging instructions for definitions.

Proceduralizing thus presents the practices of a DS^+ activity as though it were a DS^- activity. The substitution of algorithms or procedures for principles is one mode of this strategy. The text may also proceduralize through the use of exemplars which constitute specific instances which tacitly stand for, or synecdochize, a whole class. The relationship between exemplars is metaphoric. The use of exemplars in this way again renders the message more context dependent. *Proceduralizing* and *metaphor* are both instances of what I shall refer to as *particularizing* strategies.

The inverse of proceduralizing is principling. Here, the use of definitions and taxonomic classifications etc., facilitate the expression of the regulating principles of a DS^+ practice, such as school mathematics. As I have argued, these principles cannot be fully realized outside of the esoteric domain, so that principling must involve esoteric domain message. Where exemplars are used, their abstractive properties will be made explicitly available. In this way, the

Figure 6.4   Distributing strategies

Distributing Strategies

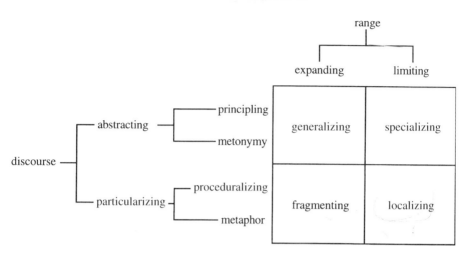

metaphorical relationships between exemplars are reduced metonymically, so that the context dependency of the message is reduced. Again, this will generally involve moving beyond the public domain. I should note, here, that the move from principles and definitions to exemplars as metaphors for the principles and definitions is a particularizing of message. It is the metonymic reduction of the metaphoric exemplars which constitutes an increase in the level of abstractive potential of message. *Principling* and *metonymy* are instances of *abstracting* strategies.

I have described the *range* of the message as being expanded or limited and the *discourse* as being abstract or particularized. These combine to generate the two-dimensional strategic space shown in *Figure 6.4. Generalizing* refers to the combination of expanding and abstracting. In the context of esoteric domain message, this might constitute an articulation between topics within the more general discourse. The articulation of public domain settings must involve specialized significations, so that there must be some movement of the text outside of the public domain. This is because that which constitutes exemplars as exemplars is the gaze of the activity, the realization principles of which are precisely the regulating principles of the esoteric domain. Articulation between public domain settings, therefore, also constitutes articulation between the public and esoteric domains, which is to say, the rendering visible of the recognition principles of the gaze.

Specializing is the construction of abstract message with respect to a specific topic or setting. Again, specializing in relation to a public domain setting must entail esoteric domain message, so that the setting is constituted as an analogue of a region of the esoteric domain. An activity, such as academic mathematics, rather than school mathematics, comprises a large number of

148

Figure 6.5 *Social activity theory: The textual level*

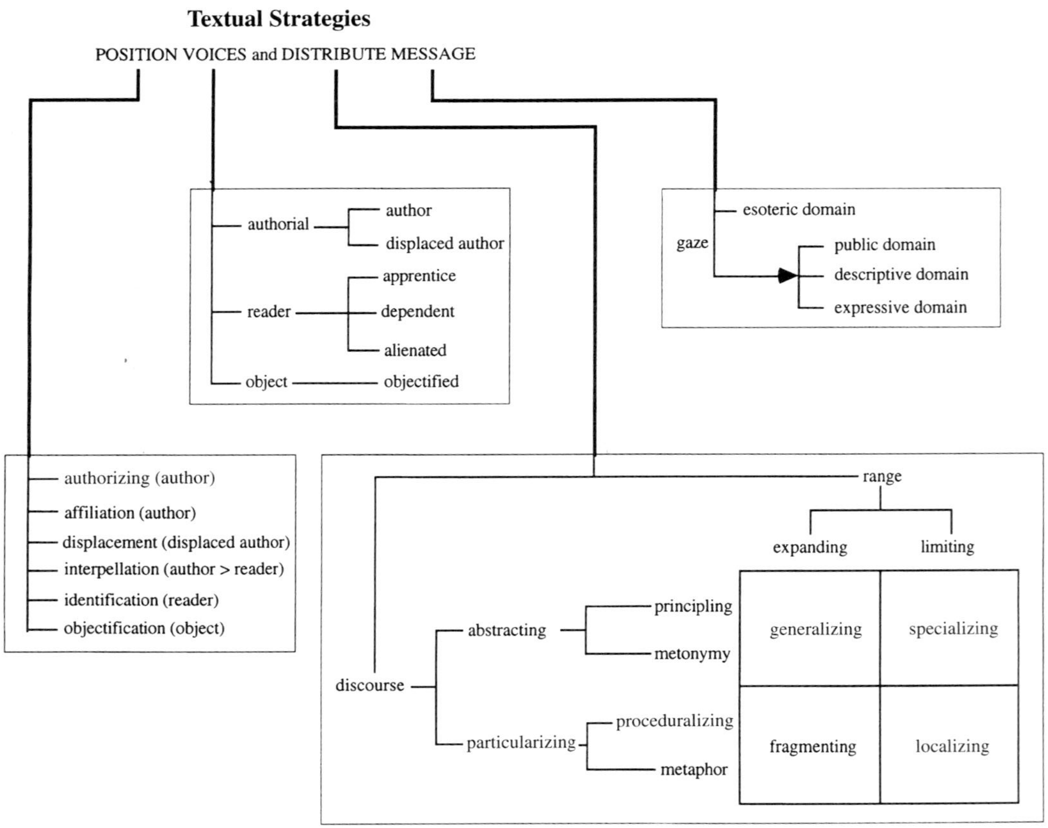

Textual Strategies

POSITION VOICES and DISTRIBUTE MESSAGE

specialist positions each of which may be described as subordinate in relation to the field as a whole. The subject position of mathematics, then, is not realized in any single human subject. Thus we might expect to see specializing strategies in the constitution of all apprentices at the most advanced stages of their careers. The subject position of school mathematics, on the other hand, is clearly far closer to being realizable in single human subjects. Here, we might expect to see specializing as a *career pacing* strategy, whereby the apprenticeship may be constituted as an articulation of a sequence of specialisms.

Where the discourse is particularized, expanding and limiting strategies constitute *fragmenting* and *localizing*, respectively. Fragmenting realizes the esoteric domain as segmental, rather than articulated. The public domain is constituted as an incoherent collection of settings or, alternatively, as constituted by public domain rather than esoteric domain principles. For example, the public domain settings might be justified in terms of everyday use-values, thus constituting a realization of the myth of participation described in Chapter 1. Localizing procedurally or metaphorically elaborates the instance (esoteric or public domain) rather than generating segments or collections.

Expanding and limiting strategies may both be associated with the apprenticed voice or the dependent voice. The determination is made in terms of the particular combination of these range strategies with strategies relating to discourse. Thus, when the discourse is abstract, the message is apprenticing; where the discourse is particularized, the message produces dependency. Nevertheless, limiting strategies clearly limit subjectivity and are therefore subordinating. Where they combine with abstracting strategies to produce specialization, the apprenticed voice is subordinated either in terms of career pacing, or in relation to the more general practices of the field as a whole.

Particularizing strategies are clearly associated with the dependent voice. They may be described as distributing to this voice the products of the practices of the activity without the principles whereby these products are generated. In the case of DS^+ activities, this entails the presentation of the discourse as if it were a DS^- activity. It is to be expected, therefore, that particularizing distributing strategies will be associated with positioning strategies which establish public domain identification (the objectification of the reader voice) or with a displaced authorial voice. This is, of course, not necessarily the case, although authorial identification in combination with particularizing distributing strategies would constitute a contradictory or disingenuous text.

Conversely, abstracting strategies distribute a more complete message to the apprenticed voice. They are, therefore, likely to be combined with authorial identification. However, the apprenticed voice must also be identified within the public domain if it is to be recognized. The public domain is, in this sense, the principal arena in which an activity selects its apprentices.

This completes the introduction of the textual level of the language of description, which is summarized in *Figure 6.5*. I shall now move to a consideration of the third and lowest level of the language of description, that of *textual resources*.

Resources

The Third Level of the Language of Description

Although I have introduced some illustrations, the form in which the language of description has been developed, so far, is primarily deductive. The theoretical propositions presented in the summary of Chapter 5 arose out of a discussion of a range of theoretical work, that is, out of the constitution of the academic field as antecedent texts. From these propositions has been derived the notions of activity — with its associated practices and positions — and text — with its categories of message and voice which are realized by and in textual strategies. The language, thus far conceived, contains recognition and realization principles for the description of its empirical object.

However, as I have argued in the first section of this chapter, the language cannot exhaust the empirical. Thus, whilst the deductive structure advanced above entails the theoretical possibility of the categories of textual strategy, it does not prefigure the empirical resources that will be implicated in these strategies. The category, message, for example, must logically include public domain text, but it does not specify the external activities which are the objects of the recontextualizing gaze nor, indeed, whether any such text will be incorporated into any particular empirical text. School mathematics, in general, must have a public domain, but, again, what is represented in this domain — the domestic, professional activities of various kinds, other school disciplines — is an empirical question which is to be addressed through textual analysis. Similarly, the theory can assert that there will be particularizing and abstracting strategies. However, it cannot predict how these will be realized in terms of resources that are available. For example, the production of textbooks may entail different kinds of verbal text, literary styles, pictures of various kinds, different kinds of binding, and so on.

Thus, textual strategies are realized in pedagogic texts via the implication of what will be referred to as *resources*. I have referred to certain resources in introducing the categories of textual strategy in the previous section. For example, I noted how a teacher might recruit features of the social organization of the classroom and a particular mode of address in her/his positioning strategies. There is no *a priori* limitation on what can count as a resource. Nor is there a predetermination on how they are implicated into the various textual strategies, so that such implication may be close to what Lévi-Strauss (1972) has called *bricolage*, or it may consist of a more engineered approach. There is, then, a theoretical arbitrariness about resources which does not obtain with respect to textual strategies. The relationship between these two levels is thus similar in form to the relation between 'action' and 'operation' in Leont'ev's 'activity theory' (1978, 1979). In Leont'ev's conception, 'actions' are goal-oriented, whilst 'operations' are concerned with means. The latter are therefore comparatively contingent rather than necessary. This resonance between Leont'ev's schema and my model is the principal reason for the choice of the term 'activity', although my use of it is clearly different from Leont'ev's.

It should be emphasized that the arbitrariness of resources is purely a theoretical arbitrariness. Empirically, there must always be a selection from a notional *reservoir* of resources to constitute the *repertoire* of resources which make up a particular text. The differential selection of resources in relation to different voices is crucial in the realizing of all of the principal categories of textual strategy. For example, in the analysis of the *SMP 11–16* texts, it will be demonstrated that the potential for differentiation of form of binding of the textbooks is recruited by positioning strategies in constructing different categories of reader.

Because this chapter is concerned primarily with the theoretical derivation of the language of description, I shall not introduce, here, the empirical repertoire of resources incorporated in the *SMP 11–16* texts. These will emerge from the textual analysis conducted in the following chapters. I shall, however, discuss a single main category of resource which is to be implicated in a quantitative content analysis to be described in Chapter 9. The category to be introduced is to be referred to as *signifying mode*. The reason for placing this discussion here is that it of necessity involves some theoretical considerations.

Signifying Modes: Icon, Index, Symbol

Signifying mode describes a form of the relationship between expression and content that is implicated in sign production. That is, Saussure's contention that the general relationship between signifier and signified is one of arbitrariness is being rejected, here; rather, this relationship is understood as being motivated (see Hodge and Kress, 1988, 1993; Kress, 1993). There are diverse ways in which such motivation can be realized. 'Signifying mode' refers to a particular repertoire of resources which is implicated in localizing and generalizing strategies. Furthermore, these particular resources can be described with sufficient precision to enable a content analysis of the empirical texts. This repertoire thus offers an opportunity to provide a methodological triangulation by complementing the predominant qualitative mode of analysis with a quantitative component.

Figure 6.6 shows a page from *SMP 11–16 Book Y1* which incorporates all three of the signifying modes to be discussed here, that is, the *iconic*, the *indexical* and the *symbolic*. These terms clearly refer back to Peirce's (1931–58) distinction between 'icon', 'index' and 'symbol'. However, my use of these terms does not coincide with any of Peirce's. In particular, the notion of 'index' used here has a considerable overlap with other uses of 'icon'. Furthermore, I am not ascribing essential qualities to the textual fragments which I am labelling icon, index or symbol, but am referring to conventions of signifying practice (cf Eco, 1976). Bishop's (1977) brief discussion in the professional journal *Mathematics Teaching* is illustrative of the cultural relativity of visual codes.

The picture at the bottom of the page shown in *Figure 6.6* portrays what looks like a sandy beach in front of a sizeable hotel; there are holidaymakers

Figure 6.6   SMP 11–16 Book Y1 (p. 18)

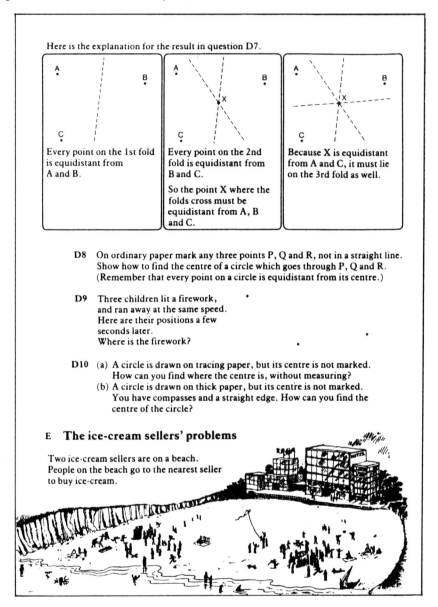

Here is the explanation for the result in question D7.

Every point on the 1st fold is equidistant from A and B.	Every point on the 2nd fold is equidistant from B and C. So the point X where the folds cross must be equidistant from A, B and C.	Because X is equidistant from A and C, it must lie on the 3rd fold as well.

D8   On ordinary paper mark any three points P, Q and R, not in a straight line. Show how to find the centre of a circle which goes through P, Q and R. (Remember that every point on a circle is equidistant from its centre.)

D9   Three children lit a firework, and ran away at the same speed. Here are their positions a few seconds later. Where is the firework?

D10   (a) A circle is drawn on tracing paper, but its centre is not marked. How can you find where the centre is, without measuring?
       (b) A circle is drawn on thick paper, but its centre is not marked. You have compasses and a straight edge. How can you find the centre of the circle?

E   **The ice-cream sellers' problems**

Two ice-cream sellers are on a beach. People on the beach go to the nearest seller to buy ice-cream.

and vendors on the beach and swimmers — in various states of distress — a shark and an octopus in the water. Our view of the scene might be from an aeroplane coming in to land at a nearby airport: we can read the text by substituting for it a potential visual image and a physical viewpoint which fixes our own virtual presence as spectator of the scene. The image, in other words, is an articulation of a visual code and a physical viewpoint. Such a text is to be referred to as an *icon*. Crucially, an icon signifies the virtual, physical presence of the viewing reader and at least one of its readings is predicated solely upon this *visual code of presence* — this is what it would look like if you were there[14]. 'Code' is being used, here, in a similar way to Eco's (1976). The reader must recognize her/his own spatial position as encoded within the icon (in terms of azimuthal and elevation angles, perspective, etc), thus producing the icon as signifying her/his presence[15].

No assertion is being made that an icon presents an actual and uncoded resemblance or replication of a scene or of an object. We could match every posited resemblance between the beach scene in *Figure 6.6* and a real beach (which, of course, may not actually exist) with a difference. Clearly, as Eco (1976) argues, iconic codes must be acquired and there are different kinds of iconic code: a line drawing may exhibit a greater or lesser degree of caricaturing, for example. A pedagogic text must make the assumption that its reader has acquired certain codes[16] and this is true of iconic codes. Again, it is the incorporation of the visual code of presence which characterizes all iconic modes[17].

The image adjacent to task D9, in *Figure 6.6*, is of a different kind, because, although producing it as a sign incorporates a visual code, the physical presence of a viewer is not signified, there is no code of presence. The image could be transformed into an icon by replacing the dots by drawings of the children. The reader would then be drawn into the unlikely position of flying above the children's heads. However, it is the signification and not the plausibility or modality of presence that is crucial. As it is produced on the page, however, the D9 image is better described as a minimalist kind of map. The positions of the children are marked in such a way that mathematics can be performed using a pair of compasses or a piece of tracing paper. There are similar images at the top of the page in *Figure 6.6*. It is not possible, from the image, to say what the points are marking, because they refer to a task (D7) on the previous page; actually, they represent, simply, points — mathematical

---

14 A sound recording might be understood as the aural analogue of an icon; such resources are not, of course, available within the context of most school textbooks, although they do feature in some modern language courses.

15 In Eco's sense as in mine, signs are not passive, but must be produced in their reading.

16 Although not necessarily all: clearly, a text can address multiple readers as is instanced by the inclusion in the SMP texts of occasional references to members of the authoring team — there is, probably, no assumption that the student reader will recognize these, although the alert teacher reader might, since the authors are listed in the Teacher's Guides. The text here fails to interpellate and so alienates the student as object.

17 Regester (1991) has developed a dual classification of 'visuals' in history textbooks. Visuals may be photographs, illustrations, tables, maps or graphs and they vary in their 'degree of visualisation' on a scale ranging from all words to no words. The motivation for Regester's study, however, is related to the apparent lack of knowledge concerning the influence of visuals on learning. This motivation has resulted in a form of classification which is inappropriate for the present purposes.

objects. This mode of signification is to be referred to as an *index*. An index incorporates visual or spatial codes, but does not assert the virtual, physical presence of the reader[18].

The final mode of signification in *Figure 6.6* is provided by the alphanumeric text on the page which, primarily, is produced as signifying via an articulation of what might be described as a linear visual code (the numbers and letters must be written in a punctuated line which encodes the syntagmatic as well as the paradigmatic) with non-visual codes. This text is *symbolic*. A symbol is alphanumeric and is visual only in linear terms; it does not incorporate a code of presence. It is clear that symbolic text may verbally signify a virtual presence. This is often the case in novels, where scenes may be described as if witnessed by the writer/reader. In the novel, the signified 'viewpoints' are often impossible 'positions', such as inside the mind of one (or more than one) of the characters or as an outsider, impossibly witnessing an intimate dialogue; they are viewpoints, nevertheless. Under such circumstances, however, it is generally the content that is signifying the 'viewpoint' and not the mode of signification which is signifying presence. Onomatopoeia may be a partial exception, but the virtual presence is, in that case, aural rather than visual. Furthermore, there is clearly a sense in which any text encodes presence insofar as it presupposes a reader; in this sense, it is the text-as-work which is signifying presence. To define 'codes of presence' in such all-embracing terms would clearly be unhelpful. It is reserved, here, to indicate the signification of a virtual physical presence of the reader in addition to their presence *qua* reader. The distinguishing feature of the iconic mode is that it is the mode of signification itself which is signifying a virtual visual presence.

A rider must be added: it is clear that symbolic text may be laid out on the page so as to incorporate more complex visual codes. Where this is the case and where it is intended to focus on the visual codes, it is appropriate to refer to the text as indexical or even iconic. For example, alphanumeric text may be tabulated, thus incorporating two linear dimensions; tables are generally referred to as indices. Plausibly, the text may be arranged so that, for example, the outline generated by the line beginnings and endings traces the profile of a human head. In such cases, it may be appropriate to distinguish between the symbolic and iconic modes incorporated by the text.

Scaling Icon, Index and Symbol

The intrinsic nature of the visual code of presence in the iconic mode renders it particularly appropriate for incorporation into strategies which particularize

---

18   It may be that certain non-representational forms of painting (some of the work of Joan Miró, for example) would thereby be described as indices rather than as icons within this language: this does not, of course, diminish them.

and limit message, which is to say, in localizing. This is because the iconic mode frequently makes a strong claim on a reality beyond itself, which is to say it frequently exhibits strong modality[19]. Iconic public domain text may, in general, be interpreted as an assertion of the reality and significance of a specific public domain setting, which is thereby foregrounded, whilst the esoteric domain is correspondingly backgrounded. The mode of signification of non-iconic (indexical and symbolic text) text, by contrast, facilitates the alienation of presence[20]. This renders it suitable for incorporation in generalizing strategies.

This suggests that a comparison between the ratios of iconic to non-iconic modes in two textbooks has face validity as a measure of the relative extent of the use of localizing and generalizing strategies, assuming, of course, that the textbooks are each consistent. Such a comparison is carried out on a sample of the G and Y series of *SMP 11–16* in Chapter 9. In anticipation of this, I shall, here, provide a little more delicacy to the categories of signifying mode which I have introduced.

Within the category 'icon', there are different degrees of localizing in terms of what might be described as interruption of the code of presence. Compare, for example, the iconic significations in *Figures 6.7* and *6.8*. The drawings of Nadia and her classmates in *Figure 6.8* is a simple, but 'straight' illustration with no exaggeration of features and without humour. John in *Figure 6.7*, on the other hand, would put Cyrano de Bergerac to shame. His brother, Charlie, has yet to reach puberty, but he seems to be able to grin almost from ear to ear and is sporting an ironic 'Big C' on his T-shirt. The caricature and humour in the drawings of the industrious John and Charlie have a tendency to interrupt the code of presence by asserting the impossibility of a viewpoint; the modality is weakened. There is no such interruption in the drawings of Nadia *et al*, even though they are clearly drawings and not 'the real thing'.

Figure 6.9 incorporates a third iconic category in the photographs of grocery items. Photographic codes — and certainly the representational photographic codes implicated here[21] — signify a real presence. This real presence is in the form of the camera which is a surrogate for the authorial/reader voice. In terms of the resources available within a textbook, the photograph, as a mode of signification, minimizes the interruption of the code of presence. Thus three species of icon are defined which respectively specialize the definition of icon given above as: photographic; non-photographic but

19 See Hodge and Kress (1988) for a discussion of modality used in this sense.
20 This is not to assert that non-iconic text necessarily alienates presence as a reading of Keats or Dickens, for example, well illustrates. Again, however, such representational writing recruits other literary resources to overcome the tendency to abstraction of the mode of signification that is being employed.
21 It may well be appropriate to consider a wider range of photographic codes when considering certain other empirical texts, for example, in the context of astronomical photography or of the use of photography in art.

Figure 6.7 SMP 11–16 Book G2 (p. 4)

---

c Making money

John is saving up for a new bike.

To earn some money he makes bird tables.
He sells them to neighbours and friends for £1·50.
Each table takes him about 2 hours to make.

He buys scrap wood for the tables
from a local timber yard.
The wood costs him 20p for each table.

C1 What other things would John need to make the bird tables?

C2 The only thing that John has to pay for is the wood.
John makes a profit on each table.
His profit is

Money I get by selling table — anything I have to pay for

(a) How much profit does John make on 1 table?

(b) How much profit does he make for each hour he works?

C3 Each weekend, John spends about 8 hours making the tables.
How much profit will he make each weekend?

Business is booming!
Christmas is coming and a lot of people
want to buy John's bird tables.

He gets his little brother, Charlie, to help him.
If they both work for 8 hours at the weekend
they can make 6 bird tables altogether.

C4 How much money will John get when he sells the 6 tables?

C5 (a) How much money do you think John should pay Charlie
for his work each weekend?

(b) How much profit would that leave for John?

(c) Which makes more money for John,
working with Charlie, or without Charlie?

4

---

representational; representational, but incorporating exaggeration of features[22]
and/or humour. These species are referred to as photographs, drawings and

22 Clearly there is commonly a certain exaggeration and certain cases may be difficult to call.
The eyes of some of the characters in the drawings of Nadia *et al* (*Figure 6.8*), for example,
are reduced to dots. However, given the scale of the drawings, this is interpreted as expe-
dient; dots (or lines) for eyes in a much larger face would constitute exaggeration.

Figure 6.8 SMP 11–16 Book G2 (p. 19)

Review: time

1   Nadia looks at her watch.
    Schools starts at 5 to 9.
    How long has she got?

2   From 5 to 9 until 9:15,
    Nadia is with the others
    in her House group.
    How long is she in her
    House group?

3   First lesson is Art.
    It starts at 9:15 and
    goes on until a quarter
    to eleven.
    How long is Art?

4   After Art, Nadia has break
    until five past eleven.
    How long is break?

5   After break, Nadia has
    Design until lunch.
    Lunch time starts at
    20 to 1.
    How long is Design?

6   Lunch lasts until 5 to 2.
    How long is lunch?

7   After lunch, Nadia has
    Games all afternoon.
    Games lasts until
    3:40, when it is
    home time.
    How long does Games last?

8   How long is Nadia at school altogether?
    (She stays at school for lunch.)

19

cartoons, respectively and, taken together, constitute an ordinal scaling of 'icon' in terms of interruption of the code of presence.

It has already been mentioned that the spatial arrangement of symbols into tabular form is interpreted as indexical, so that there are two species of index, tables and graphs, the latter being the residual category once tables are

Figure 6.9   SMP 11–16 Book G7 (p. 3)

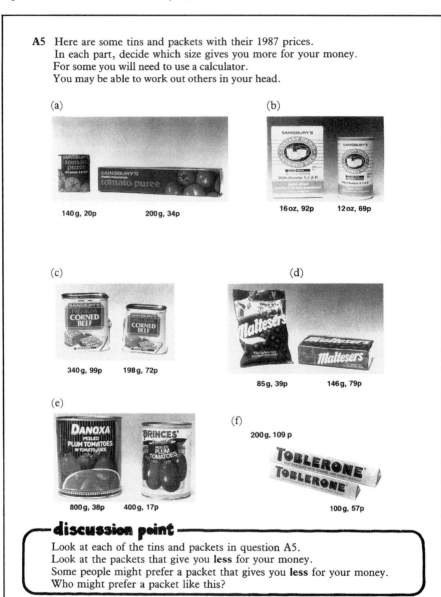

A5   Here are some tins and packets with their 1987 prices.
In each part, decide which size gives you more for your money.
For some you will need to use a calculator.
You may be able to work out others in your head.

(a)

140g, 20p   200g, 34p

(b)

16oz, 92p   12oz, 69p

(c)

340g, 99p   198g, 72p

(d)

85g, 39p   146g, 79p

(e)

800g, 38p   400g, 17p

(f)

200g, 109p

100g, 57p

discussion point

Look at each of the tins and packets in question A5.
Look at the packets that give you **less** for your money.
Some people might prefer a packet that gives you **less** for your money.
Who might prefer a packet like this?

3

removed. Graphs include those 'mathematical' diagrams that are generally referred to as graphs (line graphs, histograms, pie charts, etc), also maps and the various forms of projection (the 'viewpoints' for which are formally defined and do not signify virtual visual presence). Also included within the category 'graph' are geometric diagrams, including, for example, drawings of polygons and polyhedra. This is because, in mathematical terms, what is being signified is not a visually realizable object, but a formally defined construct; it is not possible within this language to produce an icon which signifies such a mathematical object. On the other hand, it is possible to produce an iconic signification of an index. Thus, an image might suggest that 'this is me looking down on my hands whilst drawing a regular hexagon'. Otherwise, an image might, for example, present a table showing prices on 'company headed notepaper', again evoking/being evoked by an iconic code of presence.

An additional visual code may be invoked in either indexical or symbolic signification where a deviation is made from the usual 'letterpress' form; the use of 'handwriting', for example. This use of manuscript constitutes an 'iconizing' of the symbolic/indexical text, but it is, nevertheless, the symbolic/indexical mode which is foregrounded — 'reading' rather than 'looking at' generally predominates. Nevertheless, in the analysis described in Chapter 9, it has been decided to quantify manuscript and non-manuscript symbols and indices separately.

The modes of signification are summarized in *Figure 6.10*, as an example of the resource level of the language of description. Before concluding this chapter, I shall give some consideration to some programmatic extensions of the language of description.

Extending the Language of Description

The discussion, so far, in this chapter has been concerned with DS[+] activities, with monologic texts, and with unitary subjectivity. This is entirely appropriate, because this book is directly concerned with school mathematics — a DS[+] activity — and its principal empirical research object is a school mathematics scheme which is appropriately constituted as a monologic text which, therefore, constructs a single authorial voice relating to a unitary position. However, the discussion in earlier chapters has been broader in scope as, I am sure, are the interests of the readership of this book. I feel that it is therefore appropriate to give some indication as to how the language of description can handle a greater range and complexity of empirical texts and how it might be extended in these respects. Work has been and is being done in which the descriptive power of the language of description is extended to non-mathematical texts (Dowling, 1994b), to the reading and conducting of educational research (Brown and Dowling, 1998), to the mathematical classroom (Coombe and Davis, 1995; Dowling and Brown, 1996; Johnston, 1993), and to the recontextualizing of pedagogic practices in initial teacher education

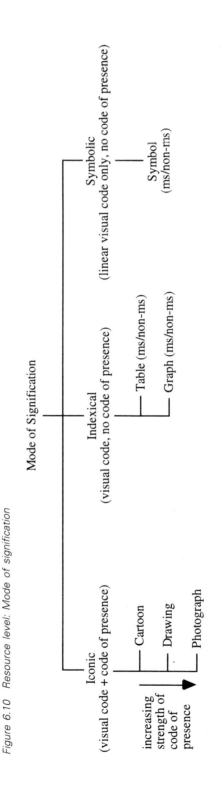

Figure 6.10 Resource level: Mode of signification

first teaching positions (Ensor, 1995, 1996). Here, I want to give some consideration to DS⁻ practices, to the analysis of dialogic texts, to multiple subjectivity, and to institutional level. The comments that follow should, at this stage, be regarded as more speculative and the issues as more programmatic than those of the previous sections. This is not, of course, to claim that the above work is, in more than a temporary sense, complete.

Low Discursive Saturation

Discursive saturation refers to the extent to which the regulation of the practices of an activity are explicitly available. I have argued that in activities, such as academic disciplines, there is a high degree of explicit availability of their regulation. This mode of practice generates discursive texts which can formulate principles and definitions and which interrogate and are interrogated by other discursive texts. In particular, such activities are able to recontextualize practices relating to other activities such that they are brought into greater or lesser discursive isomorphism with the esoteric domain of the recontextualizing activity. These activities are, in other words, able to produce languages of description which generate a discursive public domain. What is at stake in the elaboration of these activities is their regulating principles.

Other activities, including those that are generally referred to as 'manual' practices, are regulated in a more context dependent way. The texts generated by these activities exhibit far less discursivity, so that their regulation cannot be unambiguously formulated in terms of principles and definitions. What is at stake in the elaboration of these activities is not their principles so much as their sites.

These activities must still generate a public domain as the logical requirement for a point of entry into a specialized practice remains. However, this domain is far less discursive than the public domains of DS⁺ activities. Of necessity, therefore, it is not possible to capture such practices within language. We might allude to the public domains of such activities by reference to physical locations — entrances — and to elements of bodily habitus that are to be shaped to constitute esoteric domain practices which are now more aptly described as skills than as principles. At the textual level, *skilling* replaces *principling* as the strategy opposed to *proceduralizing*. The skill is that which enables the adept to dispense with algorithms. Metonymy is still available within DS⁻ activities, but it is now ostensively rather than discursively realized.

Many of the practices of everyday life might appropriately be described as incorporating neither principles nor skill, or, in any event, as being clearly context-dependent in these respects because of the limitation on the degree of public institutionalization of the details of the practices themselves. Within the general field of manual practices, then, we can propose a distinction. On the one hand, there are those practices which are acquired informally. In contemporary societies, these include everyday domestic practices, such as shopping, cooking, gardening, and so forth. The social structuring of these practices is segmental. That is, the division of labour is simple, generally being organized in terms of the patriarchal family relations of gender and age (and class, where domestic labour is waged). The organization of this region of the sociocultural space may be described as being closer to mechanical than to organic solidarity, in Durkheim's terms (1984)[23]. In general, there is no formal organization or institutionalization of pedagogy with respect to these practices which are acquired via a sharing of strategies. In this mode, the principles of evaluation of the practices reside with the acquirer rather than, or at least as much as, with the transmitter. The structure of social relationships within this mode of acquisition can be described as horizontal (other than in respect of age). Other practices in this sphere include those relating to care of the self and sexual behaviours as well as illicit practices.

Within the same societies[24], other manual practices are elaborated within the context of a more complex division of labour. That is, these practices constitute regions of specialization within the sociocultural. The acquisition of these practices is associated with more or less formally organized pedagogy, often through the kind of craft apprenticeship that I discussed briefly in Chapter 2. This will entail what Lave and Wenger (1991) have described as 'legitimate peripheral participation'. In Chapter 2 I mentioned Singleton's (1989) description of apprenticeship in a Japanese mingei pottery. For my purposes, the crucial feature of this apprenticeship was the tacit nature of much of the pedagogic action. Certainly, the process of acquisition within an apprenticeship will include the informal mode whereby strategies are shared within a horizontal structure, for example, between apprentices. Nevertheless, acquisition always takes place within the context of the formally hierarchical, or vertical, social relationship of adept/apprentice; the principles of evaluation reside with the adept.

The development of these craft practices constitutes an internal hierarchy, that is, between the adept and the apprentice. This is a career hierarchy. In this sense, it is similar to hierarchies associated with age in the patriarchal family, but distinct from gender relations, which are not resolved via career development. However, craft practices also inaugurate an external hierarchy in relation to domestic production and reproduction. This is because there is no

23 See the discussion in Bernstein (1996) from whom the horizontal/vertical opposition which is introduced below is taken. See also Dowling (1995b).

24 Durkheim (1984) attempts to characterize societies in terms of mechanical and organic solidarity. As I indicated in Chapter 5, Bernstein has described societies as hybrid. Bernstein (for example, 1977) describes different class locations in terms of different modes of solidarity. Johan Müller of the University of Cape Town (personal communication) has suggested that this effects an importing of Durkheim's evolutionary model of society into the description of contemporary society so that social class is aligned with social development. This is at least arguably the case and clearly has serious implications especially in relation to a society in which, for historical reasons, racial hierarchies are closely aligned with social class. Here, however, 'development' refers to the mode of establishing and maintaining social relations which is not to be evaluated positively or negatively.

selection with respect to domestic practices. Everyone engages in them, but there is no selection and no formal pedagogy in respect of their acquisition. Craft specialization constitutes regions of manual practice as esoteric The entry into these esoteric practices involves a more or less extended period of apprenticeship. In the course of the apprenticeship and in subsequent adept production, the subject is required to instantiate aspects of what is, within a manual craft, a tacitly regulated practice. These instantiations, then, are simulated by the craft; they are simulacra (see Baudrillard, 1993). What they achieve is constituted as skill.

However, this is not to argue that domestic practices are necessarily inferior in any sense to craft practices. The former are simply not regulated institutionally, which is to say, within a region of the division of labour which is regulated in terms of entry. In his study involving becoming an apprentice to a Kenyan Tugen blacksmith, Michael Coy (1989) indexes two kinds of 'insight':

> . . . those relating to technology, and those relating to the smith's social relations. Within the rubric of social relations I would include those aspects of the smith's craft that are supernatural. The supernatural activities of smiths are either services performed for their community, as in the curse applied to thieves, or they are protective and defensive in nature. In either case, these supernatural activities are directly related to the smith's relationships with others in his community. (Coy, 1989; p. 121)

The curse denies the thief access to the tools that the smith produces and which are needed for subsistence agriculture. Various devices ensure that only a smith is able to produce these tools and that the smith's services are regularly required. For example, the bellows, which are essential to the smith's work can be made only with access to the smith's technology. A set of smith's tools, including the bellows, are manufactured by the smith and presented to the apprentice upon completion of the apprenticeship. The axe used for cutting the hot steel is the only tool that is quenched. Unquenched steel is brittle. Thus the only smiths' products that are available to non-smiths break very quickly.

The Tugen blacksmith is thus established as an initiate into an esoteric practice. Their skills and their goodwill are constituted as essential components of the economy. Yet Coy's apprenticeship lasted only three months. Undoubtedly, he spent far longer than this learning to use a knife and fork at the dinner table and longer still learning to communicate in spoken English. These facilities are privately acquired, but they are privately acquired by everybody. Their public display does no more than affirm this. The blacksmith's tacitly regulated practice, by contrast, is acquired secretly. Its public displays, however, do not represent something acquired. This is because that which is acquired is — in respect of both technological issues and social relations — concerned primarily with the maintenance of the specialism, which is to say, with the reproduction of the division of labour. The use of cutlery and the nature of one's spoken English may also incorporate markers of social class and ethnicity. To this extent, the public display of craft simulates skill; the public display of etiquette and accent simulates 'breeding'.

This brief consideration of DS⁻ activities enables me to consider the interaction between subjectivities relating to distinct activities. Therefore, I shall now move to discuss the analysis of dialogic texts.

Dialogic Texts

I have described monologic texts as constructing a single authorial voice and, therefore, as capable of being interpreted with respect to a single activity. Dialogic texts are interactive texts which construct two or more authorial voices. These may or may not relate to positions within the same activity. Here is a section of text which has been reconstructed from fieldnotes taken during a classroom observation in a predominantly 'white' secondary school mathematics classroom in the Western Cape region of South Africa[25]:

> *teacher*: I got stuck on this at school and I was clueless after that on algebraic graphs.
> *student*: So how do you know it now?

Here, the teacher is constructing a displaced authorial voice which affiliates with the *apprenticed voice* as sharing in a difficulty in respect of entry into a region of the esoteric domain. There are clearly at least two ways of interpreting the student's response. It might be interpreted as a literal request for discursive principling: how is this difficulty to be overcome. Under these circumstances, the student, as subaltern authorial voice, would be affiliating to the apprenticed voice, thus deferring to the teacher as the dominant authorial voice. Thus, the construction of a second authorial voice by the text immediately requires the augmenting of the textual level of the language of description. Firstly, the authorial voices must be arranged hierarchically as *dominant* and *subaltern*. Secondly, the establishing of subaltern status is achieved not by interpellation, but by *deferring*.

In fact, the student uttered his response not to the teacher, but spoke very quietly, so that the most likely audience was his colleague, with whom he had been chatting for much of the lesson. The teacher could not have heard the response. Under these circumstances, an alternative analysis is appropriate. For example, the student is constructing an authorial voice, the message of which is constituted as a performance of repartee whereby the teacher's message is 'deconstructed'. The teacher is identified as an objectified voice, the message of which is to be evaluated by the student. The student's colleague was interpellated and identified as a co-evaluator with the authorial voice.

In this analysis, the hierarchical relationship between the teacher and student positions is inverted. Furthermore, there has been a reinterpretation of

25   See Dowling and Brown (1996).

the nature of the text. From the teacher's perspective, the text is a pedagogic text which constructs authorial and apprenticed voices. However, from the student's perspective, the teacher's utterance constitutes a performance which is to be evaluated by the students. In this event, the evaluation is negative. The text is not, in this interpretation, a pedagogic text, because the author is not constituted as a transmitter nor the reader — the second student — as an acquirer.

In order to produce these analyses, I have resolved the dialogic text into monologic texts. The first analysis produced two monologic texts which were both containable within the same activity. By contrast, the second monologic text of the second analysis — the text interpreted from the student's perspective — could not be contained within the same activity as the first — the text interpreted from the teacher's perspective. In this analysis, there were (at least) two activities being elaborated in the classroom; the dialogic text partitions the activity space. Alternatively, the student might have made his question audible to the teacher and clearly ironic. This again would have partitioned the activity space as a *negation* of the teacher's authority. In both cases, the first activity — school mathematics — is being objectified by the student voice, which is constituting a position within a second activity. This second activity is likely to be more appropriately described as DS$^-$ than as DS$^+$.

The general strategy, then, for dealing with dialogic texts is to resolve them into monologic texts. This entails that a crucial unit in the analysis of such texts is the utterance. This is in accord with the methodological principle proposed by Bakhtin (1986; Volosinov, 1973) wherein the utterance is defined as that which is punctuated by the voice of the interlocutor. However, the analysis of utterance can be made only with reference to the utterance or utterances to which it relates or which it may recruit. The more general unit of analysis, therefore, remains the text. The punctuation of the utterance marks out the authorial voices; their messages are constructed from the broader text. Furthermore, the approach entails a sufficiency of text to enable such a resolution to be made. Properly, the second version of the analysis of the classroom text implies that the empirical text incorporates the contextual information relating to the pattern of interaction between the two students and the sotto voce nature of the student's utterance vis-a-vis the teacher.

There is clearly scope for developing the central categories of generalizing and localizing in respect of dialogic texts and also for extending the interpretation of the possible relationships between strategies and resources. Generalizing and localizing, for example, might be interpreted as strategies of contestation which attempt to claim dominance in authority by shifting between the orthogonal axes of the general and the local. In academic dialogue, I may challenge an interlocutor either by asking for a specific example, or by offering a specific example as a challenge to their general thesis. Alternatively, I may claim access to a more general discourse which is able to objectify an example which has been offered. As a teacher in conversation with a parent of one of their students, a primary school mathematics teacher can claim access to general principles concerning the ways in which different children learn mathematics, whilst the parent can claim local knowledge of their own child. I will not develop this further at this point other than to offer the hypothesis that, where the dialogue can be contained within a single activity (as is plausibly, but not necessarily the case in the two hypothetical illustrations offered here) the dominant voice has access to both generalizing and localizing strategies, whilst the subaltern voice has access to only localizing.

In respect of the development of strategies and resources in dialogic texts, it is clear that, where the authorial voices relate to distinct activities then the strategies of each will recruit the strategies of the other as resources. That is, they are reduced in level, whence the inevitable failure of the rationalist programme. Strategies simply cannot be transported between activities which are constituted differently in terms of relations between positions.

In the hypothetical engagement between teacher and parent, introduced above, the parent attempts to define a position for themself as having local knowledge about their child. This is a strategy which authorizes the parental voice and which may, further, distribute a local message to that voice. Suppose, for example, that the parent says that the teacher must understand that the child is lacking in confidence with numbers because the child's elder sibling, who is very good at mathematics, persistently makes fun of the younger child's lack of numerical sophistication. The parent is localizing their message by referring to a very particular procedure which characterizes a highly limited relationship (that is, between these siblings). The teacher may now say, 'I'm very glad that you have told me this, because this will now enable me to plan activities that will encourage your child to experiment with numbers, but without placing them in a public situation.' The teacher is now recruiting the parent's utterance as a resource in authorizing their own voice and in distributing to that voice a potential generalizability (abstracted discourse which is applicable across a range of instances).

In this case, neither the teacher nor the parent is challenging the position of the other with respect to the activity of the other. However, each is establishing their own position within their own activity. In other cases, such recruitment may entail the kinds of challenge introduced above (or as illustrated in the Escort/B-Mer example introduced at the end of Chapter 5). Again, this development is here left as programmatic. I shall now give some brief consideration to the nature of subjectivity as it may be conceived in its instantiation in individual human beings.

Human Subjectivity

I have proposed that activity refers to a particular state or articulation of a notional Global Semantic Universe. I have further proposed that this is (re)produced in texts and also instantiated in human subjects. The human subject must, then, incorporate this structure as, in some sense, a potential in respect of the production of utterances. I want to make two points before introducing the particular metaphor for human subjectivity that has guided the production of my general methodological position. Firstly, the incorporation of the activity by the individual human subject cannot be described in simple terms as a generative grammar. This is because all practices are, in some measure, context-dependent; discursive saturation can never be complete.

Secondly, since human individuals must participate in a range of activities, they must constitute and be constituted by multiple positions of subjectivity. This raises the question of the relationship between these positions. That is, what is the nature of the relationship between object positions relating to different activities as they are instantiated in any given human individual. Clearly, they are not hermetically sealed with respect to each other. If this were to be the case, then no public domain could be established by any activity, since no human subject would be capable of casting a gaze outside of their contextually contingent position. The mathematician would not be able to recognize a supermarket shopper as anything at all other than an instance of a mathematical cipher. This would entail that apprenticeship into new activities would be impossible. The sociocultural terrain would be constituted as a static pattern.

An alternative conception is to consider that any given of subjectivity position must constitute a radical rearticulation of a region of the Global Semantic Universe. Other regions may be understood as being less radically rearticulated. Thus, as the human subject moves from one more or less context-dependent activity to another, there is a shift in the region of the Global Semantic Universe that is radically-rearticulated. It is always the radically-rearticulated region that is foregrounded by the activated activity. Thus, the mathematician *qua* mathematician must regard supermarket shopping as in the background. This conception is clearly redolent of Heidegger's (1962) conception of dassein as a lighted clearing.

It is now possible to interpret successful apprenticeship as the constitution of a new foregrounded and radically-rearticulated region of the Global Semantic Universe. The achievement of a new subjectivity by a human individual entails the potential to background previously existing subjectivities. Furthermore, the newly acquired subjectivity must now form a part of the background of each of these previously existing subjectivities. All acquisition of subjectivity, then, is also a greater or lesser transformation of all prior subjectivity.

As I have indicated, human subjectivity constitutes one element of the structural level of Social Activity Theory, the other being activity. By way of a coda to the general discussion of this level we may speculate that subjectivity, thus conceived, constitutes an appropriate arena for psychological theory. Activity, then, stands as the terrain for sociological theory. Whilst it is clear that the antecedents to my position span these spheres of academic practice, my own prioritizing of activity as that to be theorized is consistent with my specializing of this work as sociology.

Institutional Level

In introducing the term 'activity', I asserted that this constitutes an analytic space and that, activities are always ideologized in the empirical. An activity is defined as a specific articulation of a Global Semantic Universe which (re)produces (in part) a more general division of labour. Empirically, however, it is always a particular division of labour which is (re)produced. The content of an activity — its practices and positions — is always an expression of its position within a specific configuration. It is, therefore, appropriate to consider a higher level of analysis which addresses this positioning.

School mathematics has been described as an activity in its own right. However, school mathematics must, in the empirical domain, exist within schooling as an institution. That is, school mathematics is positioned in relation to other school disciplines, thus (re)producing schooling[26]. In conducting an analysis at this level, we might conceive of schooling as the structural level and school mathematics as the level of events. Schooling constructs practices (disciplines) and positions (teachers, students, parents) which are (re)produced by particular instances of activities (school mathematics in a particular school, and so on).

Schooling is similarly positioned in relation to other institutions by higher order institutions which might be said to correspond to what Bowles and Gintis (1986; Gintis and Bowles, 1988) refer to as 'sites of social practice'. Analysis at this level would (potentially) enable the consideration of the historical. This methodology constructs the social as a kind of 'Russian doll' structure or alternatively, as a 'fractal' structure. The form that the analysis takes is independent of the level of the analysis[27]. Thus the language of description might be conceived to operate, methodologically, as a lens of variable focal length, zooming in and out to produce descriptions at different levels of analysis. In this conception, there is no *a priori* highest or lowest level. Thus, whatever level is chosen, the language will always constitute an analytic space which will always be ideologized in the empirical. This constitutes a play or uncertainty in respect of an upward (in terms of level) orientation which corresponds, in a sense, to the play between text-as-text and text-as-work.

I should add a caveat. There is a danger that the Russian doll and fractal metaphors may be taken to suggest a downward determinism in respect of institutional level. This is not intended. Clearly, there is always a degree of contingency at the evental level which is precisely why I have used the expression (re)production. In developing this aspect of the language of description, it may be more appropriate to make use of the form of hierarchical organization proposed by Atkin (1981) which allows for overlapping of categories in respect of their subjacent modalities.

---

26 In an earlier publication (Dowling, 1992) I referred to this as 'framing'. I have decided to discard this term because of its potential confusion with Bernstein's use of the word.
27 Fractal geometry exhibits this property which, it has been suggested, might also be applied to the description of coastlines, telegraphic transmission, and so on (Gleick, 1988).

In this chapter I initially presented an explicit statement of my general methodological position, which I have referred to as Constructive Description. Secondly, I have introduced the main features of the language of description which will be employed in the analysis of the *SMP 11–16* texts in the following part of this book. This language of description is referred to as Social Activity Theory. I have introduced three levels: the structural, the textual, and the level of resources. This framework has, as I have indicated, been generated out of the engagement with the theoretical antecedents discussed in the previous chapter and with the *SMP 11–16* materials as the empirical text-as-work. Finally I have made some more speculative comments and raised some programmatic issues relating to the development of Social Activity Theory beyond the stage that can be illustrated in the following textual analysis. In the next chapter, I shall move to the analysis of the empirical texts.

Chapter 7

An Introduction to the Empirical Text

In Chapter 6 I introduced the principal structure of my language of description. In this chapter and the four which follow it, I shall apply this language of description to the analysis of the secondary school mathematics scheme, *SMP 11–16*. The present chapter will constitute an introduction to this analysis in two ways. Firstly, I shall give a very brief history of the development of the School Mathematics Project (SMP) and of the materials that it has produced, including *SMP 11–16*. I shall also describe the structure of the first edition of *SMP 11–16*, which is the edition that was used in the analysis (and much of which continues to be in use in schools at the time of writing). Secondly, I shall give the results and general conclusions of a content analysis of a sample of the scheme. This content analysis employed the message domains categories that were introduced in Chapter 6. The content analysis is presented in greater detail in Dowling (1995a).

SMP: An Introduction[1]

The School Mathematics Project: The 'Numbered' and 'Lettered' Books

SMP 11–16 is the current SMP text for the eleven to sixteen age range. It is the product of the School Mathematics Project which was, according to its principal founder, conceived in the garden of Culver Lodge in Winchester at 11 a.m. on Monday 18th September 1961, at a meeting of the Heads of Mathematics of Charterhouse, Marlborough, Sherborne and Winchester and Professor Bryan Thwaites, Professor of Theoretical Mechanics at the University of Southampton (Thwaites, 1987). The meeting followed a conference, organized at Southampton by Thwaites, which was 'aimed specifically at producing an "ideal" school mathematics syllabus' (Thwaites, quoted by Cooper, 1985). The project was one of a large number of initiatives arising out of a series of conferences in Europe and in the US in the late 1950s and

---

1 For further description of the development of the School Mathematics Project and of 'modern mathematics', see: Cooper (1983, 1985); Griffiths and Howson (1974); Howson (1987a); Howson, Keitel and Kilpatrick (1981); Moon (1986). More generally, regarding curriculum innovation in the 1960s in Britain and in the US, see MacDonald and Walker (1976).

early 1960s. These initiatives fall under the broad heading of 'modern mathematics' or, in the US, 'new math'. In the US, the School Mathematics Study Group (SMSG) was sponsored by the American Mathematical Society, the Mathematical Association of America, and the National Council of Teachers of Mathematics (Moon, 1986). The materials developed by this group were produced largely by mathematicians and emphasized an axiomatic and highly rigorous approach (Ling, 1987; Tammadge, 1987). Events in Europe and, particularly, in the UK followed closely those in the US. Barry Cooper has described SMP as the result of negotiation:

> . . . it required interested actors, utilizing the climate of 'crisis' resulting from the campaign on teacher supply as a major resource, to enter various arenas in order to persuade others of the 'need' for change.
>
> [. . .] such actors, especially the university pure mathematicians, with their followers in the [Association for Teaching Aids in Mathematics (ATAM)], and the applied mathematicians, with their industrial allies, did have considerable success in convincing school teachers of the 'need' for change in school practice, while fending off attacks 'from below' on their own curricular practices. In both cases, the success of the university subdisciplinary segments can be seen as having partly resulted from their having found allies outside of their own organizations. The supporters of modern algebra within the ATAM, who had come into contact with the pure mathematicians in various European-wide meetings [. . .] gradually made 'modern mathematics' more acceptable to many school teachers by combining it with those elements of their original mission concerned with Piagetian ideas, and proposing 'intuitive' and 'experiential' approaches to its study. The applied mathematicians found themselves able to claim that 'industry' also approved of 'modelling', numerical methods, and so on, as well as being able to derive resources of personnel and money from companies with which to further the promotion of their version of 'mathematics'. (Cooper, 1985; pp. 230–1)

Funding was obviously very important, indeed, the initial and continuing success of SMP is, according to Howson (1987b), due to its financial autonomy which was originally established through 'generous grants from Industry and the Leverhulme Foundation' (p. 7). In the US, federal funding for SMSG followed the successful launch of the Soviet Sputnik in October 1957 (Moon, 1986; Tammadge, 1987). Europe had only recently emerged from war and work by Vig (reported in Cooper, 1985) suggests that politicians and commentators in Britain were increasingly assuming that economic success depended upon the application of scientific research to industrial processes. Cooper also notes that the rapidly increasing number of mathematics graduates being employed in industry was 'the likely structural basis of the increased interest in mathematics education expressed by industrial employers in the late 1950s' (1985; p. 93).

The first SMP materials to be published were *SMP Books T* and *T4*, which focused on the final two years of the GCE (General School Certificate) O-level course. These were succeeded by *SMP Books 1–5* (often referred to as the 'numbered' books), which covered the whole of the secondary age range up to O-level. John Ling (the *SMP 11–16* team leader) notes that the most obvious difference between the SMP course and 'traditional' courses was in the content, which was a 'distinctive blend of pure and applied mathematics' (unsurprising, in the light of Cooper's comments).

> On the pure side, there was a highly unified development in which the concept of function/mapping/transformation played a key role. The Euclidean approach to geometry was replaced by the study of transformations, the latter being linked with vectors and matrices. The concept of function dominated the presentation of algebra, and algebra itself was enlarged to include a concrete approach to abstract algebra. On the applied side, topics such as statistics, probability, linear programming, networks and computing were introduced. (Ling, 1987; p. 34)

However, Ling points out that advocates of SMP also laid great stress on the experimental 'discovery' approach. Alan Tammadge, one of the three principal authors of *SMP Books 1–5*, has described his view of their task:

> . . . we arrived at the idea of introducing new work by means of a problem whenever possible. We tried to find problems associated with children themselves, so that they would really want to solve them. Such problems are fairly easy to find, but posing them and helping with their solution is sometimes a lengthy process. We had decided to address our books to the pupil, to talk to him or her as a person and to expect interest and willingness to participate in exploration of ideas. [. . .]
>
> The theory behind our writing was that pupils would work through the introductory problems on their own, perhaps for homework. The teacher would then pull their ideas together, correct misconceptions, go through difficult parts again and then leave them to practice their new understanding. (Tammadge, 1987; pp. 25–6)

Although Tammadge recognized that some teachers were by-passing the introductory material and 'simply telling their classes how to get on with the ensuing exercises' (*ibid*), the authors of the materials were clearly constructing an eager and essentially independent student. This, perhaps, is hardly surprising, given that SMP was directed exclusively at 'pupils in grammar schools, independent schools, and that growing number in secondary modern schools who aspired to an O-level' (Howson, 1987b; p. 3), that is to 'the top 25 per cent or so of pupils' (*ibid*). In fact, four of the original eight pilot schools were precisely those independent schools which were represented in Thwaites' garden meeting, referred to earlier. Indeed, it was these four heads of mathematics at prestigious independent schools, together with Professor Thwaites (who had received his own education at Dulwich, Winchester and Cambridge (Cooper, 1985)), who wrote the first materials (later to become Books T and T4) for the first year pupils in these schools (Tammadge, 1987). The fact that these independent schools recruited at age thirteen explains the emphasis on the

Table 7.1: *Occupational locations of participants at the Southampton conference*

Occupational location	Number
University	34
College of technology	1
College of education	1
Private industry	15
Government research	3
HMI	1
Schools	73
Uncoded	2
Total	130

Source: Adapted from Cooper, 1985

Table 7.2: *Categories and gender of students of schools represented at the Southampton conference*

Category of School	Student Gender			
	Boys	Mixed	Girls	Total
Independent	26	0	1	27
Direct Grant	7	0	3	10
Grammar	12	8	8	28
Technical Grammar	1	1	0	2
Bilateral	0	2	0	2
Comprehensive	3	1	0	4
Total	49	12	12	73

Source: Adapted from Cooper, 1985

final two years of the O-level course (Howson, 1987). A breakdown of the occupational locations of participants at the Southampton Conference is given in *Tables 7.1* and *7.2*. Comprehensive schools, in 1961, were few and far between. However, those schools attended by the majority of secondary students, that is, secondary modern schools, were not represented at all and girls schools were in a clear minority. The social class as well as the gender and 'ability' bias in the origins of SMP are clear.

SMP Book 1 was published in 1965, the year of the first CSE (Certificate of Secondary Education) examinations. SMP responded by producing a new series, *SMP Books A–H* (the 'lettered' books), the first volume of which was published in 1968. Geoffrey Howson, the editor of *SMP Books 1–3*, notes that:

> Significantly [the authors of *SMP Books A–H*] came from comprehensive schools, or from grammar or independent schools which wished to enter their average ability pupils or low attainers for the new examination. Rather than being a new course designed from first principles for those of 'average ability', the lettered books tended to present a subset of what was found in *SMP Books 1–5*. (Howson, 1987; p. 9)

173

Again, there is no inclusion of secondary modern schools. Nevertheless, Howson (writing with H.B. Griffiths) does seem to suggest, in an earlier statement, the possibility of a relationship between 'ability', as measured by the distinction between the 'numbered' and the 'lettered' series, on the one hand, and social class, on the other:

> With all types of pupil, the final teaching language may have to take account of their *social* language: it is no good using the language of mandarins to the children of factory workers, as studies by teachers of English have shown. For example, the early SMP texts T and T4 were written in the language of mathematical specialists intent on getting the mathematics right. These were rewritten in the language of grammar school boys, and the resulting books 1–5 were again rewritten (with modifications) in the language of 'CSE' children, as books A–H. (Griffiths and Howson, 1974; pp. 340–1)

In this extract, girls are, again, invisible and the identification between '"CSE" children' and 'the children of factory workers' is almost irresistible. Also encoded in the statement is a relationship between 'the language of the mandarins' and that of 'mathematical specialists', that is, the language of Head Masters Conference schools teachers (who wrote the materials) and, presumably, their male students.

As well as the 'numbered' and 'lettered' series, SMP material for the 11–16 age range included *SMP Cards I* and *II*, five booklets of supplementary questions and calculator-based supplements to the O-level material and *SMP Books X, Y* and *Z*, which provided a route to O-level from *SMP Book G*. The project also produced a scheme aimed at middle schools, *SMP 7–13*, an Advanced Level scheme (and associated publications on specific mathematical topics) and, against original intentions, a scheme for A-level Further Mathematics. SMP also produced and collaborated on the production of materials for use in other countries.

I want now to consider the second main development in the 11–16 age range, which resulted in the scheme which is the principal focus of my analysis, *SMP 11–16*.

The School Mathematics Project: SMP 11–16

The lettered series was highly successful, becoming, for a time, the most widely used textbook series in England (Ling, 1987). Despite the production of Books X, Y and Z, however, the scheme was not considered suitable for the 'upper ability' range. Nor had it been intended for use with 'lower ability' students. The corpus of materials for the 11–16 age group had all been derived from the original O-level course in rather an *ad hoc* fashion and, as John Ling comments, 'the whole collection was not organized in a way to make it satisfactory for comprehensive schools' (Ling, 1987; p. 39). SMP held a conference in Bristol in July 1976 to discuss the next development; Ling notes that:

Two major concerns emerged at the conference. One was a concern with the mathematical needs of the lower ability group, hitherto not catered for by the SMP material, the other was a concern with the organisation of course materials. It was felt strongly that material written for comprehensive schools should be flexible in use, allowing teachers to select and adapt to suit the needs of different groups of pupils. (Ling, 1987; p. 39)

In September 1977, John Ling was appointed team leader, responsible for the production of the new materials. Writing teams, initially comprising between fifty and sixty people, were set up in January 1978. According to Ling, the members of the team (which diminished in size as the work progressed) were mainly teachers in comprehensive schools. They were initially divided into five writing groups, each working on a specific topic, the list of topics comprising number, algebra, graphs, space, and statistics. The team was particularly concerned with the issue of 'learning difficulties' and received input from the Concepts in Secondary Mathematics and Science (CSMS) project based at Chelsea College[2]. Ling notes that the team's

... concern with learning difficulties became part of a much wider concern that mathematics should be *meaningful* to pupils. The considerable use of concrete materials and games derives from this concern, as does the extensive use of real life contexts which are authentic and which do not give rise to unnecessary 'noise' but facilitate a grasp of the underlying mathematical idea. (Ling, 1987; p. 40)

Ling does not provide any examples of 'real life contexts', but his brief description is redolent of Tammadge's description of the principle underlying his production of the 'numbered' texts. Ling's 'real life contexts', like Tammadge's problems, which were 'associated with the children themselves', were there to facilitate mathematical knowledge. The team decided upon an organized collection of booklets for the first two years of the scheme. Illustrators and writers met to work together on the booklets and the team received specialist help in respect of readability.

The booklet scheme comprises levels 1, 2, 3 and 4, each divided into sub-levels, (a) and (b), the latter level being at a marginally higher level of difficulty, but this is 'not so great as to prevent pupils doing some **(b)** before **(a)**', although an order is specified in some cases (publisher's publicity materials). Levels 2–4 each have an additional (e) or 'extension' level which is described in the publicity materials as intended:

2 The relevant report of this project is available in Hart (1981). This has been a highly influential study, boasting, on its cover, a representative sample of some 10 000 children. In fact, this claim is, arguably, disingenuous, given that the figure represents the aggregate of a large number of very much smaller samples. The study is also seriously flawed in a number of other respects, see O'Reilly (1990).

Table 7.3: *Numbers and length of SMP 11–16 booklets*

Level	8-page booklets	16-page booklets	Total pages	Total booklets
1(a)	3	5	104	8
1(b)	2	6	112	8
1	5	11	216	16
2(a)	2	9	160	11
2(b)	1	11	184	12
2(e)	3	4	88	7
2	6	24	432	30
3(a)	3	7	136	10
3(b)	2	7	128	9
3(e)	6	9	202	15
3	11	23	466	34
4(a)	6	3	96	9
4(b)	5	3	88	8
4(e)	11	7	200	18
4	22	13	384	35
Total	44	71	1498	115

. . . for pupils who would find little difficulty with the corresponding **(a)** and **(b)** booklets. They are not designed to be worked through as a block, but as challenging material to be used as appropriate.

The booklets all have the same basic cover design and are colour-coded according to the five topics: red = number; green = algebra[3]; blue = graphs; grey = space; mauve = statistics. Each booklet has either eight or sixteen pages; the numbers of booklets in each level and sub-level is given in *Table 7.3*. The shift in emphasis (in terms of number of booklets and number of pages) from the (a) and (b) sub-levels, in levels 1 and 2, to the (e) booklets, in levels 3 and 4 suggest that there is a widening of differentiation of students. Ling also notes that there is a 'widening gap between the mathematical levels of the "main" and the "extension" material' (p. 41) which militated against the production of a unitary 'level 5'. Thus:

> A split into differentiated courses was inevitable. In theory these differentiated courses could have taken the form of parallel booklet schemes rather than parallel series of textbooks. The argument in favour of textbooks was strongest in the case of the upper ability group. To be economical, a booklet scheme must contain units of work which can be done in many different orders, otherwise queuing will occur in the classroom and can only be avoided by having more copies of each unit. But as the subject progresses, topics become increasingly inter-related, and this restricts the number of possible

---

3 It might be noted, in passing, that the colour denoting algebra, perhaps the most 'esoteric' of the topics, is also the colour used to denote the G series for 'low ability' pupils in the third and subsequent years. By and large, the covers of the G books are not, in fact, green.

routes through them. Also, the writers who worked on the level 4 extension booklets on algebra felt that they were reaching the limit of what could be taught effectively in algebra, to all but the ablest of pupils, through the medium of the printed page. (Ling, 1987; p. 41)

Although the argument in favour of more conventional books rather than booklets was weaker in respect of the 'middle and lower levels of ability', there was some concern about overburdening schools with organizational complexity. Accordingly, it was decided to produce three parallel series of books, with the middle series branching into two after the first two books. The structure of the whole course is shown in *Figure 7.1*. The G series is clearly the most complex. There are eight books in the main G series compared with five in each of the B, B/R and Y tracks. The G series also includes Supplementary Booklets, Resource Packs, G Booklets, and Topic Booklets. In addition to the five main books, the B series shares the Topic Books with G, and the Y series has two 'extension' books (YE1 and YE2); there are no additional R materials[4].

These materials were produced by two sub-teams of writers, one working on the G books, the other on the B, R and Y books. The Teacher's Guides list nineteen G authors and twenty-one B/R/Y authors; six individuals are on both lists. John Ling, who was a B/R/Y author as well as being overall team leader, describes some of the differences between *SMP 11–16* and its predecessors:

There are important differences in mathematical content between SMP 11–16 and the earlier SMP courses. The syllabus of the G series, which has no counterpart in earlier SMP materials, conforms closely to the 'Foundation list' given in the Cockcroft Report. Compared with *SMP Books A–H, SMP Books 1–5*, etc., the syllabus content of the other SMP 11–16 series is reduced, this being more true at the middle and lower levels of ability. Algebra is confined to the 'traditional' algebra of generalised arithmetic; there is no mention, except in the extension materials for the Y series, of other 'algebras', and no work on sets or operations on sets. The explicit concept of function is introduced much later in SMP 11–16, and then only in the Y series. The concepts of ratio and proportionality are given greater weight. In geometry, the topic of transformations does not have the central importance it had in the original course (but there is no 'return to Euclid'). Spatial work in three dimensions is more prominent at all levels of ability. Matrices were included in the draft version of the Y series, but were later omitted. Some other innovations of the original course remain, such as work on probability and statistics, the latter being taken further to include practical work on sampling. (Ling, 1987; p. 43)

4   There are also worksheets associated with each series (the number of worksheets decreasing in the sequence G, B/R, Y) and more recent publications on specific topics, for example, including work on mathematics and microcomputers.

Figure 7.1 SMP 11–16 Scheme structure (from publishers publicity materials)

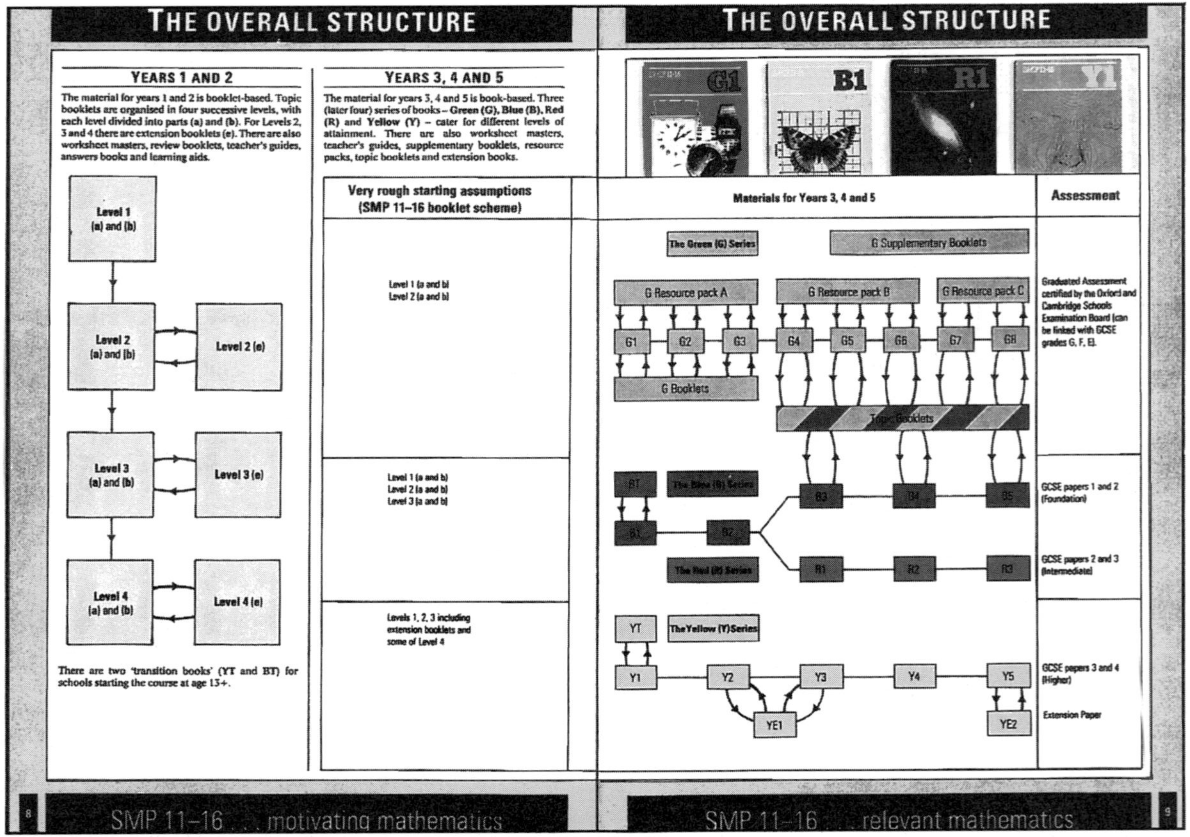

THE OVERALL STRUCTURE

YEARS 1 AND 2

The material for years 1 and 2 is booklet-based. Topic booklets are organised in four successive levels, with each level divided into parts (a) and (b). For Levels 2, 3 and 4 there are extension booklets (e). There are also worksheet masters, review booklets, teacher's guides, answers books and learning aids.

Level 1 (a) and (b)

Level 2 (a) and (b) → Level 2 (e)

Level 3 (a) and (b) → Level 3 (e)

Level 4 (a) and (b) → Level 4 (e)

There are two 'transition books' (YT and BT) for schools starting the course at age 13+.

YEARS 3, 4 AND 5

The material for years 3, 4 and 5 is book-based. Three (later four) series of books – Green (G), Blue (B), Red (R) and Yellow (Y) – cater for different levels of attainment. There are also worksheet masters, teacher's guides, supplementary booklets, resource packs, topic booklets and extension books.

Very rough starting assumptions (SMP 11–16 booklet scheme)

Level 1 (a and b)
Level 2 (a and b)

Level 1 (a and b)
Level 2 (a and b)
Level 3 (a and b)

Levels 1, 2, 3 including extension booklets and some of Level 4

THE OVERALL STRUCTURE

Materials for Years 3, 4 and 5

The Green (G) Series

G Resource pack A — G1 G2 G3
G Resource pack B — G4 G5 G6
G Resource pack C — G7 G8
G Booklets
G Supplementary Booklets

Topic booklets

The Blue (B) Series — B1 B2
The Red (R) Series — R1 R2 R3
The Yellow (Y) Series — Y1 Y2 Y3 Y4 Y5
YT — YE1 YE2
BT

Assessment

Graduated Assessment certified by the Oxford and Cambridge Schools Examination Board (can be linked with GCSE grades G, F, E)

GCSE papers 1 and 2 (Foundation)

GCSE papers 2 and 3 (Intermediate)

GCSE papers 3 and 4 (Higher)

Extension Paper

Two of the members of the G team (Afzal Ahmed and John Hersee) were also members of the Cockcroft Committee of Inquiry, the report of which was published in 1982, three years before the publication of Book G1. The 'Foundation list', referred to in the above extract was intended by the Cockcroft Committee to form a part of the curriculum for all students and 'by far the greater part of the syllabus for those pupils for whom CSE is not intended, that is those pupils in about the lowest 40 per cent of the range of attainment in mathematics' (Cockcroft, 1982; p. 134). This is the group targeted by the G series. The Committee also noted that:

> . . . as has been pointed out in official publications of various kinds over many years, formal algebra is not appropriate for lower-attaining pupils. (Cockcroft, 1982; p. 141)

Although it was believed 'that efforts should be made to discuss some algebraic ideas with all pupils' (*ibid*). Algebra is marked out in two of the extracts from Ling's paper which are quoted above. Ling argues that algebra 'is not needed in everyday life' (1987; p. 42) and that the 'return', in terms of wider applicability, on effort in algebraic manipulation is not apparent until one has mastered a number of techniques, so that the applicability of these techniques is unlikely to be immediately apparent. The principle that was employed in respect of algebra in the production of the *SMP 11–16* books is described in the following terms:

> As it is not known for certain which pupils will need algebra and which will not, and as it appears that algebraic skill needs to be built up over a period of time, the only safe policy seems to be to include algebra in the course to the extent that pupils can succeed at it, and to accept that it is likely to be unnecessary for many of them. (Ling, 1987; p. 42)

The singling out of algebra by Ling and by the Cockcroft Committee suggests that its treatment in *SMP 11–16* is worthy of some particular consideration in the analysis of the materials. This is further supported by the results of the content analysis which are presented in the next section of this chapter.

The G series was targeted at a group of students who were not expected to take either GCE O-level or CSE examinations. Ling states that:

> Working outside the framework of the public examination system gave the G series team the freedom to design a graduated assessment scheme for its target group. (Ling, 1987; p. 43)

The resulting assessment scheme looks very different from the conventional CSE or O-level examinations of the time and includes practical, oral and mental tests as well as written papers. The scheme is certificated by the Oxford and Cambridge Examinations Board. The summative assessment for students following the B, R and Y series was within the mainstream public examination system, and a joint GCE/CSE 16+ syllabus was set up for first examination in June 1985. This scheme also differed from other contemporary mathematics examinations at this level in that it included a 30 per cent coursework element. More recently, two National Curriculum GCSEs (General Certificate of Secondary Education) were approved by the Schools Examination and Assessment Council (SEAC): SMP 11–16 and SMP Graded Assessment.

Draft *SMP 11–16* materials were trialled in approximately thirty pilot schools from September 1980 following pre-draft trialling in authors' own schools. Following revision, the scheme proper began being used in schools in September 1983. The first 16+ awards were in 1985 and the first GCSE awards in 1989. Currently, *SMP 11–16* is by far the most popular secondary mathematics text in the United Kingdom, being used, according to the publishers (Cambridge University Press, private communication) by more than 50 per cent of schools. A National Curriculum Council Report (NCC, 1991) found that 48.5 per cent of schools sampled used the scheme and that the next most popular scheme was used in only 8 per cent of the sample schools. There is also a Welsh language version of the scheme and a Dutch scheme which is based on the English materials. There is some considerable diversity in the form of current secondary mathematics texts, ranging from the workcard-based SMILE[5] scheme to the more 'traditional' *ST(P) Mathematics*, published by Stanley Thorne. Nevertheless, the popularity of *SMP 11–16* clearly lends credibility to the assertion that it is representative of a dominant position in school mathematics.

Having given a brief discussion of the background and structure of the *SMP 11–16* materials, I shall move on to an introduction to their analysis.

A Preliminary Content Analysis

The language of description which was introduced in Chapter 6 is designed to reveal the nature and distribution of practices with respect to positions within the context of an activity, in this case school mathematics. This structure of an activity is (re)produced through its texts in the (re)production and distribution of message and the positioning of voices. A decision has been taken to analyse *SMP 11–16* because of its singular popularity within UK secondary school mathematics. The principal method of analysis which is to be employed is semiotic. This form of analysis entails the elaboration of denotations and connotations incorporated into the text via a detailed reading. The total number of pages in the Levels 1–4 booklets and the four series of books (G, B, R and Y including the Teacher's Guides and the two extension

5 Secondary Mathematics Individualised Learning Experience: an Inner London Education Authority (ILEA) scheme which first appeared in the early 1970s. A card from this scheme is discussed in Chapter 3.

books, YE1 and YE2) is 4918. In addition to this, there are ancillary materials and Guides associated with the booklets and the additional G and B materials shown in *Figure 7.1*. Clearly, a detailed semiotic analysis of such a large body of text is not plausible. It was therefore necessary to sample the material.

I decided to focus attention on the G and Y series of books, because it is in the division between these two series that differences in the structuring of message in relation to voice will be most explicit. Whereas the booklet scheme acknowledges differences between students in terms of pacing, many individual booklets (all those in Levels 1 and 2 with the exception of 2(e)) are intended to be attempted by all students and all of the (a) and (b) booklets in Levels 1 to 3 are intended to be attempted by the majority of students. At the start of the third year of the course, however, the scheme effectively divides students into G-students, B-students and Y-students. The greatest differentiation within the mainstream should therefore be visible through a comparison of the G and Y series[6]. Even with this restriction, however, there remains a need to sample. I decided, firstly, to concentrate my attention on the main series of books in each case, that is, books G1–8 and Y1–5, together with the relevant Teacher's Guides. I decided to organize the analysis such that it both illustrates the language of description and reveals the 'findings' of the reading of the SMP texts that the language produces.

My intention is to begin with a general overview of the two series in terms of the proportion of each book and of each chapter that consists of esoteric domain text. Each chapter in the G and Y series was analysed in order to produce an estimation of the number of pages (in units of one quarter of a page) of esoteric domain text. The details of the procedure that was employed are given in Dowling (1995a). Essentially, however, esoteric domain text is recognized according to the following principle:

> The significations carried by a particular section of text (ie excluding connectives etc) are mathematically specialized in terms of both expression and content, that is, they are strongly classified with respect to the non-mathematical.

Clearly, it is being asserted that mathematically specialized significations are recognizable by me. This is not unproblematic, because the esoteric domain is accessed only through its realizations in the text. That is, the esoteric domain can neither be operationally defined *a priori*, nor, because of its extensiveness, can its possibilities be listed exhaustively. The esoteric domain must be elaborated in the reading of the text. However, this part of the analysis of the SMP texts is intended to assist in providing a general picture of an extensive text. This would be impossible using a closer reading.

---

6 It might be argued that it would be useful to make a comparison between the Y and B books, since these were produced by the same team of authors, whereas only a subset of this team worked on the G books. However, the intention of this analysis is not to retrieve the intentions of the authors. It is the activity of school mathematics generally which gives authority to *SMP 11–16* within which scheme this authority is to be revealed.

Since the analysis in the chapters which follow will incorporate much closer reading of the text, it is felt that some play can be allowed in terms of validity and reliability, here. The results of this chapter are, in other words, to a certain extent triangulated by the finer grained analysis in the chapters which follow. Furthermore, it is also clear that specialized text is more easily recognizable in mathematics than in many other areas, sociology, say. It may be that the kind of quantitative analysis which is presented in this chapter would not be possible in sociology without extensive preliminary close analysis.

Even in mathematics, however, practical difficulties can arise. One such difficulty concerns the distinction between number and quantity. The distinction between number and quantity (or between number as noun and number as adjective) is an important point of splitting between the esoteric and the non-esoteric. Thus, for the purposes of this analysis, the general rule was applied that the inclusion or exclusion of dimensions will effect a shift from esoteric to non-esoteric or vice versa, respectively. Thus, if the text moves from £3.4285714 to 3.4285714, it is considered to have shifted into the esoteric domain (unless there are contradicting significations). Clearly, however, there are occasions when quantities are incorporated into esoteric domain text, specifically, in the topic of geometry, where number is used to quantify lengths and angles, etc. Thus, degrees and centimetres occur within esoteric domain text. However, other units of length were generally taken to indicate a non-esoteric domain referent[7].

From the analysis we can describe a coarse measure of the relative visibility of the esoteric domain in each of the Y and G series in terms of the proportion of the text that constitutes esoteric domain message. This measure clearly has face validity as an indicator of the potential level of operation in the texts of the abstracting strategies. This is because it is only within the esoteric domain that the principles and metonymic connectivity of the discourse is fully available, as was argued in Chapter 6.

From the results shown in *Tables 7.4* and *7.5* it can be seen that more than 40 per cent of the Y text, but less than 10 per cent of the G text is within the esoteric domain. Furthermore, the Y series increases its proportion of esoteric domain text in that the figure for the first three books in the series is a little below 40 per cent, whilst books Y4 and Y5 are both above 50 per cent. The G series, on the other hand, decreases its esoteric domain representation: the average for the first five books in the series is 12.8 per cent and that for the final three books is 3.1 per cent.

Thus, the abstracting potential in the Y series exceeds to a significantly greater extent that of the G series. Furthermore, this potential increases as the Y series progresses, suggesting that its reader voice might appropriately be described as an apprenticed voice. In the G series, by contrast, the abstracting

---

7 Geometrical generalizations are independent of absolute dimensions and centimetres are conventionally used, presumably because of the size of the textbook page. The G series sometimes uses centimetres and millimetres rather than the decimal form of centimetres.

Table 7.4: SMP 11–16 *Y series: Esoteric domain text*

Book	Total number of chapter pages	Total number of esoteric domain pp.	% of text in esoteric domain
Y1	129	47.25	36.6
Y2	142	53.5	37.7
Y3	136	52.0	38.2
Y4	143	73.5	51.4
Y5	125	68.0	54.4
Y series overall	675	294.25	43.4

Table 7.5: SMP 11–16 *G series: Esoteric domain text*

Book	Total number of chapter pages	Total number of esoteric domain pp.	% of text in esoteric domain
G1	44	6.25	14.2
G2	49	9.0	18.4
G3	47	7.75	16.5
G4	49	2.0	4.1
G5	50	5.5	11.0
G6	52	0.5	1.0
G7	51	1.75	3.4
G8	48	2.5	5.2
G series overall	390	35.25	9.0

Table 7.6: *Esoteric domain text in Y series chapters*

% of text in esoteric domain	No. of chapters (n = 75)
0–10	24
11–20	3
21–30	8
31–40	3
41–50	3
51–60	5
61–70	5
71–80	5
81–90	9
91–100	10

potential is far lower than in the Y series to begin with and decreases as the series progresses. This clearly has face validity as an indicator of a dependent reader voice.

The proportion of the text which distributes esoteric domain message is not evenly distributed between the chapters within each series. The distribution for the Y books is shown in *Table 7.6*. This information suggests a polarizing between two sets of chapters. Twenty-four Y chapters comprise 10 per cent or less esoteric domain text. This is less than or approximately equal

Table 7.7: Y series chapters having minimum esoteric domain text

Chapter	Chapter title	% of text in esoteric domain
Y1.02	Loci	9
Y1.08	Investigations	0
Y1.10	Percentage	6
Y1.12	Probability	3
Y2.04	Rates	0
Y2.07	Investigations (1)	0
Y2.08	Distributions	10
Y2.10	Points, lines and planes	7
Y2.15	Investigations (2)	0
Y2.16	Periodic graphs	0
Y2.17	Probability	3
Y3.04	Percentage (1)	0
Y3.06	Investigations (1)	0
Y3.07	TV programmes survey	0
Y3.11	Percentage (2)	0
Y3.12	Investigations (2)	0
Y3.15	Problems in planning	0
Y3.17	Distributions	0
Y4.01	Selection and arrangements	0
Y4.08	Types of proportionality	8
Y4.13	Optimisations	0
Y4.14	Sampling	8
Y5.02	Optimisations	0
Y5.06	The Earth	0

to the mean esoteric domain text per G series book (9.0 per cent). Nineteen Y chapters comprise more than 80 per cent esoteric domain text. This amount is more than the approximate minimum of non-esoteric domain text in a G book (81.6 per cent in G2). The Y chapters having minimum esoteric domain text are listed in *Table 7.7* and those having maximum esoteric domain text are listed in *Table 7.8*.

Of the nineteen chapters represented in *Table 7.8*, eleven explicitly concern algebra[8]. On the other hand, there are only two chapters in the entire G series which relate explicitly to this topic (chapters G1.03 and G6.01, both titled 'Formulas'). The G chapters remain almost entirely outside of the esoteric domain apart from a section of less than a half of a page in G6.01. This section relates to the equivalence of different forms of expression of the arithmetic operation 'division' and not specifically to algebra. The high representation of the topic 'algebra' in *Table 7.8* marks it out as a key topic of the esoteric domain. This is consistent with the singling out of this topic by John Ling which was mentioned earlier in this chapter. The status of this topic is also confirmed by its virtual exclusion from the G series other than in the context of non-esoteric domain text.

There are a number of other chapters in the Y series which signal algebra in their titles, but which are less confined within the esoteric domain. These

8 These chapters are: Y2.05, Y2.09, Y2.11, Y4.03, Y4.05, Y4.09, Y4.15, Y4.17, Y5.03, Y5.05, Y5.07.

Table 7.8: Y series chapters having maximum esoteric domain text

Chapter	Chapter title	% of text in esoteric domain
Y2.05	Algebraic expressions	93
Y2.09	Re-arranging formulas (1)	83
Y2.11	Re-arranging formulas (2)	100
Y2.13	Area	88
Y3.13	Right-angled triangles	87
Y4.03	Linear equations	100
Y4.05	Algebraic fractions	86
Y4.06	Vectors	94
Y4.07	Sequences (1)	92
Y4.09	Manipulating formulas	88
Y4.11	Sequences (2)	100
Y4.15	Functions	89
Y4.16	Three dimensions	81
Y4.17	Quadratic functions and equations	85
Y5.03	Algebraic fractions	100
Y5.05	The sine and cosine functions	100
Y5.07	Equations and graphs	89
Y5.09	Iterations	98
Y5.12	Vector geometry	97

Table 7.9: Y series algebra chapters

Chapter	Chapter title	% of chapter in esoteric domain
Y1.03	The language of algebra	43
Y1.09	Brackets	80
Y2.01	Relationships	36
Y2.05	Algebraic expressions	93
Y2.09	Re-arranging formulas (1)	83
Y2.11	Re-arranging formulas (2)	100
Y2.12	Proportionality	38
Y2.14	Linear equations and inequalities	35
Y3.02	Linear relationships	67
Y3.08	Direct and inverse proportionality	25
Y3.16	Linear equations	55
Y4.03	Linear equations	100
Y4.05	Algebraic fractions	86
Y4.08	Types of proportionality	8
Y4.09	Manipulating formulas	88
Y4.15	Functions	89
Y4.17	Quadratic functions and equations	85
Y5.03	Algebraic fractions	100
Y5.05	The sine and cosine functions	100
Y5.07	Equations and graphs	89
Y5.11	Inequalities	67

chapters, together with the eleven algebra chapters from *Table* 7.8, are listed in *Table* 7.9. As is illustrated by the information in *Table* 7.9, the algebra chapters exhibit a wide spread in terms of their proportion of esoteric domain text, one (but only one, chapter Y4.08) also being included in *Table* 7.7 which lists the Y chapters having minimum esoteric domain text. We might infer from this (on the basis of titles only, at this point) that, in the Y series, not only is the esoteric domain in relation to algebra highly visible, but so is the gaze of this topic. This is crucial. Algebra may be glossed as the topic in school mathematics concerned with the structure of systems which is explored and described through the introduction of variables. Algebra, in other words, is concerned with objectification, it comprises what might be described as a language of description (and is described as a 'language' in Y1.03) which facilitates a degree of context independence[9]. The other topics represented in *Table 7.8* are: trigonometry (two chapters); vectors (two chapters); other geometry (two chapters); and sequences (two chapters).

In contrast to algebra, the chapters signalling (by their titles) the compound topic 'probability and statistics' are almost all listed in *Table 7.7*, which comprises those chapters having not more than 10 per cent of esoteric domain text[10]. These seven chapters are supplemented in the Y series by just one more, chapter Y4.10 which falls only just outside of the criterion for inclusion in *Table 7.7*, having only 11 per cent of esoteric domain text. However, the whole of the esoteric domain text in Y4.10 concerns the addition of fractions, and is not explicitly related to probability. Thus, all eight chapters concerned with statistics and probability effectively fall within the category of minimum (not more than 10 per cent) esoteric domain text. Statistics and probability are, it seems, presented without theory. These topics represent, in a sense, the limits of visible pedagogy in the Y series. The mathematical objects that constitute the interpretants constructed by the statistical and probabilistic gaze are never elaborated so that the message may appear to be concerned with essential properties of that world, but not with mathematics. As mentioned in Chapter 6, this constitutes a rare instance of exclusion of the apprenticed voice from the esoteric domain and may be appropriately interpreted as a career pacing strategy.

Also included in *Table 7.7* are all five chapters headed 'Investigations' and all three headed 'Percentages'. These eight chapters are in the first three books in the Y series. There are two chapters concerning rates and proportion, two concerning geometry and one concerning graphs, all of which topics appear in other chapters having greater esoteric domain text. There are four chapters, 'Problems in planning', 'Optimisations' (two chapters) and 'The Earth', the titles of which index the public domain.

The distribution of esoteric domain text in the G books is shown in *Table 7.10*. Of the fifty-nine G series chapters, only twenty-three enter the esoteric domain. The amount of text which is esoteric domain in these twenty-three chapters ranges from 2.3 per cent (G1.01) to 66.7 per cent (G1.06 and G2.04). These twenty-three chapters are listed in *Table 7.11*. As is clear from *Table 7.11*, the chapter titles in the G series are sometimes rather more ambiguous than the Y chapter titles in terms of their indexing of esoteric domain topics. In deciding upon which topics are represented, it

9   Arithmetic, of course, also does this, but in a much more limited way.
10   These chapters are: Y1.12, Y2.08, Y2.17, Y3.07, Y3.17, Y4.01, Y4.14.

Table 7.10: Esoteric domain text in G series chapters

% of text in esoteric domain	No. of chapters (n = 59)
0–10	43
11–20	5
21–30	5
31–40	3
41–50	1
51–60	0
61–70	2
71–80	0
81–90	0
91–100	0

Table 7.11: G chapters incorporating esoteric domain message

Chapter	Chapter title	% of text in esoteric domain
G1.01	Estimating and scales	2.3
G1.05	Chains	28.6
G1.06	Calculate . . .	66.7
G2.03	Working backwards	37.5
G2.04	Polygon patterns	66.7
G2.05	Further beyond the point	16.7
G2.06	Button pressing	3.1
G2.07	Percentages	11.1
G3.02	Percentage scales	41.7
G3.03	Area of rectangles	36.4
G3.05	Carrying on	21.4
G4.02	Thousandths	29.2
G4.05	Long and short numbers	5.0
G5.02	Times 10, times 100	28.1
G5.04	Dividing by 10 and 100	35.0
G5.06	Percentages and your calculator	25.0
G6.01	Formulas	4.2
G6.08	Averages (2)	8.3
G7.02	Sixteenths and all that!	5.0
G7.03	Circles	18.8
G8.01	Calculating well	20.0
G8.03	Large numbers	16.7
G8.08	Cones, cylinders and spheres	10.0

was therefore necessary to refer to the chapter contents. The topics represented in the twenty-three G chapters are listed in *Table 7.12*.

The text represented in *Table 7.12* represents only 9 per cent of the G series text, 35.25 pages in all. Nevertheless, more than one-third of this is concerned with arithmetic operations and more than one-sixth with the representation of number (mainly decimal representation). Percentages and statistics are also included here: these topics are amongst those with minimum esoteric domain text in the Y series, although two of the Y chapters on statistics and probability have comparable esoteric domain text in the respective chapters (10 per cent of Y2.08 and 8 per cent of Y4.14 compared with 8.3 per cent of G6.08).

Table 7.12: *G series topics incorporating esoteric domain message*

Topic	No. of chapters	No. of pages	% of chapter
arithmetic operations	8	13.0	3.3
representation of number	6	6.75	1.7
geometry	3	6.0	1.5
percentages	3	5.0	1.3
area	1	4.0	1.0
statistics	1	0.25	0.1
linear measurement	1	0.25	0.1
Total	23	35.25	9.0

Algebra is completely absent from *Table 7.12* as are vectors, sequences and trigonometry: all of these are represented in *Table 7.8* as amongst those topics with maximum esoteric domain text in the Y books. There is evidence, then, that a number of those topics which involve the most esoteric domain text in the Y books do not occupy esoteric domain text in the G series. Correspondingly, percentages and statistics, which occupy very little esoteric domain text in the Y series, are amongst those maximizing esoteric domain text in the G books. This chiastic prioritizing in the Y and G schemes is another consistency with the description of the former scheme as apprenticing and the latter as constructing dependency with respect to esoteric mathematics: where the Y books apprentice, the G books render dependent; where the Y books constitute dependency, the G books apprentice. This will be a familiar finding in the analysis in the following chapters.

This quantitative analysis has limitations in terms of validity and reliability, as has been noted. In addition, the distance of the analysis from the substance of the text must also place limitations on the delicacy of the description that it produces. Nevertheless, it does reveal a considerable difference between the Y and G series in terms of the amount of 'textual time' spent in the esoteric domain. More than 40 per cent in the Y books, but less than 10 per cent in the G series is within the esoteric domain. In other words, 90 per cent of the G series concerns or is expressed in terms of something other than mathematics. The esoteric domain is all but invisible in the G series. Furthermore, the proportion of esoteric domain text increases as the Y series progresses, whilst it decreases in the G series, so that there is what might be described as a general career towards the esoteric domain in Y and towards the public domain in G. Finally, certain topics are marked in terms of their high degree of representation within the esoteric domain in the Y books; algebra, in particular, stands out in this respect. Other topics, notably, probability and statistics and percentages, minimize esoteric domain text within the Y books. In terms of their representation in the G books, however, there is a degree of reversal of the relationship between topic and domain. Whilst it is the case that the absolute amount of esoteric domain text is very small, statistics and, particularly, percentages occupy rare esoteric domain text within the G series, whilst algebra is entirely absent from this domain. Certain topics occupying maximum esoteric domain text within the Y series, notably, vectors, sequences and trigonometry, are excluded from the G series altogether.

This comparison of the two series of books has revealed evidence of a reversal of priorities in terms of domain, in aggregate amount of text, in respect of career, and in terms of particular topics. These distinctions between the series are consistent with the claim that where the Y series is apprenticing, the G series is constituting dependency. The careers of their respective reader voices move, it would seem, in opposite directions. Ultimately, the Y reader is to be identified with the esoteric domain subject of the activity and the G reader with its public domain objects.

The purpose of this chapter has been to provide some background information on the School Mathematics Project and, in particular, to the first edition of its current main secondary school mathematics text, *SMP 11–16*. In this introduction, the middle class and masculine base of at least the early activities of the project are made quite apparent. The comments by John Ling on the *SMP 11–16* materials also mark out algebra as mathematically important but, in some sense, 'difficult'.

I have also introduced an initial coarse grained analysis of the Y and G materials which has begun to characterize these texts in relation to the language of description introduced in Chapter 6. This analysis has suggested that the topic algebra, in particular, is worthy of closer analytic scrutiny. In the next chapter, I shall present a close and comparative reading of the first chapter in each of the Y and G series which is explicitly concerned with algebra[11].

11 In Dowling (1995a) I have included a similar close comparative analysis of the first chapter in each series which deals explicitly with probability.

Chapter 8

The Textualizing of Algebra

In this chapter I shall present a close and comparative reading of the first chapters in each of the *SMP 11–16* Y and G series which explicitly concern algebra. These chapters are Y1.03 and G1.03. In Chapter 7, algebra was indexed as having a particular significance in the scheme. I have therefore decided to use the analysis of these chapters in order to begin to socialize (apprentice) the reader into the use of the language of description that was introduced in Chapter 6. Thus, in the presentation, there is a sense in which the language of description is being presented as 'emerging' from the text. This is also intended to represent the importance played by induction in the production of the language of description. This was discussed briefly in Chapter 6, but could not be illustrated in its strongly deductive format. In following the reading, it may be helpful to refer back to *Figure 6.5*, which shows in diagrammatic form the main structure of the textual level of the language of description.

I should note that there is some tension between the demands that the reading be 'close' and that it be 'comparative'. By 'close' reading, I mean, simply, that the reading follows the order of the empirical text and that a substantial amount of the empirical text be explicitly referred to in the reading. However, there are two textual components (the G and Y books) and I intend that the reading should highlight the differences between them, that is, that the reading should be 'comparative'. Clearly, comparisons are to be made in terms of my language of description. This entails that I shall need, upon occasion, to prioritize the categories of the language over the strict sequencing of the text. The difficulty in reconciling the demands relating to close and comparative readings is, to a certain extent, exacerbated by the fact that the Y chapter is rather more extensive than the G chapter with which it is being compared.

I noted, in Chapter 7, that algebra is prevalent amongst those chapters in the Y series which have the highest proportion of esoteric domain text. 'Algebra' was glossed, in that chapter, as 'that topic in school mathematics which is concerned with the structure of systems which is explored and described through the introduction of variables'. School algebra is often particularly concerned with the manipulation of formulas (and other variable expressions) and the solution of equations. It is difficult to find a single chapter, in the Y series, which does not involve the use of symbolically expressed variables to highlight an abstracted structure (although a few, such as Y1.02, do not take this very far). By contrast, the G series is almost completely free of the use of such variables[1] and only two G chapters (G1.03 and G6.01, both titled 'Formulas') explicitly involve algebra in their titles. This contrast raises two issues. Firstly, it indicates that the reader voices constructed by the Y and G series are respectively included and excluded from the topic of algebra by the distributing strategies which are deployed in the *SMP 11–16* text. That is, the range of esoteric domain message is relatively expanded and limited, respectively, by these texts. This is clearly consistent with the intentions of the authors as discussed in Chapter 7.

Secondly, however, insofar as algebra constitutes the 'language' of mathematics which facilitates the exploration and description of structure in esoteric domain topics, exclusion of the G reader voice must also tend to delimit the abstracting potential. Thus, the treatment of algebra by these texts would seem to push towards generalization, in the Y series, and localizing by the G books.

The first two sections of the present chapter describe the introductory sections in the Y and G chapters, respectively. The third section contrasts the subsequent development in the Y chapter with the continued rehearsal in the G chapter. The fourth section compares the use of a particular symbol used by both texts. Here, it is necessary to consider a second chapter in Book G1 in order to sustain an optimum comparison between the texts. The fifth section contrasts the insistence upon mathematical convention, by the Y text, with the idiolectical description of mathematics in the G chapter. The sixth section describes the introduction of an exposition on calculators in the Y1 chapter and compares this with the treatment of calculators in the final book in the G series. The seventh section returns to a comparison of Y1.03 and G1.03, this time in respect of the development of the gaze. Finally, the eighth section compares the endings of the Y and G chapters.

'The Language of Algebra'

Y1.03 is titled *The Language of Algebra*. Its first section is called 'A review of some shorthand' and involves a number of textual strategies. Firstly, the section is exclusively typeset, foregrounding the symbolic mode of signification. As was discussed in Chapter 6, the prevalence of the symbolic mode has face validity as an indicator of generalizing strategies.

Secondly, the section is a celebration of esoteric domain competence. The section is labelled as a 'review', but the initial exposition is not a straightforward repetition of something which has gone before, but an extension of the currency of that which has already been acquired:

---

1 All significations are variables in that they are essentially repeatable, that is, they can stand for any instance of any of their connotations or denotations. The use here, however, is restricted to the use of specifically mathematical significations, normally expressed non-verbally (*e.g.* using letters).

The language of mathematics is international.
You may not know what language this problem is written in,
but the algebra is the same as you would find in an English book.

      I.82.   Sa se arate ca expresia

$$E = 4n^2 - 2n + 13$$

        nu se imparte exact la 289, pentru nici un numar n intreg.

           (Y1, p. 21; accents omitted)

The reader must be able to recognize as algebra the specifically mathematical expressions included in this extract in order to be able to make sense of the exposition. S/he is constructed as being able to do this because the extract is apparently taken from a school textbook and because algebraic strings have arisen before in the scheme (hence 'review' in the title of the section)[2]. The extract given above is followed by an extract in Japanese and another in Arabic, the latter (but, unexpectedly, not the former) requiring some transliteration in the English text. These are, predominantly, positioning strategies, because there is relatively little elaboration of the content of the message.

Essentially, the authorial voice is affiliating to an international community of mathematicians: 'The language of mathematics is international'. The section carries an internationalizing of mathematics itself, specifically, esoteric domain mathematics, which is elevated above particular linguistic differences. Algebra has the status of a language which is, furthermore, international and here it is, appearing in an unidentified, European language, in Japanese and in Arabic. 'Language', in the chapter heading, might signify simply a code, like a computer language; however, the play on the word language in the first two lines of the above extract and the extracts in Japanese and Arabic emphasize 'language' and 'international' as foregrounded significations. The reader voice is also being identified as a competent student within an international community of competent students and already has access to some of the principles which will enable them to recognize the international language of the mathematical message. The reader, then, is being identified as a potential author, which is to say, as an apprentice.

To the extent that the foreign language extracts are expressed in non-mathematical terms (the foreign language words and symbols are not unambiguously mathematical since they cannot be recognized as such within an English language context) and signify a non-mathematical content (foreignness) they are located within the public domain[3]. However, the extracts also implicate specifically and recognizably mathematical signifiers (the letters 'x'

2 The text does not state that the 'problem' is taken from a school textbook, but it appears to concern the solution of a quadratic equation which is compatible with school mathematics at a slightly more advanced level than that signified by Y1; the item reference, 'I.82.', is also associated with textbooks.

3 Public domain refers to the domain of weak classification of mathematical message in terms of expression and content and so does not necessarily imply general familiarity: in most instances, public domain message does have a wider semantic currency than esoteric domain message, but this is clearly not the case in these instances.

and 'y' are conventionally italicized) which are examples of (*i.e.* they are metonyms for) algebra, to which attention is also drawn in the text: in this respect, the extracts are within the esoteric domain. The foreign language extracts thus carry contradictory significations.

Within the textual context, there is no elaboration of the public domain element other than the note that 'Arabic is written from right to left' and an associated ironic 'translation' of the Arabic algebra which is reprinted as mirror writing. This ironic 'translation' effects an alienation of the public domain context (the foreign language) thus diminishing its priority. The irony also emphasizes the foreign connotation of the extract and so enhances the signification of mathematics as international. Mathematics extends even to the most foreign parts, unreached, we might suppose, by other, less international disciplines. The esoteric domain significations, on the other hand, are elaborated within the English text. Furthermore, the final quarter of the page (after the mirror writing) is more or less exclusively esoteric domain and so confirms the priority of the esoteric over the public domain. This is a further affiliation which lends esoteric domain mathematics a universal currency: it doesn't matter what the *words* in the extracts mean, the extracts themselves all contain metonyms for the language of algebra.

The section also carries an imperative invitation into the esoteric domain practices of the international community of mathematicians through the indexical emphasizing (in red print) of its agreed rules of expression:

> It would be confusing if everyone used their own shorthand, so mathematicians have agreed that

$$3a \text{ means } 3 \times a \qquad\qquad a^2 \text{ means } a \times a$$
$$ab \text{ means } a \times b \qquad\qquad a^3 \text{ means } a \times a \times a$$
$$\frac{a}{b} \text{ means } a \div b \qquad\qquad 2ab \text{ means } 2 \times a \times b$$

(Y1, p. 21; rules of expression emphasized by red print in original)

The rules employ different variable labels from the preceding exposition (which implicate n and x and y, but not a or b). This marks them out in the text as does their emphasis in red print. Both of these contribute to their exemplary status, as does their subsequent rehearsal in specific realizations (*i.e.* tasks). The rules are thus produced as general features of the 'language', rather than particular statements.

This exposition is followed by task A1 which constitutes an imperative action in which these rules of expression are rehearsed by the reader, confirming her/him as an apprentice mathematician. This is, again, an affiliation of the authorial voice and an identification of the reader voice with the international community of mathematicians. The alienation of the public domain and the rehearsal of esoteric domain forms constitutes an introductory movement from the public to the esoteric domain, confirming the reader as a neophyte mathematician who must speak the agreed language.

Figure 8.1   SMP 11–16 Book G1 (p. 23)

3 Formulas

A Hiring

Peter works for the
Blagdon Hire Company.
They hire out ladders,
paint sprayers, floor cleaners
and so on.

You can hire them for
a number of days.

When you bring them back
Peter has to work out how much you pay.

There is a card for each item the company hires out.
On each card there is a machine chain.
The machine chain shows how to work out the cost of hiring the item.
Here is the card for a paint sprayer.

A1 (a) Copy the machine chain
for the paint sprayer.
Write it like this.

(b) How much does it cost to hire a paint sprayer
for 3 days?

A2 How much does it cost to hire a paint sprayer for 4 days?

A3 Work out how much it costs to hire a paint sprayer
(a) for 6 days   (b) for 5 days   (c) for 7 days

23

'Formulas'

Chapter 3 of Book G1 — *Formulas* — is quite different. To begin with, half
of the first page of the G chapter (*Figure 8.1*) is taken up by cartoons and
drawings. This page thereby contrasts with the Y page by its foregrounding
of the iconic rather than the symbolic. As was argued in Chapter 6, the

prevalence of the iconic mode has face validity as an indicator of localizing strategies. This is supported by the content of the first cartoon and by the opening exposition which, together, constitute a closed narrative by specifying the public domain work setting in some detail. In the cartoon, the reader is shown the front of the company building and a man who appears to be the proprietor. The exposition introduces Peter (the main character of this part of the chapter) and gives some details regarding the nature of the company business and of Peter's role. Peter is also represented in the cartoon at the bottom of the page.

The cartoon of the 'Blagdon Hire Company' — open for business — is at the head of the chapter, almost on a level with and much more prominent than the chapter title. This is a scene setter, announcing the public domain setting of the chapter far more forcefully than the title announces its esoteric domain topic (six of the seven pages of the chapter concern the Blagdon Hire Company). As is the case with the mirror writing in the Y text, the cartoon incorporates irony. The display window of the Blagdon Hire Company denotes a manager wearing a suit, what might be a watch and chain and a bow tie — unlikely garb in a contemporary establishment of this kind. The display also includes a broom amongst the items for hire. It is not at all clear who might want to hire a broom; the manager appears to be looking at the broom with raised eyebrows, perhaps he wonders what it is doing there as well.

These ironies effect an alienation of the public domain setting. However, the irony in the Y text is resolved through a prioritizing of the esoteric over the public domain. The ironies in the G text can be resolved only within the public domain, because there is no esoteric domain text. The irony signifies 'not this', allowing a connotative signification to come to the foreground. This connotative signification is a mapping of the G text onto comic literature: the setting is transformed into a joke. The work setting which apparently motivates almost the entire G chapter is satirized at the very instant of its announcement.

A drawing of a 'card', incorporating an algorithm used in the company and, alongside it, what is presumably a paint sprayer neatly bisect the page and bisect the content, exposition/tasks. The card incorporates *descriptive domain* significations through the use of the 'flowchart' symbols referred to as 'machines'. The strong classification (with respect to the non-mathematical) of the flowchart formula is muted by its appearance on a public domain icon. Both the formula itself (incorporating non-mathematical expressions) and its signifying mode (as manuscript on a drawing) are markedly less mathematical than the formulae in the Y text, discussed above. The G text thus draws away from the descriptive domain significations (the flowchart symbols), again foregrounding the public domain. The text moves on from the card (which is further localized by the drawing of the paint sprayer) to an instruction to the reader to copy it. Accompanying this instruction is a drawing denoting the appearance of the current page of the reader's exercise book when they are part way through copying the algorithm. A pencil (not a pen) point is poised in mid-trace. The second part of this task asks how much it costs to hire the paint sprayer for 3 days and includes a cartoon showing Peter thinking about the problem. The final two tasks on the page require the reader to rehearse the same algorithm for different numbers of days.

Peter represents an objectified voice. He appears as a junior in the company (Peter works 'for' the company, the proprietor is shown in the cartoon) and so stands in a possible career relationship with the reader: *you might be doing this 'manual' job when you leave school.* Metonyms that are thereby attached to Peter thus ionize the character with respect to the reader. This identification is sustained in the rest of the chapter, where the other characters are at a greater semantic distance. The manager and supervisor are Peter's superiors in age and rank and all of the hirers have titles (Mr, Mrs, Miss) rather than first names; Mr Evans appears to be the school caretaker[4]. The identification of the reader voice with the object, Peter, locates the former within the network of public domain relationships which Peter occupies. This is reinforced by the considerable amount of detail which is given regarding this public domain setting. In addition, the descriptive domain significations are, as I have suggested above, backgrounded in relation to the public domain setting: the flowchart symbols are presented as if they were public domain signs. The overall effect is the projection of the reader voice into the public domain narrative. This narrative is a plausible realization of the reader's own future. The text objectifies the reader. Additionally, the public domain context is satirized, as has been noted, so that the reader voice is, at least partially, shifted within the public domain to be identified with another object, the reader of comic literature. This is an infantilizing identification/objectification.

Mathematically, we might describe the formula that is used in the tasks as linear in one variable and might abstract it as $C = An + B$. This is the mathematical form of all of the formulae in the chapter, yet there is no exposition concerning either its esoteric domain structure or (more pertinently) its public domain origin. It is not clear, from the text, why this particular formula should be used by the Blagdon Hire Company to price the hire of its paint sprayer (and, indeed for all of its hirings). There is no principling, either in esoteric or public domain terms. The message is entirely procedural.

Both the Y and the G pages incorporate exemplars. However, whilst the algebraic recognition rules of the Y text have general significance within

---

4 The reader identification with Peter is somewhat confused by the form of address used in the above extract: '*You* can hire them for a number of days . . . When *you* bring them back *Peter* has to work out how much *you* pay'. However, the strong career association between Peter and the reader, the fact that the reader is to do Peter's job (*i.e.* calculate the cost of hiring), the clear semantic distance between all of the hirers and the reader certainly outweigh the apparent addressing of the reader as hirer. In fact, an alternative to 'you' would possibly render the exposition too specific for an exemplar (an individual's name might be used which would also involve an introduction) or, perhaps, too vague (by using, 'someone'). Thus 'you' is being used as a sort of generalized other which is, nevertheless, not too alien: the reader might, after all, become a hirer in due course; all of the hirings do, after all, connote manual labour.

the esoteric domain, the G exemplar (the algorithm which appears on the 'card', in the 'think bubble' and, partially, on the exercise book fragment) is highly limited in range. The algorithm is confined not only to the public domain setting, but to a specific item of equipment. This is clearly a localizing strategy.

The first pages of these two algebra chapters operate together. They are parts of the same text, although they clearly constitute distinct utterances, because they address different reader voices. Together, they effect a partitioning of these reader voices. The Y reader voice is identified as a member of an international community comprising mathematicians and student mathematicians. This voice is further identified as already competent; it is to recognize its message encoded in the foreign language extracts. These strategies, combined with the rehearsal of esoteric domain rules and the ironizing of the public domain contribute to its apprenticing into the esoteric domain.

The G reader voice is identified with the object, Peter, and so with a public domain setting about which a considerable amount of information is given. The modality of this setting is increased via the extensive use of an iconic mode of signification. The text does enter the descriptive domain, but the specialized nature of the expression is backgrounded by its superimposition on a public domain icon. Thus the G reader voice is projected into the public domain, the range of which is limited to a single procedural operation within a narrowly defined context. Furthermore, the ironizing of the public domain setting can be resolved only via the identification of the reader voice with a second object, the consumer of comic literature. This is an infantilizing of this voice. These two introductory pages, then, clearly indicate the status of the Y and G reader voices as, respectively, apprenticed and dependent: the Y reader is to recognize its mathematical, which is to say, esoteric domain message; the G reader must recognize its public domain life, but without access to the esoteric domain principles which have structured it.

The two pages also constitute the authorial voice in rather different ways. The Y text affiliates the authorial voice to the international community of mathematicians. The G text, on the other hand, must simulate an interest in the public domain setting, because its esoteric domain message, visible in the Y text, is not revealed in the G text. The G text thus projects a displaced author into the public domain. Mathematics, here, is being presented as being for something other than itself, in other words, the text is elaborating the myth of participation. This myth constitutes the interest of both the dependent G voice and the displaced G author.

Developing the Language of Algebra: Rehearsing Formulas

Section B of Y1.03 begins on the second page of the chapter and opens with the following exposition:

> When you **say** $3a^2$ ('three a squared'), it is not clear what you mean. You could mean 'three **a-squared**' or '**three-a** squared'. These do not give the same answers. For example, if $a = 5$,
> 'Three **a-squared**' gives three times **5-squared** or $3 \times 25 = 75$.
> '**Three-a** squared' gives **15** squared or $15 \times 15 = 225$. (Y1, p. 22)

This initiates a generalizing of the esoteric domain message introduced in the previous section by addressing a possible ambiguity arising out of a combination of two of the rules that were given before. The initial approach is empirical. The empirical approach is, of course, highly localized and generalization depends upon making the move from the particular numbers used in the example to numbers in general. This move is made in the rule which is printed, in red, below the example and in the subsequent exposition:

> The squaring symbol ^{2} only squares the number or letter it is written against.
> If you want to square more than that, you use brackets.
> ... (*ibid*)

Thus far, the rule has simply been asserted and barely extends beyond procedure. However, the text moves on to provide an exposition which is more abstracting.

Figure 8.2 Diagrams from SMP 11–16 Book Y1 (p. 22)

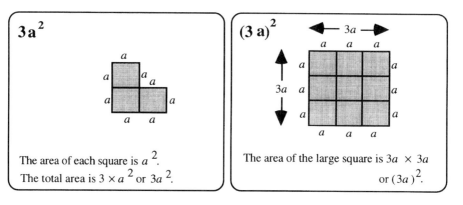

The two diagrams (indices) in the middle of page 22 (*Figure 8.2*) firstly map the two algebraic expressions, $3a^2$ and $(3a)^2$, respectively, onto two geometric figures which can be compared in terms of area. Although the figures have specific shapes, that they have different areas is not dependent upon the absolute value of a (provided that it is not zero), so that the comparison is a form of proof that $3a^2$ and $(3a)^2$ have different values. The proof is achieved via a mapping between topics within the esoteric domain, that is, between algebra and geometry. This is a metonymic rather than a metaphorical mapping, because the text makes the links explicit. This is achieved, for example, through the labelling of the diagrams. The text thus confirms the general status of the need for the disambiguating rule which is printed in red on the page, it also generalizes, increasing the connectivity of the esoteric domain by articulating topics.

Following the indexical 'proof' above are a worked example and a number of tasks which relate to the syntactical rules given in the current and in the previous section. However, the tasks are not simply rehearsals of the rules, but involve the extension of their application, which is to say, the esoteric domain topic is being expanded (relative to the highly limiting strategies of the G text described above). One task, for example, includes a fractional coefficient and others introduce a number of variations, including exponents in the denominator of an algebraic fraction.

The next section of Y1.03 — section C — covers page 23 and half of page 24 of the book. This section follows the same pattern as section B: an exposition of esoteric domain principles; worked example; tasks (rather more, this time) which also expand the application of the principles. The tasks are, additionally, punctuated by the provision of an additional rule concerning the omission of the multiplication sign in algebra. The whole of this section fore-grounds the symbolic mode of signification. Task C6, however, can be read as iconically signifying part of a page of an exercise book with mathematical expressions in manuscript. The task instructs the reader to '. . . put brackets in the correct places to make these statements true'. This device is distin-guished from the exercise book fragment appearing on page 23 of the G text (*Figure 8.1*) because the former cannot be identified with the reader's own exercise book which must show the same mathematical expressions, but with correcting brackets. The manuscript and iconic mode facilitate a shift towards the public domain. The use of symbolic mode is muted by the intrusion of the iconic, which localizes the mathematically false statement. This use of the iconic mode to localize mathematically false statements is also used elsewhere in Y1 and also in the G series.

The second and third pages of the G text are again dominated by the iconic mode and incorporate three prominent cartoons, thus extending the con-notation of comic literature introduced on the first page of the chapter. The tasks on these pages involve a rehearsal of the basic algorithm introduced on the first page. Each task is accompanied by the 'card' relating to the relevant item of equipment which is 'for hire'. In the case of the first task, the card is produced as part of a drawing which also shows part of a hand holding a scrap of paper on which are written the details of the hire. The hand is a left hand: this could be Peter's hand, offering the paper to the reader whilst standing at her/his shoulder. Alternatively, it might be the reader's own hand. The reader is placed either in Peter's position, or in a position in which Peter is supervising the reader who is to calculate the hire charge. In either case, the identification of the reader voice with the public domain setting — and hence its objectification by the text — is established.

In the lower left-hand corner of the same page is a cartoon showing Mr Evans using the floor cleaner that he has hired from the Blagdon Hire

Company[5]. Behind him is the Blagdon High School noticeboard on which three notices and two graffiti are legible. 'Do More Maths', advises one of the notices, 'Yes Please!' reads a graffito. The second graffito, 'Wow! Maths is Fun!', is just above one of the other notices, 'Extra Maths Club: Tues. Evening'. These two notices are, ironically, identifying school mathematics with a leisure activity through their out-of-school timing (do *more* maths, *extra* maths *club*) and through their juxtaposition with a Disco notice. This is a leisure activity, furthermore, about which the students are thoroughly enthusiastic — 'Wow! Maths is Fun!' The fun in this chapter, however, is all in the ironies contained in the cartoons: the broom and the overdressed manager on the previous page; Mrs Jones wobbling dangerously on her hired ladder on the next page; manual road workers being violently shaken and deafened by a pneumatic drill at the bottom of page 27; a hired road roller and a hired mechanical digger sporting bandages and band-aids; Mr Ling trying to sell a 'new 24-volume pocket edition' of mathematics exercises. Mathematics is fun, because mathematics textbooks contain comic cartoons[6].

The reader voice is, firstly, projected into the public domain via its exclusion from the esoteric domain message — a localizing strategy — combined with the extensive and extended narrative detail about the public domain setting. But, once more, the public domain setting that apparently motivates the tasks is satirized by the repeated irony. It is the scene-setting cartoons that carry the real fun of mathematics which is comic literature. The third legible notice on the board behind Mr Evans is an advertisement for a 'Disco' for which the main attraction is 'The Idiots' — presumably, a live band, what might be a guitarist also appears on the notice. This notice signifies, literally, student leisure activities; the name, 'The Idiots', satirizes the reader her/himself.

The second and third pages of each of these two chapters extend the positioning and distribution of the opening pages. The Y text abstracts by elaborating metonymic connections and principles within the esoteric domain topic of algebra (specializing) and between algebra and geometry (generalizing). The text is almost exclusively esoteric domain, so that the local, public domain conditions of the reader are alienated. As I argued at the end of Chapter 6, apprenticeship entails precisely the foregrounding of the specialized practices which are to be acquired and the backgrounding of other practices. This backgrounded material must include aspects of the subjectivity of the apprentice which cannot be assimilated by the esoteric domain. It is consistent with this interpretation to describe the Y text as constructing an apprenticed reader voice.

The G text, by contrast, sustains the infantilizing of its reader voice via the repeated emphasis on cartoons. The satirizing of mathematics in the ironic notices on the school board produces a spurious collusion between the authorial and reader voices, thereby constructing a displaced authorial voice. This

5 It is not entirely clear why a school caretaker might need to do this: it seems odd that the school would not possess its own cleaning equipment.
6 And this is a construction of the reader in relation to what they consider to be 'fun'.

renders invisible the authority of the authorial voice. The pedagogic action is also invisible because the reader voice is excluded from the esoteric domain principles which have structured the text. The reader voice is dependent upon the authorial voice to which these principles are exclusively distributed. Peter, on the other hand, is highly visible as is the public domain setting within which he is placed. It is Peter who, as surrogate for the teacher, apprentices the G reader into his own public domain setting. However, the public domain always recontextualizes the non-mathematical resources which are appropriated by the gaze. In the case of the Blagdon Hire Company, we might imagine that the cost of hiring the paint sprayer would be more easily expressed as £5 plus £4 per day; the tendency of the firm's customers to return the equipment an hour before the deadline is also somewhat suspicious[7]. The apprenticeship of the G reader, unlike that of the Y reader, is a spurious apprenticeship as the collusion of the displaced G author is a spurious collusion. Both strategies project the dependent voice into the ironized public domain.

Flowcharts and Machines

Section D of Y1.03 is titled *Chips* and represents the first substantial move of the Y text outside of the esoteric domain. The section opens in the public domain, employing a relatively open narrative. That is to say, very little detail is provided, so that the text does very little to localize the interpretations which may be made by the reader in respect of a specific setting. 'Chips' are integrated circuits which 'you can buy' and which add, multiply, etc voltages. However, it is not certain who will be buying the chips, a school science department, perhaps, although task D3 refers to a 'micro-electronics kit' which connotes a hobby; the pronoun, 'you' may or may not identify the reader voice.

The electronics setting is sustained throughout the whole of the section, but mathematical expressions are first introduced to the setting and are ultimately prioritized over it. The text moves into the descriptive domain with the first icon which superimposes a flowchart symbol on a drawing of a part of a circuit. The subsequent icons move further into the descriptive domain through the introduction of algebraic notation. At task D3 (and for the remainder of the section), the chips are signified by flowchart symbols only, the drawings being replaced by indices, and the algebraic expressions are now foregrounded. The section constitutes a textual trajectory from the public domain into the descriptive and, by foregrounding the mathematical expressions, points towards the esoteric which is where it returns in the subsequent section.

The flowchart symbol which is incorporated into section D is basically the same symbol as is used in G1.03, although, in the latter case, it always

---

7 The Teacher's Guide notes that 'We have not included examples of the type 'Monday 10 o'clock to Tuesday 11 o'clock for the sake of simplicity'.

appears in manuscript. In G1, the symbol is referred to as a 'machine' which is glossed, in the Teacher's Guide, as 'a box containing a single operation' (G1TG, p. 25). This metaphor occurs again in G1.05 and also in G2.03[8]. G1.05, in particular, opens with a cartoon. The cartoon shows students using chains to drag what appear to be large and heavy 'machines' — three-dimensional reifications of the flowchart symbols — towards a 'scrap heap'. The chains presumably pun the reference to a series of flowchart symbols as 'chains' in section A of G1.05. Through an ironic reification of the metaphor, the flowcharts are satirized as superfluous pedagogic props, to be scrapped, like their metaphors. The flowcharts make brief reappearances on the following page and in G2.03 (still referred to as 'machine chains'), but their use in the G books ends there.

The G reader is provided with imaginary machines; it is not at all clear what the non-mathematical purpose of such machines might be. Their introduction into a mathematical setting shifts the text into the expressive domain, which is to say, a non-mathematical term is being used to express a mathematical content. The reader of Y1.03, on the other hand, is provided with real, albeit recontextualized, machines in terms of integrated circuitry. In the Y chapter, the relationship between the mathematical signs (flowcharts, arithmetic operations and algebraic expressions) and the 'machines' is not metaphorical, because the former are not identified with the latter, but, rather, they describe them; this is descriptive domain text. The flowchart is, initially, superimposed on a drawing of the 'machine' and is constituted as a mathematical description of the operation of the chips which 'instead of numbers [. . .] add and multiply voltages'. The relationship between mathematics and machinery is made more explicit, so that they stand as metonyms for one another. In other words, the gaze is made comparatively visible and this is enhanced by the textual trajectory referred to above. Furthermore, the flowchart symbols are not, as in the G series, a dispensable pedagogic prop, but are used, albeit fairly infrequently, throughout the Y series[9].

As is the case with the public domain setting in G1.03, the electronics setting in Y1.03 has been recontextualized. Quite apart from the descriptive domain significations, a certain amount of violence has been done to the setting. Although the manufacturing of integrated circuits such as those described in the section is entirely possible, it is not clear that they are actually available. Furthermore, the voltages mentioned are very high, for this kind of circuitry, and voltage is represented in the icons and indices as a flow rather than a difference, which is to say, as something closer to current.

In other words, although the public domain setting is electronics, the text is clearly not about electronics, just as the G1.03 text is not about hiring equipment. Both are about formulae. As has been argued, however, the G

---

8 This chapter is called 'Working backwards' and is a representation of inverse arithmetic operations as 'number puzzles', thereby contextualizing algebra within the public domain.

9 More conventional flowcharts are also introduced in the Y series (in Y4 and Y5) and also appear in B1.

text is presented as entirely motivated by the public domain setting and so constitutes a spurious apprenticeship which projects the dependent voice into that domain. The Y text, by contrast, through its textual trajectory and through its use of a comparatively open narrative, backgrounds the public domain in favour of the descriptive algebraic expressions which are clear metonyms for the esoteric domain algebra in the sections before and after section D.

Mathematical *vs* Idiolectical Shorthand

Section E of Y1.03 returns to the esoteric domain and expands the algebraic conventions introduced in sections A and B. Section B of G1.03 also expands mathematical message, but, again, without entering the esoteric domain. The first page of the G section is even more heavily dominated by the iconic than the previous pages in this chapter, yet, mathematically, it is making the transition between flowchart and algebraic conventions. The algebra is initially referred to as a 'shorthand', which is the term used in the first section of Y1.03. The Y text makes it quite clear that idiolects are unacceptable: 'It would be confusing if everyone used their own shorthand, so mathematicians have agreed that . . .'. By contrast, the G narrative positions Peter as the author of the shorthand and the public domain setting as the motivation for its production: 'I can use a shorthand for this', Peter thinks, on being told that he will have to copy out all of the cards, not 'I remember what we used to do in maths when I was at school'.

Even the introduction of the term 'formula' is expressed in public domain terms, it is 'this way of writing the card'. A right hand holding a pencil and copying out the new card appears at the bottom of the page; there are three of these in this chapter and one idle left hand. The hand icons emphasize the manual aspect of writing and balance the 'think bubbles' in two of the cartoons. The mathematics, which is mental, optimizes the public domain, which is manual. In this case, of course, the optimizing works only because a rather long-winded form of mathematical expression was adopted in the first place. Furthermore, it is Peter, within the public domain and identified with the dependent voice, and not the authorial voice of school mathematics which appears as the subject of this optimizing.

The descriptive domain expressions, such as $n \times 3 + 2 = c$, incorporated into the G text are certainly mathematical. However, these expressions represent a restructuring of esoteric domain syntax. Firstly, the dependent variable, c, is placed last, rather than its more conventional place at the beginning of a formula. Secondly, the independent variable, n, is positioned before rather than after its coefficient ($n \times 3$ rather than $3 \times n$). In addition, the multiplication sign has been retained, counter to the rule on the first page of the Y chapter. The restructured syntax has the advantage of being in accord with that of the 'machine chains' and this localizes the algebra more effectively than would be the case if a more conventional, and therefore more abstract, syntax were imposed.

Calculators

Section F of Y1.03 is titled *Using a calculator* and opens with a classification of calculators in terms of their logic of operations, generating four categories, LTR (left to right) with or without bracket keys and MDF (multiplication and division first) with or without bracket keys. There follows an exposition on bracket keys and the classification described above together with a worked example corresponding to each type of calculator. The final part of the initial exposition is emphasized through the use of red type:

> If you are ever in doubt whether a key sequence is correct, try it out on some simple numbers where you know what the answer should be. (Y1, p. 28)

This is followed by task F2:

> The following calculations are simple ones. First work out each answer without using a calculator. Then experiment with your calculator until you find the key sequence which agrees with the answer. Write down the key sequence . . . (Y1, p. 29)

Having described the principles of the classification of calculators the task of classifying specific calculators and so generating specific calculating sequences is delegated to the reader. Between tasks F4 and F5 is another fragment of exposition which gives a generally applicable procedure:

> In very long calculations such as this one:
>
> $$\text{Calculate } \frac{a^2 - 2ab}{3b^2 + 4} \text{ when } a = 6.3 \text{ and } b = 0.75$$
>
> it is risky to try to find a single key sequence. It is safer first to write the calculation with the numbers in, putting in brackets where necessary, and then use the calculator to work out each separate part, like this . . . (*ibid*)

Again, however, it is left to the reader's discretion in assessing the level of 'risk' and so determining whether to apply this or the previous procedure.

The issue of calculator logic does not appear in G1.03, but is introduced towards the end of the G series, in G8.01. The opening exposition and task describe the syntax for the mental computation of a 'bill' and contrast this with the operation of 'most calculators'. The text introduces brackets to 'tell you to do the multiplying first' and provides an algorithm for using calculators: '. . . work out any multiplying first, and then write down the answers. Then add up your answers at the end.' The subsequent tasks rehearse this algorithm, first with reference to a 'bill' and then, using brackets, in the esoteric domain. The following section provides an alternative algorithm (in the form of a simplified, esoteric domain flowchart) for use with calculators which have a memory. This algorithm is subsequently to be rehearsed in a series of public domain tasks.

The G8 text is a rare example, in the G series, of a textual trajectory which moves between the esoteric and public domains. However, the esoteric domain text is entirely proceduralized and the chapter ends where it began, in the public domain with comparatively closed narratives. The public domain is constituted so as to motivate the chapter, including its esoteric domain sojourn which is presented as a subroutine for the facilitating of public domain tasks. The algorithms which are provided will work with any calculator, the choice between them being contingent upon whether or not the machine has a memory. There is thus no need to discuss the variations in calculator logic. This is not, however, a generalizing strategy; rather, it localizes the use of the calculator, which is untheorized. The G8 reader has no options within the esoteric domain; its subjectivity is dependent upon the instructions provided by the authorial voice. The message distributed to this reader voice is limited and proceduralized, which is to say localized. The Y1 reader is provided with an esoteric domain schema which will help to enable them to optimize their own use of the calculator. This limited region of the esoteric domain is, for the apprenticed voice, principled, so that the strategy being employed is specialization.

Expanding and Limiting the Gaze

The mathematical object which acts as the esoteric domain interpretant for all of the algorithms in G1.03 remains, as has been noted, unchanged throughout and, until the final page of the chapter, is projected, mythically, onto a single public domain setting. This setting is described in some detail, generating a very closed narrative. Furthermore, only small natural numbers are involved in the tasks and, as was mentioned above, there has been a restructuring of esoteric domain syntax in the algebraic expressions. This high degree of localizing is only minimally disturbed in the final section of G1.03, where two additional public domain settings are introduced. Here, again, closed narrative is employed. In these cases, a single alteration has been made to the formula, p is substituted for n. The restructured syntax is retained to the end of the chapter. Algebra, within the G text, is localized in both form and setting.

The Y text, by contrast, has approached algebra via the use of generalizing strategies. Abstracted and expanded message is distributed to the apprenticed voice in the form of principles for the interpretation and formulation of algebraic formulae and metonymic links within and between topics. Thus, any formula which lies within the scope of the rules becomes comprehensible, regardless of setting. Apart from section D ('Chips'), the Y1.03 text discussed so far remains within the esoteric domain. Following the exposition and first five tasks in section F, however, the chapter moves out of the esoteric into the descriptive domain, where it more or less remains until its conclusion. These final tasks in section F and those in section G minimize detail of the settings, thus employing more or less open narratives. In most cases, the open narratives connote, rather than denote, a range of settings. There is also a wide variation of predominantly public domain settings as the text moves between tasks. Thus, mathematics is represented as itself constituting a powerful language of description. I will discuss a number of these tasks, although there are no comparable G tasks with which to compare them.

Task F8 begins, 'The weight in kg that can be supported at the middle of an oak beam is given by the formula . . .'. The formula for the weight is simply stated without explanation. Most of the chapter has been esoteric domain text and has been concerned with the evaluation of formulae. In F8, however, the reader is provided with a public domain instance of the descriptive power of mathematics. Whilst there is a certain ambiguity in the setting (the narrative is fairly open) the advantage of being able to calculate the load that can be supported by a beam without actually having to test it is clear.

F9 is a little different, because the narrative is more closed, particularly via the provision of a marginal cartoon. The formula, which concerns the stopping distance when driving a car, is again stated rather than derived, but this time there is a weak hint as to where it comes from: it must incorporate thinking time and braking time. The task involves the completion of a table and drawing a graph, similar tasks were introduced in chapter Y1.01, so that there is a reference back to another topic (metonymic abstraction). This implicit reference to another topic, the visible similarity between the formula and esoteric domain formulae which appeared earlier in the chapter, and the hint about the origin of the formula are beginning to make explicit the action of the gaze of school mathematics. In this case, the result of this action is to produce a graph which describes an aspect of motoring. The graph is drawn in the Teacher's Guide. Although the narrative in this task is closed, the task, unlike those in G1.03, does not point to participation in the public domain setting; the appearance of a child in the road when driving a car would suggest braking rather than drawing a graph. Rather than denoting participation, the task constitutes a rationalizing description, which is to say, a referential mythologizing of the setting.

The final task in section F illustrates the effectivity of the recontextualizing gaze of school mathematics. The narrative is again fairly closed and a marginal cartoon is again included. The text provides a formula which is used by nurses in calculating children's doses of drugs.

Reference books of medicines and drugs usually give the size of an adult dose of each drug. One of the rules used by nurses to work out the children's doses is called 'Young's rule'. It is

$$C = \frac{An}{n + 12}.$$

C stands for the child's dose, *A* for the adult's dose, and *n* for the child's age in years. (The rule is not used for babies less than 1 year old.)

(a) Use the rule to calculate the dose for an 8 year old child when the adult dose is 15 milligrams (mg).

(b) At what age does a child receive half the adult dose?

(c) A Rule used to calculate the dose for a child less than 1 year old is called 'Fried's rule'. It is

$$C = \frac{am}{150}.$$

m is the child's age in months.

Calculate the dose for a 9 month old child when the adult dose is 400mg.

(Y1, p. 30; marginal cartoon omitted)

The formula introduced as 'Young's rule' is not fictitious, its mathematical equivalent being cited by Pirie (1981), who was investigating the 'uses' of mathematics in medical practice. Pirie cites the formula as follows:

$$\text{Childs dose} = \frac{\text{Age} \times \text{Adult dose}}{\text{Age} + 12}$$

Although this is mathematically the same formula, the variables are, in Pirie's version, expressed in words rather than letters. Furthermore, Pirie's formula breaks with mathematical convention because the variables are quantities rather than numbers. The formula itself does not specify the units in which 'Age' and 'dose' are to be measured and would clearly produce different results if the age of a child were to be measured in months rather than in years[10]: a child's dose of one-thirteenth of the adult dose if an age of 1 year is used as opposed to a child's dose of one-half of the adult dose if 12 months is used instead. The formula in the Y1 text, by contrast, is presented as a numerical relationship insofar as *n* represents the *number* of years in the child's age. This convention is, to an extent, also broken by the Y1 text in that no allusion to units is made with reference to *C* and *A* (it is clearly important only that they refer to the same unit of measurement). Thus mathematical forms of expression are being imposed upon a non-mathematical setting, so that the formula constitutes a shift into the descriptive domain.

A second point concerns part (b) of the Y1 task. 'At what age does a child receive half the adult dose?' Essentially, it is difficult to conceive of circumstances in nursing practice when such a computation would be necessary; the nursing setting cannot motivate the task. School mathematics, on the other hand, can, because the task involves solving a linear equation (formally or informally) and 'the solution of linear equations' is a sub-topic of algebra

10 Pirie does provide this information which would presumably be available to and/or known by nurses, the point here, however, concerns the mode of expression of the formula itself.

(although this sub-topic has yet to appear explicitly in Y1). This particular equation, furthermore[11], is somewhat more complex than those which have appeared explicitly in the course as a whole, for example in the level 4e booklet 'Equations'. The action of the gaze has thus transformed the mode of expression of the formulae so that it conforms more or less with mathematical, not nursing, convention and it has incorporated the formula into a strategy which is (albeit implicitly) expanding the esoteric domain message. In this latter respect, the gaze has reduced the level of the formula from that of textual strategy (it is a procedure within nursing) to that of resource. It is hypothesized that this reduction in level is a general effect of recontextualization between activities. This hypothesis was introduced in Chapter 6 in the discussion relating to dialogic texts.

Both of these final tasks in section F begin with a scene-setting introduction which includes a marginal cartoon. The first cartoon (F9) signifies a child chasing a ball out into the road in front of a car and being urgently hailed by another. There is no irony within the cartoon, indeed, this particular cartoon is very close to being a drawing in terms of the criteria introduced in Chapter 6. Nor does the Y cartoon satirize the public domain activity as do many of the G chapter cartoons. Indeed, there is a literal relationship between the verbal scene setting introduction and the cartoon: both signify an inherent danger in the situation. However, as the elaboration of the task progresses to its specific imperatives — 'Copy and complete this table . . .', 'Draw a graph . . .' — both the verbal introduction and the marginal cartoon are revealed as ironic. The problem is not, after all, how to make sure we can stop the car (or stop children from running out into the road), but to complete a table and to draw a graph, neither of which would be very likely to be of assistance to the driver who, were they to be looking at their speedometer at the time, would probably hit the child anyway.

Precisely the same trajectory is rehearsed in the nursing task. The cartoon accompanying this task shows a female nurse standing at a child's bedside and pouring a dose of medicine from a bottle into a spoon. Again, the cartoon does not, alone, contain its irony (although the nurse's uniform is, perhaps, a decade or so out of date). On the contrary, it stands in literal relationship with the verbal scene-setter. As noted above, however, the nursing activity cannot motivate the task as a whole, so that there is a textual trajectory out of the public domain and into the descriptive domain which is thereby prioritized.

Section G, the final section in the Y1 chapter, includes, very near the beginning, a cartoon which is somewhat different from those in section F in that it is a rare instance in the Y series of hyperbole in the caricaturing of an (anonymous) individual. The section also contains five other cartoons which implicate puns or elements of the ironic or ludic. These cartoons are not simply scene setters, but humorous elaborations of an aspect of the verbal

11 The equation may be formalized as $\dfrac{A}{2} = \dfrac{An}{n+12}$ or $\dfrac{n}{n+12} = \dfrac{1}{2}$.

text; they carry their own humour. Task G4 is accompanied by a cartoon showing a cat sitting on a box of tins of 'moggy food' and clutching the end of a ball of string which seems to have rolled across the page underneath the verbal text of the task. The cat and box are weakly associated with the task. The latter does not specify that the '*n* tins in a box' are catfood and part (b) refers to tins which each weigh 3kg and which are, therefore, certainly not catfood (at least, not the catfood signified by the cartoon). The playfulness of the cat, with its ball of string which intrudes in the serious business of doing mathematics, and the ironic labelling of the box lighten the page of otherwise symbolic text and diagrams.

The setting for G10 (*Figure 8.3*) is ludicrous: why are the children in separate rooms; why do we not, initially, know how many there are or how much the trifle weighs; whoever heard of a trifle weighing 60kg; how are the children going to eat 3kg of trifle each (the same weight as is to be eaten by the virtual cat in G4 part (b))? The verbal text is accompanied by a cartoon which visually balances the cat in G4 (they are in the top right-hand and top left-hand corners of the double page spread respectively). This G10 cartoon signifies two doorways out of each of which children (apparently standing on top of each other or, alternatively, of conveniently graduated heights) are staring at a huge trifle in the foreground. This task contrasts with the section F tasks, F9 and F10. The latter fix their public domain settings with little ambiguity via the use of closed narratives, even though they implicate an ironic trajectory out of the public domain. G10, on the other hand, certainly connotes a recontextualized domestic setting, but implicates irony right from the start. This ironizing of the public domain setting exceeds even that in the introduction to the G1 chapter, because the verbal text as well as the cartoon is ironic.

The effect of the irony is to alienate the public domain setting. However, and in contrast to the G chapter, there remain the descriptive domain significations which themselves connote the esoteric domain expressions in previous sections of the chapter. The public domain setting is almost entirely driven by the esoteric and the descriptive domain denotations and their esoteric connotations allow this to be seen. The trajectory is from public to descriptive domain and, connotatively, to esoteric domain. The ludic nature of the setting simply ensures that priority is given to the esoteric domain.

Section G is specifically referred to in the generally laconic Y1 Teacher's Guide:

> Section G is particularly important, and if it is felt that the chapter is taking a long time, or if the pupils find the first few questions in section G very difficult, then the section can be postponed. However, whenever the work in section G is introduced it is likely to be difficult for many pupils. (Y1TG, p. 18)

Concessions may be made for the many pupils who will find this section difficult, but only by postponing the work, that is, by reducing the pacing.

Figure 8.3   SMP 11–16 Book Y1 (p. 33)

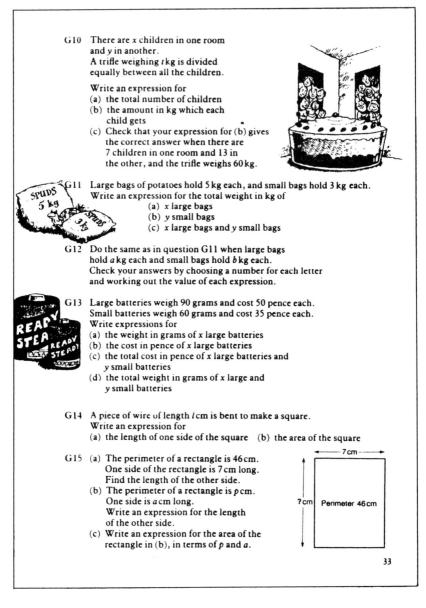

G10   There are *x* children in one room
and *y* in another.
A trifle weighing *t* kg is divided
equally between all the children.

Write an expression for
(a) the total number of children
(b) the amount in kg which each
     child gets
(c) Check that your expression for (b) gives
     the correct answer when there are
     7 children in one room and 13 in
     the other, and the trifle weighs 60 kg.

G11   Large bags of potatoes hold 5 kg each, and small bags hold 3 kg each.
Write an expression for the total weight in kg of
          (a) *x* large bags
          (b) *y* small bags
          (c) *x* large bags and *y* small bags

G12   Do the same as in question G11 when large bags
hold *a* kg each and small bags hold *b* kg each.
Check your answers by choosing a number for each letter
and working out the value of each expression.

G13   Large batteries weigh 90 grams and cost 50 pence each.
Small batteries weigh 60 grams and cost 35 pence each.
Write expressions for
(a) the weight in grams of *x* large batteries
(b) the cost in pence of *x* large batteries
(c) the total cost in pence of *x* large batteries and
     y small batteries
(d) the total weight in grams of *x* large and
     y small batteries

G14   A piece of wire of length *l* cm is bent to make a square.
Write an expression for
(a) the length of one side of the square   (b) the area of the square

G15   (a) The perimeter of a rectangle is 46 cm.
        One side of the rectangle is 7 cm long.
        Find the length of the other side.
     (b) The perimeter of a rectangle is *p* cm.
        One side is *a* cm long.
        Write an expression for the length
        of the other side.
     (c) Write an expression for the area of the
        rectangle in (b), in terms of *p* and *a*.

33

The section cannot be postponed indefinitely, however, because the work is 'particularly important'. In any event, postponement will not necessarily make the tasks any easier. This Teacher's Guide statement signifies a possible lack in competence in the reader, which is also signalled in the student's book by the introduction of the ludic in the cartoons and the trifling tasks in this section.

The mathematical distinction between section G of Book Y1 and the previous section is that, now, the algebraic expression, the formula, is not given, but is to be derived by the reader. There is, however, a further distinction in the plausibility of the settings. The section F tasks that involve public domain settings (F6, F8, F9 and F10) vary in terms of the openness or closedness of the narratives that are employed. However, it is clear that they all concern plausible mathematical descriptions, that is, a plausible casting of the gaze onto something plausible — the setting. This is the case even where the setting cannot itself motivate the mathematical task as in the 'nursing' task in F10. The application of the gaze effects a recontextualizing which appropriates strategies within non-mathematical activities (braking within motoring, Young's Rule within medicine) and reduces them to resources within school mathematics.

Plausibility breaks down almost entirely, however, in some tasks in section G. G10 has already been described as implicating a ludicrous setting. Elsewhere, it is the effect of the gaze itself which is ludicrous. Consider the final task, G19, for example.

A woman has a husband, *m* sons and *n* daughters.
When she dies, she leaves a sum of money, *a* pounds to be shared out among her family.
Write an expression for
(a)   the amount each person gets if the money is shared out equally among all the members of her family
(b)   the amount each child gets if the husband gets *b* pounds and the rest is shared out equally among the children
(c)   the amount each daughter gets if the husband and sons get *c* pounds each, and the rest is shared out equally among the daughters (Y1, p. 34)

The setting is signified by a comparatively closed narrative and is certainly grave in comparison with the earlier trifle. However, the specificity of each of the three possibilities for the will is starkly contrasted with the indeterminacy in the numerosity of the woman's offspring[12]. The opening words of the text also seem to specify the woman ('A woman has . . .') and to place her death in the past ('When she dies, she leaves . . .'); her identity and her death are fixed, how many sons and daughters she has is not.

It is also interesting that the political validity of constructing a will on the basis of gender (and of ensuring that the male beneficiaries get their share before the daughters share the rest) is not questioned . This would be to engage the setting at the level of strategies rather than resources (see, also, Brown and Dowling, 1989).

Most of the other tasks in the section avoid the ludic (although G17 apparently mathematizes a strawberry picking expedition). However, the mathematical gaze in most of the public/descriptive domain tasks remains

12   A contrast which is reproduced elsewhere in the *SMP 11–16* scheme, as I noted in Chapter 4.

very distant from any possible recontextualized activity. In G6, for instance, one answer — the total weight of a train — might plausibly be of interest to railway managers/engineers in relation to the power of the engine (although algebraic generalizing would be unlikely to be of procedural value). However, there is no attempt to motivate the task in this or in any other way. This contrasts starkly with the tasks in the G chapter. What the task is achieving, on the other hand (and this applies equally to the ludic tasks discussed above), is an apprenticing into the action and validity of the mathematical gaze, a metonymic abstraction. The question, 'What does nb tell you?' invites the reader to describe a public-descriptive domain trajectory by giving the answer in public domain terms: 'nb tells you the total weight of the train' (Y1TG, p. 21). The question also celebrates, through the use of the word 'tell', the descriptive power of mathematics; mathematical expressions can *tell* us about non-mathematical things, which affirms the myth of reference. But the reader must beware of profligacy. The gaze is to be applied with discrimination: $a + b$, for example, has no meaning, in this case, because 'It makes no sense to add the weight of a coach to the total length of the train' (*ibid*). The general nature of this answer, given in the Teacher's Guide, again creates a distance from any possible setting. The fact that very few of the tasks in this section seem to make any sense (outside of school mathematics) is left unaddressed.

Concluding the Chapters

Both Y1.03 and G1.03 end in irony, the Y chapter with the testate woman and her family, and the G chapter with the second of two new settings introduced in its final section. The G chapter is finally completed with a cartoon drawing of Mr Ling posting a notice — 'Buy them today!!' — on a copy of his 'New 24 volume pocket edition' of 'Ling's Exercises'.

> The Maths Publishing Company print and sell books.
> They use a formula to work out the cost of printing a book.
> The formula is $p \times 2 + 60 = c$.
> p stands for the number of pages in the book.
> c stands for the cost of the book in pence.
> (a) How much will a book with 25 pages cost?
> (b) How much will a book with 80 pages cost?
> (c) Mr Ling wants to sell 200 pages of maths exercises.
>   He can sell them in 1 book with 200 pages, or in 2 books, each with 100 pages. Which is cheapest? (G1; p. 29)

As with the other settings, motivation for the task is located within the public domain. The objectified voice, Mr Ling can do the necessary calculation himself and so structure his texts appropriately. Again, mathematics is optimizing the public domain in terms of participation. The cartoon, however, carries its own ironic significations: a 24 volume *pocket* edition (each volume appears to be of encyclopaedic proportions); who, particularly a 'less able' reader of the G text, would want to buy such a publication? By juxtaposition with the symbolic text, the cartoon emphasizes the otherwise weak irony in the task, part (c) in particular. Again, there is no esoteric domain to resolve the irony, so that the comic cartoon comes to the foreground. Furthermore, it is the institution of school mathematics itself which is being satirized, here, as is the case with the noticeboard behind Mr Evans. Mr Ling also connotes John Ling, the *SMP 11–16* team leader (see Chapter 7), so that the irony also infects the *SMP 11–16* project itself, by signifying the futility of producing mathematical texts for such readers[13].

The page opposite the final page of Y1.03 is the first of three pages entitled 'Mathematics of Yesteryear'. These pages appear at intervals in Y1. They implicate extracts from old school mathematics textbooks, this one apparently from *Rural Arithmetic*, published in 1916. In terms of content, this text constitutes a return to the kind of task at the end of section F, in which a formula relating to a public domain setting is presented. Following an initial exposition, there follows a worked example and a list of wind velocity ranges corresponding to verbal descriptors. Underneath the extract appears a drawing of Saxtead Green windmill and a task. It is not made clear whether or not the task is also taken from *Rural Arithmetic*[14]. The extract, task and drawing are on a black background which is bordered by Corinthian order columns and indeterminate (but classical-looking) stylobate and entablature. The title, 'Mathematics of Yesteryear' appears on a scroll which is mounted on the entablature. The mathematical content of the extract connotes the formulae in section F, thus metonymically linking this page with the preceding chapter and effecting its punctuation. The chapter thus opens with a synchronic universalization of mathematics — the language of mathematics is international — and ends with a European diachronic universalizing extending from ancient Greece through early twentieth century Britain to contemporary times. The authorial voice thus affiliates to a pan-cultural and pan-historical (eurocentric) metadiscourse.

In general, the final part of the Y chapter which concerns 'formulas' extends the contrast with the G chapter which is entitled 'formulas' in terms of the differential textual strategies that are implicated in the two texts. Five areas of contrast, in particular, should be emphasized. Firstly, the Y text continues the apprenticeship of the reader voice with respect to the esoteric domain through the denotative and connotative prioritizing of the latter by the domain trajectories which it incorporates. This is achieved, in particular, by the resolution of irony which projects out of the public domain and into

13 Clearly, this latter connotation is likely to be missed by most readers, especially since John Ling's name does not appear in the student texts (other than ironically). The analysis here, however, is concerned with the construction of the reader voice by the text as an exemplar of the activity of school mathematics; the reader's response is not under consideration, nor should it be in the absence of appropriate empirical text.

14 There is a windmill in Saxtead Green in Suffolk.

the descriptive domain and, connotatively, into the esoteric domain. The G text, by contrast and as has been argued earlier, prioritizes the public domain by locating task motivation within recontextualized settings. Because the G text never enters the esoteric domain and only weakly enters the descriptive, irony can only be resolved within the public domain, by emphasizing comic literature which, through its association with children (and with working class literature, see Dowling, 1990a, 1991b, 1991c and Chapter 9 of this volume), infantilizes the G reader voice relative to the Y reader. Thus, a hierarchy measured explicitly in terms of mathematical 'ability' (in the Teacher's Guides) is brought into correspondence with a public domain hierarchy measured in terms of maturity (and class). The apprenticed voice is identified with middle class maturity, albeit only weakly, at this stage; the dependent voice is identified with working class immaturity.

Secondly, the Y text apprentices the reader into the action of the mathematical gaze. This has been partially achieved in the opening sections of the chapter through the introduction of generalized esoteric domain text. In the later sections, the application of the gaze is practically and metonymically demonstrated in worked examples and in tasks. Clearly, it is necessary for the text to move beyond the esoteric domain in order to establish the gaze. The use of multiple public domain settings fragments the public domain because the relations between the settings are given within that domain only metaphorically. These metaphors, however, are reduced metonymically, within the esoteric and descriptive domains. The Y text thus fixes the focus on the gaze itself, rather than on the object of the gaze. Such apprenticing is not achievable by the G text which never enters the esoteric domain wherein lies the subjectivity of the gaze. On the contrary, the G text constructs mathematics as idiolectical in contrast to the Y text which celebrates the power of mathematics to generate valid references within the descriptive domain.

Thirdly, the Y text implicates a diverse, if fragmented, public domain. This expansion constructs the generalizability of the mathematical gaze in comparison with the very narrow public domain in the G text. The latter limitation of the message confirms the context-specificity of the procedures which are implicated. Fourthly, it is only in the Y text that there is any generalizing between esoteric domain topics. The G text, as has been stated, does not enter the esoteric domain at all. Finally, whilst the G chapter ends with a satirizing of school mathematics itself, the Y chapter — through its extension into 'Mathematics of Yesteryear' — ends as it began, with a celebration of the wide-ranging validity of mathematical reference, which is to say, an affiliation to a universal metadiscourse.

Conclusion

The textual strategies which are implicated in these two chapters (re)produce quite fundamental differences in voice and message. In the Y chapter, there is a consistent foregrounding of generalized esoteric domain message via abstracting and expanding strategies. Where the text involves public domain settings, there is always a movement away from the public domain which prioritizes the esoteric. This movement is sometimes achieved via the use of irony, as is the case in the ironic 'translation' of Arabic as mirror writing and in the bizarre and ludic settings at the end of the chapter. Then, the text might 'peel off' the public domain significations, foregrounding the descriptive, as occurs in the 'chips' section (cf Walkerdine's (1982) 'stripping away the metaphors', see Chapter 5). Alternatively, the text may constitute a mathematical rationalizing of the setting, objectifying it as a field to be described rather than one which invites participation; this is the strategy involved in the tasks on braking distances and children's doses. Finally, the text may incorporate many diverse and metaphorically related settings which are weakly fixed by open narratives. This fragmentation backgrounds the specificities of the public domain settings and renders more visible the structured action of the recontextualizing gaze. Crucially, it is always the mathematics that must be recognized in the text and which must apprentice the reader voice. There is no room for the individual particularities of the reader voice in this chapter. The chapter opens with an invitation to the reader to join an international community of mathematicians, we might call this a recruiting strategy. The chapter ends with historical and, particularly, classical references which celebrate the pan-historical (and the class and Eurocentric basis) of mathematical authority.

The G chapter is entirely different. Throughout the chapter, the text never enters the esoteric domain and never transcends the procedural. Localizing strategies recruit extended and closed narrative and combine with positioning strategies which identify the reader voice with a public domain setting in order to project the dependent voice into that domain. At the same time, localizing strategies recruit irony and the cartoon mode of signification to ironize and infantilize that domain. The dependent voice is thereby itself constituted as an object of fun. There is to be no recognition of mathematics. The algebraic content (defined in terms of the esoteric domain) is highly particularized, that is, to a single expression. Esoteric domain syntax, in respect of the rules of expression given in the Y chapter, are, in the G chapter, negated in simplifying the tasks. Furthermore, mathematical authority is replaced by mathematics as idiolect, as the object, Peter, invents his own shorthand. Finally, the public domain referents in the G chapter are predominantly low in terms of socioeconomic class. Only Mr Ling stands out as a professional and he is clearly dominant with respect to the reader. The satirizing of this particular teacher as altogether too earnest is consistent with a tendency, in G1, to construct a displaced authorial voice which colludes with the reader in opposition to mathematical authority.

This concludes the close comparative reading of the Y and G chapters. I shall now move to consider the operation of textual strategies more widely in the two series of *SMP 11–16* books.

Chapter 9

Genres of Production

In the previous chapter, I introduced the practical use of the language of description via a close comparative reading of, primarily, two of the *SMP 11–16* chapters. I attempted to show how textual strategies combined in the positioning of authorial, reader and object voices and in the distribution of message across the voice structure. The result was the apprenticing of the reader voice by the Y texts and the rendering dependent of the reader voice by the G text. I indicated how the strategies operated by recruiting resources, in particular: public domain settings; openness and closure of narrative; tropes, such as irony; and mode of signification. I also illustrated the way in which the gaze of the mathematical activity recruited strategies from the non-mathematical settings as resources for its own strategies. In both Chapters 7 and 8 I also illustrated the substantial difference between the two series in terms of abstracting potential. This was measured by the relative proportions of esoteric domain text incorporated by the schemes.

The analysis of two chapters of the *SMP 11–16* scheme in Chapter 8, has taken a whole chapter of over 11 000 words of my own book. Since there are seventy-five chapters in the Y series and fifty-nine in the G series, it is clear that a more economical form of presentation is needed. The content analysis presented in Chapter 7 represents one attempt to achieve this and a second content analysis will be presented in this chapter. The other strategy that I shall employ is to arrange the presentation of the analysis so as best to highlight features of the language of description and features of the empirical texts. This clearly entails that the selection of exemplars will be less complete than in the close comparative reading and less systematic than the content analysis. In respect of the reliability of the description, I am claiming that the three approaches constitute a triangulation. That is, they complement each other in respect of the range and detail of the empirical text that can be covered; they expand my empirical setting (see Brown and Dowling, 1998).

The approach that I have decided to take in this chapter and in the two which follow is to focus on key areas of resource which are recruited by the positioning and distributing strategies. The evidence produced so far describes the G and Y series as 'generically' different texts. I am using this expression with metaphorical reference to Mikhail Bakhtin's (1986) conception of speech genres. That is, the nature of the texts depends upon the social context of their production. In this case, the texts participate differently within the activity of school mathematics in that the Y text addresses the apprenticed reader voice, whilst the G text addresses the dependent reader voice. The relationship between author and reader is, therefore, distinct in each of the series. Signifying modes are recruited by distributing strategies in the (re)production of these distinctive genres. Further, they are recruited specifically in the material production of the texts. Thus, the G texts are produced with more pictures and the Y texts with more alphanumeric text and so forth. For this reason, I want to refer to distinctive *genres of production*. In the present chapter I shall consider the genres of production that characterize the two series. In Chapter 10 I shall focus particularly on the constitution of the public domain in the two series and finally, in Chapter 11, I shall discuss the direct objectification of the reader voices in terms of the instructional theories incorporated by the scheme.

I shall begin the work of this chapter by presenting a content analysis of the use of the different modes of signification by the *SMP 11–16* books. It will be recalled that it was argued that analysis in these terms had face validity as an indication of the orientation of the texts towards generalization or localization. In the content analysis, I shall include some reference to the B and R series, although these remain backgrounded for the purposes of the main study.

Signifying Modes

Quantifying Signifying Modes

Signifying modes are textual resources that were introduced in Chapter 6. They are listed in *Figure 6.10* as: icon (cartoon, drawing, photograph); index (table, graph); and symbol. Index and symbol can be non-manuscript or manuscript. It was argued in Chapter 6 that the use of different signifying modes can orientate the text towards generalization or towards localizing. In particular, the *visual code of presence*, which is intrinsic in iconic signification, itself effects a semiotic localizing. Thus a measure of the relative use of iconic and non-iconic modes (and of the categories of iconic mode) in the G and Y books has face validity as an indicator of the extent of localizing within each series. This being the case, I have conducted a quantitative comparison of the incidence of the different categories of signifying mode in these texts.

The operational difficulties involved in quantitative content analysis are readily acknowledged. The validity of indicators in relation to concepts and the reliability of operational recognition rules can never be guaranteed. On the other hand, quantitative methods can be far more representative in the sense that they can achieve a more exhaustive coverage of the empirical text. Crucially, the quantitative content analysis here and in Chapter 7 is being used in support of and, occasionally in dialogue with, the more detailed semiotic analysis and not in any sense as a replacement for it.

Because signifying modes are textual resources, they are, by definition, analytically very low level constructs. By virtue of this, the definitions given in Chapter 6 were, in terms of operational recognition, more or less sufficient to make a start on the practical analysis. One additional qualifier was made at the outset[1]: indices such as arrows and emphatic borders were to be ignored completely unless they are clearly part of (or where they overlapped with) another section of text. This is principally because a decision to include them in the analysis would render decisions concerning spaces enclosed by such indices highly problematic.

There are two obvious ways of quantifying signifying modes, that is, to count them in terms of frequency or in terms of area. A measure in terms of frequency would clearly problematize the validity of a comparison between symbolic and non-symbolic text, because an iconic or an indexical text visually terminates itself in a way that a symbolic text does not[2]. Furthermore, there is clearly a positive relationship (although not necessarily a linear one) between the size of an icon or index and its visual impact. An area measure will also give an indication of how much of the book or series as a whole comprises each signifying mode. I therefore decided to compare signifying modes in terms of the area occupied by each mode on each page of a sample of each of the G and Y series and also to include a sample from the B series (one of the median tracks). Each page of the books is a portrait sheet of approximately 24 cm by 17 cm. A centimetre grid of this size was prepared on a transparent, plastic sheet, this was laid over each page and the number of grid squares containing any part (however small) of text interpreted within each category of signifying mode were counted. Where a square contained more than one mode, a decision had to be taken as to which dominated in terms of coverage.

The intention was, firstly, to compare the G series with the Y series. However, it is also apparent from the most cursory inspection of the two series that there are trajectories, in terms of modes of signification, within each. I therefore decided to analyse the beginning and end of each series. The beginning and end of a series of books are, to an extent, naturally punctuated by, respectively, the first and last books in the series. However, Books G1 and G8 constitute a smaller proportion of the main G series as a whole[3] (approximately 25 per cent) than do Books Y1 and Y5 with respect to the

---

1 Further minor qualifications were made in the course of conducting the analysis (see Dowling, 1995a).
2 Regester (1991) uses a frequency count of 'visuals' of different kinds in her analysis of history textbooks. However, she is comparing the visuals in two categories of textbooks and is not directly concerned with the ratio of visuals to verbals.
3 *i.e.* Books G1–8, excluding ancillary materials such as worksheets and cards, supplementary booklets etc.

main Y series[4] (approximately 40 per cent). I therefore decided to analyse Books G1 and G8 and an equivalent proportion of the Y series, the latter being defined by the first and last 100 pages of the Y course. Book Y5 ends with a forty page 'General review', which comprises tasks but not exposition and, in a sense, comes after the end of the course. I decided to omit the 'General review' section and analyse the 100 pages immediately preceding it, that is, pages 48 to 147 inclusive, together with the first 100 pages of Y1. A random sample of forty pages from Book B3 (total ninety-two pages) was also analysed[5]. B3 is the middle book in the five-book series and so nominally represents the central book in the book-based part of the SMP scheme. The results of this analysis are given, in *Tables 9.1–3*, and discussed in the section below on 'Localizing via Signifying Modes' (page 221).

Two further counts were made. Firstly, since the type sizes in the G and Y series appear to be different — the G type appearing to be bigger — the number of non-manuscript, alphanumeric characters on each page was counted for a random sample of forty pages from Book G1 and for another of forty pages from that portion of Book Y5 which was sampled in the previous analysis (*i.e.* pp. 48–147). The number of characters on each page of the random sample of forty pages from book B3 were also counted. Characters are letters or numerals or mathematical or other symbols which are included under the heading 'symbol' in the earlier analysis of signifying modes[6]. The mean number of characters per page was counted for each sample and a measure of 'character density' for each page was computed by dividing the number of characters by the amount of symbol space on the relevant page (taken from the analysis of signifying modes). The mean character density for each sample was also computed. The results are given in *Tables 9.4–6*.

Secondly, an alternative measure of the relative use of photographs in the books was made by counting the number of photographs in each. In addition to the G and Y series, the photographic content of the B and R[7] series was also measured, in this way. Photographs vary considerably in size and some of them are overlaid on other photographs. I decided to count, as individual

4 *i.e.* Books Y1–5, excluding worksheets and the two extension books.

5 Pages 54 and 55 were omitted *a priori* from the sample from Book B3. This was because the symbolic text on these pages is produced as if it were newspaper text (although not fully iconically). These pages thus contain very high numbers of characters and are wholly unrepresentative of Book B3 and of the B scheme as a whole. The occurrence of one or more of these pages in the random sample would have dramatically distorted the sample. The choice of forty pages was made in relation to an additional form of analysis which is described below.

6 It was decided that a fraction, such as $\frac{3}{4}$ would count as three characters (because of the way in which such text is produced), but that the per cent symbol, %, would count as one (for the same reason). There were, in fact, few instances of either. Symbols signifying calculator keys were counted as single characters.

7 Books R1–3 are intended to substitute for books B3–5 for 'more able' students who initially follow the B, or middle, track.

Table 9.1: Mean page coverage by each signifying mode

| Book | Icon | | | Index | | | | Symbol | | Total |
| | Cartoon | Drawing | Photo | MS | | non-MS | | MS | non-MS | |
				Graph	Table	Graph	Table			
G1	44.8±15.3	67.7±15.4	4.0± 5.6	5.4±4.2	4.6±4.2	11.5± 8.4	0.5±1.0	10.2±5.9	104.2±10.2	252.9±9.2
G8	0.3± 0.6	43.7±12.8	32.9±16.5	5.6±6.2	2.3±3.4	23.7±12.6	3.1±2.9	7.3±3.6	127.0±10.3	245.7±8.4
B3	6.7± 6.2	23.7±13.6	6.1± 9.8	2.8±4.4	0.0±0.0	53.1±15.0	4.2±4.6	1.8±1.9	133.4±15.5	231.7±8.0
Y1	8.6± 5.0	29.3± 9.6	1.1± 1.6	1.4±1.5	0.0±0.0	32.7± 9.5	3.9±2.3	4.0±2.4	157.8± 9.7	238.7±6.2
Y5	4.0± 3.3	6.9± 5.0	2.1± 2.8	0.0±0.0	0.0±0.0	73.4±11.7	5.0±3.5	0.8±0.8	151.1±10.7	243.3±5.9

means and 95 per cent confidence intervals; all data to 1 decimal place

Tables 9.1–3 refer to mean numbers of cm squares per page containing the relevant signifying mode (one page is approximately 408 square centimetres)

The data relates to the whole of each of Books G1 and G8 (pp 0–61 in each case), to pp 1–100 of Book Y1 and to pp 48–147 in Book Y5 (i.e. the last 100 pages before the 'General Revision' section which concludes the Y series) and to a random sample of forty pages from Book B3 (the central book in the B series, pp 54–5 excluded).

MS = 'manuscript form'

Table 9.2: Mean page coverage by symbol, index, icon

	Book G1	Book G8	Book B3	Book Y1	Book Y5
Symbol	114±11	134±12	135±16	162±10	152±11
Index	22±10	35±14	60±17	38±10	78±12
Icon	116±20	77±17	37±16	39±11	13±7
Non-Icon	136±15	169±16	195±17	200±10	230±10
Page Coverage	253±9	246±8	232±8	239±6	243±6

means and 95 per cent confidence intervals; all data to nearest whole number

Table 9.3: Ratios of signifying modes

	Book G1	Book G8	Book B3	Book Y1	Book Y5
non-symbol:symbol	1.2	0.8	0.7	0.5	0.6
icon:non-icon	0.9	0.5	0.2	0.2	0.1

all data to 1 decimal place

photographs, images that had obviously been produced separately and then overlaid. Where an enlargement of an image was overlaid on the 'original', they were not counted separately. The numbers of photographs in each book in the G, B, R and Y series are given in *Table 9.7*.

Localizing via Signifying Modes

As I have indicated, four sections of text for analysis were selected from the G and Y series on the basis that they constituted the beginnings and ends of each series. The sections of text were: i) Book G1; ii) Book G8; iii) pages 1–100 of Book Y1; iv) pages 48–147 of Book Y5. Viewed in this way, a comparison of the absolute quantities of each signifying mode in each section of text — that is, without reference to the variations within each section — is valid as a description of trajectories within each series and of differences between the beginnings and between the ends of the two series.

However, it is also conventional to test for the statistical significance of the results of quantitative analysis with respect to a null hypothesis. In this case we must construct an imaginary text from which samples — assumed to be (but actually not) random — were taken and calculate the probabilities of obtaining the actual results shown in *Tables 9.1* and *9.3*. In consideration of the questionable relevance of the null hypothesis, in this case, I have decided to discuss the results of this analysis, firstly, as repeated comparisons of 100 per cent samples of the 'beginnings' and 'ends' of each series. In this discussion, the confidence intervals given in *Tables 9.1* and *9.2* will be ignored.

Table 9.4: Character densities in Book G1

| | **Book G1** | | |
page	characters	symbol space	character density
0	194	48	4.04
1	306	78	3.92
5	744	114	6.53
6	531	87	6.10
7	420	83	5.06
8	377	73	5.16
9	161	41	3.93
10	424	78	5.44
11	503	85	5.92
13	286	60	4.77
17	901	184	4.90
18	487	94	5.18
19	557	100	5.57
21	498	104	4.79
22	486	102	4.76
23	574	109	5.27
24	586	113	5.19
25	658	123	5.35
26	285	55	5.18
31	718	150	4.79
32	0	0	—
33	484	86	5.63
36	839	155	5.41
37	307	67	4.58
38	602	114	5.28
41	310	51	6.08
42	720	158	4.56
43	300	79	3.80
44	499	88	5.67
45	512	95	5.39
47	1006	155	6.49
49	641	148	4.33
50	787	167	4.71
53	496	109	4.55
54	522	116	4.50
55	330	57	5.79
56	527	107	4.93
58	783	159	4.92
59	1022	196	5.21
60	905	165	5.48
mean	532	104	5.11*
std error	36	7	0.11*

* Omits page 32

Each of *Tables 9.4–6* represents a random sample of forty pages from the relevant book. Pages 54 and 55 of Book B3 were omitted from the sampling frame. Page 32 in G1 and page 65 in Y5 contain no symbolic text and so data relating to these pages had to be omitted from the character density calculations.

Table 9.5: *Character densities in Book B3*

	Book B3		
page	*characters*	*symbol space*	*character density*
2	506	92	5.50
5	422	89	4 74
6	916	147	6.23
7	263	50	5.26
10	655	124	5.28
13	1162	242	4.80
15	538	95	5.66
18	607	90	6.74
22	384	75	5.12
23	815	212	3.84
25	253	61	4.15
30	873	182	4.80
31	618	139	4.45
33	658	180	3.66
34	1006	219	4.59
35	490	83	5.90
36	1358	238	5.71
37	647	121	5.35
39	616	140	4.40
41	924	163	5.67
43	1127	179	6.30
44	820	146	5.62
48	840	115	7.30
50	582	96	6.06
53	556	97	5.73
57	778	118	6.59
58	801	130	6.16
59	1034	173	5.98
60	245	55	4.45
64	780	146	5.34
65	553	154	3.59
68	965	158	6.11
72	586	87	6.74
73	703	112	6.28
76	315	71	4.44
82	1203	198	6.08
85	826	138	5.99
86	982	164	5.99
90	508	134	3.79
92	646	121	5.34
mean	714	133	5.39
std error	42	8	0.15

Subsequently, some qualifying comments will be made on the basis of significance tests made using an estimate for χ^2. The data relating to Book B3 is not central to the analysis and was obtained rather differently from that relating to the G and Y books. Nevertheless, some mention of this data will be made within each part of the discussion.

Table 9.6:   *Character densities in Book Y5*

| | **Book Y5** | | |
page	characters	symbol space	character density
48	1121	168	6.67
49	941	144	6.53
52	562	108	5.20
53	1114	179	6.22
56	1129	176	6.41
57	1921	263	7.30
58	1037	180	5.76
59	958	163	5.88
64	1162	181	6.42
65	0	0	—
69	974	137	7.11
70	1336	179	7.46
72	850	133	6.39
74	586	85	6.89
78	513	93	5.52
79	985	183	5.38
83	701	131	5.35
87	792	121	6.55
92	585	85	6.88
95	390	65	6.00
97	630	112	5.63
102	716	130	5.51
106	1362	235	5.80
108	1242	221	5.62
111	1181	238	4.96
113	1176	239	4.92
114	1215	234	5.19
115	1232	218	5.65
116	1469	228	6.44
117	954	182	5.24
121	1297	201	6.45
130	465	89	5.22
131	815	149	5.47
133	1332	203	6.56
137	695	122	5.70
138	585	143	4.09
140	871	173	5.03
141	1114	195	5.71
145	531	98	5.42
147	614	119	5.16
mean	929	158	5.89*
std error	57	9	0.12*

* Omits page 65

Tables *9.8* and *9.9* show direct comparisons between the sections of texts (to be referred to as 'books', for simplicity) in terms of the ratios of the mean values represented in *Tables 9.1* and *9.2*. *Table 9.8* expresses the mean value of each signifying mode for each book as a ratio with respect to the smallest

Table 9.7: Numbers of photographs in SMP 11–16 Books

G Series		B Series		R Series		Y Series	
Book	Photos	Book	Photos	Book	Photos	Book	Photos
G1	3	B1	0	R1	6	Y1	4
G2	1	B2	5	R2	1	Y2	5
G3	0	B3	4	R3	12	Y3	3
G4	6	B4	21			Y4	2
G5	11	B5	6			Y5	6
G6	18						
G7	80						
G8	75						
pp/photo	2.5	pp/photo	15.9	pp/photo	23.8	pp/photo	40.6

Table 9.8: Ratios and order of means of signifying modes

mode	G1	G8	B3	Y1	Y5	order
icon	8.9	5.9	2.8	3.0	1	G1>G8>Y1>B3>Y5
non-icon	1	1.2	1.4	1.5	1.7	G1<G8<B3<Y1<Y5
cartoon	149.3	1	22.3	28.7	13.3	G1»Y1>B3>Y5»G8
drawing	9.8	6.3	3.4	4.2	1	G1>G8>Y1>B3>Y5
photo	3.6	29.9	5.5	1	1.9	G8>B3>G1>Y5>Y1
index	1	1.6	2.7	1.7	3.5	G1<G8<Y1<B3<Y5
ms graph	3.9	4.0	2.0	1	0.0	G8>G1>B3>Y1>Y5
ms table	2.0	1	0.0	0.0	0.0	G1>G8>B3>Y1>Y5
non-ms graph	1	2.1	4.6	2.8	6.4	G1<G8<Y1<B3<Y5
non-ms table	1	6.2	8.4	7.8	10.0	G1<G8<Y1<B3<Y5
symbol	1	1.2	1.2	1.4	1.3	G1<(G8,B3)<Y5<Y1
ms symbol	12.8	9.1	2.3	5.0	1	G1>G8>Y1>B3>Y5
non-ms symbol	1	1.2	1.3	1.5	1.5	G1>G8>B3>(Y1,Y5)
total	1.1	1.1	1	1.0	1.1	(G1,G8,Y5)>(B3,Y1)

The table shows the ratios of each signifying mode per book expressed to the smallest non-zero value as base (which appears in the table as 1) and the ordering of the books in terms of these ratios; » indicates a factor greater than 10.

non-zero value as base. The final column shows the ordering of the books. *Table 9.9* shows the ratios of the mean values of each signifying mode relating to the books shown in the left-hand column, for example, the first figure in the second column, 6.6×10^{-1}, is the ratio of iconic signification in G8 to that in G1, that is, 0.66:1.

Most of the sequences in the right-hand column of *Table 9.8* are in a direction which, on the face of it, suggests an increase in generalizing strategies within each of the series and an increase in generalizing strategies in moving from the G to the Y series. Thus icons are decreasingly implicated as resources within the sequence G1 → G8 → Y1 → Y5. However, there are some notable exceptions which will be referred to in the following discussion.

Table 9.9: Ratio of means of signifying modes

Comparison	icon	cartoon	drawing	photo	index	ms graph	ms table	non-ms graph	non-ms table	symbol	ms symbol	non-ms symbol	total
G8:G1	0.66	0.0067	0.64	8.3	1.6	1.0	0.50	2.1	6.2	1.2	0.71	1.2	1.0
Y1:G1	0.34	0.19	0.43	0.28	1.7	0.26	0	2.8	7.8	1.4	0.39	1.5	0.90
Y5:Y1	0.33	0.46	0.24	1.9	2.1	0	—	2.3	1.3	9.3	0.20	1.0	1.1
Y1:G8	0.51	29	0.67	0.033	1.1	0.25	0	1.3	1.3	1.2	0.55	1.3	0.90
Y5:G8	0.17	13	0.16	0.064	2.2	0	0	3.0	1.6	1.1	0.11	1.3	1.0

The table shows the ratios of signifying modes between the books in the left-hand column. Numbers are expressed to two significant figures.

The use of cartoons is a minimum in Book G8 and not, as we might have expected, in Book Y5. With reference to *Table 9.1*, it is clear that cartoons represent a substantial (greater than 5 per cent of the average page coverage) resource only in Book G1 and that they are almost entirely absent from Book G8. By contrast, in the 'photo' column of *Table 9.1*, Book G8 stands out as the only book for which photographs constitute a substantial resource. We can describe a trajectory within the G series which constitutes a substitution of photographs for cartoons and drawings. In other words, there would appear to be an overall increase in localizing strategies within the G series. This reading is supported by the data in *Table 9.7* which points to a massive increase in the use of photographs in the last two books of the G series. However, an alternative interpretation may be more apposite.

Whilst it does constitute a strengthening of the visual code of presence, the exchange of cartoons for photographs also connotes a trajectory from the playful and fictional world of childhood to the real world of adulthood. For example: *Figure 9.1* includes a G1 image of shopping[8] incorporating puns ('J. Nare'/Jane Eyre[9]; 'Pseudo'/Cluedo[10]) and imaginary magazine and trade names; *Figure 6.9* (p. 158) shows a G7 image which incorporates the 'real thing'. There are similar shifts in the representation of other settings, such as work. For example, a humorous cartoon image of a building site, in G1 (mentioned in Chapter 8), contrasts with photographs of nurses, in G8. As I argued in Chapter 8, the connotative value of cartoons may be interpreted as localizing within childhood. In other words, although cartoons involve a weaker visual code of presence and are, to this extent, less localizing than photographs, their connotative values are highly localized within childhood. Thus, G1 localizes via the connotations of the particular category (cartoons), G8 localizes via the enhanced visual code of presence of its preferred category (photographs). The G series may thus be understood as constituting a continuity of localizing strategies in its exchange of iconic signifying modes. In both cases, the mode of distributing strategy is the projection of the dependent voice into the public domain.

It is apparent from *Table 9.1* that not all of the reduction in cartoons and drawings between G1 and G8 can be accounted for by the increase in photographs, because there is an overall reduction in icon space between these two books. Corresponding to this decrease, there has been an increase in both indexical and symbolic space, most substantially in terms of non-manuscript graphs (a doubling) and non-manuscript symbol (an increase of about 25 per cent). Thus, two trajectories can be described: an exchange of cartoons and drawings for graphs; and an exchange of cartoons and drawings for symbols. These trajectories represent shifts from the modes indicating greatest localizing

---

8   This G1 chapter does include a photograph, apparently of a greengrocer's shop, but it is a
    rare instance in the early G books.
9   By Charlotte Bronte.
10 A popular board game.

Figure 9.1   SMP 11–16 Book G1 (p. 19)

to those indicating most generalizing. The overall trajectory, therefore, is towards an increase in generalizing. However, the content analysis presented in Chapter 7 concluded that only about 5 per cent of Book G8 comprises esoteric domain text. Indeed, approximately one third of the graphs in G8 are road maps and most of the others are diagrams of boxes. The strategy which generalizes via the implication of graphs and symbols is, in other words, opposed within the G8 text by strategies which localize via public domain settings (see, further, Chapter 10).

Within the Y series, there seems to be a reduction in symbolic space between Y1 and Y5. However, this is entirely accounted for by the increase in index space. The principle trajectory in the Y series represents an exchange of icons, mainly drawings, for non-manuscript graphs. But, as is apparent from the data in *Table 9.2*, the increase in indices in Y5 as compared with Y1 exceeds the decrease in icons. This accounts for the difference in symbol space. Again, with reference to the content analysis presented in Chapter 7, the amount of esoteric domain space in Y5 is more than ten times that in G8 at over 50 per cent. Y5 graphs are generally mathematical objects. Although Y5 does include projections of the globe and of other objects, in each case it is the nature of the projection which is foregrounded, rather than the resulting 'map'. The generalizing, icon → index trajectory between Y1 and Y5 is therefore not countered within the text as it is in the G series.

As noted above, *Tables 9.8* and *9.9* indicate that the differences between the use of different signifying modes by each book considered are generally such as to suggest an increase in generalizing strategies within each series (G and Y) and between the G and Y series. Thus, there is a reduction by a factor of approximately 0.66 in iconic space between G1 and G8, a reduction by approximately 0.51 between G8 and Y1, and a reduction by 0.33 between Y1 and Y5. Indexical space increases by a factor of 1.6 within the G series. Thus the indexical space within G8, the last book in the G series, is approximately the same as that in Y1, the first book in the Y series (the factor shown in *Table 9.9* is 1.1). Indexical space is increased by a factor of 2.1 within the Y series. Symbolic space increases within the G series[11] and is greater in Y1 than in G8 (the subsequent slight reduction between Y1 and Y5 has been explained above). B3 (nominally, the median book in the textbook scheme) is close to Y1 in terms of iconic space, close to G8 in terms of symbol space and between Y1 and Y5 in terms of indexical space. The difference between the G and Y series in terms of symbolic text is probably underestimated by the use of textual space as a measure. This is illustrated by the data in *Tables 9.4–6* which indicate a statistically significant difference[12] in character density between G1 and Y5 symbolic text.

The use of manuscript in indexical and symbolic space was described (in Chapter 6) as constituting an iconicizing of the indexical/symbolic and hence measures the incidence of localizing strategies. In absolute terms, the amounts of manuscript space are small (always less than 10 per cent of page coverage). Nevertheless, there are substantial differences between the books

---

11 The factor of this increase is small. However, since the starting point (symbol space in G1) is approximately 45 per cent of the total page coverage, factors are of somewhat less importance than additive quantities.

12 $\chi^2 \approx 4.856$ which indicates significance at the 0.05 level.

Table 9.10: *Incidence of manuscript text*

Book	manuscript text	
	mean space	% of page coverage
G1	20.2	8.0
G8	15.1	6.1
B3	4.6	2.0
Y1	5.4	2.3
Y5	0.8	0.3

'Mean space' is the mean area per page (in cm^2) which is produced in 'manuscript'. Each page has an area of approximately 408 cm^2.

as is shown in *Table 9.10*. Basically, manuscript text is about three times more common in the G series than in Y1 (and B3) and has almost disappeared by Y5[13]. This confirms the increase in generalizing strategies within the Y series and between G and Y. Tables do not occupy a great deal of space, their representation being only about 2 per cent of page coverage. When the quantities of manuscript and non-manuscript tables are added, the mean representation of tables in G1, G8, B3, Y1 and Y5 are, respectively, 5.1, 5.4, 4.2, 3.9 and 5.0 square centimetres per page. So, there appears to be more use of table space in the G series than in the Y series. However, since manuscript tables generally use far more space than non-manuscript tables and since most of the tables in G1, nearly half of those in G8, but none of those in Y1 or Y5 (or B3) are manuscript, this measure probably fails to give a valid comparison. The larger manuscript tables are, of course, also constituted iconically, so that they are, in this respect, localizing.

As mentioned earlier, a simpler count was also made of the number of photographs in each of the *SMP 11–16* books. The results of this count are shown in *Table 9.7*. The figure at the bottom of each column gives the average use of photographs in terms of the number of pages per photograph for each series of books. Clearly, these data confirm that the G series as a whole makes far greater use of photographs. The occurrence of photographs in the G books is 6.4 times as frequent as that in the B series, 9.5 times that in the R series, and 16.2 times that in the Y series. Furthermore, whilst there is a low but relatively steady presence of photographs in the Y series, there is a trajectory which increases photographic presence in the G books. Similarly, *Table 9.1* indicates a low presence of cartoons throughout the Y series which, again, stands in contrast to the trajectory of decreasing cartoon presence in the G books. This illustrates the very different extents to which these signifying modes are incorporated into distributing strategies in the two series. Specifically,

13 Manuscript text in the Y5 sample occurs once as 'handwritten' algebra and three times as headings to the public domain 'Money matters' sections in the book.

they mark the respective modes of localizing in G1 and G8, whereas both are present, but marginalized in the Y books.

It should be noted that eighteen of the twenty-one photographs in B4 and nine of the twelve in R3 are incorporated into tasks and exposition in which photographic enlargement is used as a metaphor for mathematical enlargement. In these texts, it is the photograph as photograph that is foregrounded and not its scene, so that there is a weakening of the visual code of presence. Thus, the photograph count tends to overestimate the use of localizing in the R books. This argument, of course, weakens the validity of the use of the occurrence of photographs as a sole indicator of localizing. The same is true of the qualifications made in respect of increasing generalizing in the G series as a result of the increase in indexical and symbolic space. However, the use of quantitative content analysis is being used here in support of the more detailed semiotic analysis and is not intended to stand alone.

As was mentioned earlier, estimates for χ^2 were made in relation to the data for which the means and 95 per cent confidence intervals are shown in *Tables 9.1* and *9.2*. For this purpose, the data was treated as repeated comparisons between random samples drawn from normal populations. An estimate for χ^2 (1 degree of freedom) was calculated for each comparison; these values are shown in *Tables 9.11–14*. In these tables, the results of the tests are given at two levels: all comparisons shown in bold typeface are significant at the 0.05 level, in addition, those which are capitalized are significant at the 0.01 level. *Table 9.15* displays those differences between books (in terms of signifying modes) which are referred to in the above analysis.

By referring the comparisons in *Table 9.15* to *Tables 9.11–14*, it is clear that all of them apart from the three bracketed items are statistically significant and that those marked with an asterisk are significant only at the 0.05 level. Thus the tests may be taken to qualify, or, perhaps, to append caveats to, statements made concerning the indexical trajectory within the G series and the symbolic and manuscript trajectories within the Y series.

Signifying Modes: Summary

This quantitative analysis of signifying mode space has pointed to trajectories within each series and to differences between them. Within the G series, there is a trajectory which exchanges iconic text in G1 for symbolic text within G8. Insofar as this comparison is reliable, the G series thus becomes less iconic, signalling a reduction in the use of localizing strategies[14]. On the other hand, the trajectory which exchanges cartoons and drawings in G1 for photographs

---

14 This trajectory is, to an extent, countered by the localizing use of public domain settings (see Chapter 10).

Table 9.11: Differences of means of signifying mode space per page between Book G1 and Books G8, B3, Y1 and Y5

G1–G8 mode	χ²	+/-	G1–B3 mode	χ²	+/-	G1–Y1 mode	χ²	+/-	G1 — Y5 mode	χ²	+/-
ICON	**9.25**	+	**ICON**	**39.50**	+	**ICON**	**47.12**	+	**ICON**	**97.69**	+
NON-ICON	**9.05**	–	**NON-ICON**	**27.55**	–	**NON-ICON**	**49.06**	–	**NON-ICON**	**113.12**	–
CARTOON	**33.48**	+	**CARTOON**	**21.00**	+	**CARTOON**	**20.05**	+	**CARTOON**	**26.95**	+
drawing	**5.66**	+	**DRAWING**	**17.89**	+	**DRAWING**	**17.67**	+	**DRAWING**	**55.58**	+
PHOTO	**10.89**	–	photo	0.14	–	photo	0.98	+	photo	0.34	–
index	2.15	–	**INDEX**	**15.19**	+	**index**	**5.35**	+	**INDEX**	**51.49**	+
ms graph	0.00	+	ms graph	0.68	+	ms graph	3.17	+	**ms graph**	**6.33**	+
ms table	0.76	+	**ms table**	**4.85**	+	**ms table**	**4.85**	+	**ms table**	**4.85**	+
non-ms graph	2.54	–	**NON-MS GRAPH**	**22.86**	–	**NON-MS GRAPH**	**11.09**	–	**NON-MS GRAPH**	**72.76**	–
non-ms table	2.86	–	non-ms table	2.42	–	**NON-MS TABLE**	**7.57**	–	non-ms table	6.23	–
symbol	**6.07**	+	symbol	4.45	–	**SYMBOL**	**39.67**	–	**SYMBOL**	**22.85**	–
ms symbol	0.71	+	**MS SYMBOL**	**7.33**	+	ms symbol	3.75	+	**MS SYMBOL**	**9.87**	+
NON-MS SYMBOL	**9.64**	+	**NON-MS SYMBOL**	**9.64**	–	**NON-MS SYMBOL**	**56.81**	–	**NON-MS SYMBOL**	**39.50**	–
ms text	0.68	+	**MS TEXT**	**9.93**	+	**MS TEXT**	**14.89**	+	**MS TEXT**	**33.58**	+
total	1.30	+	**TOTAL**	**11.79**	+	**total**	**6.44**	+	total	3.02	+

In *Tables 9.11-14*, bold type indicates significance at at least 0.05 level, capitals indicates significance at at least 0.01 level. The +/– column indicates the direction in the difference, + indicating that the space per page consisting of the relevant signifying mode in the first book named in the heading is greater than that in the second named book. The estimation for χ^2 is given by the formula

$$\frac{(M_1 - M_2)^2}{\dfrac{S_1^2}{N_1 - 1} + \dfrac{S_2^2}{N_2 - 1}} \quad \text{where}$$

M and S are the sample means and standard deviations of the samples and N are the sample numbers.

Table 9.12: Differences of means of signifying mode space per page between Book G8 and Books B3, Y1 and Y5

G8–B3			G8–Y1			G8–Y5		
mode	χ^2	+/−	mode	χ^2	+/−	mode	χ^2	+/−
ICON	**11.86**	+	**ICON**	**13.98**	+	**ICON**	**48.03**	+
non-icon	**5.23**	−	**NON-ICON**	**10.77**	−	**NON-ICON**	**44.41**	−
cartoon	4.15	−	**CARTOON**	**10.75**	+	cartoon	4.65	+
drawing	4.46	+	drawing	3.20	+	**DRAWING**	**28.36**	+
PHOTO	**7.67**	+	**PHOTO**	**14.54**	+	**PHOTO**	**13.33**	+
index	**5.43**	+	index	0.16	−	**INDEX**	**22.37**	−
ms graph	0.52	+	ms graph	1.72	+	ms graph	3.15	+
ms table	1.77	+	ms table	1.77	+	ms table	1.77	+
NON-MS GRAPH	**8.83**	−	non-ms graph	1.30	−	**NON-MS GRAPH**	**32.96**	+
non-ms table	0.17	−	non-ms table	0.21	−	non-ms table	0.76	−
symbol	0.01	−	**SYMBOL**	**12.95**	+	symbol	**4.91**	+
MS SYMBOL	**7.27**	+	ms symbol	2.28	+	**MS SYMBOL**	**12.29**	+
non-ms symbol	0.46	−	**NON-MS SYMBOL**	**18.64**	−	**NON-MS SYMBOL**	**10.39**	−
ms text	**5.38**	+	**ms text**	**4.91**	+	**MS TEXT**	**12.90**	+
total	**5.65**	+	total	1.76	+	total	0.21	+

Table 9.13: *Differences of means of signifying mode space per page between Book B3 and Books Y1 and Y5*

B3–Y1		B3–Y5	
mode	χ^2 +/–	mode	χ^2 +/–
icon	0.06 –	**ICON**	**7.23 +**
non-icon	0.22 –	**NON-ICON**	**13.16 –**
cartoon	0.21 –	cartoon	0.60 +
drawing	0.44 –	**drawing**	**5.27 +**
photo	1.00 +	photo	0.59 +
index	**5.24 +**	index	3.14 –
ms graph	0.40 +	ms graph	1.63 +
ms table	X X	ms table	X X
non-ms graph	**5.17 +**	**non-ms graph**	**4.47 –**
non-ms table	0.01 +	non-ms table	0.09 –
SYMBOL	**7.93 –**	symbol	2.98 –
ms symbol	2.11 –	ms symbol	0.81 +
NON-MS SYMBOL	**7.00 –**	non-ms symbol	3.49 –
ms text	0.05 –	ms text	1.90 +
total	1.86 –	**total**	**5.26 –**

Table 9.14: *Differences of means of signifying mode space per page between Book Y1 and Book Y5*

Y1–Y5	
mode	χ^2 +/–
ICON	**15.71 +**
NON-ICON	**18.51 –**
cartoon	2.34 +
DRAWING	**17.04 +**
photo	0.42 –
INDEX	**27.44 –**
ms graph	3.40 +
ms table	X X
NON-MS GRAPH	**28.89 –**
non-ms table	0.29 –
symbol	1.76 +
ms symbol	**6.33 +**
non-ms symbol	0.84 +
ms text	3.3 +
total	1.13 –

in G8 constitutes a strengthening of the visual code of presence and indicates an increase in localizing strategies. It has been suggested, however, that cartoons connote childish play, whilst photographs (at least, the particular photographs used in the later G books) denote specific instances of adult reality. In this respect, the G series moves between modes of localizing in time with the

Table 9.15:   Index of differences between books

Signifying mode	Directioned differences between pairs of books						
Icon	G1→G8	G8→Y1	Y1→Y5				
Cartoon	G1→G8	G1→Y1	G8→Y1	G8→Y5*			
Drawing	Y1→Y5						
Photo	G1→G8	G8→Y1	G8→Y5				
Index	(G1→G8)	Y1→Y5					
non-ms graph	Y1→Y5						
Symbol	G1→G8*	G8→Y1	(Y1→Y5)				
MS text	G1→B3	G1→Y1	G1→Y5	G8→Y1*	G8→B3*	G8→Y5	(Y1→Y5)

The Table shows differences between pairs of *SMP 11–16* books in the G and Y series in the incidence of the relevant signifying mode. In all cases, the arrow shows the direction of increase. Bracketed differences are not significant at the 0.05 level; asterisked differences are significant at the 0.05 level, but not at the 0.01 level; other differences are significant at the 0.01 level.

chronological age of the student. Trajectories relating to the use of distributing strategies within the G series can thus be described as moving in different directions. There is a trajectory from strong to weak localizing (the substitution of symbolic for iconic text); there is a trajectory from weak to strong localizing (the substitution of photographs for cartoons and drawings); and there is a trajectory from one mode of localizing to another (the substitution of photographs for cartoons). This last trajectory can be described as the progressive replacement of education by domestic and working responsibilities, as will be illustrated in the next chapter. The G books signify this change by moving from the child's world of cartoons to the apparent concrete reality of photographs.

Within the Y series, the principal trajectory is represented by an exchange of iconic for indexical. Thus, drawings in Y1 are replaced by (non-ms) graphs in Y5. This signals a progressive weakening of localizing strategies[15]. The use of cartoons and photographs remains small and more or less constant within the Y series. The trajectory which moves from stronger to weaker localizing is, at least as far as the analysis in this section is concerned, unopposed.

Comparing the G with the Y texts, we find that there is a substantial and statistically significant reduction in iconic text between G and Y and corresponding increases in indexical and symbolic text. The latter is greater when the statistically significant difference in character density per page between G1 and Y5 is considered. Within the category of iconic text, cartoons and photographs are substantial resources only within the G series. Here, they comprise approximately 18 per cent of textual space in G1 and 13 per cent of textual space in G8. The largest proportion of Y series textual space which consists of these modes is 3.6 per cent (cartoons in Y1). Finally, manuscript text is

---

15   This weakening of localizing strategies is not countered by public domain settings as is the case in the G series (see Chapter 10).

never a very substantial resource, in terms of textual space (*Table 9.10*), but is minimal in the Y series in comparison to the G books.

Overall, the analysis of signifying modes points to the comparatively extensive and effectively constant use of dependency strategies in the G series. The Y series, on the other hand, makes far less use of localizing strategies from the start. At the end of the Y series, there is even less use of these strategies and far greater use of generalizing modes (indexical and symbolic text). The results of this quantitative content analysis, then, suggest the possibility that the G books may be described as (re)producing the DS⁺ practice of school mathematics as DS⁻. That is, as context-dependent. In this case, the context is precisely the pedagogic programme itself. Thus the reader voice is constructed, by the G books, as dependent upon this programme, which is to say, dependent upon the authorial voice.

I want to move now to consider further aspects of the genres of production that are constituted by the G and Y series and which facilitate the recruitment of social class by positioning strategies.

The Recruitment of Fundamental Organizing Principles in Material Production

I have already hinted at the significance of social class in the *SMP 11–16* texts in the analysis in Chapter 8. It will recur as an organizing principle throughout the remainder of the textual analysis in this book. Here, I want to consider the ways in which the specific genres of production of the Y and G series enable class to emerge as a principle of recognition of the apprenticed and dependent voices.

If we compare the physical construction of the G and Y series, the following differences emerge. The main textbooks of the G series, books G1 to G8, not only contain fewer pages overall than those of the 'Y' series, books Y1 to Y5, (512 pages as opposed to 832[16]) but there are also more G books (8 compared with 5 Y books). This means that each G book has very much fewer pages than each Y book (G1 has 64 pages, Y1 has 160). The G books are, in fact, stapled as booklets, whereas the Y books are bound as books[17]. Considered as a whole, the G series comprises eight books of approximately sixty pages each together with G booklets, three 'G resource packs', 'G supplementary booklets' and 'topic booklets' (shared with the 'B' books).

---

16 These figures include the title and contents pages etc.
17 Since 'extension book', YE1 is stapled (having only sixty-four pages), the difference in binding seems to be a consequence of the relative lengths of the books rather than (or, at least, in addition to) any deliberate decision to produce booklets for the 'less able' and 'books' for the more able. It is not, however, the authors' conscious intentions which are at issue here.

This gives a total of thirty-one G items (apart from Teacher's Guides) listed in the price list as compared with seven Y items (the five main books and two 'extension' books). The result is that the Y materials, taken individually, are far more 'weighty' than individual G materials and this is enhanced by the difference in the binding of the main books in each series.

The analysis of signifying modes revealed that Book G1 contains three times as much iconic space per page as does the first 100 pages of Book Y1 and nearly nine times as much as the sample of 100 pages from Book Y5. On the other hand, the Y1 sample contains approximately one-point-four times as much symbolic space per page as Book G1. Although there is a reduction in iconic space between G1 and G8, Book G8 still contains nearly six times as much iconic space per page as Book Y5. The ratio of symbolic space in G8 to that in Y5 is almost unity, but this is accounted for by the substantial increase in graphs in Y5 (three times the page coverage by non-manuscript graphs in G8). Furthermore, the character density of symbolic space in the Y series is significantly greater than that in the G books, so that the symbolic text in the Y series is visually more dense than that in the G books.

This differentiation of the G and Y materials in terms of physical and textual 'weightiness' connotes similar differentiations in printed materials of other kinds. For example, the differentiation between books for young children in comparison with those intended for a more adult audience and, in particular, the differentiation between the 'popular' and the 'quality' press. 'Quality' newspapers are typically substantially more weighty. Thus, on 21st March 1990, *The Daily Telegraph* contained forty-eight broadsheet pages and *The Times*, fifty-six (in two sections). *The Sun* and the *Daily Star*, on the other hand, contained only thirty-two and thirty-six pages respectively. Since the tabloid format is only half the size of the broadsheets, the 'quality' papers cover approximately four times the page area of the 'populars'. Furthermore, as Jeremy Tunstall (1983) notes: 'typically about 60 per cent of a tabloid's contents is in fact 'looked at' material — pictures, headlines, cartoons and display advertising . . .' (p. 134).

There is, in other words, a correspondence in form between the G books and the 'popular' press, on the one hand, and the Y books and the 'quality' press, on the other. However, there is also a connotative differentiation between the 'populars' and the 'qualities' in terms of social class; *Figure 9.2* illustrates the readership of the major 'quality' and 'popular' papers by social class. As Tunstall notes, this differentiation has a considerable history:

The 1947–49 Royal Commission referred to 'quality' and 'popular' national newspapers. Other nations have had similar distinctions — in France the *Grand* and *Petit* press — but in Britain this tradition is particularly long; it dates back to *The Times* and its radical rivals of the 1830s. To some extent the distinction between the large size prestige papers of the 1980s and the popular tabloids reflects real differences in education, reader interest and

Figure 9.2 *National newspaper readership by social class* (Source: Adapted from Tunstall, 1983)

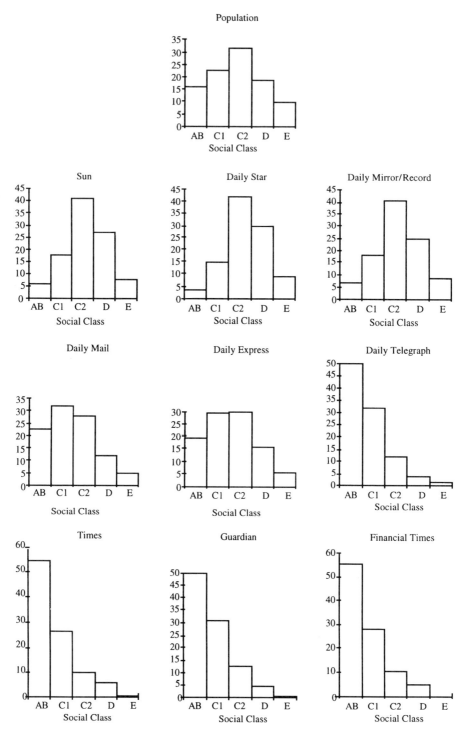

income. These real differences have become exaggerated because the two types of paper have not only, since the 1970s, acquired different physical sizes, but they rely on different prime sources of revenue. The 'prestige' papers operate primarily from an *advertising* revenue base; this forces them 'up market' more than a sales revenue base would require — because advertisers are willing to pay several times as much to reach readers who are several times as wealthy. (Tunstall, 1983; p. 77)

Economic targeting is also evidenced by the content of both reporting and advertising in different categories of newspaper. For example, in reporting income tax changes in the Budget in 1990, the *Daily Star* (21st March 1990) included tables showing weekly wages up to £700 per week, whilst *The Daily Telegraph* of the same day presented incomes as annual salaries up to £70 000 per year. This constitutes a difference in both form and substantive income (£700 per week is £36 400 per annum). In respect of advertising, we find, for example, 'SALES MANAGER Algarve, Portugal £45 – 70K + Benefits', in *The Daily Telegraph*. In the *Daily Mirror*, a Department of Trade and Industry advertisement is a photograph showing hands, holding aloft hand tools of various kinds and bearing the slogan 'HANDS UP FOR A JOB . . . *REAL TRAINING • REAL SKILLS • REAL JOBS.*'

It may well be the case that, as Williams (1961) points out, we cannot find 'quite the simple class affiliations used in popular discussion' (p. 236), particularly if readership data are presented in terms of the proportion of each social class taking each newspaper, rather than, as in *Figure 9.2*, the proportion of the readership of each newspaper within each social class. However, there is no attempt, here, to unify the Registrar General's sometime classifications in terms of cultural qualities. It is not a question of what social classes are like (insofar as such a question may have any meaningful answer). Nor is it entirely a question of what newspapers are like, although this is closer (and is, to a degree caught at by the social class profile of their respective readerships). It is more a question of what Williams describes as 'popular discussion' which enables connotative mappings, direct metonymic chains linking school textbooks to social classes via national newspapers.

I have already referred — in this chapter and the previous one — to the comic-book style of the early G materials. I have argued that this effects an infantilizing of the dependent reader voice through its identification with the objectified reader of comic literature. In similar manner, the differentiation in presentational style between the Y and G series constitutes a dichotomizing of genres of production. The result is the identification of the apprenticed, Y, reader voice and the dependent, G, reader voice with the objectified readership of broadsheet and tabloid newspapers, respectively and, connotatively, with the objectified middle class and working class voices which are more generally constructed as constituting these readerships. In this way, the *SMP 11–16* scheme is able to 'recognize' and so to recruit its high and low 'ability' readers in terms of its objectified — in this case stereotyped — class voices.

Genres of Production: Summary

In this chapter I have focused attention on some of the resources that are recruited in the material production of the *SMP 11–16* scheme to generate differentiated genres of production. As I announced at the beginning of the chapter, the activity — school mathematics — must be (re)produced through different textual genres because its pedagogic subject must address different subaltern voices. In this case, the Y text interpellates an apprenticed voice, whilst the G text interpellates a dependent voice. The genres are described via a comparison of the two schemes from which a positive description of each genre can be abstracted.

Thus, the genre characterized by the Y books employs, firstly, distributing strategies which recruit predominantly symbolic and indexical resources. These facilitate the generalizing strategies that are necessary in the (re)production of DS^+ practices and which, therefore, must feature in the construction of the apprenticed voice. Secondly, this genre recruits a style of presentation which recalls a social class-specific object via the stereotypical readership of the 'quality' press. This recruitment enables the text to identify the apprenticed voice with the middle class object voice.

The genre characterized by the G books, by contrast, incorporates distributing strategies which recruit substantially from iconic resources. This, firstly, delimits the potential for generalization, whilst facilitating localizing strategies. The latter can only present the DS^+ practices as DS^- and so construct the reader voice as dependent. Positioning strategies recruit differentially from iconic resources within the trajectory of the G series. Thus, the early part of the scheme recruits the cartoon mode, which identifies the dependent voice with an infantilized object voice — the reader of comic literature. The latter part of the scheme recruits from the photographic mode, commonly within domestic and other everyday settings. This identifies the dependent voice with a more mature, but nevertheless mundane object voice. The style of presentation of this genre now recalls the stereotypical readership of the 'popular' press. This enables the identification of the dependent voice with the working class object voice.

These specific differences in genre of production are not unique to the *SMP 11–16* scheme. If they were, the scheme would stand as a critical rather than a representative case study. Examples of similar differentiation in the genre of production of pedagogic texts are easy to find. For example, on one visit to the bookshop nearby my office, I visited the medical department, looking for a book on medical education. There was no section on medical education which would correspond to the mathematics and science education section in educational research. The book that I had been looking for was *A Handbook for Medical Teachers* (Newble and Cannon, 1994); I found it under 'general practice'. The foreword bemoans the general indifference to, even contempt for, pedagogy by medical and other academics. It recounts a story about a young assistant professor of mathematics at a 'leading research university' who won the 'best teacher' award one year. His department chairman summoned him and announced, '"You will win no 'brownie points' with me or this department for that kind of crap"' (p. ix). Ironically, the handbook reproduces itself as precisely 'that kind of crap'. It is in A4 format, with cartoons on the cover and as marginal illustrations throughout the text; books on endocrinology don't look like this.

In the next chapter I shall move to a consideration of the differential recruitment of settings by textual strategies employed in the SMP texts.

Chapter 10

Setting and the Public Domain

In the previous chapter I was concerned with what might be described as the expressive matrix which constitutes distinctive genres of production in the SMP materials. Now, I shall look at content, rather than expression. By way of orientation, I want first to describe the connotative construction of intellectual and manual objects by the Y and G books, respectively, in the construction of their cover illustrations. This analysis links to that of the previous chapter in underscoring the importance of social class as a principle of recognition. It points towards the subsequent work of the present chapter in moving towards a focus on content rather than on form of expression.

Getting Attention: The Cover Illustrations

The cover illustration of a book is an important scene setter which, if read with reference to the activity in which it participates, must minimally constitute an affiliation of its authorial voice and an identification of its reader voice. Take, for example, the doctoral thesis of the University of London. This is an A4 format book, bound in plain blue cloth and bearing only the degree — PhD — the year of submission and the name of the candidate in gold letters on the spine. The doctoral thesis must be considered as the 'masterpiece' of the apprenticed academic which confirms them as a worthy member of a community of academic peers. The almost singular lack of individuation of the thesis binding facilitates this affiliation. The reader is identified as already having made their selection, already having accepted a reader voice. This is because the only identification that can be made is with the readership of theses (of a specific period and of a specific university, perhaps) and with the audience — critical or acquisitive — of the specific candidate, whose topic must already be known. The potential reader must order the thesis from the librarian; they won't be allowed to browse the shelves.

The covers of the *SMP 11–16* Y and G books are more obviously sententious. The pictures on the front of Books Y1 and G1 (*Figure 10.1* and *10.2*) might serve as emblems for their respective series. The Y1 picture, a contour map of a face, is intellectually ambiguous: is it a mathematizing of humanity or a humanizing of mathematics? It is a janusian celebration of the mythical: mathematics can describe us; we can participate in mathematics. The picture also foregrounds the ambiguity of its own mode of signification. Depending

Figure 10.1   *SMP 11–16 Book Y1* (cover)

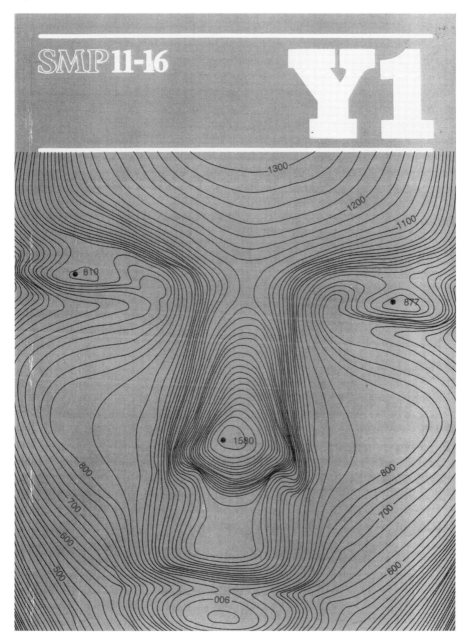

Figure 10.2   SMP 11–16 Book G1 (cover)

upon how you read it, it is both icon and index. The icon/index is, in other words, enigmatic, signalling the mysteries to be explored between the covers, in Chapter 11, 'Gradient'.

Contrast this cover with that of Book G1 (*Figure 10.2*). There is nothing very ambiguous here. The icon signifies three everyday items, foregrounding the quotidian. Mathematics is backgrounded in a quite literal sense; the digital calculator watch is partially obscured by its analogue. The juxtaposition of the three images might possibly suggest a historical narrative, not a mathematical one. There is no mystery, nothing intellectual. Even the calculator, in a sense, manualizes the intellectual and wristwatches are manual things. Taken together, these two covers inaugurate the recruitment of social class objects that I have referred to in the previous two chapters.

Social class may be understood as a fundamental organizing principle in the social spheres of commodity production and exchange[1]. The description of class as an organizing principle demands an empirical analysis of commodity production and exchange. This is clearly beyond the scope of the current project. Were such an analysis to be carried out, it is undoubtedly the case that class would emerge as a complex structure of dominant and subaltern positions[2]. Nevertheless, social class stratification is connoted by certain discursive oppositions, such as intellectual/manual[3] and by institutional oppositions such as quality/popular press. Social class is thus available as a resource which can be appropriated in the positioning of voices within activities such as school mathematics. Positioning strategies attach class-oriented metonyms in the (re)production of the voice hierarchy. This entails the identification of apprenticed and dependent voices with class-specific object voices. Insofar as this is achieved, it can be argued that Y and G reader voices are constructed in terms of social class.

The arcane/mundane opposition between the two series is restated on the covers of each book. The manual theme of G1 is sustained on the covers of G2 — a technician weighing a mouse — and G3 — surveyors using a tape measure on a building site. The hands of the technician (a scientist wouldn't be doing this) are foregrounded along with the physical act of weighing the mouse. The manual act of measuring on a building site also seems a long way from the intellectual classroom. Y2, by contrast, shows an M.C. Escher print, the mathematics ('Points, lines and planes' in Chapter 10) is again indexed by the enigma proposed by the icon.

Books G4 — plan and elevation drawings, rather than diagrams, of a windmill — and G5 — a plan drawing (again, not a diagram) of the ground

---

1 Race being another, that is, in relation to international divisions of labour, see Dowling (1990b, 1991a).

2 The complexity of the structure being attested by the diversity of forms that class analysis has taken; see, for example: Dahrendorf, 1959; Miliband, 1969; Poulantzas, 1975; Sohn-Rethel, 1978; also Parkin, 1978.

3 Indeed, Alfred Sohn-Rethel (1973, 1978) uses this opposition as the fundamental organizing principle of social class, as was discussed in Chapter 5.

floor of a house (complete with occupants) projected out of a street map — signal very practical skills, again all outside of the classroom. These covers iconize the indexical in their replacing of diagrams with drawings. The windmills show light and shade and grass bents are drawn in. Mum, dad and dog (the reader's?), watching TV/reading, find their way into an iconized plan of their own house which is graphically mapped onto a map of their town. The girl on the cover on Y3 might be a girl in the reader's class, but she is not the subject of the picture. She appears to be facing herself and this image is repeated in an ever reducing sequence. Something tricky is going on here and it has something to do with mirrors. How is it achieved, why does it work: mathematics will explain on page 54, where another picture of the girl in the mirror is printed.

G6 shows an 'exploded diagram' of what might be a single roomed crofter's cottage. 'People use exploded diagrams to fit things like cassettes together, or to take them apart', we are told on page 26, under the heading 'Exploded diagrams (1)'. It is, perhaps, unlikely that such diagrams are used in the construction or demolition of crofters' cottages, but 'Exploded diagrams (1)' is about the construction of an audio cassette. 'Exploded diagrams (2)' (pp. 53–6) is about a plastic kit of a model Mercedes 540 which 'you can buy' and, presumably, assemble manually. Y4 produces a metaphor which maps the shadow cast by the lampshade onto the graph of a mathematical function. There is, again, nothing manual about this image, even the hand which draws the graph is absent. Nor is there anything useful about the image, the mythical potential of mathematics as arcane reference to the mundane is celebrated, but not, on this Y cover, its use value for participation. Indeed, the image almost dismisses the public domain as having minimal intrinsic value.

The covers of the final two books in the G series take us farther afield than the homeliness of the G5 and G6 covers. The sprinting feline, on the G6 cover, blurring its exotic savannah setting connotes speed, the title of chapter 6. But the significations remain in the world, in the public domain. It is the speed of a motorbike or a car that constitutes the topic of the chapter. The giant 'golf ball' on the cover of G8 is somewhere else in the world, Disneyland. The 'golf ball' is 'almost spherical', like some other buildings, two of which are shown in Chapter 8, 'Cones, cylinders and spheres'. The chapter also includes photographs of a football and a globe: the mundane made literal. The final cover in the Y series returns to an ambiguity similar to that in the Y1 image. Has the world been mathematized: it's not a spherical but an icosahedral 'globe'? Or has the face of the world been superimposed on a mathematical index. The arcane and the mundane compete with the former coming out on top. The only practical thing about this 'globe' is that it won't roll away.

All of these covers move beyond the esoteric domain. Some (Y1, Y4, Y5, G4, G5) being (without consideration of the chapters that they index) descriptive domain, and the rest public domain. Insofar as they involve narratives, the Y covers are far more open and the G covers relatively closed, so that the latter more effectively than the former localize the public domain settings. The enigmatizing of the world by the Y covers identifies the reader voice with the intellectual. What might be described as the factualizing of the world by the G series covers identifies its reader voice, perhaps, with the anti-intellectual; the world is as it is, safe, known and risk-free, not dangerous, mysterious, risky. Furthermore, the emphasis on the manual skills in some of the G covers (G1, G2, G3, G6 (by connotation)) identifies the reader voice with manual practices. Through the respective attachment of the metonyms, intellectual and non-intellectual or manual, the two sets of covers achieve a connotative mapping of ability onto social class.

The covers signal the public domain, with varying degrees of openness, as invitations, interpellating the reader voice in the different ways that I have described. I now want to consider how the books incorporate the public domain into the mathematical tasks that comprise their principal content.

Public Domain Settings

I want to use the term *setting* to refer to a recognizable space for social prac-tice. Examples of settings might be 'domestic' (refinable as, for example, 'shopping', cooking, gardening, DIY, etc), 'work', 'school', 'travel'[4]. The category is not being defined sufficiently tightly to enable a quantitative ana-lysis to be carried out. I have, therefore, decided to present illustrative cases from the SMP texts. I am asserting, however, that similar descriptions could be made using virtually any extracts from these books. I should emphasize, that the referent activity remains school mathematics. The description of that activity is to be achieved, in part, through an interrogation of the way in which it acts selectively on its carriers, which are precisely the settings through which it is realized. The settings that occur most commonly in these texts are the domestic, work and school settings and I shall focus on each of these in turn.

The Domestic Setting

The domestic space may be glossed as that social region which is concerned with consumption, production and reproduction within the context of a kin-ship network. Domestic settings are common and often textually extended, in the G series. They are rare and generally brief, in the Y series. I shall discuss examples from three categories of domestic setting, shopping, DIY and cook-ing. Although the domestic setting is the focus of this section, its rarity of representation in the Y texts requires that I make reference to some text

---

4 That 'setting' is not coterminous with 'activity' is exemplified in the plausible overlapping of 'travel' with each of the other examples of settings: 'travel' may be indexed as a movement between social spaces.

relating to other settings in order to highlight the contrasts between the two books. Essentially, the domestic is used to localize in G, but not in Y.

Pervasive throughout the G series are settings related to shopping, almost invariably produced as narratives 'from the shopper's perspective'. Here is an example from Book G4, the shoppers being represented, in this instance, in the third person:

> Soap powder is sold in 'Euro-sizes'.
> These are Euro-sizes E5, E10 and E20.
> In the McGee family
> there are 2 adults and 3 children.
> The McGees use six E10
> packets of soap powder each year.
>
> C5   What weight of soap powder do the McGees use in a year?
>
> C6   The E10 packet costs £2.59.
>   How much does soap powder cost the McGees each year?
>
> C7   The E20 packet contains twice as much
>   powder as an E10 packet. It costs £3.89.
>   (a) How many E20's would the McGees use in a year?
>   (b) How much would powder cost them if they used E20's?
>
> C8   (a) How many E5 packets would the McGees
>   use in 1 year.
>   (b) The E5 packets are on special offer.
>   At the moment, an E5 packet costs 95p.
>   How much would the McGees soap powder
>   cost in a year if they used E5 packets? (G4, p. 18[5]; drawing
>   omitted)

As I have indicated in Chapter 1, there is evidence that 'best buy' decisions are efficiently and appropriately made in context (that is, in the supermarket) with very little reference or debt to school mathematics (see Lave, 1988). However, recourse to such research is hardly necessary to reveal some of the violence that has been done to the setting in this case. For example, the long timescale of this narrative (a year) ought, perhaps, to make allowances for inflation[6], and the answer to C8 (b) given in the Teacher's Guide (£11.40) suggests that either the 'special offer' lasted all year (rendering it rather 'ordinary') or the McGees bought a year's supply all at once. This, despite the family's apparent storage problems indicated by their customary use of the middle sized packet rather than the 'better value' E20 size. The conditions have to be fixed in order to allow the exercising of the mathematical intention of the chapter, which is 'to provide pupils with experience of ratio problems' (G4TG, p. 14). This recontextualizing is, however, apparently belied by the realism of the task formulation. The reader is provided with some 'factual'

---

5   The vulgar use of the apostrophe to indicate a plural — as in 'How many E20's ...' — is representative of a common inelegance in language.

6   The possibility of prices going down is mentioned in the 'discussion points' in the Teacher's Guide, as noted below.

information about shopping (Euro-sizes) and is introduced to a family. The task, itself, apparently concerns the optimizing of the McGees' domestic routine. Thus the narrative is comparatively closed: this might be the reader's family, either now or in the future; or it might connote a 'soap' family with which the reader voice is identified. The setting, in other words, is limited to the specific community space of this family and to this specific aspect of their domestic activity.

This is a mathematics task, but the text is silent on the matter of how it is to be read and on how the task is to be carried out. There is, deliberately, no explicit pedagogizing of method in this chapter, as is common in the G series:

> There are many methods of solving problems where ratio is involved. We have deliberately not set out a 'standard method'. After pupils have done a few questions, we hope that discussion with them will bring out these various methods, and thus help them tackle the next batch of problems. (G4TG, p. 14)

There is an assumed transparency in the task text with regard to its reading and a repertoire of 'strategies' within the classroom. The repertoire is activated by the 'realistic' task and made explicit in 'discussion'. Thus, pedagogic practice, here, is a celebration of already existing competencies through official recognition and sharing in discussion. At the end of the chapter there is a bordered set of 'discussion points', the first two of which are, 'Why are things cheaper when you buy them "in bulk"?' and 'Sometimes it is not sensible to buy in bulk. When is it silly to buy huge packets?'; the Teacher's Guide gives the following answers to these discussion points:

> Cheaper in bulk: easier to handle, less packaging costs, less transportation costs, take up less space etc.

> Large packs not best when you have little money, you can't store large packs, food might go off before you can eat it, prices might go down etc. (G4TG, p. 16)

However, the inclusion of such discussion only serves to accentuate the domestic setting which has apparently been incorporated by school mathematics. In other words, we might ask why shopping should appear in a mathematics textbook. One reason might be to initiate a route into the esoteric domain. This would constitute a metonymic articulation of the public and esoteric domains which would contribute to the apprenticing of the reader voice. Alternatively, the performance of the shopping tasks might be constructed as mathematically therapeutic. But the text does not leave the public domain and, furthermore, there is very little (if any) explicit articulation of these shopping tasks with other tasks and exposition in the G series; they stand in metaphorical relation to each other. Thus, in broader view of the G series, any expansion of the public domain is constituted as a fragmentation.

249

At the same time, the elaboration of the public domain setting through the closed narrative and the identification of the reader voice with the setting effect a projection of the dependent voice into a highly localized region of the public domain. The tasks seem to be constituted for the benefit of optimizing shopping practices themselves. Mathematics, even if this is signified only by the subject or book title, is being constructed as a prior condition for optimum participation in the public domain. This is the *myth of participation* that was introduced in Chapter 1.

There are two points to be made, here. Firstly, as there is no pedagogizing of method, methods are constructed as residing within the reader or within the setting. The reader's competence in participation is constructed as the prior condition for mathematics, whilst the latter is constructed as the prior condition for the reader's competent participation in the setting. The myth is thereby deconstructed[7]. Secondly, the setting, itself, is a recontextualizing of shopping. The criteria for successful completion of the tasks within the mathematics context are not the same as those structuring the domestic activity. There is, in other words, no basis for the reader's competence. The myth of participation is precisely a shibboleth.

The 'best buy' problem is the setting for the whole of Chapter 1 of Book G7. Localizing in this chapter is enhanced by the extensive use of photographs of 'real' supermarket commodities (see, for example, *Figure 6.9*) and prices which 'were accurate in 1987' (G7TG, p. 7). Furthermore, the teacher is, here as throughout the series, urged to carry the localizing further:

> [Discussion] is central to the chapter. The pupils' own stories of 'bargains' and 'best buys' should be exploited. [. . .]

> The prices will, inevitably, be out of date. It would be useful to bring in (or list) actual tins, packets and so on. You could make a collection of labels if you prefer not to use actual tins etc. — this is not quite so good, but better than nothing!

> Comparing prices in different supermarkets may be possible.

> All the prices used in the chapter were accurate in 1987 — you will (like the authors!) need to search hard to find tins or packets where 'biggest gives more for your money' is not true. (G7TG, p. 7)

The stated intention of the chapter has moved completely into the public domain in the expression of the 'aims' in the Teacher's Guide:

> To develop various strategies for working out 'which packet gives you most for you [sic] money.'

----

7 See Derrida, 1981; Sturrock, 1979.

To show that 'value for money' depends on more than this, and to encourage
examination and discussion of other factors. (G7TG, p. 7)

Here, the intention explicitly concerns participation in a domestic setting
which is, again, produced as providing the rationale for the tasks. Again,
mathematics is the prior condition for this participation (or, at least, for effective participation). This chapter is distinguished from the previous one discussed in that it does include prescribed methods, presented as algorithms, or
procedures, with reference to specific cases. In one piece of exposition, for
example, two tins of 'Sainsburys Garden Peas' are shown in a photograph
and their value for money is compared by calculating the weight of peas per
1p using division on a calculator (G7, p. 2). The procedure, however, is
entirely restricted to commodities sold by weight and is nowhere abstracted
to the more general topic of ratio (although this topic is mentioned in the G4
Teacher's Guide).

Whereas the G4 example signifies a highly limited public domain through
the introduction of a family, the G7 chapter effects limitation through the use
of 'actual' commodities and real prices, etc. The earlier example presented a
vision of future participation, the tasks in the G7 chapter make the reader the
grammatical subject of the narrative, identifying the reader voice with the
public domain setting. There are few cases of a third person, everything is
expressed in terms of what 'you' can buy and which gives more for 'your'
money. The trajectory from G4 to G7, supported by the shift from drawings
to photographs, is towards a greater realism and, perhaps, immediacy of
participation. Again, there are 'discussion points' covering almost identical
areas and having almost identical answers as those in the earlier chapter.

Distributing strategies are operating, in these examples, to limit the public domain setting to specific instances which are particularized. The latter may
be achieved through the introduction of algorithms. Alternatively, there is a
presumption of competence which is exterior to the text itself. The implicit
nature of this competence constructs the esoteric and public domains and
settings within the public domain in metaphorical relation to each other. This
combination of limitation and particularizing constitutes a localizing of the
public domain message which is distributed to the dependent voice.

There are very few shopping settings in the Y series, two instances were
cited in Chapter 1. These tasks, concerning shopkeepers A and B and Britannia
and Uncle Sam's flour, establish a clear semantic distance between the reader
voice and the shopping setting by employing comparatively open narratives
and clearly contrived settings. In other words, the tasks include elements of
generality and strangeness which ensures their dislocation from the domestic
setting to which they now only indirectly relate.

These examples signal a chapter (Y1.04) which incorporates an exposition
on the mathematical method which is to be applied in such cases, the 'unitary
method'. Like the G7 exposition, the unitary method is introduced by reference to a specific case, that of a length of steel rope (not a domestic setting):

Figure 10.3 SMP 11–16 Book Y1 (pp. 46–47)

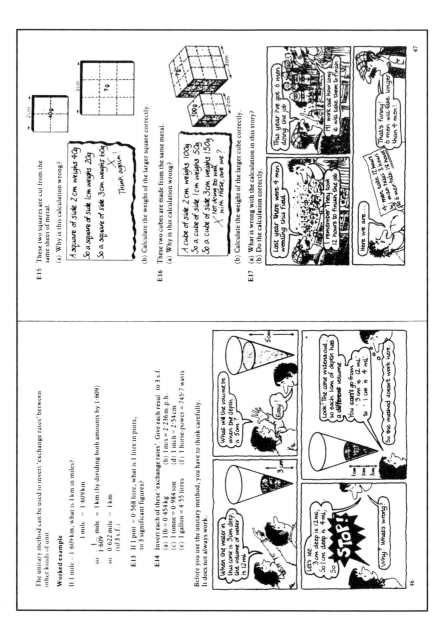

Here is a problem of a very common type.

> 12.3 m of steel rope weighs 10.6kg.
> How much does 17.5m of the rope weigh?

You can solve this problem by first working out how much 1 metre of the rope weighs. This method is called the **unitary** method. It can only be used when the rope is **uniform**, so that every metre weighs the same amount. (Y1, p. 43; drawing of rope and border omitted)

The exposition goes on to describe and carry out the computation. The first point to note is that the exposition marks out the 'problem', but not the setting, as being of a common type. The tasks that follow concern the weights of bolts and of gold, the alcoholic content of wine, the revolutions of a wheel, the thickness of paper, the iron yield from iron ore, the weights of links of a chain and of ball bearings, the petrol consumption of a car and of a motor-bike, the vitamin C content of orange juice, the weights of squares and cubes of metal, foreign exchange rates, and the conversion of units; the last two of these are also signalled by the second of the two tasks quoted above. Most of the tasks employ objects which might participate in a diversity of settings (or in none at all) and, in any event, no setting is elaborated, the narratives are very open because the settings are comparatively arbitrary. It is the mathematical structure that is being foregrounded, an abstract structure that may be imposed upon many settings and thereby articulating them metonymically. The reader voice is identified, potentially, with the voice of this structure, which is to say, as an apprentice to the authorial voice.

The section also includes several instances (again, none of them implicating domestic settings) in which the unitary method cannot be applied. The first is a strip cartoon representing a discussion between a girl and a boy about the relationship between the depth and volume of water in a cone (as is often the case in these books, the girl has the correct answer). The final tasks in the section are shown in *Figure 10.3*. This last case, task E17, satirizes the setting and its characters both through the mode of expression and the content.

Thus, although the opening exposition (which is considerably more extensive than the extract above) is expressed with reference to a specific case, the variation in settings in the subsequent tasks expands the public domain. This expansion is not unprincipled. On the contrary, a limited region of the esoteric domain is signalled in metonymic terms[8]. The text specializes the esoteric domain and generalizes the expanded public domain via the abstracted esoteric domain discourse. Without this generalizing discourse, the public domain is fragmented, as was found in the descriptive domain tasks at the end of Y1.03 (discussed in Chapter 8). These abstracting strategies contrast with the particularizing of the G text.

---

8 The text does not move fully into the esoteric domain, so that principling as such cannot be fully achieved.

The Teacher's Guide includes a comment at the head of the answers to this chapter which promises future discursive generalization:

> Please note that questions E15 and E16 are introduced to be merely 'counter examples' involving misuse of the unitary method. The important (and difficult) topics of the effects of the enlargement on area and on volume are dealt with later in the series. (Y1TG, p. 21)

This topic is begun in Chapter 1 of Book Y3. The unitary method is developed in Chapter 1 of Book Y2 and in subsequent chapters in the series. The Y2 chapter includes more shopping settings. Again, narrative detail is minimal, 'dress material' and 'crisps' being represented as instances of something which can be bought and which are possible instances of proportionality and non-proportionality (previously defined in the esoteric domain). There is also a varying in the form of address in the exposition, 'suppose *you* buy . . .', '. . . if *we* buy . . .' and, in the subsequent task, 'when a *motorist* buys . . .'. These texts exhibit: a variation in settings and in form of address; a minimizing of setting detail; textual movement between the esoteric and public domains; and longer term trajectories which facilitate discursive abstraction and, again, the esoteric domain generalization of the public domain.

These features all serve to minimize the local importance of the setting and to accentuate the mathematical grammar. The setting is backgrounded whilst the mathematics is foregrounded. Mathematics, in other words, is abstracted in relation to the public domain. This contrasts with the particularizing G texts which frequently concentrate on a given setting for an extended amount of textual time, sometimes an entire chapter. Closed narratives, in the G texts, give far more setting detail. There is a greater consistency in projecting the reader into the public domain setting and, thereby, in the incorporation of non-mathematical regimes of truth. The G reader voice is thus frequently identified with the object voices of the public domain. This is at the expense of esoteric domain text and abstracted discourse. The content of background and foreground is reversed between the two series of books as is the domain of principal identification of their respective reader voices.

Participation in a public domain, domestic setting is not entirely absent from the Y texts, A task in Y3, for example, shows a rare Y instance of a DIY setting. The reader is introduced to and identified with Jan, Rob and Cathy who are decorating their flat. This introduction connotatively signifies a possible future for the reader, sharing (and decorating) a flat with some friends. However, the task, which entails making a work plan for Jan, Rob and Cathy, involves a recontextualizing from management practice, this being made clearer, perhaps, by reference to the other tasks in the chapter. The chapter opens with a problem involving the planning of staff holidays at 'Mayhem's stores'[9], there follows: a task which involves planning the holidays of a sports centre

---

9 A metaphor which presumably signifies an erroneous use of 'mayhem' and also a satirizing of the setting.

staff; another which concerns the planning of the building of an office complex; and another which is about managing the manufacturing process in what appears to be a dressmaking factory. The last two tasks in the chapter follow the first by satirizing their settings. C1 concerns the problems involved in getting a passport in 'Ruritania' (an optimising of the imaginary) and C2 is about 'Cold Comfort farm museum' (complete with besmocked yokel holding a pitchfork and uttering 'oooo Aaaarr', an 'ancient farm worker').

The method to be employed in these tasks involves, essentially, the transcription of listed data into a form of graph (a transcription which is far more radical than anything in the G series). The chapter presents an apparently generalizable heuristic through the introduction of a range of public domain settings, although without ever entering the esoteric domain. The planning heuristic indexes an abstracted discursive space via the diversity of settings which are presented. A generalizing potential is being asserted, so that the decorating task is less about participation in DIY than about exploring the range of application of the heuristic. Mathematics is presented, not as a precondition for participation in the domestic setting, but, again, as generalizing its structure, linking it metonymically with an indefinite number of other settings. Thus, the generalizing strategy operates by backgrounding the specificities of the setting or, as in the first task and last two tasks of the chapter, by satirizing the setting, enabling metonymic abstraction and weakening the public domain positioning of the reader voice.

In contrast, DIY settings are very common in the G series. *Figure 10.4* shows one instance from Book G7 in a chapter which, rather unusually, has been given an esoteric domain title, 'Ratios'. As with the McGees' shopping, the narrative is comparatively closed, introducing a familial setting, in this case, fairly strongly gender-stereotyped. It is dad, not mum, who is doing the work. Jane is somewhat inappropriately dressed and is only handing dad the bricks[10]. This stereotyping is, however, disrupted in task A6 and the associated drawing, which introduce a female builder. The drawing in *Figure 10.4* is 'straight', it is not a cartoon, so that the code of presence is minimally disrupted. The opening task gives further narrative details, 'first they dig a trench . . .'. The closed narrative and strong code of presence localizes the setting. Furthermore, this is public domain text. There is no mention of ratios and no mention of method which must reside as a local competence within the reader-setting. Indeed, the term 'ratio' appears only three times in the whole chapter (which moves from a DIY to a cooking setting): once in the title, once in a recipe for fruit punch and once in the exposition associated with the latter:

10   The drawing illustrates the violence of recontextualizing in the ergonomically inappropriate positioning of the heap of bricks (they're obviously not new ones) and other materials and tools. Dad, inexplicably, has placed his mortar on the opposite side of the wall from that on which he is standing. The subordination of the feminine assistant, here, mirrors the subordination of the masculine assistant in the domestic setting in the original SMP series. See the discussion in Chapter 4.

Figure 10.4 SMP 11–16 Book G7 (p. 22)

4 Ratios

A Review

A1 Jane and her dad are building a brick wall.
First they dig a trench for the foundation of the wall.
Then they fill the foundation with concrete.

This list shows what they need
to make 1 barrow-load of concrete.

> Makes 1 barrow load
> 6 shovels sand
> 4 shovels gravel
> 2 shovels cement
> water

(a) How much sand do they need
to make 3 barrow-loads of concrete?

(b) How much gravel do they need
for 5 barrow-loads of concrete? ●

(c) Jane reckons they will need about 8 barrow-loads of concrete.
Write down how much sand, gravel and cement this needs.

A2 Jane's dad buys the cement in bags.
Each bag holds about 8 shovels of cement.

(a) About how many shovels of cement
will you get out of 4 bags?

(b) About how many shovels of cement
will 3 bags hold?

(c) If you need about 20 shovels of cement,
how many bags will you need to buy?

(d) How many barrow-loads of concrete
can you make from one bag of cement?

22

This is a recipe for fruit punch. You mix cider and apple juice **in the ratio 2 to 3.**

That means that for every 2 parts of cider, you add three parts of apple juice. So if you used 2 litres of cider, you would use 3 litres of apple juice. (G7, p. 25; bold text in red in original)

The Teacher's Guide makes it clear why the term has been generally avoided:

> The phrase 'in the ratio 2 to 3' is used only on page 25, since most ratio applications are not stated in this form. Pupils using Stage Three assessment will need this usage emphasised.

> You may need to revise m². The words 'foundation', 'coping stones', and 'ingredients' may need attention. (G7TG, p. 12)

For the most part, the esoteric mathematics is to be backgrounded in favour of the relevant domestic setting. The use of the term, 'ratio', which is used in the title of the chapter is, in fact, only a requirement for those readers involved in the highest level of formal assessment relating to the G scheme. Otherwise, mathematical signifiers are confined to 'm²', which has been met before. On the other hand, the non-mathematical terms 'foundation', 'coping stones' and 'ingredients' are important, foregrounding the setting at the expense of mathematics and ensuring that there is no weakening of the identification of the reader voice with the public domain object voices.

As with many of the G series public domain settings which have been discussed, method is not fixed:

> We have not suggested one 'correct' method. You will need to discuss with your pupils the various methods which might be used in particular circumstances. [. . .]

> There is no wish here to impose a particular method or to suggest that one is 'better' than another. (G7TG, pp. 1–13)

No method at all is provided for tasks A1–6, but four algorithmic methods are illustrated in the context of the subsequent task, A7. These algorithms are all strongly localized to the particular task and, in any event, apparently represent only a sample of the 'lots of ways to work this out'; 'what matters is getting the answer right — and checking that your answer looks about right'. The rationale for the tasks, the methods and the criteria for evaluation reside within the reader-setting articulation.

The primacy of the setting is further and explicitly emphasized in both the Teacher's Guide and in the student's text:

> [. . .] In very many of the questions, the assumption that the relationship is strictly linear ('twice as much takes twice as long' etc.) is very much open to discussion and is brought out at the very end of the chapter [. . .] (G7TG, p. 12)

The chapter closes with a 'discussion point':

> 'It take 4 minutes to boil an egg.
> How long will it take to boil 2 eggs?'
> Questions like this are meant to fool you!
> But there are other times when the methods in this chapter won't work.
> For example, it might cost £20 to have 500 posters printed.
> But it won't cost twice as much for 1000 posters.
> Why can't you just double?
> What other examples are there like this? (G7, p. 28)

The reader is, in fact, given no chance to be fooled, but is alerted to the trick straight away. This contrasts with several examples in the Y series, where the trick has to be discovered. Mathematically, this is the same qualification as is being made by the Y1 text in *Figure 10.3*. The Y text, however, focuses on the mathematical structure, 'the cone widens out, so each 1cm of depth has a different volume'. This deviates from the requirement of 'uniformity', which had been introduced earlier. Furthermore, the Y1 Teacher's Guide gives answers to E15–17 which index alternative mathematical structures:

> The weight is related to the area of the metal, not simply the length of its side.
> [. . .]
> The weight is related to the volume of the metal.
> [. . .]
> One man will take *four times* as long as four men, not a quarter of the time.
> Six men will take a sixth of the time one man takes. (Y1TG, p. 23)

Although the G text also mentions mathematical structure, this occurs only when it addresses the teacher. Even then, 'linear' is translated as '"twice as much takes twice as long" etc.' The answer to the 'discussion point' quoted above remains firmly in the public domain and incorporates further localizing strategies:

> Many things cost comparatively less when ordered in bulk.
> It should be possible to find examples of printing within the school: report forms, brochures etc.
> Pupils could be asked to find examples — personalised stationery, Christmas cards, photocopying perhaps — where rates for different quantities are sometimes advertised. (G7TG, p. 13)

The G7 'ratios' chapter represents the public domain settings as driving the mathematics, whereas the Y texts consistently present mathematics as making sense of the public domain (descriptive domain) or as illustrated by the public domain (expressive domain). The Y texts mark out the limitations of the application of the unitary method. It achieves this explicitly, in the case of the 'cone of water' discussion. In the tasks concerning the metal squares and cubes, the limitations are implied by the introduction of dotted lines on the associated 'graphs', which both reveals the inadequacy of the postulated 'answer' and suggests a more appropriate solution. The inadequacy of the 'unitary method' in E17 is indexed by the absurdity of the final utterance in the cartoon. The task is presented as a puzzle, with the solution being encoded in the equivalently absurd logic which moves from '4 men take 12 hours' to '1 man takes 3 hours' (although, looking at the men, this might be plausible). The limiting of the message is only temporary — a career pacing strategy. The minimizing and satirizing of the public domain contribute to the alienation of the objectified voices and the identification of the reader voice as apprentice.

There is no unitary method in the G7 text, however. Arrays of 'ways' are presented, *post hoc*, as methods that might have been used by the reader. The mathematical equivalence of the 'ways' is not addressed, nor are they given ultimate privilege over other methods that the reader might have used, 'what matters is getting the right answer'. The limitations of these methods (which are those of the reader her/himself) are given in the structure of the setting, for example, 'many things cost comparatively less when ordered in bulk'. The reader must, at least potentially, already be familiar with such knowledge, because there are no clues within the formulation of the 'discussion point'. The G text is, again, localizing or, alternatively, fragmenting the settings within the postulated material experiences of the reader and it is within these experiences — within the public domain — that the limitations of mathematics as well as its specific procedures reside.

The G text presents the public domain setting as paramount, but this is not to gainsay the recontextualizing achievement of the gaze. To refer back to task A1 (*Figure 10.4*): there is an elision of the process whereby dad arrives at the requirement for '8 barrow-loads of concrete' which, in any event, we might expect to result in a measure of cubic metres or yards. The recipe for the concrete, itself, is suspect. More sand than aggregate ('gravel') is unusual, and the mixture is far too strong for foundations[11]. Using 'shovel' and 'barrow-load' as units is appropriately 'manual' and 'amateur', but it is not clear that such a choice would facilitate the mixing of concrete, especially as the size of a shovel is defined in terms of the amount of cement in a bag[12]. Finally, on

---

11 The *Reader's Digest New D-I-Y Manual* (Frewing, N.J. and Wilkins, T, (eds), nd, London: RDA) suggests 1 part cement, $2\frac{1}{2}$ parts sharp sand and $3\frac{1}{2}$ parts coarse aggregate. There is no obvious reason for the practically inappropriate recipe, because using the quantities, 7 shovels of gravel, 5 of sand and 2 of cement would not render the task arithmetically more complex; nevertheless, this illustrates the arbitrariness of the practical details.

12 The *Reader's Digest New D-I-Y Manual* provides recipes both in proportions (see earlier footnote) and in the units in which the materials would be ordered (bags, in the case of cement, kg for sand and aggregate). This publication also offers the following instructions labelled 'What to specify for a ready-mixed load': 'Mix C7.5P to BS5328; medium or high workability; 20mm maximum aggregate'. As in the G text, there is a certain invisibility of the generative grammar. However, we can assume that this message, esoteric as it is, will get us our concrete: it is not meant for us, but for the concrete mixer.

the following page of the G7 chapter, the reader is asked to estimate the number of bricks needed to build a half-brick wall $1\frac{1}{2}$m high and 4 m long. Such dimensions for a half-brick wall, especially without end or intermediate piers, seem positively dangerous[13].

Thus, firstly, the G text is presenting domestic settings which, in articulation with the reader's individual experiences, embody mathematical algorithms and the limitations on the application of these algorithms, highly localizing the message. Secondly, there is no explicit consideration of any unifying mathematical structure. Rather, various context-specific algorithms are presented, any of which (along with any others that yield the right answer) are acceptable. Thirdly, the settings are localized by the comparatively closed narratives. This is achieved through, for example, the large amount of detail given and the use of characters as object voices (often named and/or represented in an icon) which have some affinity with the reader voice. The latter is thereby identified with them and is itself objectified by the text. Mathematics, in other words, is presented as residing *within* the domestic world, as substantially particularized by context-specificity, and as a precondition for optimizing participation within domestic practices; this is the myth of participation.

However, domesticity is recontextualized, so that the generative/evaluative grammars of these 'real life' practices are elided and negated. The text announces itself as mathematics, but offers no ingress into mathematical discourse. The text promises an optimizing of domesticity, through its localizing strategies, but has shifted the material basis of domesticity from the home to the classroom, so that what is being optimized is no longer domesticity. Furthermore, the means of the proposed optimizing is algorithmic, but the text frequently assumes that these algorithms are already available to the reader and confers official sanction on those that 'work'. Under these circumstances, the myth of participation deconstructs itself by inverting its own prioritizing. Rather than mathematics facilitating participation in the domestic, it is domestic competence that facilitates participation in mathematics. Such participation is denied, however, as the text almost never leaves the public domain.

The domestic space is that space which is most highly localized and individualized in relation to the student-reader *vis à vis* school mathematics. Yet this space is minimally indexed by the Y texts. Where the text does intrude into the domestic setting, the narratives are generally open and recontextualizing is highly visible. Text is descriptive domain, but rarely public domain. Rarely is the participation of the reader indexed. It is not localized and individualized public domain competencies that are celebrated, but the power of mathematics to describe, define and control. The following task from Y2 is exemplary:

A cookery book gives these instructions for roasting pork:
25 minutes per pound, plus an extra 35 minutes.

13   We can tell that this is a half-brick wall from the information given in the text, including the pattern of stretchers and the number of bricks required per square metre.

(a) Which of these sketch graphs shows the relationship between the weight of a joint and its cooking time?

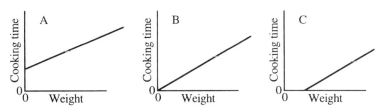

(b) Is the cooking time proportional to the weight? (Y2, p. 152)

This is a rare instance of a cooking setting in the Y series. It incorporates no characters, there is not even a specification of a particular, exemplary joint of pork. It is always the mathematical expressions — proportionality, relationship, the line graphs — that are foregrounded. There is no participation, here, even the absurdity of a joint weighing 0 lb needing 35 minutes fails to get a mention, although this consequence of the formula is represented on the 'correct' graph (A). Rather than few detailed, closed narratives which localize, the Y texts implicate many open narratives, foregrounding the abstracted mathematical structure and backgrounding the setting. But the mathematical structure resides within the esoteric domain which constitutes the gaze, rather than in the always already recontextualized setting. The myth of participation in the immediate and local is replaced by the myth of reference.

I shall now leave home for work and move to a discussion of the work setting.

The Work Setting

In Chapter 9 I illustrated the way in which the SMP scheme recruits social class as a public domain selection principle through its differentiation of genres of production in the Y and G series. In the first section of this chapter I pointed to the intellectual/manual connotations of the covers of the respective sets of books. These constitute positioning strategies which hierarchically interpellate the Y and G reader voices such that the former is identified as an intellectual voice and the latter as a manual voice. Here, I shall illustrate a continuity in these identifications in tasks settings that relate to economic activity, that is to 'work'.

As a first example, Books G8 and Y5, the terminal books in their respective series, each contain a short section relating to income tax. In G8, this section (section D of Chapter 6, 'Percentages in use') also includes Value Added Tax. Y5 has a separate section dealing with VAT. The G8 section opens with a photographic reproduction of a small collection of government information documents, including 'Income Tax and the Unemployed', foregrounded, perhaps as a threat to those who would not mathematically optimize their economic participation. The settings for the exposition and tasks include the denotations of weekly wage earners and basic rate tax payers. In fact, nearly all of the references to income in the G series refer to weekly wages, even a doctor's income (G8, p. 37) is described as 'about £350 a week'.

By contrast, the expression 'wages' is absent from 'Money matters: income tax' in Book Y5. The term 'income' is used exclusively. Throughout the Y series, incomes are generally described as annual salaries and only very rarely as weekly wages. Furthermore, the Y5 exposition on income tax also denotes above-basic-rate income tax payers and the only calculation that the reader is to perform concerns an individual with a taxable income of £50 000. The Y5 section is distinguished from the rest of the book by its comprising almost entirely of the exposition. There are four tasks, grouped in pairs, under the heading 'Find out', but only the calculation of the tax paid by a £50 000 per annum earner can be completed on the basis of information given in the exposition; the others require further investigation. A substantial amount of the information given in the exposition is in fact historical information which has no utility value in respect of the calculation of income tax. In fact, there is, generally, no need to calculate the amount of tax paid on your salary, because this is done on behalf of the government by tax inspectors (illustrated in a cartoon in Y5) or by your employers (as is stated in the G8 section). In terms of mathematics, the Y5 section appears to be almost redundant, so that the non-mathematical denotations, including high income groups, are foregrounded.

Juxtaposed, the G and Y sections denote an income hierarchy within the economic field which now maps onto the ability hierarchy denoted by the G/Y differentiation. Furthermore, insofar as salaries and wages connote middle and working class positions, respectively, there is an additional mapping of ability onto social class which is consistent with the analysis in Chapter 9 and earlier in this chapter.

This social class identification is sometimes achieved more directly through the differential recruitment of settings. For example, although neither the G nor the Y series make many direct references to 'professionals' within what used to be Social Class 1 (OPCS, 1980), where they do, the reader is differentially placed in relation to them. A one-and-a-half page sequence of tasks in Y1 relating to a geologist, for example, involves calculations using formulae relating to the growth of stalactites. The fictional geologist has derived these formulae empirically, for example:

> [. . .]
> In a wetter cave nearby, the geologist studied two other stalactites. The formula for the length of one of them was $l = 1231 + 1.8t$, and for the other it was $l = 1384 + 2.1t$.
> As before, l is in mm and t is the number of years since 1950.
> (a) Find the value of t when the two stalactites were of equal length.
> (b) In what year was this? (Y1, p. 71)

There is a sense in which the reader is participating, as an apprentice, perhaps, in the work of the geologist[14], using her equations, and so forth.

Another case concerns a 'biologist' who 'wanted to compare the lengths of worms living in two different kinds of soil' (Y3, p. 89). The final part of this task requires the reader to 'write a brief report comparing the two groups of worms' (*ibid*). The reader is again positioned alongside the professional.

By contrast, a doctor in G8 (mentioned above) is simply a wage earner. Dr Baxter, possibly an academic, is running a computer programme in G1 (p. 59). However, the G task involves calculations relating to the time that the programme takes and not anything to do with the professional activities of Dr Baxter. Another medical doctor appears in G8, taking a girl's pulse (p. 48). However, the whole section (two pages) is about heart rates, more than half of it relating to a graph of the pulse rate of an athlete. Only in two tasks is the measurement of pulse rate placed within a medical setting (an earlier task has a nurse timing a patient's pulse rate) and the last task in the section involves the reader experimenting with her/his own pulse rate. Thus the timing of a pulse is not constituted as specialized medical practice in the way that the prediction of stalactite growth is constituted as specialized geological knowledge. The G reader is watching the doctor; the Y reader is, in a sense, a proto-apprentice of the geologist or of the biologist. Only the Y reader is identified as a possible future professional.

On the other hand, where non-professional occupations are denoted, the relationship between the Y and G readers and the occupational group is often reversed. *Figures 10.5* and *10.6*, for example, both show 'police' settings and both concern the estimation of the speed of a vehicle by measuring skid marks. The two texts recruit the same public domain setting. However, they implicate the object voices — the police officers — into their narratives in quite different ways. The photograph in the G6 section (*Figure 10.5*) situates the reader at the shoulder of the officer making the measurement. This viewpoint is minimally interrupted by the strong iconic code of presence of the photographic mode. The table to be completed by the reader is drawn in manuscript, as it might be in the policeman's notebook. The final task requires the reader to estimate the speed of a car from its skid marks, thus performing a simulation of the policeman's task. In addition, the formula is stated in words, which minimizes the intrusion of specialized expression; the text barely penetrates the descriptive domain. The reader voice is a proto-apprentice of the objectified policeman, just as it was a proto-apprentice of Peter in the 'Formulas' chapter analysed in Chapter 8.

The Y text (*Figure 10.6*) is actually very different. The code of presence is now interrupted by the drawing mode and the reader is positioned as an onlooker and clearly not a participant. The formula is now stated in what looks much more like mathematical language and the tasks move well away from the activity of the police officers. The reader must draw a graph and the final task inverts the relationship between the known and the unknown

---

14 Although the effect of recontextualizing is still visible, it not being entirely clear why the geologist might wish to know the answer to this particular question.

Figure 10.5   SMP 11–16 Book G6 (p. 6)

F   Skids

When a car is in an accident,
there are often skid marks on the road.
The police measure the length
of the skid marks.
Then they can work out how fast
the car was going when it started to skid.

This formula tells you roughly how long a skid will be.

$$\text{length of skid} = \frac{\text{speed} \times \text{speed}}{75}$$

The car's speed must be in **miles per hour** (m.p.h.).
The skid length will be in **metres**.

F1   A car is moving at 30 m.p.h. and then skids to a stop.
Roughly how long will the skid marks be?

F2   (a) Work out how long a skid
will be from 20 m.p.h.
Check you get this display
on your calculator.

(b) **Roughly** how many metres long will a 20 m.p.h. skid be?

F3   (a) Copy and complete this table.
It shows the length of skid
from different speeds.

(b) The police measure
some skid marks.
They are 27 m long.
About how fast do you
think the car was going?

Speed (m.p.h.)	Skid (metres)
20	
30	
40	
50	
60	
70	
80	

F4   Here is a picture of some skid marks.
1 cm on the picture is 1 m on the real road.

About how fast do you think the car was going?

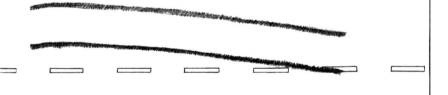

Figure 10.6   SMP 11–16 Book Y5 (p. 181)

M13

When measuring skid marks, the police can use this formula
to estimate the speed of the vehicle.

$$s = \sqrt{(30fd)}$$

s is the speed in miles per hour (m.p.h.).
d is the length of the skid, in feet.
f is a number which depends on the weather and the type of road.

This table shows some values of *f*.

		Road surface	
		Concrete	Tar
Weather	Wet	0·4	0·5
	Dry	0·8	1·0

(a) A car travelling on a wet concrete road makes a skid mark
of length 80 feet. How fast was it travelling?

(b)   (i) When the road surface is tar and the weather is dry, the
formula may be written

$$s = \sqrt{(30d)}$$

Complete this table to show the values of *s* for the given
values of *d*, to 1 decimal place.

d	50	100	150	200	250
30*d*	1500				
$s = \sqrt{(30d)}$	38·7				

(ii) Draw axes, with *d* from 0 to 250 (use 2 cm for 50) and
s from 0 to 100 (use 1 cm for 10).
Draw the graph of (*d*, *s*).

(iii) Use your graph to find how many feet a car would skid on
a dry tar road at 75 m.p.h.

181

quantity so that it is quite irrelevant to the kind of question that the police
are interested in[15]. The Y text more clearly takes into charge the police activity

15   F1–3(a) in the G text also invert this relationship, but apparently only to facilitate the more
'realistic' tasks in F3(b) and F4.

as a resource to be incorporated in what looks much more like an esoteric domain mathematics task, although it remains in the descriptive domain.

Other examples of the colonizing by Y books of a non-professional work setting for resources include drawing a graph to determine the point at which a car speedometer sticks (Y3) and the use of 'bin-packing' optimization strategies in cutting lengths of copper pipe (Y5). Again, the manual occupation is incorporated into the narrative such that the Y reader is situated as mathematical observer and commentator. There is no pretence that mechanics draw graphs (and the point at which the speedometer sticks is, in any case, irrelevant: the meter needs replacing). Nor is it implied that plumbers make use of 'bin-packing' optimization strategies which, in this chapter, are applied in a diversity of settings. These examples contrast with the 'bricklaying' tasks in the G7 section discussed earlier (see *Figure 10.4*). As was the case with the geologist in Y1, the G7 reader is using the builder's formula. In the G text, however, the reader is 'apprenticed' to a manual worker, and not to a member of the professional classes.

I want to introduce one more example of a work setting which acts in a rather different way. It is shown in *Figure 10.7*. The waiters in the cartoon in the top corner are in formal dress, but one of their number looks out of place. He has a broken nose, stubble on a lantern jaw, and a crew cut: a stereotypical image of a working class lag, perhaps. This waiter is also holding aloft a tray on which are placed a beer bottle and a foaming jug, establishing class connotations by comparison with the wine bottle and glasses carried by another waiter. The thuggish waiter strongly contrasts with the other, rather snooty waiters; perhaps a joke against pretentious restaurateurs. The joke is compounded by one of the illustrations accompanying task C10. What seems to be a composite bill for first course dishes served over a period of weeks, beginning with: 3625 soups, 1200 prawn cocktails, 2765 smoked salmon, 1490 whitebait. Patés are rather less popular, 169, but the really pretentious and, of course, foreign dishes are almost completely rejected, only 3 snails and 1 frog's leg. It is the five snooty waiters who are out of place in this restaurant in which discriminating, middle class diners, are a fantasy. The clientele is actually less than sophisticated, that is, working class. The cartoon alienates middle class pretension through the satirical presentation and thus apparently identifies the authorial and reader voices with each other and with the objectified working class.

There is no necessary assertion, here, that working class individuals have lantern jaws and stubble, or that they refuse to eat exotic food and drink beer rather than wine. This image of the working class is constructed by the text which, through the use of satire, sides with this 'Andy Capp' image and eschews the middle class image presented. At the same time, we may suspect a double irony. Just as Andy Capp is a handicap to his wife and to the broader economy, the gastronomical incompetence of the working class, mirrored by its mathematical incompetence and ultimate unteachability, is an impediment to the free elaboration of middle class sophistication and of the erudition which characterizes the authorial voice behind its virtual brutish mask. The

Figure 10.7   SMP 11–16 Book G1 (p. 47)

C9 A restaurant employs 6 waiters.
Each waiter works 8 hours a day.
Each one gets paid £2 an hour.

(a) How much does the restaurant pay
the waiters altogether each day?

(b) Each waiter works 5 days a week.
How much does each waiter get a week?

(c) What is the restaurant's total
wages bill each week?

C10 In the restaurant there are
12 tables.
Each table seats 5 people.

Each person
has 4 pieces
of cutlery.

(a) All the tables are laid ready.
How many pieces of cutlery
are there altogether?

(b) Each person has a wine glass and a water glass.
How many glasses are there altogether?

(c) The restaurant has 2 sittings each evening.
If it is full for both sittings, how many
people eat there each evening?

(d) The restaurant closes only on Sunday night.
If it is full all week, how many people eat each week?

(e) How many people could the restaurant serve
in a year if it is open for 50 weeks?

C11 You need coins and a ruler.

A miser is stacking his 1p coins in a box.
The box is 10 cm wide and 12 cm long.
It is 5 cm high.

(a) About how many 1p coins can he get in the box?
(You will have to measure some 1p coins.)

(b) How much will the 1p coins in the box
be worth when it is full?

(c) What is the largest amount of money
he can get in the box using any coins?

BILLS
3 625 soups £
169 patés £
1 200 prawn cock
2 765 smoked salm
1 490 whitebait
3 snails £
1 frog's leg £

47

cartoon images the middle class author looking at the working class reader
looking at the author in a regression which is a truncated version of the
photograph of the girl sitting between two mirrors on the cover of Book Y3.

There is, then, a consistency in the recruitment of social class as a public
domain selection principle in the SMP texts. In the examples cited settings are

used, firstly, to identify the Y and G reader voices with high salary earners and low wage earners, respectively. Secondly, the texts establish reader object identifications on a social class basis, so that the Y reader is identified as a potential professional and a describer of manual workers and the G reader is identified as a potential manual worker and an occasional watcher of professionals. The G reader is not identified as the subject of the mathematical gaze, here, because the text rarely approaches the esoteric domain. The final example constructs a displaced authorial voice which is identified with the reader voice. The effect is the alienation of middle class sophistication and the identification of both displaced author and reader voices with the mundane. However, the class basis of the authorial voice is revealed in the Y texts as professional, middle class. The construction of the displaced author is the ironic opposite of this dominant voice so that the dependent voice is satirized just as it was in the cartoon advertising 'The Idiots' in the 'Formulas' chapter earlier in G1.

I shall conclude this chapter with a short discussion of one more setting, that relating to the school itself.

The School Setting

Both the G and Y series recruit school settings other than school mathematics. A number of cases in the Y series involve students carrying out science experiments, for example:

> A student carrying out an experiment in electricity passed an electric current through a piece of copper wire. She varied the voltage across the ends of the wire and each time measured the current in the wire. (Voltage is measured in volts and current in amps.)

> Here are her results. [. . .] (Y2, p. 112)

In this as in many of these cases, the reader is required to draw a graph as, in fact, they might do in the science lesson. There is quite extensive use of non-mathematics school settings in the G series, but very rarely do these index curriculum content. The following extract from Book G4 is a very rare example:

> Ajit is weighing this empty beaker.
> The beaker weighs 0.096kg.
> (a) How many **grams** does the beaker weigh?
> (b) Ajit wants to put exactly 500g of water in the beaker.
>   What will the scales read when there is 500g of water in the beaker?
>   (G4, p. 10; drawing omitted)

This looks like a science lesson setting, but, unlike the Y2 task above, it is not about the knowledge content of a science lesson. The reader is given no indication as to why Ajit might be weighing water and, in any event, the beaker would quite possibly be marked at 500 ml level, making weighing redundant[16]. Two cartoons in G1 represent science lessons as about making bombs or noxious substances; in one of these (G1, p. 37) the science teacher manages to blow himself up. There are a number of other cases in which the reference is to the assessment of students in different lessons: History, in G6 (p. 7); Typing in G8[17] (p. 50). However, the knowledge contents of these disciplines are again absent. Very frequently, school settings in the G series concern non-curricular activities. The school timetable in G1 and G2; the school canteen, in G1, G4 and G6; and especially fundraising, usually sponsored events of one form or another, in G2, G3 and G4.

The G texts incorporate curriculum procedures (weighing the beaker, assessment) and stereotypical images (science as bomb-making), school organization (the school timetable, the school canteen), and non-curricular activities (fundraising). All of these incorporations alienate specialist knowledges, which is to say, they alienate DS+ practices in the school. The cases in the Y texts, on the other hand, index precisely the DS+ quality of school science. Science, in the Y texts, is about the empirical discovery of relationships and not making mischievous explosions or smells. The mapping, here, confirms the identification of the 'high ability' Y reader voice with the DS+ practices and of the 'low ability' G reader voice with DS− practices, now extended beyond the mathematics classroom.

The ironic construction of a displaced authorial voice by the G texts which was discussed above in the context of work settings is also achieved via the recruitment of school settings. The mathematics teacher, Mr Ling (see Chapter 8), is ironized in the narrative and cartoon: he wants to sell 200 pages of maths exercises; 'New 24-volume pocket edition'; 'Buy them today!!' Other cartoons in G1 satirize various aspects of school, mathematics, in particular: mathematics is mystifying; history sends you to sleep; comics and magazines are much more interesting than geography; a games lesson is a brawl for which it is not even necessary to get changed; the best event of the day is home time or possibly school lunch. There is an establishment of an apparently collusive relationship between the authorial voice and the student through the satirizing of the lessons. The author appears to be siding with the reader against incomprehensible maths and boring history lessons.

This satirical collusion is certainly spurious, at least in relation to school mathematics, which is treated very seriously in the Teacher's Guides. The classification between the teacher and the student is in fact strengthened by the duping of the latter, the intentionality of which is, at times, almost explicit in the Teacher's Guide:

16   The specific gravity of water being 1.
17   The trajectory from 'academic' to vocational between G6 and G8 is also worthy of note.

> If pupils have covered part of level 3, they may meet some of the work again. We have tried to ensure that level 3 work is presented in a different way so that pupils will not complain that they have 'done all this before', but on the contrary will be provided with stimulating revision material. (G1TG, p. 6)

Again, the G text is constructing an ironic, displaced authorial voice which identifies the dependent voice with the satirized object, which is to say, the disaffected and non-academic student.

The Public Domain: Summary

This chapter has been concerned with the public domain of school mathematics as (re)produced by the *SMP 11–16* texts. I have attempted to show how the positioning and distributing strategies which comprise these texts act selectively on non-mathematical activities, recontextualizing their practices and objectifying their positions. This recontextualizing effects the construction of the public domain as a differentiated repertoire of resources which enables the construction of the apprenticed and dependent voices and their associated message.

The analysis has revealed, firstly, the way in which the cover illustrations of the Y and G books identify their respective readers with intellectual and manual practices. This differential identification is consistent with the social class identifications achieved via the genres of production discussed in Chapter 9. Secondly, domestic settings are recruited differentially by the two series of books. In the Y series, the local details of the settings are backgrounded as generalizing and specializing strategies apprentice the reader voice into the abstract structures of the esoteric domain which is always prioritized. The mythical nature of the public domain is barely concealed in the (re)production of the myth of reference.

The G books, on the other hand, prioritize the public domain settings, identifying the reader voice with their object voices. Particularizing strategies ensure the fragmentation and localizing of the public domain. The G text presents mathematics as a prior condition for optimum public domain performance, but generally without entering the esoteric domain. By failing to specify methods, the text constructs the reader voice as already competent within the domestic settings. In this sense, public domain performance is constituted as a prior condition for mathematics. But since these settings are more or less radical rearticulations of domestic practices, there is no material basis for this competence. The myth of participation is thereby revealed as mythical and as contradictory.

Thirdly, the texts recruit work settings so as to identify the apprenticed and dependent voices with social class positions which are consistent with the recruitment of social class by the covers and by the genres of production. Proto-apprenticeships are constituted such that the apprenticed voice is allowed to be identified with professional occupations, whilst the G reader is identified with more obviously manual occupations. Finally, this hierarchy is sustained in the recruitment of school settings. The apprenticed and dependent voices are identified, respectively, with the academic and non-academic work of the school. The recruitment of both work and school settings is occasionally accompanied, in the early part of the G text, by a double irony which constructs a displaced authorial voice effecting a satirizing of the dependent voice by the pedagogic text.

In the final chapter in this part of the book I shall consider the elements of the SMP scheme which constitute the teacher as the reader voice, that is the Teacher's Guides.

Chapter 11

Interpellating the Teacher

In the analysis presented so far I have illustrated the ways in which textual strategies comprising the G text position its reader voice as dependent and identify it with object voices constructed by public domain settings. Distributing strategies localize or fragment the public domain by particularizing the discourse. The text employs context-dependent algorithms and backgrounds the metonymic connections which enable the abstract discourse of the esoteric domain to be made explicit. This backgrounding is often achieved via the use of closed narratives and iconic modes of signification which localize the message to a highly specific setting with which the reader voice is identified. Since the G text rarely enters the esoteric domain, the result is the projection of the dependent voice as a participant in the public domain. Since this domain has been constructed via the rearticulation of its referent practices by the gaze of the esoteric domain, it is essentially a mythical space despite its apparent strong modality in the G texts.

These strategies construct a relationship between the authorial and reader voices such that the latter is to recognize itself in the message of the former. This was apparent, for example, in the description of the first page of the 'Formulas' chapter in G1 (Chapter 8) in which the object voice, Pctcr, was constructed as a point in the potential career trajectory of the reader voice. The G texts, then, are about the mythical, yet perversely, mundane world of the reader voice which already inhabit it or already possess the potential to inhabit it. Mathematics, in these texts, is for the optimizing of performances in this mythical world.

The Y text, by contrast, is concerned to minimize the local specificities of its reader voice. Apart from the recognition principles which identify it in terms of social class and 'ability' (professional, intellectual, academic), the reader voice of the Y text is most commonly identified with the authorial voice as an apprentice. Distributing strategies highlight metonymic and principled connections between settings and topics. The Y text is about abstract, DS^+, mathematical discourse and its descriptive power over an expanded public domain, the objects of which are less commonly identified with the apprenticed voice. Metaphorically, the latter stands alongside the authorial voice as an apprentice to the mathematical gaze which constructs the public domain as its object space.

If the SMP scheme is consistent, these differences in the student texts should be accompanied by corresponding differences in those texts which interpellate the teacher as the reader voice, that is in the Teacher's Guides which accompany each student book. For example, we should expect that the G series guides would be more concerned than the Y guides with the specificities of the student voices. We would expect, in other words, the dependent voice, but not the apprenticed voice to be individualized by pedagogic considerations in the guides. I shall explore this and other features of the Teacher's Guides in this chapter.

Localizing and Generalizing the Student Voice

The Teacher's Guide to Book Y1 (Y1TG), in common with most of the Teacher's Guides, comprises a brief introductory section. In the case of Y1TG, this section is approximately five-and-a-half pages in length, of which three-and-a-half pages concern the *SMP 11–16* scheme more generally, and two pages comprise an 'Introduction to Book Y1'. The remaining thirty-six pages are the 'Notes and answers for Book Y1', divided into sections corresponding to the chapters of Book Y1, each having a, generally brief, introductory paragraph followed by lists of answers. Although the amount of text relating to pedagogic practice is very limited, there are a small number of comments present that prioritize mathematics in relation to the particular student:

> Section G is particularly important, and if it is felt that the chapter is taking a long time, or if pupils find the first few questions in section G very difficult, then the section can be postponed. However, whenever the work in section G is introduced it is likely to be difficult for many pupils. (Y1TG, p. 18)

This extract (which was also quoted in Chapter 8) suggests that concessions may be made in the face of student difficulties, but only in terms of career pacing. However, postponement may not be perpetual, because the content is 'particularly important' and, in any event, will not overcome all difficulties. Again:

> Please note that questions E15 and E16 are introduced to be merely 'counter-examples' involving misuse of the unitary method. The important (and difficult) topics of the effects of enlargement on area and on volume are dealt with later in the series. (Y1TG, p. 21)

> The use of 'awkward' numbers in the equations in section E is intentional: it focuses attention on the process of solution. (Y1TG, p. 26)

> . . . The method used for increasing an amount by 35 per cent, for example, is to multiply by 1.35. Although more difficult to grasp, this method (and the corresponding method for percentage decreases) has distinct advantages over the more usual method in that it easily extends to such problems as

'what is the overall effect, in percentage terms, of two successive percentage increases of 30 per cent and 35 per cent?' or 'what amount, when increased by 15 per cent becomes £250?' (Y1TG, pp. 38–9)

To obtain the correct answer is not enough. Attention is to be placed on the abstracted mathematical processes involved which are valued because of their generalizing potential. In the end, students' difficulties will just have to be overcome. These are to be subordinated to the mathematical message.

On the face of it, the Y1 chapter on 'Investigations' (Y1.08) allows for more individualised approaches:

Obviously, the investigations in this chapter are not important pieces of mathematics in their own right. So the teacher is not trying to teach, or the pupils to learn, any important mathematical 'facts'. The class discussion — which is essential — can focus on the ideas and efforts of the pupils themselves, comparing approaches, discussing the explanations offered, and so on. (Y1TG, p. 33)

The extract above ends the notes on the following investigation:

Two people are playing noughts and crosses.
'Nought' goes first.
How many different ways are there to make the first two moves (one move each)? (Y1, p. 98)

The notes in the Teacher's Guide suggest:

Let the class work at the problem for a while without general assistance. The point about the meaning of 'different' will come up in individual questions, but don't 'prompt' anyone who does not ask it for themselves. (Y1TG, p. 32)

However, this approach is very different from the projection of reader competencies that characterizes much of the G text as is illustrated by the following extract.

When the results of the class's labours are examined, the person with the biggest number may think of himself or herself as somehow 'the winner', but this 'score' may be reduced when some cases which are not really different from others in the list are eliminated.

Now the attention must be focused on the real nature of the problem, which is not simply to count as many cases as possible, but to have a way of knowing that all possible cases have been considered and none has been counted more than once. This can be done in two stages:

(1)   possible first moves;
(2)   possible second moves for each first move.

At each stage we try out every position on the grid in a definite sequence, for example $\begin{array}{|c|c|c|} \hline 1 & 2 & 3 \\ \hline 4 & 5 & 6 \\ \hline 7 & 8 & 9 \\ \hline \end{array}$. Then we ask if it is the same as any other already counted.

For your benefit, here is one way of listing a complete set of all possible 1st and 2nd moves.

(YITG, pp. 32–3)

It appears that the unaided work is intended to reveal incompetencies, which are subsequently to be remedied by the provision of heuristics. This is apparent in a reference to the 'Investigations' chapter in the general introduction to Book Y1:

Depending on the level of confidence of the class and the extent of their previous experience of investigations, it may be a good idea to introduce the first problem in chapter 8 (Cutting a cake) before reaching the chapter, and without any of the assistance given in the chapter. Those who try to solve the problem and 'get lost' are likely to appreciate more the need for a methodical approach. (Y1TG, p. 10)

The notes for the first of the investigations outline further general 'strategies':

Investigation 1 introduces a strategy which is often useful in tackling a problem: simplify the problem and see what can be learned from solving the simpler problem. This investigation (together with investigations 2 and 5) also offers scope for:

tabulation — making a record of the results of experimentation, which makes it easier for the results to be viewed as a whole;

looking for relationships, and expressing them in a form which other people can understand;

using the relationships discovered to help in solving problems;

trying to find explanations for why the relationships are true, and making such explanations clear to other people. (Y1TG, p. 32)

Even where mathematical content is not central, there are still mathematical processes to be elaborated. These are to be transmitted and acquired, rather than revealed as already present in the student as competencies. The career trajectory of the student voice is constructed as moving from a state of incompetence to competence in terms of the generalized message.

G1TG has only slightly fewer pages (40 pp.) than Y1TG (46 pp.), although the corresponding student's books, G1 and Y1 have 61 and 156 pages, respectively. This is partially because G1TG includes an eleven page commentary on pedagogic practice in relation to the G scheme, whereas the corresponding section in Y1TG is less than two pages in length. Furthermore, whereas approximately 85 per cent of the page space of the notes and answers section in Y1TG is devoted to answers, the rest comprising headings and introductory paragraphs, about 50 per cent of the space on the corresponding pages in G1TG are given over to pedagogic considerations for each chapter. Purely in terms of textual space, in other words, pedagogic considerations are far more visible in G1TG[1] than in Y1TG.

The differentiation of the SMP curriculum at the start of the third year of secondary schooling is explicitly made in terms of 'ability', which term is used seven times in the Guide in referring to a range of 'abilities' on what is, apparently, at least an ordinal scale:

> The Y series is for the most able group of pupils (roughly speaking, the top 20–25 per cent or so, although the proportion is likely to vary from school to school). The B and R series are for the 'middle' group (the next 35–40 per cent [or] so) and the G series is for lower ability pupils (apart from those with special learning difficulties). (G1TG, p. 4)

The exclusion of those with 'special learning difficulties' appears to be made on the basis that printed materials are, in some respect and to some extent, unsuitable for such students (G1TG, p. 6). Having excluded this group, the G1 Teacher's Guide describes its student constituency as 'lower ability' or 'less able'. These expressions are used eight times (in total) in the Guide; the expression 'lower attaining pupils' is used twice and 'weaker pupils' is also used twice. The Guide also gives various indications as to what 'lower ability' means. This is a property of the students which is unlikely to change since, once the G course is under way, there is no facility for transferring to the higher tracks (as there is for students following the median B course). At the start of the scheme, however, there may be some shuffling in the setting:

> A pupil who is started on *Book G1* but then appears to find the work too easy can be given booklets from levels 3 and 4 as individual extension work, and may be able to transfer to *Book B1* when setting is finally decided. (G1TG, p. 5)

Thus, the relative ease with which a student performs mathematics is a measure of her/his ability: mathematical performance is an indicator of competence. Furthermore, it is necessary to match the mathematical level to the competence level:

1 G1TG is unique amongst the Teacher's Guides in the *SMP 11–16* scheme in terms of its comparatively extensive introductory section. However, all of the G series Guides, but none of the other Guides, contain extensive chapter introductions relating to pedagogy.

Of course no assessment will be appealing if pupils cannot manage to do it! At the same time it is important that it is not so simple that pupils find it beneath them. In order to make the assessment sufficiently challenging to pupils we have in general fixed the 'pass mark' at 70 per cent. Passing a test when 70 per cent or more is required is generally reckoned to show that the candidate has mastered [sic] the work contained in the test, so setting the requirements this high has the double benefit of challenging the pupils and allowing them to display mastery. (G1TG, pp. 13–14)

This need for matching is clearly of far less importance in the Y scheme where, as the earlier extracts illustrate, certain 'important' mathematics is bound to be difficult for at least some of the students whenever it is introduced. However, the provision of 'extension' books in the Y series (YE1 and YE2) does reflect a need to 'stretch the most able pupils' (Y1TG, p. 6) so, here too, mathematics measures 'ability'. The extract which offers the possibility of transfer to the B scheme at the start of the course also suggests that Level 3 and 4 booklets might be used as individual extension work. These booklets are considered appropriate for all but the 'lower ability' students in the year before G1 is introduced. This suggests that mathematical performance is dependent upon some articulation of age and 'ability', so that each of these independent variables can, in a sense and to a limited degree, compensate for the other[2]. This possibility of compensation is explained by the understanding of 'low ability' pupils as slow:

> ... we feel strongly that lower attaining pupils can continue to learn provided that the pace of learning is appropriate, and the content is relevant to the pupil. (G1TG, p. 6)

> The G series proceeds slowly, moving at a pace in keeping with the pupils' understanding. (G1TG, p. 6)

However, there may be absolute limitations on performance in terms of more complex tasks:

> At first sight [problem solving] may seem far-fetched as an aim for the low attainer, but we believe it forms an essential part of the course. A 'problem' to one pupil may be routine to another. We do not wish to introduce artificial problems, and so have written in problems only where it seems appropriate[3]. The sort of activity we would call a 'problem' might be to give a pupil a parcel, some scales, a post office guide to postal charges and some stamps. The pupil is then asked to stamp the parcel. Each part of the problem is simple, but for the less able it is the joining together of the simple tasks which is difficult. (G1TG, p. 9; my footnote)

2   This is also found elsewhere in school mathematics, for example, in the documents relating to the UK National Curriculum, see Dowling (1990a).
3   Here, as elsewhere, is evidence of strained writing: a scenario in which authors of materials admit to having included problems where it did not seem appropriate is bizarre.

'Low ability' students are, in this respect, simple-minded, being generally limited to separate, simple tasks. Finally, 'low ability' students are perceived as needing diversity in terms of pedagogic materials. This perception is implicit in the structure of the G scheme, which comprises: eight books of sixty-one pages each plus associated worksheets; 'G booklets'; three 'G resource packs' each containing thirty-two cards; 'G supplementary booklets'; and 'topic booklets' (shared with the B series). This gives a total of thirty-one 'G' items as listed in the price list (many more, if the cards in the 'resource packs' are counted individually) and compares with seventeen 'B' items and seven 'Y' items. This need for diversity is also made explicit in the Teacher's Guide:

> We have taken the view that lower ability pupils need a wide variety in their mathematics — variety of presentation, content, method of working and so on. The G materials reflect this view. (G1TG, p, 7)

> We have provided a variety of G materials because we believe that pupils of lower ability need a varied mathematical diet. In the same way, we believe that any assessment they undergo should also be varied. A variety of assessment instruments are provided — short written tests, tests of practical and oral ability and mental tests. (G1TG, p. 13)

Even such diversity as is directly provided by the materials is insufficient:

> We hope that pupils will enjoy the wide range of mathematical activities in the G material. But there are a number of vital mathematical activities that cannot be written down. We have tried to include suggestions about these in the notes on each chapter, where appropriate. (G1TG, p. 8)

The Guide provides a page-and-a-half of exposition on six 'vital mathematical activities': 'discussion'; 'mental mathematics'; 'approximation and estimation'; 'practical work'; 'problem solving'; and 'further consolidatory work'. This emphasis on diversity and the consequent brevity of any instance of 'activity' might be described as an interpretation of 'low ability' students as having a short attention span. A relationship between the two independent variables, competence and age, is, again, apparent, because the booklet scheme for use in the first two years of secondary schooling also constitutes diversity through the provision of 115 booklets of eight or sixteen pages in length. A short attention span is constructed as a property which is common amongst younger students and which is still present in the older 'lower ability' students.

The G1 Teacher's Guide thus produces 'ability' as an independent variable indexing a property of the student. Some function of this variable with the other independent variable 'age' (or, at least, 'year cohort') produces mathematical performance as a dependent variable. Performance is measured (or assumed) in terms of: (i) the level of difficulty experienced with the mathematics curriculum at any given level within its own hierarchy; (ii) the pace at which transmission can proceed; (iii) the complexity of tasks that can be

Table 11.1: *Relationships between age, ability and mathematical performance in SMP 11–16*

		Difficulty (level of maths)	Pace	Complexity of tasks	Attention Span
		Mathematical Performance			
Age	High	high	X	X	long
	Low	low	X	X	short
Ability	High	high	high	high	long
	Low	low	low	low	short

'X' indicates that age is not a factor

attempted; (iv) the length of attention span. The relationship between age, ability and performance is summarized in *Table 11.1*.

Clearly, the dependent voice constructed by the G1 Teacher's Guide presents problems for the teacher voice. These problems are, in part, generalized by the abstractions indexed in *Table 11.1*. However, they are also localized in terms of the individual or localized specificities of the student. The question to be addressed now is, what are the pedagogic consequences of this construction.

Localizing and Generalizing Pedagogic Action

Trivially, perhaps, one consequence is that there should be some measure of matching between ability (the independent variable) and level of mathematics, pace, task complexity and task/topic duration. This is apparent from the extracts cited above and from the structure and content of the G scheme as discussed earlier. It has also been mentioned that diversification also extends to mode of pedagogic action as well as topic and mode of presentation. Thus 'low ability' students need the various forms of pedagogic action, 'vital mathematical activities', that have been listed above. Of these forms of pedagogic action, 'mental mathematics' is given some attention in Y1TG:

> It is assumed throughout that unless there is an instruction to the contrary calculators will be used for all but the simplest calculations which can be done mentally.

> We strongly recommend that teachers encourage mental calculation, and from time to time give short sets of questions to be answered mentally. We also suggest having occasional practice sessions on written arithmetic, but that the scope of these should not extend beyond addition, subtraction, multiplication by 2, 3, . . . 9 and division by 2, 3, . . . 9 of whole numbers and money. (Y1TG[4], p. 9)

4 In fact the requirements for arithmetic without the use of a calculator at Level 4 (the average level for 11-year-olds) of the UK National Curriculum slightly exceed that suggested here.

In this extract, mental arithmetic is presented as a skill which, like written computation, needs some practising. There is no indication as to the nature of its value, but the limiting of written arithmetic to dealing with single digit numbers might be taken to imply that the value is measured in terms of utility and that the value added by dealing with two and more digit numbers is not worth the effort. In G1TG, however, mental mathematics extends beyond arithmetic and its value, furthermore, seems to derive from its role as a kind of therapy:

> In a sense all mathematics is mental; however, we have tried to encourage more emphasis on the mental aspects of the work. By this we do not only refer to 'mental arithmetic', but to the whole range of mathematical activities. For example, 'seeing' what will happen if you cut a folded piece of paper, or reflect a shape, are valuable mathematical activities. Many mental skills need practising, and we have indicated suitable places in the chapter notes. (G1TG, p. 8)

The suggestion that there is a sense in which all mathematics is mental points to a psychologistic interpretation of mathematics as cognitive states or processes. Although practising skills seems to suggest a utility value, it is not at all clear that it is this value which is being placed upon ' "seeing" what will happen if you cut a folded piece of paper'. Rather, some kind of logico-mathematical experience seems to be being indexed, which is to say, 'mathematical activities' are cognitive therapies. This is a realization of the myth of construction that I introduced in Chapter 2. The mathematical abstraction, which is that which is to be 'seen', is being presented as if it were independent of the recontextualizing mathematical gaze. In the position which I am adopting in this book, the gaze is not the inevitable rationality of the epistemic subject of Kant or Piaget. Rather, it is the achievement of and is specific to the social activity of school mathematics. The failure of the SMP text to recognize the activity-contingent nature of recontextualization here is entirely consistent with its (re)production of the myth of participation, which also entails a failure to recognize the productivity of the recontextualizing gaze.

Any potential use-value of mental mathematics is, in fact, denied in the advice relating to the 'mental tests', which form a part of the formal assessment for the G series:

> The mental tests provide an opportunity for pupils to show their skills at doing mathematics in their heads. The tests are to be worked without a calculator and it is not intended that pupils do any working with paper and pencil. If however pupils do rough working this should not be penalised. (G1TG, p. 15)

The tests are 'opportunities' for the pupils to celebrate the success of pedagogic action, but there are to be no penalties if pupils decline this particular opportunity. The interpretation of mental mathematics as pedagogic therapy is in keeping with the nurturing pedagogic practice represented throughout the Guide:

> Pupils of lower ability need encouragement and help in learning mathematics. The particular difficulties which a pupil finds are often specific to that pupil. So when using the books, we hope that teachers will explain and discuss the work with pupils, ask them where they have seen examples of this kind of activity outside the classroom and so on. (G1TG, p. 7)

The nurturing pedagogic practice suggested in the first sentence of this extract is reinforced in the 'aims' outlined in the chapter notes:

> *To help develop* 'strategies' with numbers . . .
>
> *To help pupils develop* their skills of estimating . . .
>
> *To give pupils a feel* for what is 'more likely' or 'less likely' . . .
>
> *To help develop flexibility* in number calculations . . .
>
> *To reinforce* the equivalence of . . .
>
> *To give some primitive ideas about* equally likely events . . .
>
> . . . *To help pupils see* when multiplying is the appropriate operation . . .
>
> *To introduce simple ideas* of statistical inference . . .
>
> *To develop strategies and thinking ahead* by games playing . . .
>
> . . . *to encourage* drawing skills . . .
>
> *To provide a stimulating context* for the practice of drawing skills. (G1TG, pp. 19–36; my emphasis)

By contrast, the chapter notes in Y1TG (which, as noted above, are very brief) include few references to the students, but relate to the mathematical content. That is, to particular conventions which have been used and, sometimes, to the particular route through the content being taken in the relevant chapter and in relation to other chapters in Y1 and subsequent books in the scheme. The following extract, for example, comprises the whole of the introduction to the answers for Chapter 7, 'Polygons and circles':

> The idea of ratio, as developed in chapter 6, plays an important part in this chapter. The ratio $\dfrac{\text{circumference}}{\text{diameter}}$ in a circle is approached as a limiting case of the ratio $\dfrac{\text{perimeter}}{\text{diameter}}$ in a regular polygon. (Y1TG, p. 30)

This extract also refers to the development of an idea, but, in this case, the idea is discursive rather than cognitive as is evidenced by the comment in the introduction to the Chapter 6 answers: 'The ideas in it arise frequently in later work' (Y1TG, p. 28). The 'ideas' are immanent in the practice rather than developing in students' heads. The therapeutic pedagogic practice of G1TG starts and frequently ends with the individual student, as is suggested by a comment in an earlier extract: 'The particular difficulties which a pupil finds are often specific to that pupil'. This individualizing of mathematics is explicit elsewhere within the Guide:

> . . . Within the assessment items themselves we have not in general insisted on any particular methods being used. In this the assessment again reflects the written G materials, and the belief that teaching one single algorithmic approach to solving a problem is not the best we can do for pupils. (G1TG, p. 13)

Individual students have individual difficulties and are encouraged to employ individual approaches. The class, as a whole, is then constituted as a reservoir of strategies which can be shared in 'discussion'. Interaction, in the form of discussion, is given considerable emphasis in the G Series Teacher's Guides, the answer sections for most chapters including advice on possible areas and forms of discussion:

> Discussion between pupils, and between pupil and teacher, is perhaps the most useful mathematical activity possible; 'talking through' with the teacher may be the only way to make the work relevant. Discussion should always precede a teacher-led lesson, and discussion can often follow a class game or investigation. Pupils may be asked how they solved a particular problem, and the different methods used by pupils can then be compared. Often for these pupils, there is no single 'correct way' of doing things. Rather there is one method which suits a particular pupil best for a particular problem. (G1TG, p. 8)

As earlier extracts illustrate, 'discussion' in the Y books is valued less for its sharing potential than for its corrective effect. There is an apprenticing, for the Y student, but no negotiation of mathematics. The uncompromising position of the Y text is highlighted in the following extract (which was also reproduced earlier):

> . . . The method used for increasing an amount by 35 per cent, for example, is to multiply by 1.35. Although more difficult to grasp, this method (and the corresponding method for percentage decreases) has distinct advantages over the more usual method in that it easily extends to such problems as 'what is the overall effect, in percentage terms, of two successive percentage increases of 30 per cent and 35 per cent?' or 'what amount, when increased by 15 per cent becomes £250?' (Y1TG, pp. 38–9)

Mathematics, in the G series, is often to be individualized in terms of its procedures. The centrality of the student is also apparent in the emphasis placed upon 'relevance', in G1TG, in relation to the students' individual and collective experiences. The introduction to the G materials lays stress on the notion of relevance:

> . . . But we feel strongly that lower attaining pupils can continue to learn provided that the pace of learning is appropriate, and the content is relevant to the pupil. (G1TG, p. 6)

> . . . We hope that teachers will explain and discuss the work with pupils, ask them where they have seen examples of this kind of activity outside the classroom and so on. (G1TG, p. 7)

Furthermore, as I pointed out in Chapter 2, the Guide includes the suggestion (in its introduction as well as in the chapter notes, as mentioned in earlier sections of this chapter) that teachers will produce additional materials, which are of greater immediate relevance:

> We hope that much in the G materials will act as a 'model' for work of your own devising. Work on timetables, map-reading, shopping and so on is far more motivating for pupils if it is seen to be 'real'. Blagdon can never substitute for your own town! So in a sense, we hope that some chapters in the books never get used by pupils. They are written to be replaced by work which is firmly based on the pupils' own environment. Of course, replacement may not always be possible, but work based on the pupils' own school, town or surroundings may be added to a particular chapter. Some of the later topic booklets in the fourth and fifth years particularly can be thought of as models for a booklet based on the pupils' own environment. (G1TG, p. 8)

The subsequent section of the Guide is subtitled 'the maths we haven't written' and is arranged under the headings of the 'vital mathematical activities' that were mentioned earlier. The section includes several references to the need for relevance:

> . . . 'talking through' with the teacher may be the only way to make the work relevant . . .

> . . . Questions of the type 'about how much . . . ?' 'how far do you think . . . ?' may be asked about much of the work, and are often best based on the pupil's own environment and experience. Pupils should be encouraged to look at their answers to questions and ask 'is this a sensible answer?'.

> . . . We do not wish to introduce artificial problems, and so have written in problems only where it seems appropriate . . .

> Discussion of how to solve problems will be almost as valuable as actually solving them. A discussion of how to avoid congestion in the school corridors, which would be the best local school to amalgamate with, where to go to buy a bike cheaply — all these represent the sort of problem whose solution is mathematically valuable. They are, of course, absolutely specific to the pupils' own environs and interests. 'Problems' may arise topically from a newspaper or TV or a local incident. Valuable discussion can come out of unpromising territory.

> Some of the chapters in the book, or games in the resource pack may lead to valuable problems; you are equally likely to find them around you, in your own situation. (G1TG, pp. 8–9)

That the mathematics must be made relevant in terms of the experiences and specific situation of the student is not tantamount to a denial of the recontextualizing achievements of the gaze which can be described by reference to an example that is offered of an appropriate problem:

> . . . The sort of activity we would call a 'problem' might be to give a pupil a parcel, some scales, a post office guide to postal charges and some stamps. The pupil is then asked to stamp the parcel . . . (G1TG, p. 9)

The implied narrative is comparatively open. It could relate, for example, to a domestic or to a work setting. Even so, it is actually quite difficult to imagine a non-school-maths situation in which anyone would actually perform such a task. Within a domestic setting, the necessary range of stamps would be unlikely to be available and the parcel would be checked at the Post Office counter anyway. Within a work context, the probability that an automatic franking machine and/or scales calibrated in terms of postal charges would be available would be quite high. Furthermore, even to the extent that such a task is plausible within a work setting, the individual would be trained to perform it as a routine, it would not constitute a problem. The task, in other words, is structured in terms of esoteric domain mathematical discourse, number (linear measurement) and arithmetic (combinations of the face values of the stamps), rather than the work or domestic context.

The use of scales in the above 'problem' is an example of what is referred to in G1TG as 'practical work', which is an important pedagogic mode in relation to 'low ability' students, a mode which may actually be used in substitution for 'written work':

> We hope that it will be possible to give pupils as wide a range of practical experience as possible. Some (like weighing) we have included in the work.

In other places it is very desirable to have practical work alongside, or in place of, written work. So, for example, alongside book G1 we would hope that watches and clocks would be used in chapter 4, 'Time', and that dials, meters and scales of various types can be brought into the classroom for use in chapter 1, 'Estimating and scales'. (G1TG, p. 9)

'Scissors' are included in the list of 'essential equipment' and the Guide provides advice on how to obtain filter papers ('we suggest you ask your science department') and 'items such as dice, counters and mirrors' (the names and addresses of some suppliers of educational aids are listed). Furthermore, 'practical tests' are included in the formal assessment for the G scheme and most of the chapter notes include suggestions for 'practical activities'. 'Practical' work of the kind described in G1TG is clearly localizing insofar as it does not incorporate discursive distancing or abstraction from itself and is clearly limited in range. The suggestion that practical work may substitute for written work seems to place little value in such discursive distancing.

To summarize this discussion of the Teacher's Guides, whereas Y1TG focuses its attention on mathematical practices, G1TG theorizes the student. The G1 Guide firstly marks out its student voice in relation to the general readership of the scheme: the G student has 'low ability'. Secondly, 'low ability' is theorized as reflecting competence at a comparatively low level of mathematics, low pace of working, low task complexity and short attention span. The individual realizations of these properties in individual students must be matched by pedagogic action. The G1 Guide further prescribes an appropriate pedagogic practice for 'low ability' students as a form of therapy. This therapy is localized in terms of the 'mathematical' strategies, which may be idiolectical, and in terms of settings, which must be 'relevant' in respect of individual experiences and circumstances. There is, in a number of the extracts cited from G1TG and elsewhere in the G series Teacher's Guides, a considerable emphasis on discussion within which students share their strategies. The G students are thus constituted as a resource. Discussion between Y students, on the other hand, is generally corrective. Emphasis is also placed, in the G Guides, on localizing, 'practical' tasks.

We can describe Y1TG as proposing generalizing strategies in the sense that there is minimal reference to the student who, furthermore, must be brought to the discourse. There is no apology for the fact that 'whenever the work [. . .] is introduced it is likely to be difficult for many pupils'. G1TG, on the other hand, proposes localizing strategies in relation to a highly specified student to whom mathematics must be taken. The emphasis on pedagogic advice in G1TG, furthermore, produces the teacher, a dominant voice in school mathematics, as incompetent *qua* teacher, as if pedagogy is only an issue for 'low ability' pupils which are, naturally, of a different species from the teacher. Y1TG produces a generalized student voice in respect of an external mathematics, a potentially dominant voice. G1TG produces a localized and 'disabled' student voice which incorporates its own mathematical limitations with respect to the esoteric domain. However, the G students are constituted as a reservoir of highly localized, public domain 'mathematical' strategies.

Reading the Teacher's Guides

It will be apparent that the form of reading which I have applied to these Teacher's Guides differs from that applied in previous chapters to the student books. Clearly, it would have been possible to adopt the same approach. The Teacher's Guides are monologic pedagogic texts. They construct an authorial voice as transmitter and a reader voice as receiver. In this case, the reader voice is that of the teacher who is interpellated by the texts. Adopting this form of reading would have foregrounded the construction of the teacher voice. One example of this appears in the previous paragraph where I point out that the G guide constructs the teacher as incompetent *qua* teacher. On the other hand, since the Y student voice does not pose pedagogic difficulties, they have no need of a teacher. Rather, they need a practitioner of school mathematics. Both guides construct the teacher as competent in this regard through their minimal transmission of mathematical message.

The appearance of the myth of construction in the G guide aligns it with the Nelson primary school scheme discussed in Chapter 2. This is the case notwithstanding that the realizations of this myth differ, being, respectively, rationalist and empiricist. In this sense, the G teacher voice is being identified with the connotatively objectified primary teacher voice. This is entirely consistent with the infantilizing identifications of the G student voice described in this and in previous chapters.[5]

I shall not pursue this mode of reading of the guides further. That I have, in the main, adopted the alternative mode is a consequence of the way in which the guides have been constituted as data by the analysis in this chapter. Specifically, in the previous chapters, I have described the texts in terms of the ways in which they employ textual strategies and selectively recruit textual resources to position authorial and reader voices and to distribute message across the voice structure. Crucially, the focus has been on authorial and reader voices which are always attributed a degree of subjectivity, as I argued in Chapter 6. In the present chapter, however, I am, by continuing to focus most of my attention on the student voices, actually shifting to a consideration of object voices. This is because the Teacher's Guides address the teacher voice as their reader and objectify the student voice. This is most clearly the case in the G guides. The Y guides, as I have demonstrated, only occasionally and minimally objectify the student voice.

---

5 It is also consistent with the well-rehearsed misinterpretation of Piaget within secondary school pedagogic discourse that cognitive development ends at the primary-secondary interface at which point students will have achieved the stage of formal operations. It might be speculated that this is precisely why the secondary G teachers are in need of pedagogic advice with respect to the cognitively underdeveloped G student voice.

I am, therefore, reading these Teacher's Guides as representations of something else. That which they represent is the construction of the practices and positions of school mathematics by the Y and G student books, which are the principal objects of my analysis. The distinction in readings which I am making is metaphorically equivalent to a distinction which I might make in relation to the interpretation of interview data. Conventionally, I might interview teachers to find out about their classroom practices of their understandings of mathematical knowledge and so forth. Under these circumstances, I may feel obliged to minimize the unfamiliarity of the interview context by trying to make it feel like an everyday conversation. My analysis of the interview data might tend to treat the responses as more or less transparent with respect to that which they are supposed to represent. This analysis would correspond to the reading of the Teacher's Guides in this chapter.

Alternatively, I might focus my attention on the interview as itself constituting a very particular kind of social situation. Under these circumstances, I might tend to read the transcript in terms of how the interviewer and respondent recruit resources in positioning themselves and each other and in distributing their respective practices. This would be an analysis of a dialogic text. In other respects, it would correspond to the analysis of the student books in the previous chapters.

This now concludes my analysis of the *SMP 11–16* scheme. I shall not give a separate summary of the analysis. Rather, I shall incorporate some of its principal findings into the more speculative discussion in the next chapter which is the concluding chapter to the book.

Chapter 12

Disturbing and Re-establishing Equilibrium

The principal work that I set out to do in producing this book has been achieved. Centrally, I have derived a language for the sociological description of texts and I have applied this language to the analysis of a high profile school mathematics scheme. The result has enabled me to make a number of claims about school mathematics as an activity and I shall restate some of these in the discussion which follows. I have also contended that this work has more general applicability, beyond the analysis of school textbooks and beyond the activity of school mathematics. However, insofar as the apprenticeship of my reader voice is now complete, I shall not feel obliged to give further illustrations of this potential. Rather, in this final chapter I want to refer back to some of what I consider to be key points in the work and generalize from them in a more speculative social theorizing.

The central problematic of this chapter concerns the subjectivity of analysis and the limits placed upon it by exteriority and by non-containability. Firstly, I shall briefly reprise the marking out of my general methodological position — constructive description — from certain other constructivist approaches. Piaget's position, in particular, seems to want to hold on to the exteriority of one system with respect to another, whilst failing to recognize the *a priori* need for a higher level structure which sustains this exteriority. This higher level structure is, in Piaget's case, the subjectivity of his own theorizing. Constructive description, on the other hand, self-consciously recognizes its own subjectivity. This can operate at the same level as the systems which it constructs precisely because it does not constitute these systems as mutually exterior. Nevertheless, this places a constraint on the decriptions which are produced insofar as we may want to make comments about the totality of systems. This would be to construct a hypersystem.

The problem of the hypersystem becomes important when we make reference to general characteristics of the sociocultural such as the fundamental organizing principles of class, gender, race and ablebodiedness which I have introduced in my analysis. These may be constituted as the products of power, but this leaves open the question of the subjectivity of power. I shall consider, in particular, the intellectual/manual duality, which is associated with the class principle and also with what I have identified as the level of discursive saturation of practices. I shall argue that this duality is, in fact, inadequate to the exhaustion of the modality of practices and shall introduce a third mode. The description that I shall produce of the sociocultural is as an equilibrating hypersystem. However, this reintroduces a problem that I have identified in Piaget's theory, which is to say, that equilibrium must be constituted as a predicate of an equilibrating system. The question, then, is what is the nature of this edenic or utopian equilibrium such that it does not constitute an exteriority and hence a contradiction at the heart of the theory? In the final section of the chapter I shall make reference to some work in the field of psychoanalysis to suggest that the problem might be resolved via the substitution of exteriority with non-containability in the concepts of individual and social unconscious.

Exteriority and the Subjectivity of Analysis

In Chapter 6 I referred to the general methodological position that I introduced as *constructive description*. In choosing this term, my intention is to affiliate to constructivist forms of epistemology which reject simple reference. That is, they reject the contention that knowledge is to be construed as being about something that lies beyond or exterior to the knower; in this sense, they deny the myth of reference. However, I also need to distance my position from those that adopt the alternative myth of construction. The first version of this myth — pedagogic constructivism — appeared in Chapter 2 in consideration of the Nelson primary mathematics materials. What appeared to be being presented was a conception of mathematical knowledge as originating in the physical world and acquirable through physical engagement with this world. This empiricist epistemology constitutes a denial of the subjectivity of the acquirer/constructor.

The far more sophisticated, genetic epistemology of Jean Piaget, from which pedagogic constructivism derives, is nevertheless a version of the myth of construction. As I indicated in Chapter 6, Piaget conceives of cognitive development as occurring via the interaction of three systems; the sensorimotor; the operational; and the symbolic. These systems, he contends, must be understood as distinct. However, it is clearly the case that interacting systems can interact only to the extent that their mutually interactive features are predicated of each.[1] Separate systems, then, must either be inert with respect to each other, or they must be contained within a higher order system of which they constitute subsystems. It further follows that subsystems within a dynamic system are always defined in a way which is motivated by the

---

1 Partial separation is also not possible. This is because it would constitute an internal division between the interactive and non-interactive elements of the system which constitute an internal 'exteriority', which would constitute a negation of systematicity.

defining subject position[2]. Piaget's definitions are highly imaginative and highly productive, but not essential. In other words, Piaget ultimately denies his own constructive subjectivity.

If, ultimately, the essential exteriority of systems with respect to each other cannot be sustained theoretically, then the world must be theoretically conceived as in some sense unitary. This is not to deny other ways of relating to the world which would constitute it as sundered. The following extract from St Matthew's Gospel is illustrative:

> 20 The young man saith unto him, All these things have I observed: what lack I yet?
>
> 21 Jesus said unto him, if thou wouldest be perfect, go sell that thou hast, and give to the poor, and thou shalt have treasure in heaven: and come, follow me.
>
> 22 But when the young man heard the saying, he went away sorrowful: for he was one that had great possessions.
>
> 23 And Jesus said unto his disciples, Verily I say unto you, it is hard for a rich man to enter into the kingdom of heaven.
>
> 24 And again I say unto you, It is easier for a camel to pass through a needle's eye, than for a rich man to enter into the kingdom of God.
>
> 25 And when the disciples heard it, they were astonished exceedingly, saying, Who then can be saved?
>
> 26 And Jesus looking upon *them* said to them, With men this is impossible; but with God all things are possible. (*The Holy Bible, the revised version*, Oxford: OUP; Matthew, 20, 16–26)

The young man had approached Jesus in an attempt to look behind the simulacrum of goodness constructed by the Commandments. But he was not offered an option in verse 21. To be perfect is to be God: '*One* there is who is good' (*ibid*; verse 17; my emphasis). The rich man cannot become that which he is not, but this neither gives nor denies him access to heaven. What he lacked was not poverty, but faith and no strategy is offered for the achievement of either.

Genuine exteriority, then, is accomplished only by faith. Exteriority must mark the limits of analysis. Heaven and Earth can stand only in metaphorical

---

2 I initially phrased this sentence as follows: 'It further follows that subsystems within a dynamic system are always defined arbitrarily.' Kress (1993; see also Hodge and Kress, 1988) argues against Saussure's description of the sign as arbitrary. Rather, Kress wants to claim that the relation between signifier and signified is motivated by the sign producer. This is clearly a position which is consistent with Bakhtin and Eco and, indeed, with that being adopted here. I do not wish to reinstate Saussure. Nevertheless, Kress tends to reinstate arbitrariness through a lack of theoretical resources which would motivate his own description of the sign producer. This is also true of Bakhtin and Eco, as was argued in Chapter 5. My original choice of the term 'arbitrary' was intended to recall Bourdieu and Passeron's expression, 'cultural arbitrary', which I have referred to, in Chapter 5, as an ideology-in-particular or, in other words, as an activity. I finally rejected the term, here, because of its suggestion that the recognition principles referred to are non-theoretically motivated.

relationship to each another. This is a metaphor which cannot be metonymically resolved. In this sense, there is no apprenticing into faith.

I have, therefore, explicitly denied exteriority a meaning within my theory. Nevertheless, constructive description must recognize and locate its own subjectivity in recontextualizing the texts-as-work which it constitutes as texts-as-texts. It must do this in a way which does not constitute a retreat into rationalism — the antithesis to the empiricist thesis which denies any voice to the text-as-work.

The GSU, the Hypersystem and Fundamental Organizing Principles

I have referred to Eco's notion of a Global Semantic Universe (GSU) as a heuristic device in constituting notional sociocultural unity. Thus, the world is to be understood as a GSU which incorporates discursive and non-discursive elements — the distinction between these being given by the form of my theory, which is my analytic subjectivity. Social activity is to be understood as entailing the (re)production of radical-rearticulations of the GSU as specialized regions of practices and positions. This achievement is precisely the operation of power in the social. These regions are referred to as activities. Activity defines, in context-specific terms, who can say or do or think what. My own analytic subjectivity can be construed as an (emerging) activity and is, therefore, at the same level as the activities which it objectifies (and which may objectify it).

The totality of activities is (re)productive of what might be referred to as the division of labour in the social as a hypersystem. The hypersystem is characterized by fundamental organizing principles. These are constituted as fundamental by their ubiquitous recruitment as resources by positioning strategies. As examples of fundamental organizing principles, I have mentioned social class, gender, race and ablebodiedness and I have given some discussion of these dimensions in Chapter 3. Class is clearly important in my analysis of the SMP texts. I shall give a further indication of what is meant by the recruitment of fundamental organizing principles through a brief consideration of gender, which has been present, but not always foregrounded in my analysis.

Essentially, gender is a defining and hierarchical category of positions within domestic activities. However, the gender hierarchy is pervasively (re)produced within all activities as a resource in the (re)production of their position structures. The result might be described as patriarchy. A modernist feminist description might regard this pervasion as a patriarchal hegemony of which the patriarch is the subject. However, the model of the social which is being applied here regards patriarchy as the universalization of a fundamental resource. It is not so much that the patriarch actively penetrates school mathematics, rather, school mathematics recruits, appropriates and recontextualizes the patriarchal hierarchy. This is not an idealist conception (as is, arguably, 'hegemony'). Gender is understood as a fundamental and material organizing principle (others being age and kinship) within a central domain of social structure, the family. School mathematics can hardly fail to implicate it. Crucially, gender within school mathematics is recontextualized gender. The recontextualizing may, for example, be realized as a mapping of gender onto mathematical competence.

The recontextualizing of gender within the original SMP scheme was referred to in Chapter 4. These texts certainly retained an element of gender stereotyping. In this sense, gender was not 'recognized' by these texts as a dimension of social inequality (or, alternatively, this form of social inequality was 'recognized' as necessary). The *SMP 11–16* scheme, on the other hand, does 'recognize' gender and its recontextualizing is often realized in terms of idealized states in which gender is no longer relevant. There are women farmers, women builders (but not, it appears, women tax inspectors or men doing needlework).

Whether this is an 'adequate' tactic in the politics of 'equal opportunities' is not my central concern in the present study. Here, the subject is not tied to one essential identity or to a small number of possible and competing identities (gender, class, ethnicity, etc). Rather, the subject is constructed whenever an activity can be described. As was discussed in Chapter 6, the empirical (human) subject is to be considered as a complex of positions relating to different activities. Insofar as gender is a resource which is universally involved in positioning strategies by texts (re)producing these activities, then it is reasonable to speak of the social as characterized, but not caused, by patriarchy. In my model, the relationship between the social and its cultural (re)production is dialectical rather than causal. Nevertheless, to the extent that we wish to speak of the sociocultural as patriarchal, we must be conscious of a subject of this particular principle of recognition. My particular focus in this study has been on the class principle. I shall continue this discussion with a reprise and some extension of its mythologizing in school mathematics.

Texts, Myths and Class Strategies

My analysis of the *SMP 11–16* texts in Chapters 8–11 constructed school mathematics as an activity through its (re)production by the positioning and distributing strategies which comprise these texts-as-texts. In particular, I illustrated how the Y and G series of books constructed a hierarchy of reader voices through the distribution of the myths of reference and of participation. As I established in Chapter 1 and in the subsequent textual analysis, the myth of reference must constitute the sociocultural as a divided space. This enables its prioritized practices — its esoteric domain — to appear to refer to practices other than themselves. These practices are recontextualized and constituted by the gaze of the activity as its public domain. What the myth achieves is the concealing of the productivity of social activity in constituting its esoteric domain as very substantially self-referential. This is to say that the esoteric domain refers to the practices of other activities only as a system of exchange values which therefore simulates its referents. It is the constructive nature of this simulation that is concealed by the myth of reference.

Consistent with the position described above, the division of the socio-cultural space is never substantively achieved. Rather, the activity must establish a differentiation in the strength of classification of the positions and practices that it constructs in the radical-rearticulation of the GSU. Specifically, it must establish a Subject and apprenticed positions, to which a relatively high degree of subjectivity is attributed. Because the activity must select its apprentices, it must also establish dependent and objectified positions, to which low or zero subjectivity is attributed. The activity must also differentially specialize its practices through the construction of esoteric, public and hybrid domains.

The activity, thus described, is (re)produced in its texts through the construction of voices and message. The Y text constructs the apprentice voice through the selective alienation of localized identities (objectified voices) and practices (public domain message). Metonymic links and explicit principles are incorporated into the text so that the apprenticed voice is given access to the esoteric domain at the expense of its public domain identity. The apprenticed voice is also given access to the principles of operation of the gaze. The public domain, in these texts, is presented as fragmented, but as generalizable via the abstract discourse of the esoteric domain. This is to say, the myth of reference is distributed to the apprenticed voice by the Y texts.

The myth of participation constructs the sociocultural as a unified space. Now, social activity is more fully concealed by the myth. The operation of power in and as the construction of arcane radical-rearticulations of the GSU is completely denied by the myth of participation. The G texts distribute this myth in the construction of the dependent voice. In order to avoid revealing the esoteric domain discourse, the text must construct a displaced author which affiliates to the dependent voice. The dependent voice is also identified with public domain object voices, facilitating the construction and/or retention of an alienated and localized identity for the dependent voice. This localized identity is also elaborated in the direct objectification of the student voice in the Teacher's Guides, as was revealed in Chapter 11.

The myth of participation clearly did not originate with the *SMP 11–16* G series of books. Elbert Fulkerson, for example, espoused it some time ago:

> One of the main purposes of mathematics is to provide the student with those mathematical abilities, meanings, and concepts which will assist him [sic] later in making satisfactory adjustments to the various problems of life. (Fulkerson, 1939; p. 27)

The myth constitutes the sociocultural as a virtual plane of domestic and other mundane practices. Participation in these practices is optimized through the application of mathematical rationality. Where this form of rationality is not applied, the object voices are pathologized as in Sewell's (1981) report to the Cockcroft Committee. Sewell savagely describes shoppers as using an 'avoidance strategy' if they take a chequebook to the supermarket rather than keeping a running total of what they spend as they fill up their trolley. Even demonstrable success is to be read, by the myth, as evidence of incompetence, as is illustrated by Mike Cooley's anecdote about the aircraft factory, which was quoted in Chapter 1.

The mythology which I have presented must be augmented by two more myths which correspond to, but which are distinct from the myths of reference and participation. The first has already been introduced in Chapter 1. This is the myth of emancipation. As I argued in the earlier discussion, it corresponds to the myth of participation by constituting the sociocultural as a unified space. This is achieved in two stages. The myth initially establishes the dual space of esoteric and public domain mathematics. However, it proceeds by declaring that these practices are the same. Ubiritan D'Ambrosio, for example, declares that academic mathematics is expropriated from mathematical practices conceived of more generally:

> Now we include as mathematics apart from the Platonic ciphering and arithmetic, mensuration and relations of planetary orbits, the capabilities of classifying, ordering, inferring and modelling. This is a very broad range of human activities which, throughout history have been expropriated by the scholarly establishment, formalized and codified and incorporated into what we call academic mathematics. But which remains alive in culturally identified groups and constitute routines in their practices. (D'Ambrosio, 1985; p. 45)

The productivity of social activity in the radical-rearticulation of the sociocultural is denied, here. Indeed, radical-rearticulation is substituted by expropriation. It is as if the 'scholarly establishment' waits, like a spider at the centre of its web, in anticipation of that which it will expropriate and which in no sense constitutes or is constituted by its booty. Rather, mathematical practices lie at the heart of diverse practices in diverse sociocultural contexts. This is consistent with the positions adopted by Bishop and Gerdes and the other ethnomathematicians mentioned in Chapter 1. As is the case with the myth of participation, the myth of emancipation conceals the extent of the operation of power in and as the radical-rearticulation of the GSU.

Corresponding to the myth of reference is what I shall refer to as the *myth of certainty*. This myth is (re)produced in the philosophical position described (and critiqued) by Paul Ernest as 'absolutism'. Here are two illustrations:

> Only in mathematics is there verifiable certainty. Tell a primary child that World War 2 lasted for 10 years, and he [sic] will believe it; tell him that two fours are ten, and there will be an argument. Children know what is wrong at their own level of competence in mathematics and can verify it themselves, even if they may not always be encouraged to do so. (Howson and Wilson, 1986; p. 12)

So far as we can tell, mathematical relationships should be valid for all planets, biologies, cultures, philosophies. We can imagine a planet with uranium hexaflouride in the atmosphere of a life form that lives mostly off interstellar dust, even if these are extremely unlikely contingencies. But we cannot imagine a civilization for which one and one does not equal two or for which there is an integer interposed between eight and nine. (Sagan, quoted in Cockcroft *et al*, 1982; p. 3)

As with the myth of reference, the sociocultural is again presented as divided between mathematical and non-mathematical practices. This time, however, there is no attempt to constitute referents for the former within the latter. Rather, the mathematical authorial voice is affiliating to a platonist realism. Mathematical practice is represented by elementary arithmetic which constitutes the essential truth residing at the heart of the universe. In this, if in no other area of the social or natural sciences, humanity has achieved certain knowledge. Like the myth of reference, the myth of certainty exposes some of the self-referential nature of mathematical practices. Like the myth of reference, the myth of certainty conceals the constructive subjectivity of mathematics and so the operation of power in and as its (re)production. By affiliating to a transcendental truth, the myth of certainty is exchanging faith for a constructed rationality. Mathematics simulates its own regime of truth. Once the Peano axioms have been constructed and articulated with number signs it is trivial to assert that one and one equals two and that there is no integer interposed between eight and nine, even if it does take eight-hundred pages of metonymic elaboration by Russell and Whitehead in order to establish the basis for the revelation of the triviality of the former (Restivo, 1984).

The myths of certainty and emancipation do not feature in the *SMP 11–16* texts. Their correlates, however, are distributed by these texts. The myth of reference is distributed to the apprenticed voice and the myth of participation to the dependent voice. These voices are respectively identified by the text with the intellectual and with the manual. In other words, school mathematics as (re)produced by these texts recognizes its voices in terms of social class. Textually, this entails that the Y and G books 'apprentice' in opposite directions. The Y books apprentice their reader voice to abstract esoteric domain discourse in generalizing and specializing strategies. They identify their reader voice as a potential Subject of school mathematics and of its gaze and also with other academic and professional activities. The G books construct a virtual apprenticeship by projecting its reader voice into the public domain. Here, it is identified exclusively with manual activities. In the next section I shall consider the manual/intellectual modality more generally.

The Manual/Intellectual Modality

In my discussion of manual practices in Chapter 6, I distinguished between those that could generally be characterized as segmentally organized and those that were constituted within a more complex division of labour. Domestic and other quotidian activities were given as examples of the former. Commonly, there is minimal or no institutionalizing of pedagogy within these activities, so that acquisition is achieved informally, via a sharing of strategies within a structure of relations which is basically horizontal. This is because there is generally no selection in segmentally organized activities: everyone is constituted as a participant or as a potential participant. These activities do not constitute discourse in the way in which I have defined it in this book. They are, in other words, DS⁻ activities.

Manual craft practices do institutionalize hierarchical pedagogic relations in the selection of apprentices and in the constitution of manual skills. We might interpret manual craft activities as the achievement of the specialization of positions and practices in, for example, symbolic and physical locational terms, but largely without the generation of discourse. Again, these are DS⁻ practices.

I have contrasted such practices with others which are DS⁺, that is, practices which are commonly described as 'intellectual'. Alfred Sohn-Rethel (1978) associates the division between intellectual and manual labour with class society. This association is valid, at least in part, if we can refer to the opening up of an 'intellectual' sphere of practice as an organizing of manual practices which operates at an analytically higher level than the simple marking out of areas of specialization such that the hierarchy is not resolved by career. With respect to material production, for example, the 'intellectual' practices associated with management and with engineering may be described as an objectification and organization of the 'manual' practices of production. Private sphere 'manual' practices associated with the care of the self are objectified and organized by the 'intellectual' practices associated with medical knowledge. The intellectual practices codify the manual practices which are abstracted into esoteric systems of knowledge which are substantially self-referential, which is to say, which are far less context-dependent in their elaboration. These DS⁺ practices organize, but — precisely by virtue of their context-independence — cannot facilitate the manual practices. The intellectual incompletely describes the manual because discourse can never fully saturate practice. The hierarchy which is established is close to a splitting-off of the intellectual from the manual. The manual subject is objectified by the intellectual and is, therefore, alienated from intellectually apprenticed positions. The relations between these categories of practice are, therefore, more like gender than age, which is to say, they are 'class' rather than career relations.

The intellectual/manual splitting is illustrated in the recontextualization of manual domestic practices by the intellectual practice of school mathematics as it is (re)produced by the *SMP 11–16* texts. As I have argued, any given activity is always a radical-rearticulation of the GSU. DS⁺ activities construct more or less extensive public domains, but these are always recontextualizings of their referent practices. The analysis of the public domain in Chapter 10, in particular, demonstrated the mythical nature of the myth of participation;

mathematics can codify and describe domestic practices, but the recontextualizing productivity of the mathematical gaze ensures that it cannot facilitate, far less optimize, domesticity.

Similarly, intellectual practices associated with the production of the mass media (management, engineering, journalism, etc) and with governance (the law, statistics) facilitate the codification and dissemination of illicit behaviour. Thus a violent assault on a woman by a stranger is sublimated from a unique event within a community to an instance of a practice which is thereby publicly reified. The intellectual extends the effectivity of patriarchy by establishing a fear of rape. In the UK, at least, it is men who are overwhelmingly the victims as well as the perpetrators of violent assault by strangers. Yet it is women who are deterred from going out at night unless accompanied by a man[3]. The rape is a unique and localized event. Its codifications do not so much represent it as simulate a crime as a generalized category. In this simulation patriarchy is recruited and (re)produced.

Intellectual practices are facilitated, in the first instance, by the technologies of literacy. As I noted in Chapter 5, it is literacy that, for Luria (1976), indexes the transition from 'primitive' societies, structured by individualized production, to 'modern' societies organized on the basis of collective production. Luria associates the acquisition of literacy with the development of higher forms of reasoning. It is my contention, however, that intellectual practices do not produce rationality. Rather, intellectual practices in general simulate rationality as that which is actually or potentially achieved exclusively by discursive practices. This simulation is realized in the various myths that I have described in this book. In each case, the myth conceals the operation of power in and as the work of social activity and the hypersystem of the division of labour in general in terms of fundamental organizing principles. In particular, the myth of reference, on the one hand, and that of participation, on the other, might be referred to as the ideologies of class because of their subordination of manual practices to the intellectual gaze. Correspondingly, the opposing myths of certainty and emancipation ideologize race by locating truth exclusively within a specifically European activity.

The rationalizing recontextualization of the manual by the intellectual gaze constitutes context-independent accounts of context-dependent practices. That is to say, it has a tendency or, at least, a potential, to publicize the private. Manual practices are, in this sense, potentially publicly accountable and so subject to intellectual reorganization. This is nowhere better illustrated than in the process of industrialization of production in nineteenth century Europe and in the progressive 'de-skilling' of manual labour culminating in the 'scientific management' of Fordist practices in the early twentieth century (see, for example, Braverman, 1974). The result has been the virtual elimination of extended craft apprenticeship. Alongside this there has been, during the

---

3 Rather, they are encouraged to stay at home, where they and their children are the overwhelming majority of victims of domestic violence by men who are known to them.

twentieth century, a massive expansion in terms of intellectually-oriented higher education. Mathematics is an intellectual, DS$^+$, activity. The social class principles of selection of its apprentices and its rationalizing of the manual are precisely in accord with these more general developments in the division of labour.

However, the developments do not appear to have terminated with the hegemonizing of intellectual practices. Such is hinted at in the South African White Paper which was discussed in Chapter 1. Here, it appeared that manual and intellectual practices were both being called to account by the bureaucratizing State. In Chapter 1 I suggested that the managerial practices of government were constituted as just another form of intellectual activity. Thus the assault on academic intellectualism by the State constituted an attempt to replace one form of intellectual practice with another, thus leaving undisturbed the fundamental organizing principle of the intellectual/manual hierarchy. It may be, however, that we should reconsider this.

The Development of the Sociocultural Modality as an Equilibrating Hypersystem

In terms of the distributing strategies introduced in Chapter 7, we might refer to craft activities as specializations in terms of their selection of limited ranges of manual practices and their production of these practices as skilled. Correspondingly, everyday activities confront the range of craft activities as standing in metaphorical relationship to one another insofar as the content of the craft activities cannot be addressed within the everyday. Everyday activities thus fragment the field of craft practices. Everyday activities are conceived as horizontally, which is to say, essentially non-hierarchically related to each other.[4] Craft activities act selectively on these practices and their positions and so stand in vertical relationship to them. However, these activities stand in a more horizontal relationship to each other to the extent that they mutually alienate or are mutually dependent, but do not recruit (from) one another.

Now, intellectual activities may be conceived of as generalizing in relation to both craft and everyday manual practices. That is to say, their discourses are able to traverse the range of manual activities, abstracting from them and constituting them as equivalent. I have illustrated this in the case of mathematics. However, it is also true of, for example, the natural and social sciences — biology and psychology may both recontextualize craft pottery and domestic cooking within their public domains — as it is for the law, medicine, literature, and so on. In this respect, intellectual activities stand in vertical relationship to manual activities. The strategic relationship between intellectual and manual activities is one of generalizing/localizing: the intellectual generalizes the manual; the manual localizes the intellectual. However, the generalizing

---

4   Although, clearly, these practices will entail internal hierarchies including those of gender and age.

potential of intellectual activities entails that they are far more likely than craft activities to recruit (from) one another in constituting their public domains. Again, this has been illustrated in relation to mathematics. The strategic relation between intellectual activities is specializing/generalizing. They constitute specialisms of the intellectual plane in part by generalizing each other.

The strategic relations that I have described might be interpreted as facilitating the interrogation and testing of one activity by and of others. I am conceiving of activities as being realized by human subjects who are, of necessity, multiple. However, they are not, as I argued in Chapter 7, internally fragmented. Non-activated activities remain as the background of the particular radical-rearticulation of the GSU that constitutes the activated activity. It is precisely this which enables constructive, which is to say transformative interaction between activities. Because of the dominance of the activated activity, however, such constructive interaction cannot be predictive. To this extent, the relationship between, say, mathematics and the non-mathematical or, more generally, between theory and practice, may be construed as interrogative and testing, but not as prescriptive.

In formulating the above paragraphs, I have been conceiving of intellectual activities as comprising the academic and professional fields. However, it is clear that activities within these and the craft and everyday fields are themselves being generalized by a mode of practice which we must begin to think of as qualitatively different from both DS$^+$ and DS$^-$ practices. These practices are represented, perhaps, by the managerial and bureaucratizing State, the voice of which authors the South African White Paper. Here, there is a clear generalizing of intellectual and manual as 'falsely' divided. Indeed, following on from the White Paper, the South African State is moving towards the production of a National Qualifications Framework which codifies and generalizes within a single system everything which might conceivably be thought of as education, from everyday spoken interaction, to a PhD[5].

We can see further evidence of the work of this third mode of practice in current developments within education in the UK. The National Curriculum and associated national assessments and programmes and procedures for the inspection of schools is clearly a move towards the codification of academic practices by and within a generalizing structure (see, for example, the discussions in Dowling and Noss, 1990). Within Higher Education, the evidence is equally apparent. The modularization of undergraduate and postgraduate studies has been progressing for some considerable time now. The effect is to equate limited gobbets of academic practice in terms of both range and career stage. One of the newest developments is the accreditation of prior learning which constitutes the university as a crediting agency as distinct from a pedagogic institution. It is now possible at certain UK 'universities' to obtain a 'professional doctorate' on the basis of a year's registration plus what might be only a little flippantly referred to as the contents of one's filing cabinet.

5   See, for example, Human Sciences Research Council, 1995.

The dynamic field of activities which articulate with each other strategically and in horizontal and vertical relationships is constitutive of the sociocultural as an equilibrating system. The system is, furthermore, a hierarchical one in terms of the general level of social organization that is entailed. Thus, as we move from the everyday through the craft and intellectual to bureaucratizing practices, the practices themselves become increasingly disembodied and organized by and as technology. Skill in the deployment of manual tools must be embodied in the user. Skilled crafts construct the embodiment of these skills in relatively extended apprenticeships as well as in secret knowledge. There is a limited extent to which the book — the archetypal technology of intellectual practice — can incorporate the knowledge which facilitates its own reading. This is precisely the nature of the context-independence of intellectual practices. However, it will generally require a specialist to read a research paper and the acquisition of the specialism is, again, an extended process.

Bureaucratic practices constitute and are constituted by informational matrices and data sets. These technologies facilitate the storage, retrieval and communication of information in standardized forms with, by and large, a minimum of knowledge or skill embodied in the human subject. This is perhaps most apparent in the field of information technology, which is merely the most recent form that developments in this third mode of practice have taken. In particular, apparently universal and unlimited access to the internet has inveigled some groups to imagine the existence of a new utopia in cyberspace. John Perry Barlow, for example, has led in the proclamation of 'A Declaration of the Independence of Cyberspace'. Barlow's 'Declaration' is politically and sociologically naive[6]. Essentially, it weaves together members of the pantheon of American and European liberalism with a claim to a technological realization of the Cartesian mind/body dualism:

> We will create a civilization of the Mind in Cyberspace. May it be more humane and fair than the world your governments have made before. (Barlow, forwarded by Chislenko, 1996)

Barlow indexes his own cybernetic-colonist — which is to say, mental — identity in the form of his world wide web 'Home(stead) Page' and admits to a corporeal location in what he describes as 'Meatspace'. He signs off with a quotation from Thomas Jefferson:

> It is error alone which needs the support of government. Truth can stand by itself. (*ibid*)

But whose truth? Jefferson's own Declaration of Independence did little for the indigenous population who were scape-goated by Samuel Adams *et al* in their Boston protest against British support for the East India Company (a party alluded to by Barlow). John Stuart Mill, also applauded by Barlow, was

6   Barlow is the co-founder of the Electronic Frontier Foundation (EFF).

himself an official of the East India Company. Sins of the flesh (in meatspace) versus the heady ideals of the intellectual utopia, perhaps.

Barlow is constituting technology as a revolutionary tool which enables the transcendence of the embodiment of mind. Cyberspace itself is presented as a virgin territory awaiting colonization by subjects who will transform and release themselves. Cyberspace is neutral. Power is eliminated and there are no aboriginal inhabitants to be dispossessed. Subjectivity is a utopian version of Descartes' cogito.

But cyberspace is no more virgin territory than was America prior to the European invasions. This time, however, the colonizing infrastructure is already substantially in place. Barlow is not a pioneer, so much as an immigrant. Barlow can post his message to discussion lists and I can post papers on the world wide web only because we have access to the internet which is materially constituted and so is subject to the economics of appropriation and exploitation.

For affluent intellectuals information technology looks very much like a set of tools which we can grasp in facilitating and expanding our activities. But this is because we are in a transitional phase. Intellectual practices still dominate or, at least, are still tolerated in certain domains. I am still paid to engage in intellectual labour and my technology is provided free. But not, perhaps, for very much longer. In addition to the bureaucratizing of qualifications which I mentioned earlier, academics are increasingly being held to account in respect of the totality of their intellectual labour. Artificial currencies are constructed which measure, and thereby equate, their publications (of all types), their teaching (at all levels), their research and their administrative duties. Research, in particular, is measured virtually exclusively in terms of funding brought in and number of publications it produces.

These developments must result in the degeneration to the level of bureaux of those universities which collaborate with them, which is to say, the overwhelming majority. A few, no doubt, will follow the approach of further specialization and will survive as elite centres of intellectual activity, just as there remain elite centres of craft activity[7]. Neither, of course, will be central to mainstream economic activity.

Infinite access to information within an economics of appropriation entails the automation of intellectual practices. Intellectual products, like manual products, are beginning to be corporately generated. The CD-ROM encyclopaedia presents a transparent certainty which anticipates and excludes the possibility of intellectual virtuosity. The game is no longer conceptual, but navigational.

Cybernetic practices operate at an even greater degree of context-independence than do intellectual practices. CD-ROMs and internet journals only transitionally stand in the place of the contents of a traditional library. This is not simply a matter of commodification, the products of intellectual labour were commodified a long time ago. Cybernetic activities are not concerned

---

7 Indeed, there is already some evidence of this in attempts at the establishment of a university 'superleague' in the UK.

with these products themselves, but with the modality of their encoding, with the subordination of potentially all areas of human practice to a single code. Donna Haraway perceives a parallel development:

> ... communications sciences and modern biologies are constructed by a common move — *the translation of the world into a problem of coding*, a search for a common language in which all resistance to instrumental control disappears and all heterogeneity can be submitted to disassembly, reassembly, investment and exchange. (Haraway, 1991; p. 164)

The binary coding of the digital computer is perhaps more radical than the highly complex codes of the double helical DNA molecule, but the move is, indeed, the same. All information must be numerically realizable; the minutest variations in life must be traceable to a genetic site. Cognitive science begins to make the same move with respect to psychology. Chaos theory returns us to the security of a universe operating according to simple laws[8]. We are, perhaps, only just beginning to appreciate that the productions of these fields are simulating a yet higher order of absence, a mathematical code which, ultimately, organizes all fields of practice and which is the stake within the newest site for the play of power.

Barlow's 'Declaration' fails to recognize and so conceals the constructive nature of bureaucratic practice which is constituted by and constitutive of power. It constitutes the final myth; this is the *myth of cyberspace*. Like the other myths, it constructs a utopia in which power is neutralized.

So, the sociocultural is constituted as a hierarchical and equilibrating system or, more properly, a hypersystem. Activities within the various levels of this hypersystem are constituted by and constitutive of the strategic relations of fragmentation, localization, specialization and generalization, which operate within and between them. I have, however, argued that equilibrium must itself be predicated of an equilibrating system. This raises the possibility of an original or edenic state of equilibrium. In the conclusion to this concluding chapter I want to suggest a meaning for such a state by drawing on the psychoanalytic writings of Ignacio Matte-Blanco.

The Individual and the Social Unconscious

I shall start with an illustrative narrative, as follows: a schizophrenic is bitten by a dog and so visits a dentist[9]. Such an action is clearly not to be resolved using

---

8 Cognitive science involves the construction of computer models of mind. Chaos theory proposes that a simple system is capable of generating chaotic behaviour. See Gleick (1988) for a non-technical exposition on chaos theory.

9 My comments on and interpretation of this narrative are not those offered by Matte-Blanco, who introduces the narrative in the work cited. In particular, his interpretation is far more complex and articulates more completely with the details of his theory. My simplified analysis is intended to be illustrative rather than exhaustive and the interested reader is directed to Matte-Blanco's own text.

conventional logic. An initial attempt to make sense of the narrative might constitute a chain of metonyms as follows: dog-bite, teeth, dentist. This would enable the narrative to be interpreted in terms of a displacement, but it would not explain the principles of selection of the particular metonyms involved. Suppose, however, that we make an assumption that the unconscious operates according to an alternative logic. In particular, we might assume that, whereas the conscious operates according to a logic which distinguishes between asymmetrical and symmetrical relations, the unconscious operates, at least in part, on the basis of symmetrical relations only. Thus, 'dog bites person' is an asymmetrical relation, because it does not imply that 'person bites dog'. The symmetrizing unconscious, however, would interpret these two statements as equivalent. The narrative can now be interpreted as follows. The dog bites the schizophrenic. This event is interpreted, by her/his unconscious, as equivalent to the schizophrenic biting the dog. The dog-bite causes pain. But this pain is now interpretable as consequent upon the human doing the biting. That is, when the schizophrenic bites, they experience pain, This provides entirely adequate grounds for the visit to the dentist that concludes the narrative.

The schizophrenic of the narrative can be interpreted as acting according to two modes of logic: asymmetric and symmetric. Her/his action can be described as an alternating sequence of these logics; it is 'bi-logical'. Matte-Blanco proposes that the very deepest level of the unconscious does not operate according to differentiation at all. In this sense, there is no thinking, only being. Asymmetric relations are inaugurated by the earliest encounters of this original state with the world. Specifically (drawing on Melanie Klein, 1975), the breast may be offered (good) or withdrawn (bad). At the deep levels of the unconscious, symmetric logic identifies the good breast with every member of the class of things which are good and the bad breast with every member of the class of things which can be bad. Since these are potentially infinite classes, symmetrizing here constitutes an infinitized polarization of pleasure and discomfort. This identification of a member of a class with every member of the class entails that the unconscious operates in propositional form. That is, the perception that mother is happy results in the association of mother with every member of the class of things that can be happy. Thus, 'mother is happy' is transformed into 'x is happy', which is to say, 'there is happiness'. This, again, is a state of being which contrasts with the state of happening which characterizes the differentiating action of consciousness.

Because the class, in the unconscious, is represented simultaneously by many and potentially infinite elements, the mode of operation of the unconscious can be described as multi-dimensional. Matte-Blanco argues that consciousness must conform to a four-dimensional (three dimensions of displacement plus time) world. There is, thus a 'fundamental antinomy' between the original, which is to say, unconscious human being and their worldly consciousness.

Matte-Blanco makes a great deal of use of mathematical resources to describe this fundamental antinomy. However, it may be more appropriate to interpret mathematics itself as a technological means of resolving the antinomy which can be described in simpler terms. Essentially, the original human is constituted as an unconscious *being*. This being emerges into a world which is populated by other beings, interactions between which of necessity disrupt the symmetry of *being* with asymmetrical *thinking*. The conscious human subject is constituted through the repression of the unconscious human being.

The social is necessarily agonistic. Social activity is concerned with the construction of organized spaces, in metaphorical and metonymical terms and with extended or limited ranges of practice, and with the dissolution of such spaces[10]. The existence of social solidarity in the face of an antagonistic social milieu is, of course, precisely the problem that Durkheim (1984) attempted to resolve in *The Division of Labour in Society*. Durkheim's mechanical solidarity is constituted by a collective social consciousness. However, to the extent that this consciousness can be contained within the consciousness of individuals, it cannot resolve the antinomy with being. Embodied subjectivity — social *consciousness* — is, as I have argued, multiple and, therefore, internally (re)constructive. However, I have described the sociocultural system as an organization of activities which hierarchically disembody practices in the construction of technologies. These technologies are capable of containing the symmetric, multidimensionality of the individual unconscious. This is most apparent, perhaps in the universal codifying of bureaucratic practices and, particularly, in the binary coding which lies at the heart of information technology.

This code, which is totalizing in its public domain, mirrors the good/bad code of the earliest disturbance of the state of equilibrium of individual being. In this sense, we can interpret social equilibration as the movement towards the re-establishing of the edenic state which has been constituted by the social as the individual unconscious. However, the social form is no more containable within conscious subjectivity than is the individual form. The telos of social equilibration, then, is not social consciousness, but a social unconscious.[11] Between these two sites of the unconscious — individual and technological being — is the site of subjectivity. This is not an assertion that information technology is the exclusive or even the most advanced form of the social unconscious. The most advanced form is given by that which totalizes the sociocultural. The relationship between societies is not, then, one of relative primitivity or advancement, but one of technological mode.

The relationship of the site of subjectivity to the unconscious sites might appropriately be referred to as respectively psychoanalysis and *socioanalysis*. My socioanalysis is precisely the revealing of mythical forms and their relationship

10　I am using the term 'space' in a manner similar to its use in mathematics and physics, for example, as a vector space or a momentum space. That is, as a radical-rearticulation of the GSU such that practices and positions can be described in terms of activity-specific principles.

11　This is clearly very different from the genetically constituted archetypes that comprise Jung's 'collective unconscious' (1959).

to the strategies that constitute the pedagogic texts that have been the empirical objects of my sociology in this book.

In terminating this socioanalysis, I want to make one further claim. In this book I have introduced a general methodology — constructive description — a specific language of description — social activity theory — and an analysis of school mathematics as (re)produced in and by a set of mathematical texts. I want to claim that each of these discursive presentations is consistent with the others in terms of its general structure. That is, they constitute an authorial subjectivity which organizes and principles its space through positioning and distributing strategies. Since this is a discursive subjectivity (DS⁺), the extent of its explicitness and systematicity is a fundamental evaluative criterion. Regrettably, lucidity is of secondary importance, from this point of view. Still, my intention in constructing this text has been to construct my own ideal reader as an apprenticed voice. My hope is that the empirical reader has accepted the position which this voice (re)produces. The apprenticeship is now complete. The relationship between the author and reader of a book is less geometrically defined than that between a teacher and their class. Nevertheless, insofar as you have rotated my book through one-hundred-and-eighty degrees, you now stand as its adept critical Subject.

References and Bibliography

ABRAHAM, J. and BIBBY, N. (1992) 'Mathematics and society: Ethnomathematics and the public educator curriculum', in NICKSON, M. and LERMAN, S. (eds) *The Social Context of Mathematics Education: Theory and Practice*, London: Southbank Press.

AGGER, B. (1989) 'Do books write authors? A study of disciplinary hegemony', *Teaching Sociology*, **17**, 3, pp. 365–9.

AHIER, J.G. (1987) Representations of town and country in the production of a national identity: An analysis of school textbooks for English children 1880–1960, unpublished PhD, Kings College, London University.

AL-ABDULJADIR, F.F. (1987) Islamic values and biology texts in Kuwait, unpublished MEd, University of Wales, Cardiff.

ALTHUSSER, L. (1971) *Lenin and Philosophy,* London: New Left Books.

ANUAR, M.K. (1990) The construction of a 'National Identity': A study of selected secondary school textbooks in Malaysia's education system with particular reference to peninsular Malaysia, unpublished PhD thesis, City University.

ANYON, J. (1979) 'Ideology and United States history textbooks', *Harvard Education Review*, **49**, 3, pp. 361–86.

ANYON, J. (1981a) 'Ideology and United States history textbooks' (abridged), in DALE, R. *et al* (eds) *Education and the State Volume II: Politics, Patriarchy and Practice*, Lewes: Falmer Press.

ANYON, J. (1981b) 'Schools as agencies of social legitimation', *Journal of Curriculum Theorizing*, **3**, 2, pp. 86–103.

ANYON, J. (1983) 'Workers, labor and economic history, and textbook content', in APPLE, M.W. and WEIS, L. (eds) *Ideology and Practice in Schooling*, Philadelphia: Temple University Press.

ANYON, M. (1986) *Teachers and Texts: A Political Economy of Class and Gender Relations in Education*, New York: Routledge.

APPLE, M. (1989) 'The political economy of text publishing', in CASTELL, S. de, LUKE, A.L. and LUKE, C. (eds) *Language, Authority and Criticism: Readings on the School Textbook*, London: Falmer Press.

ATKIN, R. (1981) *Multidimensional Man*, Harmondsworth, Penguin.

ATKINSON, P. (1985) *Language, Structure and Reproduction: An Introduction to the Sociology of Basil Bernstein*, London: Methuen.

ATKINSON, P. (1990) *The Ethnographic Imagination: Textual Constructions of Reality*, London: Routledge.

BAGCHI, J.P. (1985) 'Indian biology textbooks in sex education, a comparative study', *Journal of Science and Mathematics Education in Southeast Asia*, **8**, 2, pp. 180–23.

BAILEY, D.E. *et al* (1981) *Mathematics in Employment (16–19)*, Bath: University of Bath.

BAKHTIN, M.M. (1981) *The Dialogic Imagination*, ed. Michael Holquist, Austin: University of Texas Press.

BAKHTIN, M.M. (1986) *Speech Genres and Other Late Essays*, ed. Caryl Emerson and Michael Holquist, Austin: University of Texas Press.

BANNET, E.T. (1989) *Structuralism and the Logic of Dissent*, Basingstoke: MacMillan.

BARTHES, R. (1972) *Mythologies*, London: Granada.

BARTHES, R. (1974) *S/Z*, London: Jonathan Cape.

BARTHES, R. (1981a) 'Theory of the text', in YOUNG, R. (ed.) *Untying the Text: A Poststructuralist Reader*, London: Routledge and Kegan Paul.

BARTHES, R. (1981b) 'Textual analysis of Poe's "Valdemar"', in YOUNG, R. (ed.) *Untying the Text: A Poststructuralist Reader*, London: Routledge and Kegan Paul.

BAUDRILLARD, J. (1987) *Forget Foucault and Forget Baudrillard*, New York: Semiotext(e).

BAUDRILLARD, J. (1993) *Symbolic Exchange and Death*, London: Sage.

BAUDRILLARD, J. (1994) *Simulacra and Simulation*, Ann Arbor: The University of Michigan Press.

BAUDRILLARD, J. (1995) *The Gulf War Did Not Take Place*, Sydney: Power Publications.

BENACERRAF, P. and PUTNAM, H. (eds) (1983) *Philosophy of Mathematics: Selected Readings*, second edition, Cambridge: Cambridge University Press.

BENSON, H. (1990) Dialogues and interactional skills — A study of English textbooks use in Japanese senior high schools, unpublished MA dissertation, Exeter University.

BERNSTEIN, B. (1971a) *Class, Codes and Control Volume 1: Theoretical Studies Towards a Sociology of Language*, London: Routledge and Kegan Paul.

BERNSTEIN, B. (1971b) 'On the classification and framing of educational knowledge', in YOUNG, M.F.D. (ed.) *Knowledge and Control: New Directions for the Sociology of Education*, London: Collier-MacMillan.

BERNSTEIN, B. (1977) *Class, Codes and Control Volume 3: Towards a Theory of Educational Transmissions*, second edition, London: Routledge and Kegan Paul.

BERNSTEIN, B. (1982) 'Codes, modalities and the process of cultural reproduction', in APPLE, M.W. (ed.) *Cultural and Economic Reproduction in Education*, London: Routledge and Kegan Paul.

BERNSTEIN, B. (1985) 'On pedagogic discourse', in Richards, J. (ed.) *Handbook of Theory and Research for the Sociology of Education*, New York: Greenwood Press.

BERNSTEIN, B. (1988) 'On pedagogic discourse: Revised', *Collected Original Resources in Education*, **12**, 1.

BERNSTEIN, B. (1990) *Class, Codes and Control, volume 4*, London: Routledge and Kegan Paul.

BERNSTEIN, B. (1996) *Pedagogy, Symbolic Control and Identity: Theory, Research Critique*, London: Taylor and Francis.

BEYER, L.E. (1983) 'Aesthetic curriculum and cultural reproduction', in APPLE, M.W. and WEIS, L. (eds) *Ideology and Practice in Schooling*, Philadelphia: Temple University Press.

BIBBY, N. (1988) 'Social History of Mathematical Controversies: Some implications for the curriculum', mimeo, London: KQC.

BISHOP, A. (1977) 'Is a picture worth a thousand words', *Mathematics Teaching*, 81.

BISHOP, A. (1988a) 'Mathematics education in its cultural context', *Educational Studies in Mathematics*, **19**, 2, pp. 179–91.

BISHOP, A. (1988b) *Mathematical Enculturation: A Cultural Perspective on Mathematics Education*, Dordrecht: Kluwer.

BLAU, P.M. and MEYER, M. (1971) *Bureaucracy in Modern Society*, second edition, New York: Random House.

BLOOR, D. (1976) *Knowledge and Social Imagery*, London: Routledge and Kegan Paul.

BOS, W. (1990) 'On mother tongue teaching material of ethnic minorities: A comparative content analysis', *Research in Education*, 43, pp. 45–62.

BOURDIEU, P. (1977) *Outline of a Theory of Practice*, Cambridge: Cambridge University Press.

BOURDIEU, P. (1984) *Distinction: A Social Critique of the Judgement of Taste,* London: Routledge and Kegan Paul.

BOURDIEU, P. (1990) *The Logic of Practice*, Cambridge: Polity.

BOURDIEU, P. and PASSERON, J-C. (1977) Reproduction in Education, Society and Culture, London: Sage.

BOWLES, S. and GINTIS, H. (1976) *Schooling in Capitalist America*, London: Routledge and Kegan Paul.

BOWLES, S. and GINTIS, H. (1986) *Democracy and Capitalism: Property, Community, and the Contradictions of Modern Social Thought*, London: Routledge and Kegan Paul.

BOWLES, S. and GINTIS, H. (1988) 'The correspondence principle', in COLE, M. (ed.) *Bowles and Gintis Revisited: Correspondence and Contradiction in Educational Theory*, London: Falmer Press.

BRAVERMAN, H. (1974) *Labor and Monopoly Capital: The Degradation of Work in the Twentieth Century*, New York: Monthly Review Press.

BRITTON, G. *et al* (1984) 'The battle to imprint citizens for the 21st century', *Reading Teacher*, **37**, 8, pp. 724–33.

BRITTON, G. and LUMKIN, M. (1983) 'Basal readers: Paltry progress pervades', *Interracial Books for Children Bulletin*, **14**, 6, pp. 4–7.

BROWN, A.J. (1993) 'Participation, dialogue and the reproduction of social inequalities', in MERTTENS, R. and VASS, J. (eds) *Partnerships in Maths: Parents and Schools*, London: Falmer Press.

BROWN, A.J. (1994) 'Exploring dialogue between teachers and parents: A sociological analysis of IMPACT diaries', presented at Research into Social Perspectives on Mathematics Education, Kings' College, University of London, December 1994 (available from the author at Culture, Communication and Societies, Institute of Education, University of London).

BROWN, A.J. and DOWLING, P.C. (1989) 'A critical alternative to internationalism and monoculturalism in mathematics education', Centre for Multicultural Education, Occasional Paper Number 10, London: Institute of Education, University of London, Centre for Multicultural Education, also in Gardener, R. (ed.), 1992, *An International Dimension in the National Curriculum: An Imperative for Britain for 1992 and Beyond*, London: Department of International and Comparative Education, Institute of Education, University of London.

BROWN, A.J. and DOWLING, P.C. (1992) '"Who's been restructuring my primary socialisation?" the impact of school mathematics on domestic space', Ruling the margins: Problematising parental involvement, Institute of Education, University of London, September 1992, conference proceedings obtainable from IMPACT project, University of North London.

BROWN, A.J. and DOWLING, P.C. (1993) 'The bearing of school mathematics on domestic space', in MERTTENS, R., MAYERS, D., BROWN, A.J. and VASS, J. (eds) *Ruling the Margins: Problematising Parental Involvement*, London: IMPACT, University of North London.

BROWN, A.J. and DOWLING, P.C. (1997) *Doing Research/Reading Research*, London: Falmer Press.

BROWN, S.I. (1981) 'Ye shall be known by your generations', *For the Learning of Mathematics*, **1**, 3, pp. 27–36.

BROWN, S.I. (1984) 'The logic of problem generation: From morality and solving to de-posing and rebellion', *For the Learning of Mathematics*, **4**, 1, pp. 9–20, also in BURTON, L. (ed.) (1986) *Girls Into Maths Can Go*, London: Holt, Rinehart and Winston.

BROWNE, J. (1990) 'Gender bias in physical education textbooks', *ACHOER National Journal*, 127, pp. 4–7.

BUERK, D. (1982) 'An experience with some able women who avoid mathematics', *For the Learning of Mathematics*, **3**, 2, pp. 19–24.

BULMER, M. (ed.) (1984) *Sociological Research Methods: An Introduction*, second edition, London: MacMillan.

BURTON, L. (ed.) (1986) *Girls Into Maths Can Go*, London: Holt, Rinehart and Winston.

BURTON, L. (1988) 'Images of mathematics', in ERNEST, P. (ed.) *The Social Context of Mathematics Teaching: Perspectives 37*, Exeter: School of Education, University of Exeter.

BURTON, L. *et al* (1986) *Girls Into Mathematics*, Cambridge: Cambridge University Press.

CAIRNS, J.E. (1988) A cultural analysis of primary level history textbooks with a special focus on the history of women, unpublished MEd, Stirling University.

CAIRNS, J. and INGLIS, B. (1989) 'A content analysis of ten popular history textbooks for primary schools with particular emphasis on the role of women', *Educational Review*, **41**, 3, pp. 221–6.

CAIRNS, M.E. (1984) Schools Mathematics Project 7–13: Comparative content analysis and a study of implementation in primary and junior schools, unpublished MPhil, University of Lancaster.

CARLSON, D.L. (1989) 'Legitimation and delegitimation: American history textbooks and the Cold War', in CASTELL, S. de, LUKE, A.L. and LUKE, C. (eds) *Language, Authority and Criticism: Readings on the School Textbook*, London: Falmer Press.

CARRAHER, D.W. (1991) 'Mathematics in and out of school: A selective review of studies from Brazil', in HARRIS, M. (ed.) *Schools, Mathematics and Work*, London: Falmer Press.

CARRAHER, T.N., CARRAHER, D.W. and SCHLIEMANN, A.D. (1987) 'Written and oral mathematics', *Journal for Research in Mathematics Education*, **18**, 2, pp. 83–97.

CARRAHER, T.N. *et al* (1985) 'Mathematics in the streets and in the schools', *British Journal of Developmental Psychology*, **3**, 1, pp. 21–9.

CARRAHER, T.N., SCHLIEMANN, A.D. and CARRAHER, D.W. (1988) 'Mathematical concepts in everyday life', in SAXE, G.B. and GEARHART, M. (eds) *Children's Mathematics: New Directions for Child Development*, San Francisco: Jossey-Bass.

CARRELL, D. (1991) 'Gender scripts in professional writing textbooks', *Journal of Business and Technical Communication*, **5**, 4, pp. 463–8.

CARROLL, H. (1991) 'Educational levels', *The Aboriginal Child at School*, **19**, 1, pp. 3–5.

CENTRAL STATISTICAL OFFICE (1995) *Social Trends 25*, London: HMSO.

CERTEAU, M. de (1988) *The Practice of Everyday Life*, Berkeley: University of California Press.

CHIMOMBO, M. (1989) 'Readability of subject texts: Implications for ESL teaching in Africa', *English for Specific Purposes*, **8**, 3, pp. 255–64.

CHISLENKO, A. (1996) 'FWD: A Cyberspace Independence Declaration' at http://www.mailbase.ac.uk/lists-a-e/cyberspace-and-society/1996-02/0010.html.

CLARK, L.L. (1980) 'The education of French schoolgirls: Pedagogical prescriptions and social and economic realities during the Third Republic', working paper, Mary Bunting Institute, Radcliffe College, Cambridge, Mass.

COARD, B. (1971) *How the West Indian Child is Made Educationally Subnormal in the British School System*, London: New Beacon.

COCKBURN, C. (1983) *Brothers: Male Dominance and Technological Change*, London: Pluto.

COCKBURN, C. (1985a) 'Caught in the wheels: The high cost of being a female cog in the male machinery of engineering', in MACKENZIE D. and WAJCMAN J. (eds) *The Social Shaping of Technology*, Milton Keynes: Open University Press.

COCKBURN, C. (1985b) 'The material of male power', in MACKENZIE D. and WAJCMAN J. (eds) *The Social Shaping of Technology*, Milton Keynes: Open University Press.

COCKBURN, C. (1985c) *Machinery of Dominance*, London: Pluto.

COCKCROFT, W. *et al* (1982) *Mathematics Counts*, London: HMSO.

COHEN, I.J. (1987) 'Structuration theory and social praxis', in GIDDENS, A. and TURNER, J.H. (eds) *Social Theory Today*, Cambridge: Polity.

CONNELL, R.W. (1985) *Teachers' Work*, Sydney: Allen and Unwin.

CONNELL, R.W., ASHENDEN, D.J., KESSLER, S. and DOWSETT, G.W. (1982) *Making the Difference*, Sydney: Allen and Unwin.

CONNOR-GREENE, P. *et al*, (1988) 'Gender issues in psychology: A content analysis of introductory psychology textbooks', paper presented at the Annual Meeting of the Southeastern Psychological Association, New Orleans, March 1988.

COOK-GUMPERTZ, J. (ed.) (1973) *Social Control and Socialization: A Study of Class Differences in the Language of Maternal Control*, London: Routledge.

COOLEY, M. (1985) 'Drawing up the corporate plan at Lucas Aerospace', in MACKENZIE, D.A. and WAJCMAN, J. (eds) *The Social Shaping of Technology*, Milton Keynes: Open University Press.

COOMBE, J. and DAVIS, Z. (1995) 'Games in the Mathematics Classroom', in Z. Davis (ed.) *Exploring Mathematics Teaching and Teacher Education*, Rondebosch: Mathematics Education Project.

COOPER, B. (1983) 'On explaining change in school subjects', *British Journal of Sociology of Education*, **4**, 3, pp. 207–22.

COOPER, B. (1985) *Renegotiating Secondary School Mathematics*, Lewes: Falmer Press.

CORRAN, G. and WALKERDINE, V. (1981) *The Practice of Reason, Volume 1: Reading the Signs*, mimeo, London: University of London, Institute of Education.

COY, M.W. (1989) 'Being what we pretend to be: The usefulness of apprenticeship as a field method', in *Apprenticeship: From Theory to Method and Back Again*, Albany: State University of New York Press.

CRESSWELL, M. and GUBB, J. (1987) *The Second International Mathematics Study in England and Wales*, Windsor: NFER-Nelson.

CRISMORE, A. (1989) 'Rhetorical form, selection and use of textbooks', in CASTELL, S. de, LUKE, A.L. and LUKE, C. (eds) *Language, Authority and Criticism: Readings on the School Textbook*, London: Falmer Press.

CURRIE, J., KISSANE, B. and PEARS, H. (1992) 'An enriched mathematical program for young aboriginal children', *The Aboriginal Child at School*, **20**, 1, pp. 15–37.

DAHRENDORF, R. (1959) *Class and Class Conflict in Industrial Society*, London: Routledge and Kegan Paul.

D'AMBROSIO, U. (1985) 'Ethnomathematics and its place in the history and pedagogy of mathematics', *For the Learning of Mathematics*, **5**, 1, pp. 44–8.

D'AMBROSIO, U. (1990) 'The role of mathematics in building up a democratic society and the civilizatory mission of European powers since the discoveries', in NOSS, R. *et al* (eds) *Political Dimensions of Mathematics Education: Action and Critique, Proceedings of the First International Conference*, revised edition, London: Department of Mathematics, Statistics and Computing, Institute of Education, University of London.

DAVIS, P.J. and HERSH, R. (1981) *The Mathematical Experience*, Brighton: Harvester.

DEAN, E. *et al* (1983) *History in Black and White: An Analysis of South African School History Textbooks*, Paris: UNESCO.

DEPARTMENT OF EDUCATION (1995) *White Paper on Education and Training*, Cape Town: DOE.

DEPARTMENT OF EDUCATION AND SCIENCE (1975) *A Language for Life*, (The Bullock Report), London: HMSO.

DEPARTMENT OF EDUCATION AND SCIENCE (1985) *Mathematics From 5 to 16*, London: HMSO.

DEPARTMENT OF EDUCATION AND SCIENCE (1988a) *Mathematics for Ages 5 to 16*, London: HMSO.

DEPARTMENT OF EDUCATION AND SCIENCE (1988b) *National Curriculum Task Group on Assessment and Testing: A Report*, London: HMSO.

DEPARTMENT OF EDUCATION AND SCIENCE (1989) *Mathematics in the National Curriculum*, London: HMSO.

DEPARTMENT OF EDUCATION AND SCIENCE (1991) *Mathematics in the National Curriculum*, London: HMSO.

DERRIDA, J. (1981) 'Semiology and grammatology', in *Positions*, London: Athlone Press.

DESFORGES, C. and COCKBURN, A. (1987) *Understanding the Mathematics Teacher: A Study of Practice in First Schools*, London: Falmer Press.

DONALDSON, M. (1978) *Children's Minds*, Glasgow: Fontana/Collins.

DOWLING, P.C. (1985) 'Does Cuba educate for freedom?', discussion paper (available from the author at Culture Communication and Societies, Institute of Education, University of London).

DOWLING, P.C. (1989) 'The contextualising of mathematics: Towards a theoretical map', in *Collected Original Resources in Education*, **13**, 2 also in HARRIS, M. (ed.) (1990) *Schools, Mathematics and Work*, Basingstoke: Falmer Press.

DOWLING, P.C. (1990a) 'The shogun's and other curricular voices', in DOWLING, P.C. and NOSS, R. (eds) *Mathematics versus the National Curriculum*, Basingstoke: Falmer Press.

DOWLING, P.C. (1990b) 'Some notes towards a theoretical model for reproduction, action and critique', in NOSS, R. *et al* (eds) *Political Dimensions of Mathematics Education: Action and Critique, Proceedings of the First International Conference*, London: Department of Mathematics, Statistics and Computing, Institute of Education, University of London.

DOWLING, P.C. (1990c) 'Mathematics in the marketplace: The National Curriculum and numerical control', *Teaching London Kids*, **26**, pp. 28–31.

DOWLING, P.C. (1991a) 'A dialectics of determinism: Deconstructing information technology', in MCKAY, H., YOUNG, M.F.D. and BEYNON, J. (eds) *Understanding Technology in Education*, London: Falmer Press.

DOWLING, P.C. (1991b) 'Gender, class and subjectivity in mathematics: A critique of Humpty Dumpty', *For the Learning of Mathematics*, **11**, 1, pp 2–8.

DOWLING, P.C. (1991c) 'A touch of class: Ability, social class and intertext in SMP 11–16', in PIMM, D. and LOVE, E. (eds) *Teaching and Learning School Mathematics*, London: Hodder and Stoughton.

DOWLING, P.C. (1992) 'Textual production and social activity: A language of description', *Collected Original Resources in Education*, **16**, 1.

DOWLING, P.C. (1993) 'Theoretical "Totems": A sociological language for educational practice', in JULIE, C. *et al* (eds) *Political Dimensions in Mathematics Education: Curriculum Reconstruction for Society in Transition*, Cape Town: Maskew Miller Longman.

DOWLING, P.C. (1994a) 'Discursive saturation and school mathematics texts: A strand from a language of description', in ERNEST, P. (ed.) *Mathematics, Education and Philosophy: An International Perspective*, London: Falmer Press.

DOWLING, P.C. (1994b) The sociological analysis of pedagogic texts and English for educational development, presented at the Academic Development Centre, University of the Western Cape, April 1994, available from the author.

DOWLING, P.C. (1994/5) 'Spectres of schooling and utopia', *Arena Journal*, new series no. 4, pp. 191–200, Jan/Feb 1995.

DOWLING, P.C. (1995a) 'A language for the sociological description of pedagogic texts with particular reference to the secondary School Mathematics Scheme SMP 11–16', *Collected Original Resources in Education*, **19**, 2.

DOWLING, P.C. (1995b) 'Discipline and mathematise: The myth of relevance in education', *Perspectives in Education*, **16**, 2, pp. 209–226.

DOWLING, P.C. (1996a) 'A sociological analysis of school mathematics texts', *Educational Studies in Mathematics*, **31**, 389–415.

DOWLING, P.C. (1996b) *Baudrillard 1 - Piaget 0: Cybernetics, Subjectivity and The Ascension*, at http://www.ioe.ac.uk/ccs/ccsroot/ccs/dowling/1996.html.

DOWLING, P.C. (1996c) 'Apprenticeship and educational research: A mode of interrogation', in HENDRICKS, A. (ed.) *Southern African Association for Research in Mathematics and Science Education Third Annual Meeting, Proceedings, volume 1*, Bellville: University of the Western Cape.

DOWLING, P.C. and BROWN, A.J. (1996) *Pedagogy and Community in Three South African Schools: A Classroom Study*, at http://www.ioe.ac.uk/ccs/ccsroot/ccs/dowling_brown/1996.html.

DOWLING, P.C. and NOSS, R. (1990) 'Multiplying by zero', in DOWLING, P.C. and NOSS, R. (eds) *Mathematics versus the National Curriculum*, London: Falmer Press.

DOWLING, P.C. and NOSS, R. (eds) (1990) *Mathematics versus the National Curriculum*, London: Falmer Press.

DREYFUS, H.L. and RABINOW, P. (1982) *Michel Foucault: Beyond Structuralism and Hermeneutics*, Brighton: Harvester.

DURKHEIM, É. (1951) *Suicide: A Study in Sociology*, London: Routledge and Kegan Paul.

DURKHEIM, É. (1984) *The Division of Labour in Society*, Basingstoke: MacMillan.

ECO, U. (1973) 'Social life as a sign system', in ROBEY, D. (ed.) *Structuralism: An Introduction*, Oxford: Clarendon.

ECO, U. (1976) *A Theory of Semiotics*, Bloomington: Indiana University Press.

ECO, U. (1979) 'The semantics of metaphor', in *The Role of the Reader*, London: Hutchinson.

ECO, U. (1984) *Semiotics and the Philosophy of Language*, Basingstoke: MacMillan.

ECO, U. (1989) *Foucault's Pendulum*, London: QPD.

ECO, U. (1990) *The Limits of Interpretation*, Bloomington: Indiana University Press.

EICHINGER, D. and ROTH, K.J. (1981) *Critical Analysis of an Elementary Science Curriculum: Bouncing around or Connectedness?*, Elementary Subjects Center Series No. 32, E. Lansing: Center for the Learning and Teaching of Elementary Subjects.

ELLINGTON, L. (1986) 'Blacks and Hispanics in high school economics texts', *Social Education*, **50**, 1, pp. 64–7.

ENSOR, P. (1991) Upsetting the balance: Black girls and mathematics, unpublished MSc dissertation, Institute of Education, University of London.

ENSOR, P. (1993) 'Boundaries at the Centre — differentiating pupils in mathematics classrooms', in The NECC Mathematics Commission, PDME.2: Curriculum Reconstruction for Society in Transition, 2nd–5th April, 1993, Broederstroom, Pre-conference papers.

ENSOR, P. (1993/4) 'Boundaries at the centre — Differentiating pupils in mathematics classrooms', *Perspectives in Education*, **15**, 1, pp. 101–14.

ENSOR, P. (1994) Constructing Good Practice: issues of apprenticeship and alienation in an initial mathematics teacher education programme, presented at KEA Conference, Gordon's Bay, October 1994 (available from the author at the School of Education, University of Cape Town).

ENSOR, P. (1995) From student to teacher: Continuity or rupture, presented at the Kenton Educational Association Conference, Grahamstown, October 1995 (available from the author at the School of Education, University of Cape Town).

ENSOR, P. (1996) Learning to teach in the New South Africa, presented at the annual AMESA Conference, Cape Town, July 1996 (available from the author at the School of Education, University of Cape Town).

ERNEST, P. (1988) 'Editor's introduction', in ERNEST, P. (ed.) *The Social Context of Mathematics Teaching: Perspectives 37*, Exeter: School of Education, University of Exeter.

ERNEST, P. (1991) *The Philosophy of Mathematics Education*, London: Falmer Press.

ETIM, J.S. (1988) 'Sex role portrayal in 15 YA books used in Nigerian secondary schools', *Journal of Reading*, **31**, 5, pp. 452–7.

FAIRCLOUGH, N. (1989) *Language and Power*, London: Longman.

FARWELL, R. and KNEE, C. (1990) 'Demystifying mathematics: Popular mathematics as education', in NOSS, R. *et al* (eds) *Political Dimensions of Mathematics Education: Action and Critique, Proceedings of the First International Conference*, London: Department of Mathematics, Statistics and Computing, Institute of Education, University of London.

FASHEH, M. (1991) 'Mathematics in a social context: Math within education as praxis versus math within education as hegemony', in HARRIS, M. (ed.) *Schools, Mathematics and Work*, London: Falmer Press.

FASHEH, M. (1993) From a dogmatic, ready-answer approach of teaching maths towards a community-building, process-oriented approach', in The NECC Mathematics Commission, PDME.2: Curriculum Reconstruction for Society in Transition, 2nd–5th April, 1993, Broederstroom, Pre-conference papers.

FENNEMA, E. (ed.) (1985) 'Explaining sex-related differences in mathematics: Theoretical models', *Educational Studies in Mathematics*, **16**, 3, pp. 303–20.

FEYERABEND, P. (1975) *Against Method: Outline of an Anarchistic Theory of Knowledge*, London: Verso.

FILLMER, H.T. and MEADOWS, R.E. (1984) The portrayal of older characters in five sets of basal readers', paper presented at the Annual Meeting of the International Reading Association, Atlanta, May.

Fiske, J. (1989) *Reading the Popular*, London: Routledge.

Foucault, M. (1965) *Madness and Civilization: A History of Insanity in the Age of Reason*, London: Tavistock.

Foucault, M. (1970) *The Order of Things: An Archaeology of the Human Sciences*, London: Tavistock.

Foucault, M. (1972) *The Archaeology of Knowledge*, London: Tavistock.

Foucault, M. (1973) *The Birth of the Clinic*, London: Tavistock.

Foucault, M. (1977a) *Discipline and Punish: The Birth of the Prison*, London: Penguin.

Foucault, M. (1977b) 'The political function of the intellectual', *Radical Philosophy*, **17**, pp. 12–14.

Foucault, M. (1978) *The History of Sexuality: Volume 1, An Introduction*, Harmondsworth: Penguin.

Foucault, M. (1980) *Power/Knowledge*, Brighton: Harvester.

Foucault, M. (1981) 'The order of discourse', in Young, R. (ed.) *Untying the Text: A Poststructuralist Reader*, London: Routledge and Kegan Paul.

Foucault, M. (1982) 'The subject and power', in Dreyfus, H.L. and Rabinow, P. *Michel Foucault: Beyond Structuralism and Hermeneutics*, Brighton: Harvester.

Foucault, M. (1984) *The Use of Pleasure: Volume 2, The History of Sexuality*, Harmondsworth: Penguin.

Foucault, M. (1986) *The Care of the Self: Volume 3, The History of Sexuality*, New York: Vintage.

Frankenstein, M. (1989) *Relearning Mathematics: A Different Third R — Radical Mathematics, Volume 1*, London: Free Association Books.

Freeman, D.J. *et al* (1983a) 'Consequences of different styles of textbook use in preparing students for standardized tests', research report, E. Lansing: Institute for Research on Teaching, Michigan State University.

Freeman, D.J. *et al* (1983b) 'Do textbooks and tests define a National Curriculum in elementary school mathematics?', *Elementary School Journal*, **83**, 5, pp. 501–13.

Freeman, D.J. *et al* (1983c) 'The influence of different styles of textbook use on instructional validity of standardized tests', *Journal of Educational Measurement*, **20**, 3, pp. 259–70.

Freeman, D.J. and Porter, A.C. (1989) 'Do textbooks dictate the content of mathematics instruction in elementary schools?', *American Educational Research Journal*, **26**, 3, pp. 403–21.

Freud, S. (1973a) *Introductory Lectures on Psychoanalysis*, London: Penguin.

Freud, S. (1973b) *New Introductory Lectures on Psychoanalysis*, London: Penguin.

Freud, S. (1976) *The Interpretation of Dreams*, London: Penguin.

Fulkerson, E. (1939) 'Teaching the law of signs in multiplication', *The Mathematics Teacher*, **32**, 1, pp. 27–9.

Gadamer, H-G. (1976) *Philosophical Hermeneutics*, Berkeley: University of California Press.

GAIM, (1987) *Graded Assessments in Mathematics Development Pack: Teachers' Handbook*, King's College, University of London.

Garcia, J. *et al* (1990) 'The portrayal of females and minorities in selected elementary mathematics series', *School Science and Mathematics*, **90**, 1, pp. 2–12.

Garcia, J. and Sadowski, M. (1986) The treatment of minorities in nine recently published basal series, paper presented at the Annual Meeting of the American Educational Research Association, April.

Garfinkel, H. (1967) *Studies in Ethnomethodology*, Englewood Cliffs: Prentice-Hall.

GERDES, P. (1985) 'Conditions and strategies for emancipatory mathematics education in undeveloped countries', *For the Learning of Mathematics*, **5**, 1, pp. 15–20.

GERDES, P. (1986) 'How to recognize hidden geometrical thinking: A contribution to the development of anthropological mathematics', *For the Learning of Mathematics*, **6**, 2, pp. 10–12.

GERDES, P. (1988a) 'On culture, geometrical thinking and mathematics education', *Educational Studies in Mathematics*, **19**, 2, pp. 137–62.

GERDES, P. (1988b) 'On possible uses of traditional Angolan sand drawings in the mathematics classroom', *Educational Studies in Mathematics*, **19**, 1, pp. 3–22.

GERTH, H.H. and MILLS, C.W. (eds) (1948) *From Max Weber*, London: Routledge and Kegan Paul.

GIDDENS, A. (1984) *The Constitution of Society: Outline of the Theory of Structuration*, Cambridge: Polity.

GILBERT, R. (1986) '"That's where they have to go" The challenge of ideology in geography', *Geographical Education*, **5**, 2, pp. 43–6.

GILBERT, R. (1989) 'Text analysis and ideology critique of curriculum content', in CASTELL, S. de, LUKE, A.L. and LUKE, C. (eds) *Language, Authority and Criticism: Readings on the School Textbook*, London: Falmer Press.

GILLBORN, D. and GIPPS, C. (1996) *Recent Research on the Achievements of Ethnic Minority Pupils*, London: HMSO.

GINTIS, H. and BOWLES, S. (1988) 'Contradiction and reproduction in educational theory', in COLE, M. (ed.) *Bowles and Gintis Revisited: Correspondence and Contradiction in Educational Theory*, London: Falmer Press.

GLASERSFELD, E. von (1987) 'Learning as a constructive activity', in JANVIER, C. (ed.) *Problems of Representation in the Teaching and Learning of Mathematics*, Hillsdale: Lawrence Erlbaum Associates.

GLEICK, J. (1988) *Chaos: Making a New Science*, London: Heinemann.

GONZALEZ-SUAREZ, M. and EKSTROM, R.B. (1989) Are U.S. elementary school reading textbooks sex stereotyped?, paper presented at the Annual Meeting of the American Educational Research Association, San Francisco, March.

GORDON, C. (1980) 'Afterword', in FOUCAULT, M. *Power/Knowledge: Selected Interviews and Other Writings, 1972–1977*, Brighton: Harvester.

GORDON, P. (1978) 'Tradition and change in the curriculum', in LAWTON, D. *et al* (eds) *Theory and Practice of Curriculum Studies*, London: Routledge and Kegan Paul.

GORDON, P. and LAWTON, D. (1978) *Curriculum Change in the Nineteenth and Twentieth Centuries*, London: Hodder and Stoughton.

GRAMSCI, A. (1971) *Selections from the Prison Notebooks*, London: Lawrence and Wishart.

GRIFFITHS, H.B. and HOWSON, A.G. (1974) *Mathematics, Society and Curricula*, London: Cambridge University Press.

GUIDER, J. (1991) 'Curriculum, classroom management and discipline for the aboriginal student', *The Aboriginal Child at School*, **19**, 4, pp. 21–32.

GUPTA, A.F. and LEE SU YIN, A. (1989) 'Gender representation in English language textbooks used in the Singapore primary schools', *Language and Education*, **4**, 1, pp. 29–50.

HAHN, C.L. and BLAKENSHIP, G. (1983) 'Women and economics textbooks', *Theory and Research in Social Education*, **11**, 3, pp. 67–76.

HALES, M. (1980) *Living Thinkwork: Where Do Labour Processes Come From?*, London: CSE Books.

HALL, E.J. (1988) 'One week for women? The structure of inclusion of gender issues in introductory textbooks', *Teaching Sociology*, **16**, 4, pp. 431–42.

HALLIDAY, M.A.K. (1978) *Language as Social Semiotic: The Social Interpretation of Language and Meaning*, London: Arnold.

HARAWAY, D.J. (1991) 'A cyborg manifesto: Science, technology, and socialist-feminism in the late twentieth century', in *Simians, Cyborgs and Women: The Reinvention of Nature*, London: Free Association Books.

HARRIS, M. (1985a) 'Wrapping up mathematics in the world of work', *Contact*, London: ILEA, 8 March.

HARRIS, M. (1985b) 'Wrapping it up', *Mathematics Teaching*, **113**, pp. 44–6.

HARRIS, M. (1987) 'An example of traditional women's work as a mathematics resource', *For the Learning of Mathematics*, **7**, 3, pp. 26–8.

HARRIS, M. (1988a) 'Common threads: Mathematics and textiles', *Mathematics in Schools*, **17**, 4, pp. 24–8.

HARRIS, M. (1988b) 'Common threads', *Mathematics Teaching*, **123**, pp. 15–17.

HARRIS, M. (1993) 'Mathematics in the experience of school and work', in The NECC Mathematics Commission, PDME.2: Curriculum Reconstruction for Society in Transition, 2nd–5th April, 1993, Broederstroom, Pre-conference papers.

HARRIS, P. (1991) *Mathematics in a Cultural Context: Aboriginal Perspectives on Space, Time and Money*, Geelong: Deakin University Press.

HARRIS, S. (1988) 'Culture boundaries, culture maintenance-in-change, and two-way aboriginal schools', *Curriculum Perspectives*, **8**, 2, pp. 76–83.

HART, K.M. (ed.) (1981) *Children's Understanding of Mathematics: 11–16*, London: John Murray.

HARTMANN, H. (1981) 'The unhappy marriage of marxism and feminism: Towards a more progressive union', in DALE R. *et al* (eds) *Education and the State Volume II: Politics Patriarchy and Practice*, Lewes: Falmer Press.

HASSAN, M.M. (1990) Political socialization in Kuwait, unpublished PhD thesis, Exeter University.

HASSAN, R. (1991) 'Questions as a mode of learning in everyday talk', in LÊ, T. and McCAUSLAND, M. (eds) *Language Education: Interaction and Development*, Proceedings of the International Conference, Ho Chi Minh City, Vietnam, 30th March–1st April.

HASSAN, R. (1992a) 'Contexts for meaning', paper presented at the Georgetown University Round Table, GURT'92, Georgetown University, April 20th–23rd.

HASSAN, R. (1992b) 'Meaning in sociolinguistic theory', in BOLTON, K. and KWOK, H. (eds) *Sociolinguistics Today: International Perspectives*, London: Routledge.

HEATH, S.B. (1986) 'Questioning at home and at school: A comparative study', in HAMMERSLEY, M. (ed.) *Case Studies in Classroom Research*, Milton Keynes: Open University Press.

HEATHCOTE, O.D. (1981) 'Sex stereotyping in Mexican reading primers', paper presented at the Annual Meeting of the International Reading Association, New Orleans, April-May.

HEATHCOTE, O.D. (1982) 'Sex stereotyping in Mexican reading primers', *Reading Teacher*, **36**, 2, pp. 158–65.

HEIDEGGER, M. (1962) *Being and Time*, London: SCM Press.

HENRIQUES, J. *et al* (1984) *Changing the Subject: Psychology, Social Regulation and Subjectivity*, London: Methuen.

HIGHER EDUCATION STATISTICS AGENCY (1996) *Students in Higher Education Institutions*, Cheltenham: HESA.

HIRSCHKOP, K. (1989) 'Bibliographical essay', in HIRSCHKOP, K. and SHEPHERD, D. (eds) *Bakhtin and Cultural Theory*, Manchester: Manchester University Press.

HITCHCOCK, M.E. and TOMPKINS, G.E. (1987) 'Basal readers: Are they still sexist?', *Reading Teacher*, **41**, 3, pp. 288–92.

HODGE, R. and KRESS, G. (1988) *Social Semiotics*, Cambridge: Polity.

HODGE, R. and KRESS, G. (1993) *Language as Ideology*, second edition, London: Routledge.

HOFSTADTER, D.R. (1979) *Gödel, Escher, Bach: An Eternal Golden Braid*, Harmondsworth: Penguin.

HOLT, E.R. (1990) ' "Remember the Ladies" — Women in the Curriculum. ERIC Digest', Bloomington: ERIC Clearinghouse for Social Studies/Social Science Education.

HOWSON, A.G. (ed.) (1987a) *Challenges and Responses: Essays to Celebrate the Twenty-fifth Anniversary of the School Mathematics Project*, Cambridge: Cambridge University Press.

HOWSON, A.G. (1987b) 'Challenges and responses', in HOWSON, G. (ed.) *Challenges and Responses: Essays to Celebrate the Twenty-fifth Anniversary of the School Mathematics Project*, Cambridge: Cambridge University Press.

HOWSON, A.G., KEITEL, C. and KILPATRICK, J. (1981) *Curriculum Development in Mathematics*, Cambridge: Cambridge University Press.

HOWSON, A.G. and WILSON, B. (1986) *School Mathematics in the 1990s*, Cambridge: Cambridge University Press.

HUDSON, B. (1985) 'Social division of adding up to equality? Militarist, sexist and ethnocentric bias in mathematics textbooks and computer software', *World Studies Journal*, **5**, 4, pp. 24–9.

HUGHES, M. (1986) *Children and Number: Difficulties in Learning Mathematics*, Oxford: Blackwell.

HUMAN SCIENCES RESEARCH COUNCIL (1995) *Ways of Seeing the National Qualifications Framework*, Pretoria: HSRC.

HUNTER, I. (1994) *Rethinking the School: Subjectivity, Bureaucracy, Criticism*, St Leonards: Allen & Unwin.

ILYATJAR, N. (1991) 'Traditional aboriginal learning: How I learned as a Pitjantjatjara child', *The Aboriginal Child at School*, **19**, 1, pp. 6–12.

INNER LONDON EDUCATION AUTHORITY (1983) *Race, Sex and Class: 1. Achievement in Schools*, London: ILEA.

INNER LONDON EDUCATION AUTHORITY CENTRE FOR LEARNING RESOURCES (1985) *Everyone Counts: Looking for Bias and Insensitivity in Primary Mathematics Materials*, London: ILEA Learning Resources Branch.

ISAACSON, Z. (1988) 'The marginalisation of girls in mathematics: Some causes', in PIMM, D. (ed.) *Mathematics, Teachers and Children*, London: Hodder and Stoughton.

IVES, R. (1984) 'The maleness of science', *Australian Science Teachers' Journal*, **30**, 1, pp. 15–19.

JAKOBSON, R. (1956) 'Two aspects of language and two types of aphasic disturbances', in JAKOBSON, R. and HALLE, M. *Fundamentals of Language*, The Hague: Mouton and Co.

JANVIER, C. (ed.) (1987) *Problems of Representation in the Teaching and Learning of Mathematics*, Hillsdale: Lawrence Erlbaum Associates.

JOHNSON, R. (1981) ' "Really useful knowledge": Radical education and working class culture 1790–1848', in DALE R. *et al* (eds) *Education and the State volume II: Politics Patriarchy and Practice*, Lewes: Falmer Press.

JOHNSTON, J. (1993) The construction of mathematical ability: An analysis of text, presented at Research into Social Perspectives of Mathematics Education, Institute of Education, University of London, December.

JOSEPH, G.G. (1987) 'Foundations of ethnocentrism in mathematics', *Race and Class*, **28**, 3, pp. 13–28.

JOSEPH, G.G. (1990) 'The politics of anti-racist mathematics', in NOSS, R. *et al* (eds) *Political Dimensions of Mathematics Education: Action and Critique, Proceedings of the First International Conference*, revised edition, London: Department of Mathematics, Statistics and Computing, Institute of Education, University of London.

JOSEPH, G.G. (1991) *The Crest of a Peacock: Non-European Roots of Mathematics*, London: Penguin.

JUNG, C.G. (1959) *The Archetypes and the Collective Unconscious*, London: Routledge.

KEARINS, J. (1991) 'Number experience and performance in Australian aboriginal and western children', in DURKIN, K. and SHIRE, B. (eds) *Language in Mathematics and Education: Research and Practice*, Philadelphia: Open University Press.

KESSLER, S.J. and McKENNA, W. (1978) *Gender: An Ethnomethodological Approach*, New York: John Wiley.

KIM, H. (1993) 'A comparative study between an American and a Republic of Korean textbook series: Coverage of measurement and geometry in first through eighth grades', *School Science and Mathematics*, **93**, 3, pp. 123–6.

KIRK, L. *et al* (1985a) *Confronting the Stereotypes: Kindergarten to Grade 4. Volume I*, Winnipeg: Manitoba Department of Education, Curriculum Development Branch.

KIRK, L. *et al* (1985b) *Confronting the Stereotypes: Grades 5–8. Volume II*, Winnipeg: Manitoba Department of Education, Curriculum Development Branch.

KLEIN, M. (1975) *Envy and Gratitude: And Other Works 1946–1963*, London: Virago.

KNEE, C. (1983) The Incarnation of reason: Geometry as a case for a sociology of mathematics, unpublished PhD thesis, University of London, Institute of Education.

KNIJNIK, G. (1993) Pedagogy of the oppressed in practice: Ethnomathematics and the landless of Southern Brazil, in The NECC Mathematics Commission, PDME.2: Curriculum Reconstruction for Society in Transition, 2nd–5th April, 1993, Broederstroom, Pre-conference papers.

KOGAN, M. (1978) *The Politics of Educational Change*, Glasgow: Fontana/Collins.

KOZA, J.E. (1992) 'Picture this: Sex equity in textbook illustrations', *Music Educators Journal*, **78**, 7, pp. 28–33.

KRESS, G. (1993) 'Against arbitrariness: The social production of the sign as a foundational issue in critical discourse analysis', *Discourse and Society*, **4**, 2, pp. 169–91.

KRESS, G. and LEEUWEN, T. van (1990) *Reading Images*, Geelong: Deakin University Press.

KUHN, T. (1970) *The Structure of Scientific Revolutions*, second edition, Chicago: University of Chicago Press.

KUMAR, K. (1982) 'Literature in the reading textbook: A comparative study from a sociological perspective', *Research in the Teaching of English*, **16**, 4, pp. 301–19.

KUO, C-H. (1993) 'Problematic Issues in EST materials development', *English for Specific Purposes*, **12**, 2, pp. 171–81.

LACLAU, E. (1984) 'Transformations of advanced industrial societies and the theory of the subject', in HANNINEN, S. and PALDAN, L. (eds) *Re-thinking Ideology*, Berlin: Argument-Verlag.

LACLAU, E. and MOUFFE, C. (1985) *Hegemony and Socialist Strategy: Towards a Radical Democratic Politics*, London: Verso.

LAVE, J. (1988) *Cognition in Practice: Mind, Mathematics and Culture in Everyday Life*, Cambridge: Cambridge University Press.

LAVE, J., MURTAUGH, M. and de la ROCHA, O. (1984) 'The dialectic of arithmetic in grocery shopping', in ROGOFF, B. and LAVE, J. (eds) *Everyday Cognition: Its Development in Social Context*, Cambridge, Mass.: Harvard University Press.

LAVE, J. and WENGER, E. (1991) *Legitimate Peripheral Participation*, Cambridge: Cambridge University Press.

LAWTON, D. (1975) *Class, Culture and the Curriculum*, London: Routledge and Kegan Paul.

LAWTON, D. (1980) *The Politics of the School Curriculum*, London: Routledge and Kegan Paul.

LEDER, G.C. (1987) 'Teacher student interaction: A case study', *Educational Studies in Mathematics*, **18**, 3, pp. 255–71.

LEE, L. (1992) 'Gender fictions', *For the Learning of Mathematics*, **12**, 1, pp. 28–37.

LEMKE, J.L. (1995) *Textual Politics: Discourse and Social Dynamics*, London: Taylor and Francis.

LEONT'EV, A.N. (1978) *Activity, Consciousness, and Personality*, Englewood Cliffs: Prentice-Hall.

LEONT'EV, A.N. (1979) 'The problem of activity in psychology', in WERTSCH, J.V. (ed.) *The Concept of Activity in Soviet Psychology*, New York: M.E. Sharpe.

LÉVI-STRAUSS, C. (1964) *Totemism*, London: Merlin Press.

LÉVI-STRAUSS, C. (1972) *The Savage Mind (La Pensée Sauvage)*, London: Weidenfeld and Nicolson.

LIEBECK, P. (1986) 'In defence of experience', *Mathematics Teaching*, 114, pp. 36–8.

LIGHT, P. (1986) 'Context, conservation and conversation', in RICHARDS, M. and LIGHT, P. (eds) *Children of Social Worlds: Development in a Social Context*, Cambridge: Polity.

LIGHT, B. *et al* (1989) 'Sex equity content in history textbooks', *History and Social Science Teacher*, **25**, 1, pp. 18–20.

LING, J. (1987) 'SMP activity in the 11–16 sector: 1961–86', in HOWSON, G. (ed.) *Challenges and Responses: Essays to Celebrate the Twenty-fifth Anniversary of the School Mathematics Project*, Cambridge: Cambridge University Press.

LIVINGSTON, E. (1986) *The Ethnomethodological Foundations of Mathematics*, London: Routledge and Kegan Paul.

LORIMER, R. and KEENEY, P. (1989) 'Defining the curriculum: The role of the multinational textbook in Canada', in CASTELL, S. de, LUKE, A.L. and LUKE, C. (eds) *Language, Authority and Criticism: Readings on the School Textbook*, London: Falmer Press.

LOVE, A.M. (1991) 'Process and product in geology: An investigation of some discourse features of two introductory textbooks', *English for Specific Purposes*, **10**, 2, pp. 89–109.

LUKES, S. (1982) 'Introduction', in Durkheim, É. *The Rules of Sociological Method (and Selected Texts on Sociology and its Method)*, London: MacMillan.

LURIA, A.R. (1976) *Cognitive Development: Its Cultural and Social Foundations*, Cambridge: Harvard University Press.

MAC AN GHAILL, M. (1988) *Young, Gifted and Black*, Milton Keynes: Open University Press.

McBRIDE, M. (1989) 'A Foucauldian analysis of mathematical discourse', *For the Learning of Mathematics*, **9**, 1, pp. 40–6.

MACDONALD, B. and WALKER, R. (1976) *Changing the Curriculum*, Shepton Mallet: Open Books.

MACKENZIE, D.A. (1981) *Statistics in Britain 1865–1930*, Edinburgh: Edinburgh University Press.

MACKENZIE, D. and WAJCMAN, J. (eds) (1985) *The Social Shaping of Technology*, Milton Keynes: Open University Press.

McTAGGART, R. (1989) 'Aboriginalisation implies empowerment and disempowerment', *The Aboriginal Child at School*, **17**, 2, pp. 37–44.

MAIER, E. (1980) 'Folk mathematics', *Mathematics Teaching*, 93, pp. 21–3.

MARSHALL, S. and GILMOUR, M. (1993) 'Lexical knowledge and reading comprehension in Papua New Guinea', *English for Specific Purposes*, **12**, 1, pp. 69–81.

MARX, K. (1968) 'Preface to a contribution to the critique of political economy', in MARX, K. and ENGELS, F. *Selected Works*, London: Lawrence & Wishart.

MARX, K. (1973) *Grundrisse: Foundations of the Critique of Political Economy (rough draft)*, Harmondsworth: Penguin.

MARX, K. (1976) *Capital, Volume 1*, Harmondsworth: Penguin.

MARX, K. (1978) *Capital, Volume 2*, Harmondsworth: Penguin.

MARX, K. (1981) *Capital, Volume 3*, Harmondsworth: Penguin.

MATTE-BLANCO, I. (1988) *Thinking, Feeling, and Being: Clinical Reflections on the Fundamental Antinomy of Human Beings and the World*, London: Routledge.

MATTHEWS, J. (1989) *Tools of Change: New Technology and the Democratisation of Work*, Sydney: Pluto.

MAUSS, M. (1979) *Sociology and Psychology: Essays*, London: Routledge and Kegan Paul.

MAY, W.T. *et al* (1990) '"Whose" content, context, and culture in elementary art and music textbooks? Elementary subjects center series No. 23', paper presented at the Annual Meeting of the American Educational Research Association, Boston, Mass., April 1990, E. Lansing: East Lansing Institute for Research on Teaching, Michigan State University.

MICHIGAN STATE BOARD OF EDUCATION (1984) *A Study of Selected Eighth Grade United States History Textbooks. 1982–83 Michigan Social Studies Textbook Study. Volume III. Selected Sections from the Complete Report*, Lansing: Michigan State Board of Education.

MILIBAND, R. (1969) *The State in Capitalist Society*, London: Quartet Books.

MOON, B. (1986) *The 'New Maths' Controversy: An International Story*, Lewes: Falmer Press.

MOREHEAD, G. (1984) 'Nice girls don't do maths', *Mathematics in School*, **13**, 5, pp. 16–7.

MULCAHY, B.J. (1988) A study of the relationship between Ireland and England in Irish post-primary school history textbooks, published since 1922 and dealing with the period 1800 to the present, unpublished PhD, Hull University.

MULKEY, L.M. (1987) 'The use of a sociological perspective in the development of a science textbook evaluation instrument', *Science Education*, **71**, 4, pp. 511–22.

MYERS, G. (1992) 'Textbooks and the sociology of scientific knowledge', *English for Specific Purposes*, **11**, 1, pp. 3–17.

NATIONAL CURRICULUM COUNCIL (1988) *National Curriculum Consultation Report: Mathematics*, London: NCC.

NATIONAL CURRICULUM COUNCIL (1989) *Mathematics Non-statutory Guidance*, York: NCC.

NATIONAL CURRICULUM COUNCIL, (1991) *Report on Monitoring the Implementation of the National Curriculum Core Subjects: 1989–90*, York: NCC.

NEWBLE, D. and CANNON, R. (1994) *A Handbook for Medical Teacher*, third edition, Dordrecht: Kluwer.

NEW ZEALAND DEPARTMENT OF EDUCATION (1980) *Sex-Role Stereotyping in Mathematics Textbooks*, Research Report, Wellington: Department of Education.

NIBBELINK, W.H. *et al* (1986) 'Sex-role assignments in elementary school mathematics textbooks', *Arithmetic Teacher*, **34**, 2, pp. 19–21.

NORTHAM, J. (1982) 'Girls and boys in primary maths books', *Education 3–13*, **10**, 1, pp. 11–4.

NORTON, D. (1993) 'Developing social-functional numeracy materials for South African learners', in The NECC Mathematics Commission, PDME.2: Curriculum Reconstruction for Society in Transition, 2nd–5th April, 1993, Broederstroom, Pre-conference papers.

NOSS, R. and DOWLING, P.C. (1990) 'Mathematics in the National Curriculum: The empty set?', in DOWLING, P.C. and NOSS, R. (eds) *Mathematics versus the National Curriculum*, Basingstoke: Falmer Press.

NUSBAUMER, N.R. *et al* (1989) 'The discovery of war as a social problem: Teaching as sociological practice', *Teaching Sociology*, **17**, 3, pp. 316–22.

OAKLEY, A. (1981) *Subject Women*, Glasgow: Fontana/Collins.

OFFICE OF POPULATION CENSUSES AND SURVEYS (1980) *Classification of Occupations*, London: HMSO.

O'HEAR, M.F. and ASHTON, P.J. (1987) 'The substantive value of main idea statements in sociology textbook', *Forum for Reading*, **18**, 2, pp. 46–51.

O'HEAR M.F. *et al* (1987) 'Location of main ideas in composition texts', *Research in the Teaching of English*, **21**, 3, pp. 318–26.

O'REILLY, D. (1990) 'Hierarchies in mathematics: A critique of the CSMS study', in Dowling, P.C. and Noss, R. (eds) *Mathematics Versus the National Curriculum*, Basingstoke: Falmer Press.

OTTE, M. (1983) 'Textual strategies', *For the Learning of Mathematics*, **3**, 3, pp. 18–28.

OTTE, M. (1986) 'What is a text?', in CHRISTIANSEN, B. *et al* (eds) *Perspectives on Mathematics Education*, Dordrecht: D. Reidel.

PARISH, D. (1991) 'Aboriginal world view in the educational context', *The Aboriginal Child at School*, **19**, 4, pp. 14–20.

PARKIN, F. (1978) 'Social stratification', in BOTTOMORE T. and NISBET R. (eds) *A History of Sociological Analysis*, London: Heinemann.

PATTEN, S. (1988) 'English handbook selection: A feminist choice', *Feminist Teacher*, **3**, 3, pp. 23–4.

PEIRCE, C.S. (1931–1958) *Collected Papers*, Cambridge Mass.: Harvard University Press.

PENMAN, D. (1986) 'Confronting gender bias in children's books', *English for Education*, **20**, 1, pp. 2–4.

PERRUCCI, R. (1982) 'The failure of excellence in texts', paper presented at the Annual Conference of the American Sociological Association, San Francisco, September.

PETERSON, S.B. and KRONER, T. (1992) 'Gender biases in textbooks for introductory psychology and human development', *Psychology of Women Quarterly*, **16**, 1, pp. 17–36.

PIAGET, J. (1932) *The Moral Judgement of the Child*, London: Routledge and Kegan Paul.

PIAGET, J. (1953) *The Child's Conception of Number*, New York: Humanities Press.

PIAGET, J. (1971) *Structuralism*, London: Routledge and Kegan Paul.

PIAGET, J. (1972a) *The Principles of Genetic Epistemology*, London: Routledge and Kegan Paul.

PIAGET, J. (1972b) *Psychology and Epistemology: Towards a Theory of Knowledge*, Harmondsworth: Penguin.

PIAGET, J. (1980a) 'Opening the debate', in PIATTELLI-PALMARINI M. (ed.) *Language and Learning: The Debate Between Jean Piaget and Noam Chomsky*, London: Routledge and Kegan Paul.

PIAGET, J. (1980b) 'The psychogenesis of knowledge and its epistemological significance', in PIATTELLI-PALMARINI M. (ed.) *Language and Learning: The Debate Between Jean Piaget and Noam Chomsky*, London: Routledge and Kegan Paul.

PIAGET, J. (1995) *Sociological Studies*, London: Routledge and Kegan Paul.

PIMM, D. (1986) 'Beyond reference', *Mathematics Teaching*, 116, pp. 48–51.

PIMM, D. (1987) *Speaking Mathematically*, London: Routledge and Kegan Paul.

PIMM, D. (1990) 'Mathematical versus political awareness: Some political dangers inherent in the teaching of mathematics', in Noss, R. *et al* (eds) *Political Dimensions of Mathematics Education: Action and Critique, Proceedings of the First International Conference*, London: Department of Mathematics, Statistics and Computing, Institute of Education, University of London.

PIMM, D. (1995) *Symbols and Meanings in School Mathematics*, London: Routledge.

PIRIE, S. (1981) *Mathematics in Medicine: A Report for the Cockcroft Committee*, Nottingham, Shell Centre for Mathematical Education, University of Nottingham.

POTTER, E.F. and ROSSER, S.V. (1992) 'Factors in life science textbooks that may deter girls' interest in science', *Journal of Research in Science Teaching*, 29, 7, pp. 669–86.

POULANTZAS, N. (1975) *Classes in Contemporary Capitalism*, London: Verso.

RAO, J.A. (1989) Evaluation of materials for the intermediate English course in Punjab, Pakistan, unpublished MA dissertation, Exeter University.

RAYNER, E. (1995) *Unconscious Logic: An Introduction to Matte Blanco's Bi-logic and its Uses*, London: Routledge.

REGESTER, C. (1991) 'Visual and verbal content in U.S. history textbooks of the 1950s and 1980s', *Reading Improvement*, 28, 1. pp. 14–25

REMILLARD, J. (1991a) *Is There an Alternative? An Analysis of Commonly Used and Distinctive Elementary Mathematics Curricula. Elementary Subjects Center, Series No. 31*, E. Lansing: Center for the Learning and Teaching of Elementary Subjects.

REMILLARD, J. (1991b) *Conceptions of Problem Solving in Commonly Used and Distinctive Elementary Mathematics Curricula. Elementary Subjects Center Series, No. 43*, E. Lansing: Center for the Learning and Teaching of Elementary Subjects.

RESTIVO, S. (1984) 'Representations and the sociology of mathematical knowledge', in BELISLE, C. et SCHIELE, B. *Les Savoirs dans les Pratiques Quotidienne*, Lyons: CNRS.

REUSSER, K. (1988) 'Problem solving beyond the logic of things — Contextual effects on understanding and solving word problems', *Instructional Science*, 17, 4, pp. 309–38.

RICE, I.S. (1987) 'Racism and reading schemes. 1986, the current situation', *Reading*, 21, 2, pp. 92–8.

RICE, I.S. (1988) 'The portrayal of ethnic Chinese/Japanese peoples in Britain's primary reading schemes', *Reading*, 22, 1, pp. 32–9.

RIST, R. (1970) 'Student social class and teacher expectations: The self-fulfilling prophecy in ghetto education' *Harvard Educational Review*, **40**, 3, pp. 411–51.

RIVERS, J. (1990) 'Contextual analysis of problems in algebra I textbooks', paper presented at the Annual Meeting of the American Educational Research Association, Boston Mass., April.

ROBBINS, D. (1991) *The Work of Pierre Bourdieu: Recognizing Society*, Milton Keynes: Open University Press.

ROTMAN, B. (1985) 'On zero', *Mathematics Teaching*, 113, pp. 24–9.

SAAD, N.S. (1984) Content analysis of the Civics Education text books in the light of educational aims in intermediate schools in Iraq, with special attention to the methods followed in achieving them, unpublished PhD, University of Wales, Cardiff.

SALTER, B. and TAPPER, T. (1981) *Education, Politics and the State: The Theory and Practice of Educational Change*, London: Grant McIntyre.

SAUSSURE, F. DE (1983) *Course in General Linguistics*, London: Duckworth.

SCOTT-HODGETTS, R. (1986) 'Girls and mathematics: The negative implications of success', in BURTON, L. (ed.) *Girls Into Maths Can Go*, London: Holt, Rinehart and Winston.

SCRIBNER, S. (1984) 'Studying working intelligence', in ROGOFF, B. and LAVE, J. (eds) *Everyday Cognition: Its Development in Social Context*, Cambridge, Mass.: Harvard University Press.

SEDDON, T. (1983) 'Con-texts', *Radical Education Dossier*, 21, pp. 37–9.

SELANDER, S. (1990) 'Towards a theory of pedagogic text analysis', *Scandinavian Journal of Educational Research*, **34**, 2, pp. 143–50.

SELKE, B.E. (1983) 'History textbooks: Portraits of men and women?', *Southwestern Journal of Social Education*, **13**, 1, pp. 13–20.

SEWELL, B. (1981) *Uses of Mathematics by Adults in Daily Life*, London: ACACE.

SHARP, R. and GREEN, A. (1975) *Education and Social Control*, London: Routledge and Kegan Paul.

SHARPE, K. (1992) 'Educational homogeneity in French primary education: A double case study', *British Journal of Sociology of Education*, **13**, 3, pp. 329–48.

SHELL CENTRE FOR MATHEMATICAL EDUCATION (nd) Report of interviews for the Cockcroft Committee, unpublished transcripts, Nottingham: University of Nottingham.

SHUARD, H. (1986) 'The relative attainment of girls and boys in mathematics in the primary years', in BURTON, L. (ed.) *Girls Into Maths Can Go*, London: Holt, Rinehart and Winston.

SINGLETON, J. (1989) 'Japanese folkcraft pottery apprenticeship: Cultural patterns of an educational institution', in Coy M. (ed.) *Apprenticeship: From Theory to Method and Back Again*, Albany: State University of New York Press.

SKOVSMOSE, O. (1985) 'Mathematical education versus critical education', *Educational Studies in Mathematics*, **16**, 4, pp. 337–54.

SKOVSMOSE, O. (1988) 'Mathematics as a part of technology', *Educational Studies in Mathematics*, **19**, 1, pp. 23–41.

SKOVSMOSE, O. (1993) Towards a critical mathematics education, in The NECC Mathematics Commission, PDME.2: Curriculum Reconstruction for Society in Transition, 2nd–5th April, 1993, Broederstroom, Pre-conference papers.

SOHN-RETHEL, A. (1973) 'Intellectual and manual labour', *Radical Philosophy*, 6, pp. 30–7.

SOHN-RETHEL, A. (1975) 'Science as alienated consciousness', *Radical Science Journal*, 2/3, pp. 63–101.

SOHN-RETHEL, A. (1978) *Intellectual and Manual Labour: A Critique of Epistemology*, London: MacMillan.

SPRADBERY, J. (1976) 'Conservative pupils? Pupil resistance to curriculum innovation in mathematics', in WHITTY, G. and YOUNG, M.F.D. (eds) *Explorations in the Politics of School Knowledge*, Driffield: Nafferton.

STRAKA, G.A. and BOS, W. (1989) 'Socialization objectives of Chinese primary schools: Results of a comparative textbook analysis', *Studies in Educational Evaluation*, **15**, 2, pp. 257–76.

STURROCK, J. (1979) *Structuralism and Since: From Lévi-Strauss to Derrida*, Oxford: Oxford University Press.

STURROCK, J. (1986) *Structuralism*, London: Paladin Grafton.

TADROS, A.A. (1989) 'Predictive categories in university textbooks', *English for Specific Purposes*, **8**, 1, pp. 17–31.

TAHTA, D. (1985) 'On notation', *Mathematics Teaching*, 112, pp. 49–51.

TAMMADGE, A. (1987) 'A mathematics master in the 1960s', in HOWSON, G. (ed.) *Challenges and Responses: Essays to Celebrate the Twenty-fifth Anniversary of the School Mathematics Project*, Cambridge: Cambridge University Press.

TAXEL, J. (1981) 'The outsiders of the American revolution: The selective tradition in children's fiction', *Interchange on Educational Policy*, **12**, 2–3, pp. 206–28.

TAXEL, J. (1983) 'The American revolution in children's fiction: An analysis of literary content, form and ideology', in APPLE, M.W. and WEIS, L. (eds) *Ideology and Practice in Schooling*, Philadelphia: Temple University Press.

TETREAULT, M.K. (1984) 'Notable American women: The case of United States history textbooks', *Social Education*, **48**, 7, pp. 546–50.

THWAITES, B. (1987) 'Foreword', in HOWSON, G. (ed.) *Challenges and Responses: Essays to Celebrate the Twenty-fifth Anniversary of the School Mathematics Project*, Cambridge: Cambridge University Press.

TIETZE, I.N. and DAVIS, B.H. (1981) 'Sexism in texts in educational administration', paper presented at the Annual Meeting of the American Educational Research Association, Los Angeles, April.

TULL, D. (1991) 'Elementary textbooks versus the child: Conflicting perceptions of biology', paper presented at the Annual Meeting of the National Association for Research in Science Teaching, Lake Geneva, Wi., April.

TURNER, J. (1987) 'Analytical theorizing', in GIDDENS, A. and TURNER, J.H. (eds) *Social Theory Today*, Cambridge: Polity.

TUNSTALL, J. (1983) *The Media in Britain*, London: Constable.

UNIVERSITY STATISTICAL RECORD, (1994) *University Statistics 1993–94 Volume 1*, Cheltenham: USR.

VAUGHN-ROVERSON, C. *et al* (1989) 'Sexism in basal readers: An analysis of male main characters', *Journal of Research in Childhood Education*, **4**, 1, pp. 62–8.

VENTIMIGLIA, J.C. and DIRENZO, G.J. (1982) 'Sociological conceptions of personality', *Social Behavior and Personality*, **10**, 1, pp. 25–37.

VITZ, P.C. (1985) *Religion and Traditional Values in Public School Textbooks: An Empirical Study, Section 1, Part 2 of Equity in Values Education: Do the Values Education Aspects of Public School Curricula Deal Fairly with Diverse Belief Systems? Final Report*, July 1985, New York: Department of Psychology, New York University.

VOGEL, S. (1987) 'Mythology in introductory biology', *BioScience*, **37**, 8, pp. 611–4.

VOLOSINOV, V.N. (1973) *Marxism and the Philosophy of Language*, New York: Seminar Press.

VYGOTSKY, L.S. (1978) *Mind in Society: The Development of Higher Psychological Processes*, Cambridge Mass.: Harvard University Press.

VYGOTSKY, L.S. (1986) *Thought and Language*, Cambridge Mass.: MIT Press.

WALDEN, R. and WALKERDINE, V. (1982) *Girls and Mathematics: The Early Years*, Bedford Way Paper no. 8, London: Institute of Education, University of London.

WALDEN, R. and WALKERDINE, V. (1985) *Girls and Mathematics: From Primary to Secondary Schools*, Bedford Way Paper no. 24, London: Institute of Education, University of London.

WALFORD, G. (1983) 'Science textbook images and the reproduction of sexual divisions in society', *Research in Science and Technological Education*, **1**, 1, pp. 65–72.

WALKERDINE, V. (1982) 'From context to text: A psychosemiotic approach to abstract thought' in BEVERIDGE, M. (ed.) *Children Thinking Through Language*, London: Arnold.

WALKERDINE, V. (1984) 'Developmental psychology and the child-centred pedagogy: The insertion of Piaget into early education', in HENRIQUES, J. *et al*, *Changing the Subject: Psychology, Social Regulation and Subjectivity*, London: Methuen.

WALKERDINE, V. (1988) *The Mastery of Reason*, London: Routledge.

WALKERDINE, V. *et al* (1989) *Counting Girls Out*, London: Virago.

WATSON, H. (1987) 'Learning to apply numbers to nature: A comparison of English speaking and Yoruba speaking children learning to quantify', *Educational Studies in Mathematics*, **18**, 4, pp. 339–57.

WATSON, H. (1988) 'Language and mathematics education for aboriginal Australian children', *Language and Education*, **2**, 4, pp. 255–73.

WEBER, M. (1964) *The Theory of Social and Economic Organization*, New York: The Free Press.

WHITTY, G. (1985) *Sociology and School Knowledge*, London: Methuen.

WILLIAMS, R. (1961) *The Long Revolution*, Harmondsworth: Penguin.

WILLIS, P.E. (1977) *Learning to Labour: How Working Class Kids Get Working Class Jobs*, Aldershot: Gower.

WING, A. (1989) School mathematics texts: A teacher's interpretive enquiry, unpublished PhD thesis, Southampton University.

WITTGENSTEIN, L. (1958) *Philosophical Investigations*, Oxford: Blackwell.

WITTGENSTEIN, L. (1961) *Tractatus Logico-Philosophicus*, London: Routledge and Kegan Paul.

WOLF, A. KELSON, M. and SILVER, R. (1990) *Learning in Context: Patterns of Skills Transfer and Training Implications*, Moorfoot: Training Agency.

WOLFENDALE, S. (1990) *All About Me*, Nottingham Educational Supplies, Ludlow Hill Road, West Brigford, Nottingham, NG2 6HD.

WOLPE, A.M. (1981) 'The official ideology of education for girls', in Dale R. *et al* (eds) *Education and the State Volume II: Politics Patriarchy and Practice*, Lewes: Falmer Press.

WUNUNGMURRA, W. (1988) ' "Dhawurrpunaramirra" finding the common ground for a new aboriginal curriculum', *Curriculum Perspectives*, **8**, 2, pp. 69–71.

ZASLAVSKY, C. (1973) *Africa Counts: Number and Pattern in African Culture*, Westport: Lawrence Hill.

ZINCHENKO, P.I. (1979) 'Involuntary memory and the goal-directed nature of activity', in WERTSCH, J.V. (ed.) *The Concept of Activity in Soviet Psychology*, New York: M.E. Sharpe Inc.

Index

ability, 118
  age, 35, 46, 52, 277–79
  construction by the curriculum,
      49–61
  differentiation, 49–61
  'needs', 273–79
  pacing, 277
  SMP, 34, 173–79, 276–86
  social class, 247
  task complexity, 277
  task diversity, 278
Aboriginal cultures, 13
absolutism, 294
abstract practice, 88–104
abstracting, 147, 182, 253
academic activities
  discursive relations between
      performances, 32
academic field
  construction by the language of
      description, 130
activity, 20, 121, 131–42, 291
  most dominant position as subject of,
      140
  positions, 20, 131, 140–42
  practices, 20, 131, 132–40
  (re)production in human subjects, 20,
      131
  (re)production in text, 20, 131
  structural and evental levels, 131–32
  subordination of recruited practices,
      24
Adams, Samuel, 300
affiliation, 144
African National Congress, 17
age and ability, 35, 46, 52, 277–79
Ahmed, Afzal, 179
algebra, 134, 171, 172, 177, 179,
      184–86, 188, c. 8

alienated voice, 145
Althusser, Louis, 105–106
Anyon, Jean, 65, 79–80
Apple, Michael, 78–79
apprenticed position, 140
apprenticed voice, 143, 164, 305
apprenticeship, 28–33, 45–48, 162–64
  coincidence of pedagogic action and
      pedagogic content, 29
  craft, 29–33, 162, 297
  doctoral supervision, 30–33
  evaluative criteria, 29
  mingei folk pottery, 29, 162
  not specialized to manual occupations,
      30
  novice as object of pedagogic action,
      28
  pedagogic action, 113, 162
  research, 30–33
  research apprenticeship as initiation
      into a mode of interrogation,
      31–32
  SMP 11–16 Y series, 192, 200
  subjectivity, 28, 106
  Tugen blacksmith, 163
arbitrariness of the sign, 151, *290*
Atkin, Ron, 168
Atkinson, Paul, xii
authorial voice, 143, 164
authorizing, 143

Bahl, Parin, xi
Bakhtin, Mikhail, *112*, 165, 216, *290*
  materialist critique of Saussure,
      113–14
Barlow, John Perry, 300
Barthes, Roland, *2*, 127, 143
  re-reading, *73*
Baudrillard, Jean, 16, 163